THE
INDUSTRIAL REFORMATION
OF ENGLISH FICTION

THE INDUSTRIAL REFORMATION OF ENGLISH FICTION

Social Discourse and Narrative Form 1832–1867

Catherine Gallagher

The University of Chicago Press
Chicago and London

Catherine Gallagher is associate professor of English at
the University of California, Berkeley.

A portion of chapter 7 was first published in the *Arizona Quarterly*,
Spring 1980, © 1980 by *Arizona Quarterly*. Portions of chapter 9 first
appeared in *Representations*, no. 5, Winter 1984, 115–47, © 1984 by
The Regents of the University of California, and in *Nineteenth
Century Fiction* 35, no. 3 (December 1980): 372–84, © 1980 by The
Regents of the University of California. Permission to reprint the
above is gratefully acknowledged.

The University of Chicago Press, Chicago 60637
The University of Chicago Press, Ltd., London
© 1985 by The University of Chicago
All rights reserved. Published 1985
Printed in the United States of America

94 93 92 91 90 89 88 87 86 85   5 4 3 2 1

Library of Congress Cataloging in Publication Data

Gallagher, Catherine.
    The industrial reformation of English fiction.

    Bibliography: p.
    Includes index.
    1. English fiction—19th century—History and criticism.
2. Industry in literature.   3. Social problems in
literature.   4. Free will and determinism in literature.
5. Family in literature.   6. Politics in literature.
I. Title.
PR878.I62G35 1985   823'.8'09355   84-16272
ISBN 0-226-27932-4

To my mother and father,
Mary and John Sullivan

Contents

Acknowledgments

This study began as a dissertation, which was inspired by discussions with Masao Miyoshi and several of his students. It owes much to Professor Miyoshi's direction and to the advice of friends who read and commented on the various chapters: Jonathan Arac, Ann Banfield, Rosemarie Bodenheimer, Patrick Brantlinger, Carol Christ, Norman Feltes, Eric Gould, Gerald Graff, Neil Hertz, Sharon Flitterman King, Thomas Laqueur, Linda Morris, Jay Winter, and my brother Patrick Sullivan. Thanks are also due to Ralph Rader, U. C. Knoepflmacher, and Leo Lowenthal for their advice and encouragement. I am also indebted to Lois Pryor and Rhonda Rockwell for their substantive contributions and editorial skills. The last chapters of this book owe a great deal to the thoughtful and probing readings of David Miller and Stephen Greenblatt and to the enlightening responses of other members of the editorial board of *Representations*. I am especially grateful to Michael Rogin for his help in shaping and revising the entire manuscript.

From my mother and father, Mary and John Sullivan, my mother-in-law, Sari Jay, my sister, Maggie Sullivan, and my daughter, Shana Gallagher, I received help and encouragement that allowed me to complete the project, and from my aunt, Margaret Sullivan, I received material assistance that allowed me to begin it. To Rebecca Jay, my second daughter, whose arrival coincided with the first pages of the opening chapter, I owe the ability to concentrate my energies under the most pressing circumstances. Finally, to my husband, Martin Jay, I owe an inestimable debt of gratitude; he has been involved in every stage of the composition of this book, from choosing the topic to proofreading the manuscript, and he has provided the emotional as well as intellectual support that made its completion possible.

I am also grateful to Grace O'Connell for typing the manuscript quickly and accurately and to the University of California, Berkeley, for supporting the research. In addition, I would like to thank the John Rylands Library in Manchester, the Bodleian Library and the Nuffield College Library in Oxford, as well as the British Museum Library, for their hospitality.

Introduction

The expansion of industrial production in early- and mid-nineteenth-century England was accompanied by a set of controversies about English social, material, and spiritual well-being. These controversies are often collectively called the Condition of England Debate. They extended into almost every area of English intellectual and cultural life, changing the nature of many disciplines and literally bringing others into existence. Moreover, the Condition of England Debate became a discourse unto itself, creating and absorbing new fields of inquiry in metaphysics, ethics, political economy, public administration, biology, medicine, religion, psychology, and aesthetics. Hence the difficulty we have in categorizing such contributers to the debate as Thomas Carlyle, Thomas Babington Macaulay, Matthew Arnold, George Eliot, John Stuart Mill, and John Ruskin. Industrialism gave not only a new content but also a new shape to English cultural and intellectual life, creating, merging, and rearranging its constituents.

No cultural endeavor seems to have escaped these re-formations, but some were more fundamentally altered than others. In the *Industrial Reformation of English Fiction*, I hope to demonstrate that narrative fiction, especially the novel, underwent basic changes whenever it became a part of the discourse over industrialism. The works most immediately affected were those we now call the "industrial novels," the most prominent of which are Benjamin Disraeli's *Sybil*, Elizabeth Gaskell's *Mary Barton* and *North and South*, Charles Kingsley's *Alton Locke*, Charles Dickens's *Hard Times*, and George Eliot's *Felix Holt*.[1]

This book examines in detail the formal properties of these and many other works. In doing so it helps define the state of the novel in the decades between the first and second Reform Acts, for as we will shortly see, the discourse over industrialism led novelists to examine the assumptions of their literary form. Reciprocally, the formal analyses in this study enable a new understanding of the discourse itself, for the formal structures and ruptures of these novels starkly reveal a series of paradoxes at the heart of the Condition of England Debate.

I have organized this study around three specific controversies within the Condition of England Debate that profoundly unsettled fundamental assumptions of the novel form. By tracing the histories and structures of these three controversies, I attempt to show precisely how the debate and the fiction shape each other. The first dispute questions the nature and possibility of human freedom; the second, the sources of social cohesion; and the third, the nature of representation, probing in particular its methods of transforming facts into values. Specific legislative proposals for industrial and political reform stimulated these three controversies, which also had a long history in English thought, a history with consequences for the development of English novels.

As the English novel developed prior to the 1830s, one tradition within it acquired a set of conventions (later called "realism") governing the play of contradictory exigencies. The novels in this tradition, those, for example, of Henry Fielding and Jane Austen, established dynamic tensions between freedom and determinism, between public and private worlds, and between the representation of facts (what is) and that of values (what ought to be). But fiction concerned with the Condition of England Debate turned these implicit tensions into explicit contradictions because the debate was composed of controversies over the same issues that were delicately suspended to form the framework of the novel. Thus the industrial novelists found themselves uncovering the tensed structure of their own form, making the always unsettled assumptions of the novel the objects of their scrutiny. Their work, then, sometimes resembles the self-conscious, antirealism of such earlier novelists as Laurence Sterne. Unlike Sterne, however, the industrial novelists take no sly satisfaction in formal self-reflexiveness because their polemical purposes, the same purposes that lead them to question the novel's form, also lead them to make excessively naive mimetic claims for it. Even as they probe the contested assumptions of their medium, they try to insist that their fictions are unmediated presentations of social reality.

The Industrial Reformation of English Fiction analyzes the formal consequences of this paradox. The first four chapters concentrate on the dispute over free will and social determinism, showing both the disruption of narrative continuity and the formal self-consciousness that resulted from that disruption. The second section of the book (chapters five, six, and seven) examines two methods of creating coherence by reconciling social and familial needs in the industrial novel. These chapters demonstrate that, within the rhetorical contexts of domestic ideology and social paternalism, the narrative tropes linking social and private worlds could no longer be simply taken for granted. An unwonted pressure was put on these structuring tropes, again creating both incoherence and the need for new principles of social and aesthetic cohesion. As chapters eight and nine show, this need was met by redefining representation itself. This last section of the book argues that the debate over political representation impinged on the theory and practice of literary representation, calling into question previous assumptions about the right relationship between facts and values. Out of this questioning was born a new theory of culture and a new practice of realism.

The last chapter argues that the Arnoldian theory of culture (at once a reaction and a supplement to the 1860s debate over the Second Reform Bill) superseded and invalidated the Condition of England Debate out of which it grew. As literary critics, we have inherited Arnold's assumptions; our own discourse is rooted in categories partly designed to emancipate us from early Victorian social criticism. It is not surprising, then, that we have tended to exclude the industrial novels from our various canons of major nineteenth-century prose fiction. This book does not attempt to revise the canon; rather, it describes the prehistory of canon formation. It gives an account of a series of formal and discursive paradoxes that prompted the 1860s discovery of an independent realm of representation.

In writing this account, I have used a variety of critical methods, concentrating in some chapters on questions of genre, in others on structural tropes, and in still others on the more general topics of textuality, intertextuality, and representation. Underlying this variety are certain assumptions that might serve as a brief orientation for the reader.

I assume there is normally some sort of tension between ideology and literary forms, but that forms are nevertheless also historical phenomena, parts of those transideological structures that are here called discourses.[2] I am using "discourse" to designate both what is said on a particular subject (for example, the actual contents of the Condition of England Debate) and the largely unstated rules that govern what can and cannot be said. Discourse exists between and within ideologies, thereby creating the coherence and legibility of ideological conflict. Literary forms often disrupt the tidy formulations and reveal the inherent paradoxes of their ostensible ideologies. However, I try to demonstrate the the ruptures thus created are neither the automatically subversive result of all truly literary treatment nor the timeless effect of all textuality. Rather, the formal and ideological transgressions and deviations described here are elicited by and recontained within the logic of the larger historical discourse.

I assume, moreover, that an attempt to specify the ultimate sources or purposes of the discourse in either a history of material production or an account of a unitary, bourgeois class consciousness would be either futile or distorting. Hence, although I refer to the history of technological innovations, demographic developments, the reorganization of production and ownership, and changes in the environmental conditions of major industrial towns, I do not make these the ultimate sources of the discourse. Rather, I concentrate on reconceiving what ideological and literary issues were at stake, decade by decade, in the debate that itself played a crucial role in shaping the outcome of the Industrial Revolution.

I believe equally strongly that the discourse serves no single, identifiable class interest. Many readers will probably detect in the three major subdivisions of the book (free will versus determinism, private versus public, facts versus values) resemblances to Georg Lukacs's "antinomies of bourgeois thought."[3] Although sympathizing with Lukacs's attempt to historicize Kant's "antinomies of thought," in the present case I find the adjective "bourgeois" both limiting and insufficiently specific. The Condition of England Debate was primarily conducted by certain sections of the middle-class, but it nevertheless permitted the enunciation of other class interests as well. To characterize its structure as peculiarly bourgeois, one would need to be able to identify the products of working-class or aristocratic consciousness in the same period that escape its structuring contradictions. But even the most radical Chartist tracts and the most reactionary aristocratic diatribes reproduce the paradoxes ascribed by Lukács to bourgeois thought. The adjective thus seems an arbitrary attempt to limit theoretically the location of a discourse that the evidence indicates is illimitable.[4]

One could, of course, argue, along with Antonio Gramsci, that the inescapability of such structures is precisely what defines the cultural hegemony of the dominant class: the antinomies of the discourse are bourgeois in the sense that they originate in the class interests of the bourgeoisie, not in the sense that they are the differentiating characteristics, the exclusive property, of the thought of that class. Indeed, a class achieves hegemony precisely by losing the specificity of its discourse, by making that discourse the only available structure of thought. There may be much merit in this general account of hegemony, but it seems altogether inapplicable to the discourse described in these pages. For the Condition of England Debate, as this study shows, does not originate in any single, identifiable class interest, least of all that of the bourgeoisie. The ideology most often associated with the industrial bourgeoisie, laissez-faire entrepreneurialism, is on the defensive in this debate from its inception. The attacks come from all directions: the working-class, the gentry, finance capital, an increasingly differentiated state bureaucracy, various newly formed professional groups (including novelists) trying to define and protect their own authority, and middle-class women attempting (often with the aid of Evangelical religion) to extend the sphere of their social influence. The debate represented here crosses class divisions and divides a single class, the bourgeoisie, into so many competing subgroups that its interests become impossible to specify.

Rather than trace this discourse back to a single class consciousness, then, I have described the complex ideological and formal exigencies operating on each writer, noting and explaining the points of convergence and divergence while analysing in detail the narrative negotiations each writer attempted. This method reconstructs an important chapter in our literary and intellectual history, revealing that the antitheses encountered as formal paradoxes in the industrial novels are finally, at the supersession of the entire discourse, transformed into a much more general antithesis between society and its literary representations.

Part One

FREE WILL
VERSUS DETERMINISM

1

Workers and Slaves: The Rhetoric of Freedom in the Debate over Industrialism

On October 16, 1830, a ferociously indignant and yet highly sentimental letter appeared in the *Leeds Mercury* exposing the long hours, unhealthy working conditions, and general mistreatment suffered by children employed in the Bradford textile mills. Historians have noted the importance of this letter by the fiery Yorkshire industrial reformer Richard Oastler:[1] it inaugurated the Ten Hours Movement and ignited a general controversy over factory labor in the 1830s and 1840s. Commentators have not, however, paid much attention to the fact that the letter begins with an allusion to another reform movement of those decades. Entitled "Yorkshire Slavery," the letter was prefaced with a quotation from an antislavery speech delivered in Leeds a few weeks before the letter's publication. Oastler began his appeal as a commentary on that speech:

> Gentlemen, No heart responded with truer accents to the sounds of liberty which were heard in the Leeds Cloth-hall yard, on the 22d instant, than did mine, and from none could more sincere and earnest prayers arise to the throne of Heaven, that hereafter Slavery might only be known to Britain in the pages of her history. One shade alone obscured my pleasure, arising not from any difference in principle, but from the want of application of the general principle *to the whole Empire.* The pious and able champions of *Negro* liberty and *Colonial* rights should, if I mistake not, have gone farther than they did; or perhaps, to speak more correctly, before they had travelled so far as the West Indies, should . . . have sojourned in our own immediate neighborhood, and have directed the attention of the meeting to scenes of misery, acts of oppression, and victims of Slavery, even on the threshold of our homes.
>
> Let truth speak out, appalling as the statement may appear. . . . Thousands of our fellow-creatures and fellow-subjects, both male and female, the miserable inhabitants of a *Yorkshire* town; (Yorkshire now represented in Parliament by the giant of anti-slavery principles,) are this very moment existing in a state of Slavery, *more horrid* than are the victims of that hellish system—"*Colonial*

> *Slavery.*" . . . The very streets which receive the droppings of an
> "Anti-slavery Society" are every morning wet by the tears of
> innocent victims at the accursed shrine of avarice, who are *com-*
> *pelled* . . . to hasten, half-dressed, *but not half-fed,* to those maga-
> zines of British Infantile Slavery—*The Worsted Mills in the town and*
> *neighborhood of Bradford*!!!²

These paragraphs begin by professing sympathy for the antislavery
cause (the self-portrait of Oastler, deeply moved and silently praying in
the cloth-hall yard), proceed to question the humanitarian sincerity of
its leadership, and end by assuming a tone of forthright contempt for
the official organization of that cause ("the droppings of an 'Antislavery Society' "). In doing so, they encapsulate the complex and often
contradictory relationship between the antislavery movement and critics of industrial society. Industrial reformers and social critics
appropriated the images, the rhetoric, and the tone of the antislavery
movement. Simultaneously, however, they used arguments and rhetorical strategies associated with the advocates of slavery.

Oastler's ambivalent attitude toward the Anti-Slavery Society did not
stem from any disagreement with the emancipators' main purpose;
like most early nineteenth-century industrial reformers, Oastler
wholeheartedly endorsed the antislavery cause. He had been an active
worker in the antislavery cause, one who helped to promote it in
Yorkshire.³ However, his enthusiasm for the cause did not extend to all
of the anti-Slavery Society's ideological presuppositions; in particular,
he objected to the implicit model of freedom found in many antislavery
tracts, the model of a free unregulated labor force. Like critics of
industrial capitalism before him, by comparing the two work forces,
Oastler challenged the claim that free workers were necessarily better
off than slaves. He concluded that British workers who were "free" to
contract their labor or the labor of their children in an unregulated
labor market were usually forced by economic necessity to accept the
capitalists' terms of employment. The doctrine of "free labor" thus
entailed its own necessities that bound workers as tightly as the literal
chains of bondsmen. Such comparisons between British workers and
West Indian slaves had earlier belonged to the rhetorical arsenal of
pro-slavery writers; indeed, one influential critic of industrial capitalism, William Cobbett, was also an advocate of slavery, and his antiaboli-
tionism spilled over into his social criticism. However, in using the
worker/slave metaphor, most critics of industrialism, like Richard
Oastler, were not revealing pro-slavery sentiments. Rather, they were
articulating their objections to the liberal political economists' model of
freedom and developing their own alternative ideas of liberty.

The frequency of the worker/slave metaphor in their writings demonstrates the preoccupation of early industrial social critics with the question of the nature of human freedom. Beneath this general preoccupation and its common rhetoric, however, a variety of specific beliefs can be detected. It is important to uncover and examine these various beliefs about freedom, to probe typical uses of the worker/slave metaphor, to trace their history and differentiate their meanings. For the rhetoric of freedom in the discourse over industrialism is perhaps its most elusive and contradictory element; it is also, however, its most definitive characteristic in the 1830s and 1840s and the feature entailing the profoundest consequences for English narrative. As we will see, the rhetoric of freedom raised questions about such basic procedures of the fiction writer's business as plotting and character development, both of which presuppose a relatively stable set of assumptions about causality and human freedom.

Consequently, in order to explain precisely what was entailed in the rhetoric of freedom, this chapter will review the various and dissimilar circumstances under which speakers and writers compared workers to slaves. The comparison was made both to defend black slavery and to condemn capitalism; it was made both to discredit the leaders of the antislavery movement and to exploit their success. Three groups of polemicists made the comparison: (1) the spokesmen for the West Indian interests, (2) middle-class and aristocratic reformers who advocated legislation to regulate factories, and (3) working-class political radicals who sought manhood suffrage. In all of these cases the metaphor enfolded paradigms of freedom that became parts of the complex structure of both industrial social criticism and the fictional narratives that tried to embody that criticism.

In examining typical uses of the worker/slave metaphor, we will see that, for all its complexity, the body of works comprising the early nineteenth-century critique of industrialism combines three major intellectual traditions, distinguishable by their paradigms of freedom. Two of these traditions took hold among artistocratic and middle-class reformers: (1) the Enlightenment tradition that claimed man's will was externally determined but that freedom could be achieved by training the will to coincide with the dictates of reason, and (2) a tradition fed by both Arminianism and Romantic philosophy that claimed man's will was free but in need of a supporting social hierarchy to encourage its proper exercise. Although these two traditions obviously contradicted one another on the specific issue of the freedom of the will, they often coexist in works about industrialism. Many industrial novels, in particular, evince both the assumptions of the social determinists and belief in an irreducibly free will. The third major idea of freedom underlying worker/slave metaphors belonged to the political radicals. They used the word "slavery" to describe disenfranchisement and equated freedom with manhood suffrage, with the freedom to assemble and to vote. Their demand for an extended franchise had no particular metaphysical basis; it implied nothing about the ultimately free or determined nature of man's will. Yet it became a fuse that set off philosophical speculations on the nature of freedom, particularly in the industrial novels of the 1840s, which often focus on the Chartists' demands for political freedom. Chartism was the movement to which Benjamin Disraeli, Elizabeth Gaskell, and Charles Kingsley were all responding. Its political model of liberty was a locus around which the authors' own paradoxical ideas about freedom tended to cluster, paradoxical ideas that often define the novels' forms.

"Slaves of Necessity": The Worker/Slave Metaphor in the Hands of the Antiabolitionists

Oastler's letter to the *Leeds Mercury* was certainly an influential document in the history of anti-industrial literature, but it was by no means the first comparison of free English workers to slaves.[4] In the last three decades of the eighteenth century, the defenders of West Indian slavery began comparing the two work forces. The analogy, therefore, was first drawn within the context of proslavery arguments, and although it subsequently became independent of this original context, the metaphoric likening of English workers to slaves tended to retain a certain proslavery residue in both its substance and its tone. These early comparisons were made when proponents of the abolition of the slave trade called attention to the miserable conditions of the West Indian slaves; the defenders of that trade would then declare, as Coleridge later indignantly recalled, "that the Negro Slaves were happy and contented; nay, that they were far *better off* in every respect than the labouring poor . . . in England."[5] This argument was made as early as the 1770s, and by 1790 it was a commonplace in the defense of slavery to point to the allegedly greater poverty and oppression of British workers. Thus, the rhetorical strategy of the proslavery publicists contributed to a condition-of-England controversy in the late eighteenth century. The controversy was not then explicitly associated with industrialism, but the arguments of the proslavery propagandists later became fundamental to nineteenth-century criticisms of industrial society. What, then, were the style and substance of these worker/slave comparisons, and what precisely did the factory reformers and other critics of industrial society inherit from this proslavery literature?

The defenders of slavery denied the reality of a free British work force. *The Wealth of Nations*, which promoted the idea of free labor to a doctrine of classical economics, had not yet been published when in 1773 Samuel Martin declared the liberty of English workers to be chimerical:

> let us enquire into the state of our labourers . . . even in this our opulent free country. Are they not slaves to necessity? the most cruel of all Egyptian task masters; who makes no abatement for sickness or other accidents, which disable the husband and father of a numerous offspring . . . whose never-ending labours (much greater than those of our Colony Negroes) continue with life and ability. Is this a life so comfortable as those enjoy? yet these are called the sons of liberty, who really are the slaves of *necessity*. What is their great boast of liberty, but that of changing their employer? but that can neither mitigate their labours, nor increase their wages; and therefore cannot add any comfort to their existence.[6]

Martin's statement reveals that the liberal economists' model of freedom (the ability merely to contract one's labor—or other commodity—to the highest bidder on an open market) was already under attack even as it was being assembled.

The proslavery publicists continued their attack during the following decades, as abolitionists began popularizing the works of Adam Smith and the phrase "free labor" became no longer merely a descriptive but a normative term.[7] Almost all proslavery witnesses at the 1791 Parliamentary hearings on the slave trade were asked to compare the lives of West Indian slaves and British workers, and almost all reiterated Martin's main point: workers cannot properly be called free if they live in utter poverty with economic necessity dictating their actions.[8] The critics of industrialism, particularly the advocates of factory reform legislation and of manhood suffrage, incorporated this point into their own propaganda. Along with the anticapitalist substance of the argument, the reforming writers also borrowed its sarcastic tone and one of its most durable rhetorical ploys, an ironic emphasis on the word "free." That ironic emphasis, the gesture of dismissal of the political economists' model of liberty, in turn opened the door to myriad speculations about the kind of society that would make true human freedom possible.

We can trace the descent of this preoccupation with freedom from proslavery writers to critics of industrial capitalism in the works of one journalist who was both: William Cobbett. His writings illustrate the

continuity between the early proslavery propaganda and the developing criticism of industrial society. In the first decade of the nineteenth
century Cobbett began a series of attacks on the leaders of the increasingly successful Anti-Slave Trade Movement. In the 1790s Cobbett had opposed the abolition of the slave trade, but not until the
1800s did he begin to accuse the Anti-Slave Trade leadership of hypocrisy. In these attacks the mild sarcasm of the late eighteenth-century
proslavery propagandists was converted into venomous abuse, and the
interests of colonial slaves and British laborers were presented as
incompatible. Proslavery writers had long hinted that the abolitionists'
indifference to domestic poverty belied their humanitarian protesta-
tions, but these innuendoes were usually politely, even humorously,
made.[9] Cobbett's accusations of insincerity, however, were blunt and
emphatic. Even during his anti-Jacobin phase his concern for the
condition of the British poor was sincere and, combined with his
proslavery beliefs, it motivated his charges of "cant and hypocrisy"
against the abolitionists. He fulminated against the *Edinburgh Review*
liberals for advocating the abolition of the slave trade:

> while these gentlemen scruple not to applaud the system of
> government, by which the parish paupers in England have been
> swelled in number to more than a million; while, without a mur-
> mur, they behold the parish officers of Wales disposing of the
> rates in shipping off their poor to slavery in America; while they
> pass in silence over all the imprisonments, the beatings, the whip-
> pings, the tortures, the hangings, the mock-legal murders, that
> are inflicted on the white slave in certan parts of Europe.[10]

The phrase "white slaves," which recurred frequently in Cobbett's
widely read social criticism, formed a part of his legacy to later writers.
Decades after the controversies over the slave trade and colonial slavery had been settled, Victorian social critics continued to use the
phrase. They also frequently repeated Cobbett's charge of hypocrisy
against a middle class that had exerted itself to end black slavery in the
colonies but remained apathetic toward the plight of British workers.

Over the next two decades, Cobbett's emphasis shifted from colonial
slavery to domestic poverty, but the form and tone of his arguments
remained substantially the same. Agitation against the slave trade gave
Cobbett dozens of occasions to write about poverty and injustice at
home. In 1806 he promised that "so often as they agitate this question,
with all its cant, for the relief of 500,000 blacks; so often will I remind
them of the 1,200,000 white paupers of England and Wales."[11] True to
his word, when the House of Commons passed the 1806 resolution
against the slave trade, Cobbett promptly responded:

of all those who have been disappointed at the conduct of Mr. Fox [who introduced the resolution] . . . I have never yet heard of one, who even thought about the *Slave Trade* . . . as the voice of humanity called upon us much more loudly in favour of 1,200,000 paupers of England than in favour of 400,000 negroes of the West-Indies, no one of which negroes is not better fed, is not better off, than any one of those paupers; nay, than any one of the day-labouring men in England.[12]

Cobbett's antiabolitionist writings in these years provided an important nexus between the proslavery propaganda of the late eighteenth and early nineteenth centuries and the works of later writers on the condition of the poor in England.

In the 1820s Cobbett further helped to strengthen the association between the issues of industrialism and slavery by explicitly identifying England's factory workers as "white slaves." He did so in 1823 in an open letter to William Wilberforce, the leader of the Anti-Slavery Movement. By that year, factory hands had already been equated with slaves in the publicity of factory reformers; Cobbett's letter is unique among condemnations of the factory system, however, because it still shows the connection between proslavery sentiments and antagonism toward industrial capitalism. But the proslavery remarks are ultimately not central to this letter's purpose. While his contempt for Wilberforce remained undiminished, by 1823 the issue of colonial slavery had shrunk to a mere excuse for an attack on industrial capitalism, an attack that instances the ironic emphasis on the word "free" noted in Samuel Martin's 1773 essay. The letter threatens:

> Wilberforce,
>
> I have you before me in a canting pamphlet; and, upon your conduct and character, as developed in that pamphlet, it is my intention to remark fully, at some future time. At present, I shall use it only thus: to ask you what need there was, or what propriety there was, in spending your time in writing and publishing, "An Appeal to the religion, justice and humanity of the Inhabitants of the British Empire, in behalf of the Negro slaves in the West Indies"; to ask you what propriety, what sense, what sincerity, there could be in your putting forth this thing, in the present state of this country?[13]

Despite this open contempt for the emancipator, Cobbett does not defend slavery in this letter. Putting the issue off to "some future time," he spends his belligerence and exasperation, so strongly expressed by his repetitious language and syntax, on the "state of this country," specifically the state of English industrial workers; "it being at present," he wrote, "my intention to give some account of the state of the 'free British labourers' of the cotton factories in the North."[14] Although still bearing the rhetorical characteristics of his earlier tracts, Cobbett's criticism of industrialism was becoming increasingly independent of its proslavery connections.

Still, the likening of workers to slaves remains central to the letter's argument, and here the comparison reveals a preoccupation with the idea of freedom. The main purpose of the letter is to advocate repeal of the Combination Acts.[15] But it also exposes the general conditions of those working and living in industrial society. Initially questioning the rhetoric of "free labour"—"You pretend to want the Blacks to be *as free* as British labourers; but you do not tell us what you mean by the word *freedom*"[16]—Cobbett goes on to deride it:

> Away with all your trash about "*free* British labourers". . . . You seem to question in one place, whether the Blacks be, "as yet *fit for the enjoyment of British freedom*. . . . But, surely, they may be fit to be shut up in their huts from sunset to sunrise. A part of these free British labourers are so shut up.[17] . . . You never attempt to tell us; you never so much as insinuate, that the Blacks perish or even suffer for want of food. But it is notorious that great numbers of your "*free* British labourers" have actually *died from starvation.*[18]

In Cobbett's articles, then, we can see the continuity between the rhetoric of the defenders of slavery and that of the champions of the British factory workers, a continuity that includes the worker/slave metaphor, an ironic emphasis on the word "free," and accusations of hypocrisy against the Anti-Slave Trade leaders. Moreover, Cobbett's intellectual legacy contained an imperative that other early critics of industrialism found irresistible: "tell us what you mean by the word *freedom*."

Slaves of Machinery, of Ignorance and Despair: The Worker/Slave Metaphor in the Hands of Industrial Reformers

The amorphous "slaves of necessity" had assumed the distinctive, gaunt outlines of factory workers before Cobbett's open letter to William Wilberforce was published in 1823. Cobbett and other enemies of abolition made important contributions to nineteenth-century social criticism by comparing British workers to slaves and attacking the doctrine of free labor. But they were not the first writers to use the slavery metaphor specifically to describe factory workers. Cobbett's adversaries in the slave trade debate were the first to do so. Humanitarian abolitionists found new uses for the worker/slave metaphor in their long struggle for factory regulations.

The humanitarian reformers who supported both abolition of the slave trade and correction of the abuses in the factory system created an enormous body of social criticism, and it is within the context of their thought that the industrial narratives must be viewed. Such abolitionist social critics as Robert Owen and S. T. Coleridge, repeating the "slaves of necessity" arguments, shared the antiabolitionists' opposition to the doctrine of free labor. But humanitarian factory reformers added new dimensions to the worker/slave metaphor, dimensions that, we will see, had profound formal effects on the industrial narratives.

In the early decades of the nineteenth century, humanitarian reformers likened factory workers to slaves in order to stress the oppressiveness of the factory system, hoping to divert a portion of the humanitarian energy that they had set flowing in the slave trade debate into this new channel of reform. The metaphor seemed a natural one to the factory reformers because of certain obvious similarities between the objects of their concern and slaves. From 1800 to 1842, the only factory legislation written protected working children; the helplessness of these children, their total subjection to the wills of their parents and masters, easily inspired the epithet "slave." Still other facts made all factory hands seem particularly unfree: they were physically confined and had to work long hours according to the rhythms of the spinning machines; alertness and diligence were too often maintained by corporal punishment, and the sheer size of many textile mills, with their accompanying impersonality, reminded reformers of vast plantations worked by indistinguishable slaves.

It is not surprising, then, that in 1802, when the first Sir Robert Peel introduced legislation to limit the working hours and improve the living conditions of parish apprentices employed in cotton mills, William Wilberforce himself suggested that the restrictions be applied to all children working in factories. He had been told a story about a "free-labour child" who had been beaten by her overseer. Implying the comparison that was later to be made explicitly by the advocates of factory legislation, Wilberforce declared that in all his years of reading about West Indian slavery, he had seldom come across "a more artless, affecting tale."[19] The same broad humanitarianism inspired both the antislavery movement and the factory-reform movement, the latter borrowing much from the former. But the factory reformers could not accept the political economists' model of freedom; when they used the slavery metaphor, therefore, they were obliged to draw on alternative models of emancipation. Thus the writers for factory reform, attempting to capitalize on the success of the antislavery movement, helped forge a connection between the problems of industrial society and speculation about the nature of human liberty. Of course, the slavery metaphor alone did not create the issue of freedom in industrial society; there were many sources of the late eighteenth- and early nineteenth-century preoccupation with the question of human liberty.[20] But the metaphor did create a rhetorical context in which that preoccupation was both revealed and reinforced.

William Wilberforce represented an essentially Evangelical humanitarianism that first took a political form in the movement to abolish the slave trade. This religious humanitarianism was buttressed by the legacy of secular, Enlightenment humanitarianism in the first few decades of the nineteenth century. It was on the assumption of such common humanitarian sentiments that factory reformers first appealed to the constituency that had been created by the abolitionists. Robert Owen, one of the earliest analysts and reformers of industrial society, referred to the humanitarian nexus between the two movements when in 1812 he dedicated the first of his "Essays on the Formation of Character" to William Wilberforce. He did so not on the basis of shared ideologies or religious beliefs, "but rather as a *duty* which your benevolent exertions and disinterested conduct demand."[21] And it was because of the legislator's success in abolishing the slave trade that Owen asked him to "lend your aid to introduce [the essays'] influence into *legislative practice*."[22] The "legislative practice" that Owen requested was very imperfectly realized in Peel's second Factory Bill, which was debated in Parliament between 1815 and 1819.

Owen eventually disassociated himself from the compromised Bill, but the arguments of the "Essays on the Formation of Character" and his other writings on behalf of factory legislation were seminal documents in the analysis and critique of industrial society. Although Owen used the slavery metaphor in them, he developed an idea of freedom that contradicted the political economists' model. Owen did not believe that ignorant people, no matter how much at liberty, could be properly called free; consequently he stressed the need to plan rationally the "formation of human character." His ideas became essential to industrial social criticism and had a profound influence on the industrial novelists.

The thesis of the "Essays" was that human character should not be allowed to develop haphazardly but should be consciously formed through education and a "rational" social system. At first glance, Owen's theories seem hostile to all ideas of freedom, for his view of human development was a thoroughly deterministic one. For fifty years he reiterated the major premise of these essays: "*that the character of man is, without a single exception, always formed for him; that it may be, and is, chiefly, created by his predecessors*; that they give him . . . his ideas and habits, which are the powers that govern and direct his conduct."[23] Most liberal political economists agreed with Owen's basic premises.[26] Adam Smith, David Ricardo, Thomas Malthus, James Mill, and John McCulloch were all psychological determinists, intellectual heirs of John Locke and David Hume. These thinkers essentially redefined the concept of freedom by applying it to action, not to the will, and by contrasting it to external constraint, not to internal necessity. They argued that the will was the product of the convergence of various unwilled psychic entities, which were the results of one's experiences, and was therefore determined, not free. However, if one acted according to one's will, these thinkers called one's actions "free." Liberty, then, was freedom from external constraint and was entirely reconcilable with strict determinism.

Owen, then, shared intellectual ancestors with the political economists who denied the existence of free will. But Owen did not accept their liberal idea of free action. For him, action could only be free if it were rational. Industrialism held both a promise and a threat for Owen's hopes of rational freedom.

Owen's social determinism and his corresponding faith in rationality grew directly out of his industrial experiences: as a factory manager he had been able to manipulate the environment of a large industrial population and to observe the consequent improvement of the working people's "characters." Owen welcomed what he saw as the inevitable spread of industrialism because it provided the conditions for a rationally planned society: it massed and, to a certain extent, organized the population. Concentrated in industrial centers, people could be taught to subdue their animal passions and to cooperate with their fellow workers, as they had been taught at Owen's mill, New Lanark:

> They were taught to be rational, and they acted rationally. Thus both parties experienced the incalculable advantages of the system, which had been adopted. Those employed became industrious, temperate, healthy, faithful to their employers, and kind to each other; while the proprietors were deriving services from their attachment, almost without inspection.[25]

In short, the workers became free in a positive sense:[26] they could control themselves and their machines "without inspection."

If, on the other hand, the working class were left in ignorance, Owen warned, the growth of industrialism would lead to an even more disorganized and irrational society than that of the present. He reasoned that in a manufacturing society,

> All are sedulously trained to buy cheap and to sell dear; and to succeed in this art, the parties must be taught to acquire strong powers of deception; and thus a spirit is generated through every class of traders, destructive of that open, honest sincerity, without which man cannot make others happy, nor enjoy happiness himself.[27]

In order to replace this demoralizing "principle of gain" with a principle of rational cooperation, Owen campaigned for legislation to restrict the working hours of children under twelve years of age and to provide for their education. Such a bill was proposed by the first Sir Robert Peel in 1815, but it met with opposition from manufacturers who argued that Parliament ought not to interfere between employers and "free labourers." Owen's response was predictable: under the present irrational system, workers could not be called free. He used the metaphor of slavery to describe the situation of these children; at times he even echoed the old argument of the proslavery pamphlets, implying that the factory children were treated worse than slave children: "I think an intelligent slave master would not, on the sole principle of pecuniary gain, employ his young slaves even ten hours of the day at so early an age."[28] He also made the familiar "slaves of necessity" argument against the doctrine of free labor:

> If the operatives in our manufactures were really free, and had the option to work nine or fifteen hours a day, it might be less necessary to legislate on this subject. But what is their actual situation in this respect? Are they, in anything but appearance, free labourers?. . . What alternative have they or what freedom is there in this case, but the liberty of starving?[29]

Beneath Owen's use of the slavery mataphor was his own model of emancipation; he continually returned to the theme of rationality, stressing the need to educate the workers. Even when poverty is not their lot, he argued, "they are overworked by their employer, and are thus rendered incompetent from ignorance to make a good use of high wages when they can procure them."[30]

Owen's idea of freedom, then, was not one to which all abolitionists would have subscribed; he rejected the free operations of the market in favor of centralized economic and social planning, and he argued that since man's will is always determined by his environment, it ought to be conditioned to choose rationally for the good of all. Additionally, he denied the religious beliefs of many pious abolitionists, arguing that established religions spread false ideas about free will and individual responsibility,[31] and that these ideas obstructed the way to a rationally planned society.

But despite his denial of most of what the antislavery leaders meant when they talked about "freedom," Owen's writing appealed to many humanitarians in the ranks of the abolitionists because of his conciliatory style. Despite his belief that industrialism would have to cease being capitalist in order to become rational, he attempted to reason with manufacturers on their own terms. In an 1818 pamphlet addressed to "British Master Manufacturers" on the issue of child labor, for example, he tried to present his proposal as a practical economic measure: "Let your minds dwell a little longer on this subject, and you will soon discover that it is most obviously your interest that your operatives should be well taught in infancy, and during their future lives rendered healthy, and put in possession of the means of being good customers to you."[32] Even when his humanitarian sentiments broke through the crust of this essay's borrowed language of self-interest, as they did when the slavery metaphor appeared, his rhetoric was still calculated to appease: "Would any of us permit our slaves, if we were obliged to maintain them, to be so treated? Surely it is but necessary to call your attention to these facts, and you must instantly be aware of the injustice and useless cruelty which we thus inflict upon the most helpless beings in society."[33] At this point there is an apparent pause in the text, as if Owen were considering the enormous implications of the fact that he had to make the "practical" arguments in this essay at all. His next sentence, however, contained no accusations; his righteousness is subdued in the stillness that seems to accompany this gentle rebuke, addressed as much to himself as to his readers: "At this moment, I feel almost ashamed to address any human being on such a subject."[34]

Although Owen abhorred both the theory and practice of industrial capitalism, his conciliatory tone and his appeals to a general humanitarianism won him the epithets of "well-meaning" and "philanthropic" even from his adversaries.[35] Some liberals, who by no means shared his ideas about freedom, did share enough of his humanitarianism to support the factory legislation he proposed. The similarities that Owen insisted on between the factory reform movement and the antislave trade movement were evidently instrumental in winning this support. For example, in speaking for Peel's second Factory Bill, Francis Horner, one of the founders of the *Edinburgh Review* and an antislavery M.P., expressed his horror at the "slave trade" in factory apprentices in 1815: "It has been known that with a Bankrupt's effects, a gang, if he might use the word, of these children, had been put up to sale and were advertised publicly as part of the property."[36] In 1813 the fervently antislavery journal *Philanthropist* seconded Owen's call for legislation and embraced his *Essays* as extensions of the abolitionists' arguments. In their review of the *Essays*, they suggest a continuity between Owen's "environmentalist" arguments and those of the emancipators: "The philanthropic enemies of the slave trade declared . . . that it had an unavoidable effect in corrupting the people of the African coast; and that it was impossible this corruption could be removed, except by removing the circumstances which created it—abolishing the nefarious traffic."[37] Owen, therefore, in combination with a few other factory reformers, succeeded at this early stage in associating the campaigns for factory legislation and antislavery legislation while playing down the challenge to the free labor doctrine that their ideas actually represented.[38]

That Owen's underlying assumptions about freedom and determinism became widely accepted as the century progressed can be detected in the industrial narratives. He was not, after all, the only polemicist to claim that workers were often too poor and too ignorant to be morally responsible. His social determinism was supported in the 1810s by the Parliamentary testimony of many medical men, and in the 1830s and 1840s advocates of further industrial legislation and of sanitary reform repeated his fundamental challenge to the doctrine of free labor. The appearance of numerous documents describing the physical and moral condition of the working class[39] reinforced Owen's claims, insisting that, under the present social system, workers were not free: they could neither choose between employers nor choose between good and evil. Much of the publicized case against industrialism, therefore, supported the deterministic view of moral development that Owen always strongly advocated.

Furthermore, the industrial novelists, who often relied heavily on Blue Book testimony, Parliamentary reports, and other published sources, tended to imbibe the determinist assumptions about working-class character underlying Owen's use of the worker/slave metaphor. Consequently, as we will see, their books often seem to deny what had frequently been tacitly asserted by English novelists: the character's moral freedom and responsibility. The industrial novels often depict working-class characters as mere victims of circumstances, powerless to control their lives or to make rational choices. And yet their narratives are seldom *consistently* deterministic; paradigms of causality clash within these stories, producing structural dissonances that cannot be traced solely to their violation of "normal" novelistic assumptions. To understand the formal peculiarities of these novels, we must recognize that their determinism contradicts a second major tradition in the growing corpus of industrial social criticism: the Romantic and Arminian tradition that insisted on the inviolability of human free will.

The deterministic view of moral development undermined a belief that activated many religious opponents of both slavery and the factory system, including most of the industrial novelists. S. T. Coleridge was one of the earliest and most influential writers to oppose what he called the laissez-faire social theory of the political economists on the grounds that it contradicted the doctrine of free will. Like Owen, he was both an advocate of factory reform and an outspoken abolitionist, who made connections between the factory reform and the antislavery movements, attacked the political economists' idea of freedom, and constructed his own ideal of a free society. Like Owen, too, Coleridge wrote pamphlets on behalf of Sir Robert Peel's second Factory Bill that were designed to draw the humanitarian attention of the abolitionists toward the abused factory children. But here the similarity to Owen ends, for Coleridge believed that freedom could be best exercised within traditional rural societies, and his social beliefs pointed to his faith in a free, undetermined human will.

In Coleridge's second Factory Bill pamphlet (1818) we can begin to see the differences between his social criticism and Owen's. Although the purpose of the pamphlet is identical to that of Owen's "Letters" on behalf of the factory children, and even though some of Coleridge's arguments against the doctrine of free labor are reminiscent of Owen's criticisms, both Coleridge's tone and his underlying assumptions set his polemic apart from Owen's. Coleridge's pamphlet is aggressively and abrasively antagonistic to the principle of a free-labor market. Indeed, the content and language of the first half of the pamphlet are often reminiscent of Cobbett's.[40] Coleridge's antipathy to the doctrine of free labor was as deep as any writer's for the West Indian interests and more outspoken than Owen's: "Can you," he asked a lawyer while preparing the pamphlet, "furnish me with any other instances in which the legislature has interfered with what is ironically called 'Free Labour,' *i.e.*, dared to prohibit *soul-murder* on the part of the rich and self-slaughter on that of the poor!"[41] As the pamphlet makes clear, Coleridge's objections to industrialism have a religious emphasis that sets them apart both from Owen's arguments and from those of the proslavery propagandists.

In the pamphlet, Coleridge nods toward the "slaves of necessity" argument used in Samuel Martin's 1773 pamphlet, but immediately moves on to a moral condemnation of the "free" contracts between master and workman under the factory system:

> But *free* Labour!—in what sense, not utterly sophistical, can the labour of children, extorted from the want of their parents, 'their

poverty, but not their will consenting,' be called *free*? . . . The argument comes to this point. Has it or has it not been proved that the common results of the present system of labour in the cotton factories is disease of the most painful and wasting kinds, and too often a premature death? . . . It is our duty to declare aloud, that if the labour were indeed free, the employer would purchase, and the labourer sell, what the former had no right to buy, and the latter no right to dispose of: namely, the labourer's health, life, and well-being.[42]

The ironic stress on the word "free" and the denial that starving workers can properly be said to exercise their will in economic matters were standard components of the factory reformers' arguments, originating, as we have seen, in proslavery propaganda, and challenging the legitimacy of the liberal model of freedom. But Coleridge opened an additional dimension of the issue by claiming that even the exercise of *real* freedom could hardly be the highest good. Ultimately, the individual is always free; his freedom is the condition of value in his life, but it is not the source of value. Using the will in accordance with religious and social responsibility is the highest good, a good that the state should actively promote even if it thus interferes with the mere *exercise* of free will for its own sake. Such interference is not a denial of free will but an assertion that precisely *because* the will is free, societies are collectively capable of sinful practices.

A Christian legislature, Coleridge claimed, had the duty to guard against the public injury that arose from the "subversion of morals." And overworking in factories constituted just such a subversion, not, as the social determinists would have argued, because it necessarily led to immorality. Working sixteen hours a day, Coleridge believed, was itself a sin: a form of slow suicide for an adult worker and of infanticide for the parents and employers of child workers. God's laws, Coleridge reasoned, necessarily limited the right of free contract, and when one transgressed against those laws, even out of material necessity, one was morally culpable.

Coleridge believed that God's laws were best expressed and enforced through a traditional hierarchy of social relationships that defined one's "duty"; his pamphlet claims that "the labourer's health, life, and well-being" belong "not to himself *alone*, but to his friends, to his parents, to his King, to his Country, and to God."[43] This traditional idea, of course, implied duties on the part of the governors as well as the governed, for if the laborer's health, life, and well-being belonged to the king, then the king was certainly responsible for them.

Coleridge was not the first to argue that such paternalistic arrangements were good for workers. Proslavery writers and other conservative critics of eighteenth-century society had used models of traditional paternalistic communities as norms from which to attack capitalist practices.[44] In using the traditional paternalistic model of society, then, Coleridge might seem to have been associating himself still further with proslavery precedents, but in reality his use of the model departed strikingly from that of the earlier propagandists. Antiabolitionists used the traditional hierarchical paradigm in order to belittle all notions of workers' freedom, substituting security or "comfort" as the highest goal to which workers should aspire. In contrast, Coleridge believed, as we shall see, that a paternalistic society could be the basis for true human liberty. Unlike the proslavery writers, he did not deny that freedom was valuable in itself. Rather, he attempted to pry the word loose from its connection with the political economists' doctrine of free labor.

Consequently, at the end of this 1818 pamphlet on factory reform, he likened the arguments of the factory owners to those of the slave traders, citing both as examples of laissez-faire reasoning. He pointed out that the defenders of the slave trade had once argued, as vigorously as the cotton manufacturers were then arguing, for the principle of legislative noninterference: "the defenders rested their argument on the impropriety and inefficiency of all legislative interference with the freedom of Commerce. The Legislature had nothing to do with traders but to levy the duties, and then grant their only request 'Let us alone.' "[45] Citing the abolition of the slave trade as a precedent for factory regulation, he concluded by firmly linking the factory reform movement to the antislavery movement, using the highly moral tone and the language of the abolitionists: "every argument of any force, which the opponents of the Bill have urged against it, has been declared invalid, as applied to the continuance of any system *admitted* to be cruel and unjust, and solemnly negatived by the British Parliament, in the glorious precedent of the Abolition of the Slave Trade."[46]

In this pamphlet, then, Coleridge combined the rhetoric of the pro- and antislavery propagandists to refute classical economic doctrine. Along with Owen, he helped to establish a connection between the ideas of factory reform and slave emancipation, while he simultaneously resurrected some of the social criticism that appeared in the defenses of slavery. His interest in emancipation and his concurrent inability to accept the liberal idea of freedom led him to construct an alternative model of a free society. However, Coleridge believed Britain's industrial problems were primarily the result of dislocations in the countryside; he never had Owen's understanding that England was being irreversibly transformed into an industrial nation. Consequently, Coleridge thought that society could be regenerated by repairing the traditional relationships of agricultural communities. It is this traditionalist element that sets Coleridge's social criticism apart from Owen's. Moreover, a closer look at the religious basis of Coleridge's social thought reveals that it not only differs from but also directly contradicts Owen's.

In 1817, the year before this pamphlet, Coleridge had written in "A Lay Sermon" that the formerly sturdy social ladder of agricultural communities had given laborers the possibility of climbing out of their social class; it had given them "hope, which above all other things distinguishes the free man from the slave."[47] To Coleridge and many of his contemporaries, the word "hope" reverberated with religious and philosophical significance. His idea of social hope was very closely connected to his notion of spiritual hope: hope for Christian redemption. Indeed, on occasion Coleridge completely failed to distinguish between social and spiritual aspirations. For example, he condemned the radical journalists (primarily Cobbett and Hunt) for addressing "the lower orders* as if each Individual were an *inseparable* part of the order—always to remain nolens volens, poor and ignorant—How opposite to Christianity . . . *as if they were Negroes."[48] This idea of hope as both a theological and social virtue is connected in Coleridge's writing to precisely the religious notion of free will that Owen sought to discredit.

If men were to hope for salvation, Coleridge argued, they must believe that their spiritual state is neither predestined by God nor determined by social and material circumstances. Although he thought God's Providence shaped human history, he also held that by exercising their free wills men implemented the divine plan. "The elements of necessity and free will," he wrote, "are reconciled in the higher power of an omnipresent Providence, that predestinates the whole in the moral freedom of the integral parts."[49] A truly providential social order, he concluded, must encourage belief in human free will. Coleridge, therefore, devoted large sections of "A Lay Sermon," primarily a work of social criticism, to refuting various deterministic doctrines. He made a triple attack on religious, psychological, and social determinism by criticizing the Unitarians, who, he claimed, "believe men's actions necessitated."[50] By emphasizing man's intellectual capability but denying his free moral will, the Unitarians and other determinists had, according to Coleridge, reduced man's reason to the status of a mere appendage to the instincts, a faculty capable (under optimal conditions) of calculating "the greatest good" but incapable of the truly transcendent aspiration that marks the Christian idea of freedom.[51] Coleridge, therefore, believed that determinists were responsible for reducing British workers to the status of slaves, for slavery consisted not in any form of economic necessity, but in the extinction of hope that resulted from the denial of free will.

According to Coleridge, commercial societies (of which industrial communities were an extreme example) weakened people's faith in free will and encouraged all kinds of mechanistic and deterministic modes of thought. His belief was a commonplace of the Romantic reaction against Enlightenment thought; it had both religious and philosophical sources and was by no means the exclusive property of Anglicans and factory reformers.[52] Although Coleridge was the most influential propagator of this line of social criticism in the 1810s and 1820s, Thomas Carlyle was primarily responsible for perpetuating and popularizing the anti-determinist point of view in succeeding decades. Carlyle's seminal essay "Signs of the Times" (1829) closely associated deterministic modes of thought with industrial modes of production.

The ideas of Coleridge and Carlyle inspired many writers of industrial narratives; their stories were partly motivated by a desire to combat the deterministic thinking that they associated with industrialism. In their fiction, however, this antideterminist intention frequently clashes with the opposing tradition in anti-industrial writings: the tradition of social determinism that we saw in Owen's works. The industrial novelists were often faced with a dilemma: they wanted to illustrate the evil consequences of industrialism, but they also wanted to avoid implying a necessary cause-and-effect relationship between a character's environment and his moral state. The tension between these two impulses causes plot incoherence, inconsistent characterization, and dissonance of both narrative voice and mode in some industrial novels. Novels in which working-class characters' motivations are closely scrutinized, such as Charlotte Elizabeth Tonna's *Helen Fleetwood,* Charles Kingsley's *Alton Locke,* and Elizabeth Gaskell's *Mary Barton,* are most noticeably torn between the poles of freedom and determinism. However, this discontinuity is what gives these books their peculiar power, making them early explorations of a theme that was beginning to dominate English realism: the difficulty of defining the psychological and social preconditions for moral action.

Slave Drivers as Slaves of the "Devil of Avarice": Determinism vs. Moral Responsibility in the Rhetoric of the Ten Hours Movement

Sir Robert Peel's second Factory Bill was passed in 1819, and for over a decade the issue of factory reform lay dormant. The antislavery movement, however, gathered momentum during these years, and by the time Oastler wrote his famous letter to the *Leeds Mercury* in 1830, the industrial North was highly agitated about the issue. Samuel Kydd, who witnessed the agitation, later recalled the early 1830s as a time

> when England was moved from centre to circumference, with appeals on behalf of the liberation of West Indian slaves, when the West Riding of the County of York was aroused to action by the eloquence of Henry Brougham, when, without exception, in Yorkshire, church, chapel and newspaper, were organs of appeal for "liberty and right" . . . and the highly nervous had their nightly sleep disturbed by hideous visions of chains, the writhings and groans of victims.[53]

Under these circumstances, no more powerful or provocative title for a letter on factory children could have been conceived than "Yorkshire Slavery." Indeed, the comparison was so timely and obvious that Oastler seems to have made it without any knowledge of the previous connections between the issues.[54] Northern writers for the Ten Hours Movement of the 1830s and 1840s used the metaphor incessantly and made detailed comparisons between the lives of slave and factory children. They also adopted the fiery and righteously indignant style of the emancipators.

But many Northern emancipators, men such as Henry Brougham and the editors of the *Leeds Mercury*, often held interests and principles that were opposed to factory legislation. Thus, despite the fact that most Northern factory reformers (Richard Oastler, Michael Wood, and John Fielden, for example) were also middle-class supporters of abolition, charges of hypocrisy against the emancipators began to appear in their propaganda; these charges were, predictably, accompanied by assaults on the doctrine of free labor. The factory-reform publicity of the 1830s and 1840s, then, evinces the same mixture of language from both sides of the slavery debate that was apparent in the writings of Coleridge and Owen. Moreover, beneath this jumbled rhetoric lay related considerations about the nature of freedom.

In some of their first attempts to disturb the consciences of Northern liberals, the reformers went so far as to claim that factory children suffered more than colonial slaves; Cobbett's arguments about the relatively benign treatment of West Indian slaves were repeated. But these comparisons only outraged the Northern abolitionists[55] and threatened to diminish support for the Ten Hours Movement; no one who said a good word for slavery could expect to be popular in those years. Much of the negative response to Oastler's 1830 letter, with which this chapter began, came from abolitionists who objected to the worker/slave comparison on the grounds that it made the condition of slavery seem less horrible than it was. Indeed, Oastler found himself obliged to remind his readers of his own role in the antislavery movement in order to prevent his new opponents from characterizing his rhetoric as proslavery. In this passage from an 1832 article, which reveals the emotional connection between the two issues, Oastler at once established his own antislavery credentials and questioned the authenticity of his opponents':

> I wish not to be misunderstood . . . by the public—I HATE BLACK SLAVERY,—I have been engaged in opposing its continuance, by the side of Wilberforce,—I have had the honour of receiving a stone on my temple, which was intended for him—I have had the clothes torn off my back for supporting his cause—I have been hissed and hooted for supporting the emancipation of the Black Slaves!!—Oh, yes, Sir—I do hate Slavery—and if possible I hate more, that SLAVERY of the mind which prevents the unworthy Members of the *Anti-Slavery Society* in this FACTORY *District* joining heart and hand with those who seek to destroy Slavery at home, as well as Slavery in the West Indies.[56]

Although in this article Oastler insisted on the accuracy of his description of Yorkshire slavery as "the more hellish system," the reformers' subsequent comparisons between workers and slaves were more cautious. This change can be seen in the pages of the *British Labourer's Protector and Factory Child's Friend*, a periodical of the Ten Hours Movement in 1832 and 1833. One of its earliest numbers rashly quoted a West Indian slave owner's opinion about the relative suffering of black slaves and factory workers. Later numbers, however, contained nothing that could be interpreted as favorable to black slavery; instead, they were full of the most indignant and abusive denunciation of both systems:

> I hate slavery in all its forms—in all its degrees. I hate it on principle, because it is opposed to the true dignity of man—I hate it on grounds of policy, because it is always in its results subversive of the real greatness of states: *I hate, therefore, with a perfect hatred, all the disgusting cant about sleek-skinned, happy, well-fed slaves, whether white or black.*[57]

Oastler was also relieved to be able to write in a later number of the same publication that he "rejoiced to find the 'Friends' and the members of the 'Anti-Slavery Society' supporting us in London." He continued, "*There* we were all brothers—I wonder when it will be so in the West Riding?"[58]

The answer was "never," for in the North antagonism between the two groups continued. The factory reformers, nevertheless, borrowed the language and tone of the emancipators, their publicity techniques, even their issue. Oastler himself acknowledged the origins of the moral language of his crusade. One of the editors of the *Leeds Mercury* had accused him of exaggeration and inflammatory language; Oastler responded by asking what right the editor had to accuse him of inflammatory language when the accuser himself used that very language against the West Indian plantation owners.[59] The cause, moreover, was promoted through the channels first used in a "disinterested" campaign by the emancipators: pamphlets, broadsides, newspapers, petitions to Parliament, parades, and public meeting, all appealing to the unselfish humanity of the "public." And to complete the connection, the following report of a Glasgow public meeting illustrates the fact that the Ten Hours Movement literally appropriated the banner of antislavery:

> We also had two poor little Factory Girls, whose stunted growth and sickly appearance might well have drawn tears from a heart of flint, placed on the Hustings, near to the Chairman. These two poor Victims of the over-working system, supported a Banner, on one side of which was inscribed—"We pray for the speedy abolition of *ALL* Slavery," and on the other side was written— "The *Christian* Slaves of Britain, beg two hours, off their daily labour."[60]

In the thirties and forties, these constant allusions to black slavery led, as they had in Cobbett's, Owen's, and Coleridge's writings, to radical reflections on the nature of industrial society. Like their predecessors, the publicists for the Ten Hours Movement heaped scorn on the doctrine of free labor. Oastler's testimony before a House Committee of 1832, which was reprinted in several publications, is typical: "Do you think that, under the circumstances which you have described, even adults can be properly regarded as perfectly free agents?—Not at all; it is perfect nonsense to call them so; they are free to starve or to obey the will of their masters."[61] In attacking the premises of the liberals' "negative" model of freedom, the leaders of the Ten Hours Movement also developed competing paradigms. Some followed Coleridge in stressing the importance of a traditional social order and religious sanctions to the operations of *true* freedom, also insisting on the ideas of free will and moral responsibility. Others followed the course that had been marked out by Robert Owen, emphasizing the rational component of real liberty and implying the determination of the will by social forces. The reformers of the 1830s and 1840s, however, often mixed these models, and in their writings the rhetoric of freedom became increasingly complicated and paradoxical. Their speeches and articles often contained the contradictory ideas about freedom and determinism that were later to make industrial narratives problematic.

Some publicists for the Ten Hours Movement argued, as Owen had, that the routine nature of factory work, coupled with its excessive duration, robbed factory workers of their rationality and therefore their self-direction. The same contributor to the *British Labourer's Protector* who expressed his hatred of slavery "black or white" went on to describe the species of white slavery that he so deplored:

> The children of the poor, it is evident, are the sinews of all states; but let us not forget that they are *intellectual* sinews; it is not enough, therefore, that they be well governed; . . . it is required for the happiness and future improvement of mankind, that they be qualified to think, to judge, to reason; in short, that they be qualified as intelligent and accountable agents, to govern themselves. The Factory System (emphatically so called) precludes these results being accomplished; it reduces the child of the poor man to the rank of an animal machine, to the condition of a breathing automaton.[62]

As oxymoronic as the phrase "animal machine" is in its mixture of organic and mechanical metaphors, it strikingly evinces the subhumanity of the factory worker who is stunted in his intellect and hence deprived of his status as a free human being, an "accountable agent."

Indeed, the only agent in the above quotation is the "system" of factory production itself. By the 1830s it was no longer just the factory hands who were likened to slaves; in the propaganda of the Ten Hours Movement, the "system" was often depicted as the enslaver of everyone associated with it. It deprived masters and overlookers as well as operatives of their rational freedom. "Now the truth is," wrote another correspondent to the *British Labourer's Protector,*

> that there are kind men—men who often weep over the sufferings of oppressed infancy, both among Masters and Overlookers, and it is vey unjust to involve them all in one common censure. In fact the present Factory System often enslaves Masters and Overlookers quite as much as factory children."[63]

This passage is reminiscent of Owen's writings in which "systems" and "circumstances" are determining and the notion of human freedom, in the present imperfect and irrational state of society, is merely a mass delusion. But Owen's ideas, although very influential, were unacceptable on religious grounds to some factory reformers. Many leaders of the Ten Hours Movement were pious Evangelicals and Anglicans who believed in individual moral responsibility; indeed, that belief inspired their reforming activities. Furthermore, social determinism had another, even more suspect, source than Owen's writings: the idea that the system overrules individual wills also derived from the classical economists themselves, who argued that impersonal market forces dictated the hours factory owners would set and the wages they would pay. The factory reformers seemed to accept in part this description of the causality of the system, but they rejected the economists' belief that it was morally innocent and inevitable. The language of social and economic determinism was still the language of the enemy. The Ten Hours Movement, however, needed to use it in order to convince Parliament that only outside intervention could solve the problems of the factories. The reformers, therefore, applied the metaphor of slavery to the entire industrial population, but in doing so they created a rhetorical dilemma: if there were only industrial slaves and no slave masters, then who could be held responsible for the suffering of the factory children? When the "system" alone was blamed, as in the above quotation, the reformers undercut essential elements in their own propaganda: its reliance on certain religious sentiments and its capacity to generate moral indignation.

This dilemma is evident in the writings and testimony of Richard Oastler. Oastler's thinking resembled Coleridge's: both believed that preindustrial, hierarchical societies had been truly free, and both asserted that individual industrialists were at liberty to change the factory system and that their failure to do so was a sin. In statement after statement, Oastler revealed that his reforming energy and his frequent use of the slavery metaphor sprung from a deeply felt indignation which required the belief that industrial capitalists were responsible for their actions. His writings contain numerous vignettes that are clearly vengeful fantasies. This little story of the Last Judgment, revealingly call the "Inquisition," is representative of the genre:

> the Inquisition will be upon *all* sin; whether it be committed in the West Riding, or in the West Indies, makes no difference.—What a sorry figure a *cruel* Factory Master will cut when he puts in his plea—"I tried to emancipate Black Slaves"—"Thou hypocrite," the Judge will say, "Thou thyself enslaved Children of they own colour."—And the Clergyman who may plead "I exerted myself to liberate the Sons of Slavery in Foreign Climes,"—may meet his

answer, "but thou silently stood by and witnessed a *more* horrid state of Slavery at Home, nor tried to remedy it, but fain would have *hindered* those who did!" —Oh, my dear, Sir, "disguise Slavery as you will—still it is a bitter cup."[64]

This doctrinal and emotional perspective made it difficult for Oastler to adopt the rhetoric of either social or economic determinism. And yet at times that rhetoric was necessary to his cause. In 1832 Owen testified before a Select Committee of the House of Commons; the friendly questioner who directed his testimony tried to elicit the idea that regulative legislation would actually benefit the factory owners as well as the workers, but Oastler seems to have struggled against the line of questioning. The counsel asked, "When you talk of the working classes not being independent, but being in the hands of the masters, on the other hand do you conceive the masters to be independent?"[65] Oastler altogether failed to address the question in his reply, delivering instead a lengthy defense of the workers' right to combine. The counsel continued to ask about the factory owners' freedom to be humane, and Oastler continued to evade the line of questioning or to give it only the most minimal furtherance. After four tries, the counsel elicited this cursory assent to his point, which Oastler then immediately undercut by reverting to his usual condemning terms: "The system operates then as a direct premium upon cruelty, giving the advantage to the least humane of the employers?—Most decidedly; and with all the contentions that I have heard upon this question, I never heard one single argument produced, which was not exactly the argument of the owners of slaves."[66] This quiet struggle between Oastler and his questioner illustrates the tension often present in the rhetoric of the Ten Hours Movement. The questioner wished to convince the Select Committee that the system of factory production could only be reformed from without by Parliamentary intervention, because all who were inside it (masters included) were trapped by it. But Oastler could not accept the implications of this idea; he could not relinquish his contention that factory owners were responsible and therefore culpable agents. The notion of an entire industrial population driven by an irrational and impersonal system contradicted his religious beliefs and threatened to dampen his indignant reforming ardor. The religious and emotional sources of reform were at variance with the language of social and economic determinism.

In trying to transcend this contradiction, some writers shifted their causal language into the idiom of religious determinism. The writer for the *British Labourer's Protector* quoted earlier, for example, after writing about the tyranny of systems and circumstances, and apparently finding very little emotional sustenance in the exercise, finally imagines a more traditional religious causality: "He [the master] makes the overlooker into a Slave and a Slave Driver, often against his will. . . . The Devil of avarice in such cases, drives the master, the master drives the overlooker, and the overlooker drives the children, this is the truth—pleasant or not."[67] In this version, the master could be regarded as the tool of the devil, and therefore evil. But the scheme was still deterministic; so thoroughly has the metaphor of slavery been applied that the "Devil of avarice" is the only clearly responsible agent present. Determinism of some kind, however, was necessary to the author's purpose, for he was trying to prove that only legislation could check the evil and irrational force that deprived workers and masters of the freedom to be their most humane selves. Propaganda in favor of rational freedom must rely on such descriptions of irrational compulsion.

Both deterministic images of industrial society appear in the novels. In Charlotte Elizabeth Tonna's *Helen Fleetwood*, for example, the factory town of M. is described both as an economically necessitated "system" and as a part of the world that the devil somehow controls. The author is not always able to make these two images cohere. More important, she is unable to reconcile either of them with her deeply held faith in absolute free will and in God's benevolent Providence. *Helen Fleetwood*, like many other Evangelical tales, reproduces Richard Oastler's quandary: it is finally unable to contain its anti-industrial rhetoric within the limits of the religious beliefs that first inspired the hatred of industrialism.

The Slaves as the True Emancipators: The Worker/Slave Metaphor in Radical Working-Class Rhetoric

Other industrial novelists as well found it difficult to reconcile the negative determinism of the critics of the factory system with their own faith in God's benign Providence or in human free will. For the novelists of the 1840s, moreover, the problem was complicated by the emergence into prominence of yet another model of freedom, another use of the worker/slave metaphor.

Writers such as Charlotte Elizabeth Tonna, who were inspired by the Ten Hours Movement, largely ignored other political issues. The factory reform movement, however, was by no means the only outlet for anti-industrial sentiments in the 1830s and 1840s. Within the working class itself, trade unionism was growing, republican ideas were being voiced, the continuing struggle for Parliamentary reform was congealing into Chartism, and, later in the 1830s, the New Poor Law became a source of violent agitation. The plethora of causes through which members of the working class expressed their opposition to the new industrial society became an object of scorn to some observers, who read confusion into the abundance. But spokesmen for the radical workers believed that the variety of grounds for dissatisfaction led to the movement's particular strength. In 1841, for example, P. M. McDouall, Chartist and republican, complained of the results of the first Reform Bill: "Promised plenty came in the shape of the accursed Poor Law Bastilles, promised security in the shape of a Russian Police, promised economy in additional taxation."[68] But he went on to argue that the myriad wrongs were the very seeds of united working-class political action: "The strong frame of labour hath almost fainted under the withering curse of whig legislation. These wrongs arrested the attention and called forth the energies of the working man to resist aggression and re-model the form of government."[69] In short, the aftermath of the Reform Bill had strengthened working-class adherence to yet another model of freedom. As McDouall expressed it, "We have been engaged in a great agitation; within the compass of a few years we have witnessed a most memorable struggle for *political liberty*."[70]

From the 1770s through the 1840s, the struggle of the working class for "political liberty," that is, its fight for the franchise, was another conduit through which the slavery metaphor entered the controversy over industrialism. The political connotations of the words "freedom" and "emancipation" are, no doubt, very ancient, but the coincidence of the American and French revolutions, the spread of political radicalism in England, and the movement to abolish the slave trade during the late eighteenth century strengthened those connotations by providing a historical situation in which it was both easy and effective to substitute the word "slaves" for the disenfranchised.

Thomas Paine often performed this metaphoric operation in the late eighteenth century in both his political writings and his antislavery pamphlets, using metaphors of slavery to express the powerlessness of the disenfranchised. To Paine and the working-class radicals whom he influenced, the forms of oppression that the factory reformers emphasized (extreme poverty, exhausting and confined labor, ignorance, etc.) seemed secondary to one seminal deprivation: the denial of political power to the working class. In *Common Sense*, Paine announced this priority and defined exclusion from the franchise as slavery: "For it is the republican and not the monarchical part of the Constitution of England which Englishmen glory in, viz., the liberty of choosing a House of Commons from out of their own body—and it is easy to see that when republican virtue fails, slavery ensues."[71] Paine's antislavery writings, moreover, show the metaphoric substitution to have been completely reversible, and its reversibility is a measure of its concrete reality in his mind. The analogy between slaves and the disenfranchised was no mere rhetorical flourish; on the eve of the American Revolution, addressing an audience that he assumed believed in political liberty, Paine argued that his readers would be inconsistent to countenance slavery and might receive a terrible but appropriate retribution if they did:

> But the chief design of this paper is . . . to entreat Americans to consider.
> 1. With what consistency, or decency they complain so loudly of attempts to enslave them, while they hold so many hundred thousands in slavery; and annually enslave many thousands more, without any pretence of authority, or claim upon them?
> 2. How just, how suitable to our crime is the punishment with which providence threatens us? We have enslaved multitudes, and shed much innocent blood in doing it; and now are threatened with the same.[72]

In Paine's scheme, slavery was nothing more than an extreme form of disenfranchisement. After the American Revolution, Paine returned to this theme, once again implying the identity of the two kinds of powerlessness:

> we conceive that it is our duty, and we rejoice that it is in our power, to extend a portion of that freedom to others, which has been extended to us, and release them from the state of thralldom, to which we ourselves were tyrannically doomed, and from which we have now every prospect of being delivered.[73]

The radical unstamped press in England continued to spread these ideas among the English disenfranchised through the 1790s. D. I. Eaton's *Politics for the People*, for example, promulgated Paine's republicanism, his antislavery opinions, and the connection between the two in articles, fables, and poems. One republican poet alternated verses on West Indian slavery and political powerlessness, uniting the themes through the refrain of natural rights: "And Nature's great charter the right never gave, / That one mortal another should dare to enslave."[74] And the analogy reappeared when the movement for Parliamentary reform spawned another group of radical periodicals in the years after the Napoleonic Wars. Like the factory reformers during the same years, Parliamentary reformers tried to capitalize on the growing antislavery sentiments. In this 1818 quotation from the radical periodical

Gorgon, the root of the problem is disenfranchisement and the result is slavery:

> We wish to shew, that it is from the people being excluded from all influence in the affairs of Government, that these evils have been entailed upon them. And we wish to shew that, had the people been concerned in the management of their affairs, they would not have been brought to the wretched state of slavery they are now in, but that they would have taken care of their interests, in the same manner the borough-mongers have taken care of theirs.[75]

By the time the *Gorgon* was published, however, relations between the Parliamentary reformers and the key leaders of the antislavery movement had become so strained that the metaphor was seldom reversed, as it had been in the earlier Republican literature. The emancipation of black slaves was not often advocated in this journal, and the emancipators were frequently abused. For his role in suppressing the working-class movements of those years, Wilberforce is depicted as a "canting" hypocrite[76] in the *Gorgon*; Brougham was also not to be trusted. Indeed, the attitude of the *Gorgon* toward the emancipators was very much like that of William Cobbett, who, as we have noted, was influenced by pro-slavery writings. By the 1820s, then, the advocates of radical working-class causes had begun using the slavery metaphor in the same ambiguous way it was used by aristocratic and middle-class factory reformers. The political reformers were trying at once to make common cause with the emancipators and to expose their hypocrisy.

In the 1830s these accusations of hypocrisy became increasingly vehement, and the marks of proslavery rhetoric became more frequent in the language of the political radicals. Whereas the disenfranchised had included most of the middle class prior to 1832, the term referred primarily to the working class after the Reform Act. Radical workers felt themselves betrayed by middle-class liberals; consequently, they were often very disrespectful of what they considered a middle-class cause: the emancipation of black slaves. Rancorous echoes of William Cobbett abound in the radical working-class rhetoric of the 1830s and 1840s.

Chartist working-class radicals, like the factory reformers, used the phrase "*free* labor" ironically when discussing their own status. But they often coupled the phrase with an ironically inflected "*free* government," a reminder of the political roots of their economic problems, as these paragraphs from an 1841 series called "The White Slaves of Great Britain" illustrate:

> The following provisions were actually put upon the labourer's table in the year 1783, after seven shillings and sixpence had been spent in the market:—One stone of flour; twenty pounds of oatmeal; one strike of malt; one joint of butcher's meat; one pound of cross butter . . . and fourpence halfpenny was left over and above. This was the measure of labour, full, pressed down, and running over.
>
> Mark the difference now, when we have advanced in CIVI-LIZATION, improved in KNOWLEDGE, and become FREE LABOURERS under a FREE GOVERNMENT![77]

Both the doctrine of free labor and the insufficiently republican Reform Bill of 1832 are implicated here as agents in the diminution of "the measure of labour."

Although Republicanism is not theoretically opposed to the tenets of political economy and, indeed, can be seen as the extension of free contract principles into the political sphere, the Chartists believed that their model of freedom would, if implemented, exclude the economists' paradigm. A Parliament responsible to the working class, they reasoned, would check rather than encourage the unrestrained growth of capital. Therefore, the Chartists vociferously attacked political economy in the name of freedom, even though they had no agreed-upon economic theory to put in its place. Like many writers for factory reform, they often contrasted industrial capitalism with the earlier domestic system of production, claiming that workers had lost their freedom when they forfeited ownership of their tools. This nostalgia is balanced in their publications by frequent references to a future dominated by cooperative production. In both cases, industrial capitalism was depicted as a system of "wage slavery," which would only be ended by manhood enfranchisement.

Thus, in addition to charging the middle class with hypocrisy, working-class writers made direct attempts to sever, in the manner of Coleridge, the association between the ideas of emancipation and liberal capitalism; for this effort, they used the language of the emancipators. Some free trade publicity of the corn law repealers gave Bronterre O'Brien the occasion for this attack:

> The Corn-law repealers should not flatter the commercial classes, at the expense of truth. Instead of rendering men "*the unflinching enemies of oppression*," commerce has hitherto been the greatest destroyer of liberty ever known to man. . . . By whom were the natives of Africa torn from friends and home, and sold to bitter bondage all their days? By commercial men. By whom is the remorseless lash wielded over the bleeding slave's back in Brit-

ain's colonies, and even in republican America? By commercial men. . . . By whom is England herself, the most enlightened and laborious nation of all times, ancient and modern—by whom is this magnificent country now enslaved and pauperized? . . . By a Parliament and ministry of commercial men. Away, away, then, with the revolting cant which would unite commerce and liberty in the same breath. Heaven and hell are not more diametrically opposed to each other than is commerce to heaven-born liberty.[78]

Here, the slave trader, the slave driver, the corn law repealer, and the Whig politician are all emanations of the same commercial spirit. As in Coleridge's pamphlet, laissez-faire principles are depicted as license for oppression. But this passage is a much more universal indictment of capitalist commerce than any that can be found in the publicity of the factory reformers. Moreover, the most important distinction between this rhetoric and that of the Ten Hours Movement is its explicitly political dimension: a "Parliament and ministry of commercial men" were specifically responsible for England's enslavement. The problem was seen as political and so was the solution: the Chartists, slaves themselves, would be the true emancipators.

Although the Chartists did not themselves enter the discussion over free will and social determinism, the working-class rhetoric of political freedom gave the entire discourse of freedom a new urgency for middle-class writers. In two industrial novels of the 1840s, Elizabeth Gaskell's *Mary Barton* and Charles Kingsley's *Alton Locke*, the radical working-class model of freedom figures prominently and disruptively; both books attempt simultaneously to explain it and to dispose of it. Gaskell and Kingsley spin their criticisms and analyses of the "condition of England" around the issue of their radical protagonists' political development. Both writers are torn between presenting the growth of the hero's radicalism as the inevitable consequence of his distorting experiences and depicting it as the emblem of his transcendent freedom. The Chartist idea of freedom, therefore, tends to sharpen the antagonism between social determinism and free will in these novels, an antagonism already present in the traditions of industrial criticism inherited by the novelists.

Industrialism, Freedom, and Narrative Form

In tracing the uses of the worker/slave metaphor, we have seen the extent to which critics of industrialism were caught up in a controversy about the sources of action and the nature of human freedom. Many formal characteristics of the industrial novels can be explained by placing them within the context of this controversy. Critics have faulted the industrial novels for their inconsistencies without tracing these to their source in the early nineteenth-century critique of industrialism. They have instead attributed the novels' formal problems either to the authors' middle-class fears and prejudices or to some necessary incompatibility between literature and social criticism.[79] Examining the rhetoric of freedom in the debate over industrialism, however, has exposed the ruptures inside the critique of industrialism itself; probing the different uses of the worker/slave metaphor has revealed the contradictory structure of the social criticism the novelists tried to embody.

Most industrial reformers were torn between the conflicting elements in their own propaganda: on one hand they wished to assert their belief in human free will and a benign Providence, and on the other to illustrate the helplessness of individuals caught in the industrial system. Similarly, working-class radicals maintained on one hand that workers were enslaved and degraded by industrial capitalism, and on the other that workers were ready for the franchise. The industrial novels could hardly be expected to escape these deep contradictions that consistently marked both middle-class and working-class social criticism.

Indeed, the contradictions are often more apparent in the novels than they are in other kinds of writing about industrialism, for extended narratives normally contain a tension between freedom and determinism regardless of their subject matter. They are often torn between the need to explain events (to make them intelligible) and the need to capture the character's sense of free choice.[80] The tension can be felt variously as a contradiction between plot and character, narrator and character, or the beginning and the end of the story. It is basic to all narrative writing in the realist tradition,[81] but it is particularly pronounced in nineteenth-century novels, for although most nineteenth-century critics of the novel expressed a bias in favor of the primacy and irreducibility of "character," the social formation of character, its contextualization, was also a necessary subject for the novelist. Thus Coleridge, who insisted on the supremacy of the undetermined "moral Being," nevertheless expected novels to present an interplay between circumstances and free individuals: "Well, therefore, may we contemplate with intense feelings those whirlwinds which are for free agents the appointed means, and the only possible condition of that equilibrium in which our moral Being subsists; while the disturbance of the same constitutes our sense of life.[82] The purpose of the novel was to capture "our sense of life" which is described as an unstable ("disturbed") equilibrium between free moral agents and the circumstances that surround them. Further, the novel was to present this vital tension in such a way as to heighten the reader's concern for the character's ultimate destiny and to focus attention on what the character deserved.[83] The selection and arrangement of events were to be not only coherent as narrative but also morally meaningful.[84] This demand gave added impetus to expunge the random and the capricious from the novelistic chain of events.

The industrial novels, then, are not unique in containing a tension between freedom and determinism, but they are unusual in converting that tension into an explicit theme. By dealing with the "condition-of-England" question, the authors found themselves explicitly treating the very issues that were the implicit, formal concerns of all extended narratives. In addition, many of the industrial novelists had related but separate reasons to be preoccupied with the controversy over free will and the nature of Providence, for as we will see in the next three chapters, that controversy was very much alive in certain religious circles. These novelists consequently tended to put too much pressure on the vital tension between freedom and determinism, and the results are the jarring narrative dissonances that have often been noticed by critics of their fiction.

The next three chapters will examine the ways in which several fiction writers adapted the paradoxical legacy of the social criticism we have just surveyed to their own combined religious and social purposes. They will allow us to see, moreover, that these novelists revealed the tensions of their form by trying simply to record social reality.

2

The Providential Plot

The Wrong Side of the Carpet: The Legacy of Evangelicalism

In spite of what the Scripture teaches,
In spite of all the parson preaches,
This world—indeed I've thought so long—
Is ruled, methinks, extremely wrong.

"Where'er I look, howe'er I range,
'Tis all confused, and hard and strange,
The good are troubled and oppressed
And all the wicked are the blessed."

Quoth John, "Our ignorance is the cause
Why thus we blame our Maker's laws:
Parts of his ways alone we know,
'Tis all that man can see below.

"Seest thou that carpet, not half done,
Which thou, dear Dick, hast well begun?
Behold the wild confusion there;
So rude the mass it makes one stare.

"A stranger, ign'rant of the trade,
Would say, 'No meaning's there conveyed;
For where's the middle—where's the border?
Thy carpet now is all disorder.'"

Quoth Dick, "My work is yet in bits,
But still in ev'ry part it fits:
Besides, you reason like a lout;
Why, man, *that carpet's inside out.*"

Says John, "Thou say'st the thing I mean,
And now I hope to cure thy spleen:
This world, which clouds thy soul with doubt,
Is but a carpet inside out."

"But when we reach the world of light,
And view those works of God aright,
Then shall we see the whole design,
And own the Workman is divine.[1]

The Weaver God depicted in these stanzas by the Evangelical Hannah More contrasts strikingly with that more famous Divine Artisan of the eighteenth century, the Deists' Watchmaker God.[2] The Divine Watchmaker was believed to have created a mechanism, the universe, that operated according to laws humans could understand. Hannah More's God, on the other hand, weaves a pattern that man cannot even perceive. Although the rules of the Watchmaker's universe limited man's freedom, they were rational and predictable, so that man could accommodate himself to them. The underside of the Weaver's design, in contrast, appears chaotic and irrational. No amount of observation and calculation could allow people to predict its ultimate configuration. Finally, the Divine Watchmaker had withdrawn from his work; the godly act was in the past, and the eternal, predictable, self-enforcing law alone remained. God the Weaver, on the other hand, worked on unceasingly, realizing in time his eternal pattern. He intervened daily in people's affairs, overturning their plans, thwarting their desires, testing them, but ultimately, if the people accepted this interference, saving their souls.

Hannah More's popular *Cheap Repository Tracts* (1795–98) constitute the earliest examples of industrial fiction.[3] The causality that operates in these stories was passed on to later industrial novels, and although the later novels are much more complicated and contradictory in their accounts of why things happen, several of them use the kind of providential explanation offered by More: daily occurrences are traced to God's active supervision. This Evangelical model is not, however, the only kind of providential explanation found in the industrial novels. The great providential watch makes its appearance some forty years later in Harriet Martineau's *Illustrations of Political Economy* (1832–34). Although they were written forty years after the publication of More's *Tracts*, Martineau's *Illustrations* nevertheless appeared several years before the bulk of Victorian industrial fiction was produced. The Victorian writers, therefore, inherited two distinct ideas of Providence, two models of causality, from the pioneers of industrial fiction. The two ideas of Providence interacted in different ways with the traditions of social criticism surveyed in the last chapter, producing many characteristics dissonances of the industrial novels. For, as we will see in this chapter, early writers of industrial fiction found it difficult to reconcile their various visions of industrial reality with either Hannah More's interventionist notion or Harriet Martineau's mechanical idea of benign Providence.

In all her fiction, Hannah More strove to convince her readers that God is the ever-active shaper of man's destiny. Her tracts are directed against both the Deist idea of an absent God and the notion that our destinies are shaped by chance, an idea she associated with Voltaire's *Candide*.[4] Consequently, every occurrence in her tracts is assigned a providential purpose. Her rule of providential necessity is even stronger than that of Coleridge, noted in the previous chapter,[5] for she applies the explanation to the smallest incidents in each individual life; a pious collier in one of her poems paraphrases the proverb that might stand as a motto for all of her tracts: "Not a sparrow by accident drops to the ground."[6] In Hannah More's fiction, all events occur for the same reason, God's reason; none is ultimately rooted in the motivations of human characters.

Despite her belief in what seems like extreme providential determinism, however, Hannah More assumed that her characters were free. Like Coleridge, the Wesleyan Evangelicals polemicized against both Calvinists and psychological determinists on the issue of free will.[7] Consequently, Hannah More tried to portray people in all conditions of life as free moral agents. But because the events of her plots are always traced to God's will, the characters' only morally permissible free act is the act of submission. In the tracts that tell the stories of pious people, therefore, the characters seem passive; only the plot, the record of the Weaver's work, is active.

Hannah More's stories thus contain a consistent form of providential causality, but in these tracts the issue of freedom and determinism is complicated by the Evangelicals' simultaneous belief in both an all-determining Providence and human free will. For although the resigned, submissive characters seem passive in their relationship to the plot, their submission is maintained only by the utmost exertion of their wills. These model characters must be extraordinarily alert, vigilant and spiritually active; they are willfully, not passively, resigned and are thus not mere puppets in God's hands. Therefore, the fact that the characters have so little control over their earthly lives seems all the stranger. If they were only emanations of the plot, its passive pawns, the connection between plot and characters would be simple and straightforward. But even though the characters are portrayed as vigilantly active, their exertions are not the motors that propel the plot. These pious characters are eventually saved through their submissiveness, but their salvation usually falls outside the compass of the story's recorded events.

Thus there is a wide gap between plot and characterization in these early tales of workers' lives. The most important events in the tales are usually not the product of human interaction, but of divine intervention. In "The Lancashire Collier-girl," for example, the heroine, Mary, is taken to work in the mines at the age of eight by her father, with the narrator's complete approbation. There the child witnesses her father's death and then works double shifts for the next ten years in order to support her mother and brothers, while God takes these loved relations from her one by one. All of this, according to the narrator, is for Mary's own good; the narrator sees both sides of God's carpet and assures us that the story will ultimately make sense: "the most grievous afflictions are often appointed by Providence to be the means . . . of calling some extraordinary virtue into exercise."[8] Mary's virtue is indeed sorely exercised, and her health is also completely ruined, but no action she takes seems to bear any causal relationship to what happens to her. Although she constantly does her duty, she sinks deeper and deeper into poverty and isolation.

Only when her physical strength is gone and she is becoming mentally unstable does any action of Mary's engage with a major event of the plot, and that action, which wins her the post of servant to a "sober private family," is her continued submission:

> The owners of the mansion happened . . . to observe her countenance, and the peculiar modesty of her manner [after the initial rejection of her application], as she was taking her departure, for her patient and silent grief touched them far more sensibly than any loud complaints could have done, and they therefore determined to make some inquiries concerning her. (Pp. 152–53)

The prospective employers are told the story that we already know, a story of quiet suffering, and they hire her. Even in this last episode, though, neither Mary nor her employers are portrayed as the real authors of the happy ending. They do their duty, but God causes the events. The incident is introduced with the phrase "it pleased God to raise up for her some kind friends" (p. 151).

Mary, however, is unusually fortunate: pious characters in other More stories are not given even her meager portion of earthly reward. The heroine of "'Tis all for the Best" dies in an almshouse insisting to the last that "God's grace, in afflicting me, will hereafter be the subject of my praises in a world of blessedness" (p. 150). These heroines are free, not to control what happens to them, but merely to submit to their salvation.

Rebellious characters have a more creative relationship to the plot than do pious characters. According to More's theology, God intends everyone to be saved; a creature who is damned, then, must damn himself.[9] In addition, the freely willed actions of rebellious characters often determine the events of the good characters' lives. In "The History of Diligent Dick," the hero, a laborer, is cheated out of a fortune by his wicked uncle. The uncle's motivations are the engines of the plot, and the events he creates shape both Dick's life and his own.

At the same time, this sinful freedom—although it closes the gap between character and plot—is not easy to reconcile with belief in an all-determining Providence. Indeed, More comes perilously close to denying the freedom of these characters by describing them as "instruments" of God's Providence. For example, after hearing the story of his uncle's evil, Dick exclaims, "Merciful Heaven . . . how covetousness hardens the heart of man! what a safeguard has my poverty been to me; riches might have ensnared my soul too."[10] His uncle's sin has fulfilled the purposes of Providence by removing temptation from Dick's life. God has worked His will for one character through the sin of another; yet the sinner is held wholly responsible for the sin. The rebellious character is at once an instrument and a creator of the plot. Thus, when the actions of characters actually do turn the wheels of the plot, a slight friction is generated: we are unsure whether the source of the events lies in God's will or in human will.

We scarcely feel the friction when reading these tracts, however, for the sins of the rebellious characters normally cause them such extreme mental pain that they finally repent. Because such determinism is thus ultimately benign, we tend to accept it: because the sinner is not simply discarded at the end of the story, his use as an instrument, an efficient cause, raises no question of justice. God does not seem to will his sin, but merely to allow it, and the fact that the sin finally fits into a divine plan for the sinner's own salvation is only intended to make us wonder at God's extraordinary economy of means.

The motives of both good and bad characters, then, are ultimately inessential to the development of More's providential plots. The ease with which More reconciles this determinism with her firmly held belief in free will is, as we have seen, a function of the benignity of the universe she envisions. Furthermore, her universe is one of absolute moral simplicity: her characters always choose between good and evil, never between greater and lesser goods or evils, and duty is almost always visible and very close at hand. Because the Evangelical doctrine of submission to Divine Providence had reduced the range of acceptable responses to an increasingly confusing and seemingly unjust social order, the Evangelicals' insistence on free will did not present complex moral choices or problems, at least not in the fiction of an eighteenth-century political conservative like Hannah More.

By the 1830s, however, even conservative Evangelicals tended to portray a more problematic social reality when they wrote about working-class life. Like others before her in the dominant Wesleyan tradition, Hannah More had grounded her recommendation of political submission in the doctrine of beneficent Providence, and this association between political conservatism and providential faith remained strong in the minds of most nineteenth-century Evangelicals. But during the 1790s and the first three decades of the nineteenth century, as we saw in the last chapter, certain social causes began to appeal, on the basis of religious arguments, to these pious people. Even earlier in the eighteenth century, the crusade against the slave trade had enlisted their support by claiming that slavery systematically corrupted its victims and denied the essence of their humanity, their free will. By the early nineteenth century zealous Evangelicals began objecting on the same grounds to child labor in the textile factories.[11] In so doing, the Evangelical reformers began to complicate their moral vision: they still held to their belief in Providence, but they no longer practiced mere submission to all facts of the social order. As the reformers began to see themselves and their reforms as instruments of God's Providence, the world of Christian social action grew larger and more complex.

In the most important work of industrial fiction to emerge from this reforming Evangelicalism, Charlotte Elizabeth Tonna's *Helen Fleetwood* (1839–40),[12] providential design and free will are no longer as easy to reconcile as they had been in Hannah More's fiction. Submission to the social system is no longer seen as the only acceptable action. Most of Tonna's pious working-class characters are properly submissive, but the narrator herself rails against the social order of the factory town and calls for root-and-branch change. She even introduces major characters who try to reform the social system.[13] Faced with an antiprovidential society, Richard, the hero of *Helen Fleetwood*, can do his religious duty only by refusing to submit to the systematically produced disorder created by his "betters."

The discrepancy between Providence and freedom in this book is further complicated by an even deeper and more pervasive contradiction between two kinds of causality—social and religious determinism. To fill the gap between the dutiful sentiments and actions of the pious characters and the events of the plot, Tonna uses a causal analysis that closely resembles Robert Owen's, one that has little to do with divine designs. Her criticism of industrialism draws heavily on the writings of critics like Owen, who insisted that character is shaped by the environment and who denied the existence of both free will and providential necessity.

Thus, even though Tonna considered herself a disciple of More,[14] *Helen Fleetwood* contains much more complicated ideas about causality and freedom than do the stories of the earlier Evangelical. Despite More's insistence that God's ways are often mysterious, they are always pellucid in her tracts. Although the pious, impoverished characters themselves cannot clearly see God's design, the top side of his carpet, it is visible to the narrator, who describes it to the reader. But this complete visibility of God's design is missing from *Helen Fleetwood*. Indeed, the characters seem to enter an antiprovidential territory shortly after the novel begins, when the pious Widow Green makes the mistake of moving herself, her grandchildren, and her ward, Helen Fleetwood, to the factory town of M. Although the widow is actually tricked into this move by the Poor Law guardians and factory owners, the narrator calls it a "prideful" act. It is as if a pious Hannah More character has wandered off into one of those dangerous bypaths. Henceforth, God's hand is seen only in the destinies of a few characters; most lives portrayed in *Helen Fleetwood* are shaped by forces that God does not seem to control.

Tonna's novel includes some providential explanations, but she, unlike More, cannot apply them to all events, for the industrial town of M. does not fit into a providential scheme. M.'s social fabric clearly is not of God's weaving: the town is a place where submission to the social system means spiritual suicide for most working-class characters. It is not simply a place where the poor suffer physically, for that could be sanctifying; it is also a place where they are systematically depraved by those in authority. M.'s dynamic is actually antiprovidential: obedience to parents and masters leads children into temptation, not into grace. Because it is impossible to explain M. in providential terms, the narrator introduces the completely different, indeed antithetical, causal scheme of economic and social determinism to account for the factory town's existence. The author thereby creates an ideological bind: her religious principles lead to her criticism of industrial society, but her criticism draws her away from a providential explanation of events.

The formal consequence of this bind is a division of the fictional world into providential and antiprovidential territories. In its simplest form, this division separates the country from the industrial town. Although we see in the opening chapters that agents of industrialism and the New Poor Law are corrupting the country, we are also made aware of the fact that in the country Widow Green did have an authoritative guide: her pastor would have advised her against moving to the industrial town. If she had sought his advice and been dutifully submissive to him, she would never have imperiled the bodies and souls of her charges. In M., however, even the ministers find it difficult to do their duty: their parishes, we are told, are crowded and mismanaged.[15] Indeed, in M. no one considers himself responsible for the physical or spiritual health of the poor: the hierarchy of Providence has collapsed and been replaced by a hierarchy of greed.

The split between providential and antiprovidential territories also exists inside M. itself. Helen Fleetwood and the Widow carry the "blessed" country into the town, and although it is hinted that they have strayed out of the "right path" (p. 57), their spiritual innocence remains intact. Consequently their industrial ordeal sanctifies them. Even in M., God's purposes in oppressing these two women are clear: for Widow Green the experience is "an humbling dispensation" (p. 46); for Helen Fleetwood it is a martyrdom that redeems several of her fellow workwomen. Sarah Wright, the crippled, town-bred grand-daughter of the Widow, is also saved by the Green family's move to M. For Helen and the Widow, then, and those few who enter into their circle of sanctification, the descent into M. might be considered a "fortunate Fall."

The rest of the industrial population, however, exists outside the providential universe: their submission to the system only brings spiritual death. In this novel, as in Hannah More's tracts, there is a great gap between the pious characters' actions and the things that happen to them; but unlike Hannah More, Charlotte Elizabeth Tonna fills that gap with distinctly unprovidential economic and social determinism. In Hannah More's fiction a slight friction was produced when sinful characters served as the instruments of God's will. In *Helen Fleetwood* this contradiction between efficient and final causes is much more abrasive: the mechanism that humbles the Widow and sanctifies Helen Fleetwood cannot be consistently recognized in the novel as God's instrument. Such a recognition would undermine the author's religiously inspired political purpose.

For, in fact, Tonna campaigned in her fiction for legislation to reform the factory system.[16] She objected to the system on religious grounds, and her religious objections inspired her descriptions of M., its population, and their work. She could not, therefore, portray this system, which she deemed thoroughly wicked, as a part of God's beneficent plan. Nor could she depict, for all her belief in free will, the triumph of individuals over the system, since her purpose was to show that the destructive machinations of industrialism could only be stopped by government interference. The causal language that she uses to explain the dynamic of industrialism is, consequently, altogether different from the providential language she uses when justifying the suffering of Helen and the Widow. The former ignores final causes and spiritual purposes, concentrating instead on the linear cause-and-effect logic of such secular theorists as Robert Owen. Ultimately, it seems to deny the existence of both free will and Providence.

The narrator's first description of industrialism, for example, emphasizes, through the slavery metaphor, its destruction of freedom. The rural parochial authorities, motivated by the desire "to decrease the burdens of their respective parishes at any cost," are compared to the slave sellers of Madagascar (pp. 41–42). The factories are like plantations, the workers like slaves. In this passage, the slavery metaphor implies a demonic economic determinism that deprives both masters and workers of their moral freedom: the factory system, like the slave trade, is driven by an unrestrained profit motive that wastes human life and in turn creates "so pressing a demand for a supply of new labourers" (p. 41). Like many of the propagandists discussed in the last chapter, Tonna insists on this economic determinism in order to prove that the factory system cannot reform itself from within. This negative determinism is central to the novel; it leads the author to depict the systematic corruption of nearly everyone in M. However, by insisting that this evil system overwhelms every individual, Tonna ensnares herself in contradictions: the descriptions of automatic corruption, which make up the largest portion of the book, undercut the narrative's own Evangelical assumptions of human freedom and moral responsibility. They also contradict the narrator's claim that divine order rules the universe.

The negative social determinism of industrialism is illustrated by the fate of half of Widow Green's family. The Widow has two families of grandchildren, one family formed in the providential countryside, the other deformed in the factory town. The latter are the children of the Widow's daughter, Mrs. Wright, who had moved to M. many years earlier. There are two boys and two girls in the Wright family, and the narrator contrasts them with the two boys and two girls from the country. The town-country contrast is emphasized in their very names and physical descriptions. Whereas the Green children are robust and sanguine, the Wright (as in "maker" or "manufacturer") children are introduced to the reader as "the withered remains of [the factory system's] poor blighted victims" (p. 52). The phrase implies that these little factory workers are stillborn into the story's action: they are not just victims, but "the withered remains" of victims. The language of death appears throughout their description and is particularly noticeable in the portrait of the older girl, Phoebe. She is called "the spectre of a very pretty girl" (p. 53), whose black hair "set off the deadly white of her complexion with such effect that she seemed like one in whose veins the current of life had already ceased to circulate." Her eyes have a "broad, unflinching stare" that the narrator calls "oppressive" (p. 53). This last detail both emphasizes her deathly state and introduces its spiritual dimension, for Phoebe's stare is both that of a corpse and that of a bold, immoral girl. Phoebe and her brothers are pathetic, physically deformed children, but it is their spiritual deadness that the narrator repeatedly confirms.

Their physical state, however, is not just a metaphor for their spiritual state, not just an outward manifestation of inner corruption. Their spiritual deadness is actually caused by their physical weakness. Exhaustion leads the boys to the gin shop; Phoebe is too tired to improve herself, so she seeks the excitement of "bad company." The causality that operates in the story of the Wright family is that of physical, economic, and environmental determinism, the causality preached by Owen and assumed by numerous witnesses before Parliamentary committees in the early decades of the century. Indeed, the characters of Phoebe and her brothers are largely drawn from the testimony of medical men.[17] They appear to be products of their destructive environment.

The factory system is shown to have corrupted Mr. and Mrs. Wright as well, turning one "into a stone . . . towards her own children" and "forcing" the other "to wink at what frets his very life" (pp. 94–95). The industrial system is presented as all-controlling and all-corrupting. Indeed, the Widow must finally return to the country in order to save the Green children from certain degeneration. But because members of the Wright family, especially the children, seem to have no choice of companions or occupations, they can hardly be held responsible for their spiritual state; and in fact they are not. Helen Fleetwood herself absolves them of guilt, stressing (like Owen) the determinism of ignorance:[18] "for indeed ignorance is the root of it all. Poor things! they have not been taught their [religious] duty, and how should they know it? What do Phoebe and Charles ever hear at home, to strengthen them against the bad examples that they have been exposed to ever since they were mere babes?" (p. 151).

The moral consequences of industrialism aroused Charlotte Elizabeth Tonna's religious indignation against the factory system, but they also finally made it impossible for her to fit the industrial world into a providential scheme. She had to avoid attributing the physical suffering of factory workers to God's will; such an attribution would seem a justification of the suffering and consequently undermine her contention that unhealthy physical conditions lead to moral degeneration. Only the suffering of crippled Sarah Wright, which has removed her from the factory, is said to be divinely ordained. But even in Sarah's case, the providential explanation is rather tentatively given. Sarah objects to her grandmother's remark that God "ordered" her affliction: "Helen Fleetwood told me that God is very good; and I don't think he would order me to be hurt in this way" (p. 108). Instead, she blames the machine and the overlooker for the accident that maimed her. The Widow, we are then told, is "greatly affected" by Sarah's speech, but she tries once again to give a providential interpretation of the accident: "I trust you will yet find that even these hurts were ordered by his great goodness, for your everlasting benefit" (p. 109). "Hush!" replies the girl; the Widow is interrupted, and the narrator never returns to the subject.

In this novel, the providential explanations of the moral condition of the workers would be even more out of place than providential explanations of their physical condition, so no such explanations are given. The intersection of the Wrights' story and the Greens' story, however, implies that God uses the victims of the factory system for His own purposes. Phoebe, in her degenerate state, becomes the instrument that scourges and sanctifies Helen, and through Helen the Widow Green. Yet the story denies that God designed the factory system in order to make a saint of Helen Fleetwood. The factory system remains hellish and seemingly beyond God's jurisdiction; it is, to use the narrator's word, "diabolical" (p. 51). Consequently, the novel's narrative logic seems most paradoxical at precisely this intersection of Phoebe's story and Helen's: the social determinism that corrupts Phoebe's character is at odds with the providential assumption of Helen's story. The narrator cannot bring herself to explain Phoebe's spiritual ruin as part of God's plan, for doing so would eclipse the necessity of reform.

The novel contains no logical solution to this dilemma, but the narrator does find a stylistic device to cover the contradiction. She tells the events of Helen's working life completely from Helen's viewpoint, filtering everything that happens in the factory through Helen's submissive and largely nonanalytical consciousness. As Helen takes up her cross, she does not ask who made it; she sees only the duties that are immediately before her: working hard and setting a pious example. In telling this part of the story, the narrator simply records Helen's own thoughts; most of the narrator's analyses of the factory system are thus separated from the recounting of Helen's providentially ordained experience.

Outside Helen's own consciousness, the social world in this novel is not presented as a God-given order that one must simply accept. The certainties of Hannah More's providential vision have become, by 1838, the complexities of a religious outlook that can neither rest on nor dispense with providential causality. The dual providential and antiprovidential worlds of this novel in their turn call forth two different models of right action. In Hannah More's stories, the pious characters always meekly bear injustice, but in *Helen Fleetwood*, because the system itself is evil, God's work of salvation can only be done if someone actively tries to dismantle the "diabolical" machinery. Helen, whose story remains within a providential framework, acts like a character in a Hannah More tract: she submits to the system that martyrs her. There is, however, an active, masculine counterpart to Helen in this novel, and it is his role to try to do God's will by changing the world.

Helen Fleetwood is a free soul who chooses submission. Richard Green, on the other hand, represents the free will actively combating evil in the world. The novel presents these two modes of freedom as feminine and masculine, respectively. Helen does her feminine duty by meekly and silently enduring both debilitating work and persecution. Richard Green's duty, on the other hand, is to do everything in his power to protect Helen. Richard is the oldest of the Widow's grandchildren; he is a country laborer who stays on the farm while the Widow and the other children move to M. His masculinity, his unselfishness, and his country life are all connected by the narrator, who calls him "a specimen of manly English character, such as it will be found where men have not herded together in pursuit of selfish ends until all the finer touches are worn away, and 'every one for himself' becomes the heartless maxim" (p. 248). As a boy, Richard had wanted to be like his pet rooster, who protected the hens and chickens. "We are good friends," Richard told Helen when they were both children; "he follows me about, and pecks from my hand; but if I catch a fowl, and frighten it, bounce he flies at me, tries to strike with his spurs, and tells me as plain as he can speak he is going to tear my eyes out" (p. 248). This masculine aggression, even toward one's master, is called "pretty" by Helen; it is justified, indeed admirable, because the cock is bound by duty to protet those in his care.

Duty and self-assertion, then, can be combined in Richard's actions. Consequently, his kind of action, which attempts to engage with and change both events and social facts, seems freer than Helen's passivity. In a sense, Richard appears out of the fissure between the book's providential and antiprovidential worlds, and he is the character who makes *Helen Fleetwood* a novel. The distance between providential and social determinism is the very space in which novelistic action emerges and, in the person of Richard, announces itself as the enemy of determinism. When Richard arrives in M. on an errand for his master, he is shocked at the state of the family. His younger brother is very ill and the older boy and his sister Mary are growing willful and impudent. Helen, moreover, the girl he intends to marry, is physically weak and mentally troubled. Richard sets out immediately to save Helen and his brothers and sister; in doing so he becomes the principle of active freedom in the novel. He is even made the spokesman for the Wesleyan doctrine of free will, and he discovers a connection between the Calvinists' belief in predestination and industrial practices. In a conversation with the Calvinist master of the mill in which his little brother works, Richard argues against the mill owner's policy of merely reading the Scripture to his young employees without correcting their conduct or interfering in their lives in any other way. The mill owner's belief in predestination coalesces with his belief in laissez-faire economic theory, producing a general policy of nonintervention. He leaves events, he tells Richard, "to God" (p. 317). Richard, however, argues that salvation should be like farming: "It seems to me that the harvest is not a miracle worked in spite of us, but a merciful gift bestowed where we honestly labour for it" (p. 318). Richard makes one final remark that completes the author's association of Calvinism with industrial capitalism, implying that the theology of an industrialist is distorted by the very means of production he uses:

> since [God] has been pleased to make use of the figure of a field, and sowing, and reaping, and harvesting, in so many parts of his blessed word, I could not do less than take notice as I went along of the way in which it holds good. Perhaps . . . you that live among machinery, and see everything done by steam, may take different views. (P. 318)

Richard, then, is the book's principle of active, conventionally novelistic, freedom. Through him the reader learns of the attempts of working men and their allies to achieve factory reform. While Richard is in M., pockets of morally free, uncorrupted workers are discovered. But Richard is finally unable to change the system he opposes, and his efforts to save Helen fail. Indeed, since the author is intent on showing that individuals cannot change the factory system without legislative interference, Richard's attempts to find justice inside the mills are doomed to failure by the book's political purpose. Richard must be defeated by the antiprovidential determinism of M.

His battle, however, turns out to be not only against the factory system and its antiprovidential causality, but also against the book's rival providential assumptions. Although Richard's mode of freedom and Helen's mode of freedom appear to be merely masculine and feminine ends of one spectrum of duty, they are ultimately opposite models of action. Like its providential and antiprovidential territories, the novel's two modes of action are not really reconciled. While Richard tries to tear her away from the factory, Helen clings to her martyrdom. She refuses to remove herself from the bad air of the carding room or the daily contact with depraved workers, for the former would be shirking her duty, and the latter would be seeking "spiritual privileges" (p. 402). She believes God put her in the factory for a reason, and she refuses to overrule his judgment. Thus Richard's efforts are opposed by Helen on providential grounds, and he is finally forced to accept her martyrdom. He leaves M. behind, hoping he can bring Helen to be buried in the countryside.

The book's principle of active freedom, therefore, is overmatched by both its providential and its antiprovidential determinisms. At the end of this novel, as at the end of a Hannah More tract, submission seems the only possible action. And yet the book cannot come to rest on this simple principle, for in M. one's own submission could bring spiritual death to others. Thus the Widow can explain the events of the story providentially only when she applies them to her own life. "I knew I wanted daily sanctifying," she tells the doctor in M., "but I did not know I wanted daily humbling. He who knew it ordered it for me; and truly I never so rejoiced in Him before falling from what was in my own mind a little height among my equals, as now I do when I seem to have reached the bottom, and have grace to be there contented" (p. 417). The doctor, however, immediately sees the exclusiveness of the Widow's little speech and reminds her that the children, who are daily weakened and corrupted by the same processes that bring about the Widow's "daily humbling," cannot "view it in so happy a light." "Ah, sir," admits the old woman, "I spoke selfishly" (p. 418).

In order to escape this contradiction between the sanctifying effects of events on the Widow and the corrupting effects of the same events on her grandchildren, the author brings the Green family back to the countryside; she must leave the antiprovidential world of M. behind, because the reforming purpose of her fiction eliminates all possibilities of spiritual salvation for the young Greens while they remain in the corrupted factories. As the Widow explains to the doctor, neither her pious example nor Helen's is an effective antidote to the evil atmosphere of the factories:

> "They are heavy and sullen, except when they talk to one another in a way that grieves me; telling silly tales, making ill-natured speeches about their companions, and repeating idle jests, often not fit to repeat; besides all that passes in whispers, and which no doubt is worse. It seems as if the weariness brought on by the dull, but fatiguing work, required something to remove it, more exciting to the bad feelings than engaging to the mind. Oh, sir, I fear these mills are slaughterhouses to the poor little lambs of the flock!" (P. 419)

Thus, in this fictional world, which has both a providential and an antiprovidential order, acceptance is not always the answer. M. is not simply given up to the devil at the end of *Helen Fleetwood*. Although

individual evildoers are punished, and even though the narrator expresses faith in legislative reform, the triumph of good over evil is by
no means complete at the story's conclusion. The antiprovidential
determinism still operates throughout most of the town. The structural
contradictions between providential and antiprovidential territories
and modes of action remain, and we are left with conflicting emotional
and intellectual responses, which are summed up in the conversation
between Richard and his pastor, Mr. Barlow. Richard has finally
adopted Helen's providential view of her own fate, whereas the pastor
focuses on the injustice that has been done to her: "The kind-hearted
minister wept outright, and Richard. . . said, 'I should like to cry too,
sir; but somehow, I can't.' " "Oh," exclaims the minister, "what have
they to answer for who laid this cruel snare in the harmless path of the
widow and the fatherless?" He then pours forth "a most touching
supplication, such as, a few days before, would have melted Richard."
But the young man is no longer capable of feeling the indignation that
motivates his pastor; his belief in the providential necessity of Helen's
suffering and death has canceled his anger at the system that caused
them: "though the 'Amen' was breathed from his inmost heart, he rose
collected and tearless as ever" (p. 409).

The distance between Mr. Barlow's and Richard's emotional re-
sponses to Helen's story reflects the split between providential and
nonprovidential interpretations that characterizes the whole novel.
Helen's story is at least conceivable in providential terms. A far deeper
contradiction lies between her story of martyrdom and that of the
Widow's wicked granddaughter Phoebe, who persecutes the saintly
Helen. We can see the heavenly side of the plot in Helen's story, but
Phoebe's has only one side, and it is not the work of godly hands.

Charlotte Elizabeth Tonna's narrative, therefore, is paradoxical because the religious purpose of her writing finally contradicts her deeply
held religious beliefs. But her social and religious purposes cannot be
separated and said to contradict one another, for they are identical.
Her objection to industrialism was religious: she believed that the
factory system bred spiritual ignorance and vice. But in tracing the
outlines of this evil causality, the author depicts a world that seems to
accommodate neither of her two fundamental religious doctrines: that
human beings are free and responsible agents, and that God is constantly at work shaping events that will lead to salvation. Only a few of
Tonna's characters can be depicted as free; only a few seem to be under
God's providential care. The lives of the rest are determined in a
manner that was new to English fiction: they are completely creatures
of the evil social system that surrounds them. Slaves of necessity, of
ignorance, of vice, these are not characters who could have been

imagined by Hannah More. Although they aroused the pity and indignation of many Evangelicals, they ultimately cannot inhabit a world ruled by Providence.

The Devout Science: Unitarianism's First Phase

> Now that I had got leave, as it were, to apply the Necessarian solution, I did it incessantly. I fairly laid hold of the conception of general laws, while still far from being prepared to let go the notion of a special Providence. Though at times almost overwhelmed by the vastness of the view opened to me, and by the prodigious change requisite in my moral views and self-management, the revolution was safely gone through. My labouring brain and beating heart grew quiet, and something more like peace than I had ever yet known settled down upon my anxious mind.
>
> —Harriet Martineau
> *Autobiography*[19]

Harriet Martineau's industrial narratives resemble Hannah More's in several important ways. Both assume a generally benign Providence at work in the world and see the social order as the product of that Providence. The world's seeming injustices ultimately advance the general good.[20] Consequently, the most enlightened characters in both authors' works find their greatest freedom in submitting to providential necessity. In short, both try to illustrate a determined but ultimately benevolent universe.

Their notions of Providence and of the God who created it, however, are incompatible in important respects. As the epigraph for this section suggests, Harriet Martineau came to deny expressly the existence of the kind of Providence that More's stories illustrate: the special Providence of a God who intervenes in the lives of individuals. Her God is very much like the Watchmaker of the Deists,[21] a God whose Providence works automatically and impersonally. In Harriet Marineau's fiction, the plots are deterministic, but they are not, as in Hannah More's stories, the record of God's active interventions in the world. Rather, Harriet Martineau's plots show the disposition of individual destinies by immutable natural laws.

As she tells us in her *Autobiography*, the Necessarian doctrine inspired and pervaded her writings, which were designed to show that "eternal and irreversible laws [work] in every department of the universe, without any interference from any random will, human or divine."[22] Indeed, the religious and philosophical tradition to which Harriet Martineau belonged denied the very possibility of a random will, a free, undetermined, or self-determined, will. Raised as a Unitarian, she adopted the radical views of her coreligionist, Joseph Priestley.[23] In the last quarter of the eighteenth century, Priestley incorporated David Hartley's associationist psychology into a providential view of the universe.[24] He and his followers, Harriet Martineau among them, considered the human will to be a natural phenomenon, formed according to the laws of materialist psychology, powerless to escape those laws.

Consequently, Harriet Martineau's idea of Providence excluded free will; she attacked the very idea, not just as theoretical error, but also as a barrier in the path of progress. Indeed, her polemical insistence on the immoral effects of the doctrine of free will reminds one of Robert Owen's. In the *Autobiography*, for instance, she deplores "the evils which arise from that monstrous remnant of old superstition,—the supposition of a self-determining power, independent of laws, in the human will."[25]

The world of Harriet Martineau's didactic fiction, then, is in one sense more completely determined than that of Hannah More's *Cheap Repository Tracts*: there are no free wills in Martineau's work, either human or divine.[26] But in another sense, Harriet Martineau's fictional world allows its inhabitants more effectiveness of action than does Hannah More's. The reason for this lies in the nature of the particular laws that Martineau chose to illustrate. She set out to portray the workings of the providential laws of economic life, which she thought the classical political economists had already discovered. Before she began her famous *Illustrations of Political Economy*, she had published her belief that that science was an "apt and beautiful"[27] example of the Necessarian doctrine. Martineau believed the phenomena that political economy explains are the actions of men and women themselves, that the movements of the science's human subjects, even at their most automatic and unconscious, are still the motor force of the providential machine. Consequently, they become the motor force of the plots in the *Illustrations of Political Economy*.

Martineau's characters never have to confront random divine interference, and there is no disjunction between their activities and their worldly destinies. As Martineau confidently asserts in her *Autobiography*, "according to the Necessarian doctrine, no action fails to produce effects, and no effort can be lost."[28] Mundane actions have mundane consequences in the *Illustrations*. The gap between human effort and the events of the plot, which made Hannah More's characters seem helpless, is closed in Martineau's stories by the complete conflation of religious and social-economic determinism: God is present only in the laws that govern human behavior, and human behavior turns the wheels of the plot.

Moreover, because political economy explained regular and recurrent phenomena, Martineau believed that it could enable one to predict and thereby manipulate or provide against economic change. Like most political economists, whose views of liberty were derived from Locke and Hume, she believed that one's will was necessarily determined by forces beyond one's control, but that one's actions could be said to be free whenever they were not coerced against one's will. The major thinkers in Harriet Martineau's intellectual and religious tradition advocated free choice and free action, but they denied the existence of free will. Knowledge, however, could become an important determinant of the will, making one's actions more effective.

Even the greatest prescience and latitude of action, however, could not produce all that an individual might intend. The marketplace of the political economists is, after all, a mechanism for adjusting competing interests: the desires of all cannot be satisfied, and the interests of some must be completely denied, especially in times of vast technological change. Those who suffered most while the market adjusted itself, Martineau knew, were workers. Although Harriet Martineau's Providence is, like that of the Evangelicals, generally benevolent, she realized that its mainspring, competiton, often brought about a very hazardous existence for the working class. But she thought their suffering could be minimized by education, frugality, and limitations on family size; her own _Illustrations_ are examples of the kind of help she believed the middle class should give to workers. Still, she did not believe that their suffering could be altogether alleviated. Although she overtly clung to the idea that class interests are identical, she had imbibed from Malthus and Ricardo[29] a notion of the necessity of class conflict, a conflict that the working class could never win. It is not surprising, then, that despite her general optimism, her working-class characters often seemed doomed to struggle, doomed to lose.

Like Hannah More, therefore, Harriet Martineau depicts workers who are destined to suffer; unlike More, however, she cannot cheerfully explain the suffering of these victims of the competitive process as the purchase price of a glorious afterlife. She seldom mentions any afterlife, but we might assume that she accepted Priestley's idea of the Kingdom of God, which was material and ultimately pleasant for everyone.[30] She even admitted that because there was never any sharp division between the saved and the damned in her mind,[31] she felt there was no spiritual justification for the suffering of the poor. She could only optimistically interpret that suffering in secular terms: after generations of futile struggle, the working class might learn to control the labor market by restricting its own numbers. This was Martineau's hope for the distant future, but it does not make her working-class characters seem freer in the contemporary world of her fiction.

In short, although Martineau's working-class characters often seem powerful, they are also restricted. While the events of the plot grow partly out of their motives, and even though they have the potential for partially controlling their own lives, that potential is usually stultified by the circumstances that surround them. Indeed, as we will see, their very power is often self-destructive because it is ignorantly used. Furthermore, because their wills are not free, and a God to whom they might appeal for special treatment is absent, there are no transcendent elements in their existence, no reasons for discounting the importance of mundane events. There is no "otherworldliness"[32] in Martineau's stories, no implied heavenly happy endings or special Providence. There is no realm of freedom above earthly causality.

The earthbound nature of the *Illustrations* rules out the development of the gap between character and plot created by the Evangelicals' idea of Providence. In these stories, plot and character are reciprocally active. However, the conflation of earthly and providential causality ultimately spawns another formal problem. Martineau followed the political economists in giving the working class a higher stature than it had formerly received. Its members, after all, comprised that important category "labor." But again following her mentors, Martineau also viewed workers as severely limited by the often gloomy determinism of economic necessity. Because they also lacked even the possibility of a special Providence to rescue them from their plight, Martineau's working-class characters seem tragically determined. Indeed, the author deliberately uses tragic drama as a generic reference point for her tales. The narrator's emotional tone, however, is dispassionate when it is not downright cheerful. It implies satisfaction with the causality that produces the misery. The result, as we will see, is a series of discrepancies between the tale's content, its form, and its emotional tone.

Commentators on Martineau's works have noticed that the tales are gloomy but the teller is cheerful. This noted inconsistency has been traced both to Martineau's own personal confusion and to certain common contradictions within classical political economy itself.[33] The truth, however, lies somewhere between these explanations. The formal discrepancy between content and tone, plot and narration, originates in the contradiction that runs through the author's model of causality, her combination of religious and "scientific" elements. This model should not be confused with classical political economy in general.[34] The political economy that Martineau developed was a popular but peculiar blend of optimistic, providential beliefs and pessimistic, mechanical doctrines; it forced the ideas of the economists into the mold of a theodicy. Her providential beliefs implied that the gloomy determinism pervading the working-class characters' lives would lead ultimately to the greatest good for the greatest number. The narrator's tone is consequently suffused with a consciousness of the beneficent providential determinism that causes the suffering of individuals, even when nothing in the story justifies her long-term optimism.

The peculiar quality of her fiction grows out of her attempt to maintain these two perspectives simultaneously: the universal, providential outlook and the more limited, pessimistic outlook of certain classes and individuals. Nowhere is her double perspective more evident and discordant than in her short novel *A Manchester Strike*, the ninth of the stories that comprise the *Illustrations*. The workers in this short novel seem doomed to engage in a self-destructive strike; Martineau fills the story with tragic elements, but her style deliberately empties the tale of tragic emotions.

The tale is designed to illustrate that strikes cannot permanently raise the rate of wages. As the sympathetic capitalist, Mr. Wentworth, tells a delegation of Manchester weavers, it is not "a matter of pure choice with us, what wages we give."[35] The labor market itself determines wages, he explains. In the long run, workers are collectively capable of controlling that market by understanding that Providence's "usual course" would be aided if they limited their own numbers: "The power of the masters is considerable, for they hold the administration of capital; but it is not on this that the rate of wages depends. It depends on the administration of labour; and this much greater power is in your hands" (p. 34).

The workers, however, cannot wait for the usual course of Providence to raise their wages, and Martineau considers their reaction to the bad times natural. The strike leader, William Allen, voices the views of both Martineau and the political economists she read[36] when he celebrates the 1825 repeal of the Combination Laws ("combinations are ordered by laws more powerful than those which, till lately, forbade them," p. 481) and describes the regrettable inevitability of class conflict: "The best of the masters say, and probably with truth, that their interests demand the reductions under which we groan. Be it so: we have interests too, and we must bring them up as an opposing force, and see which are the strongest" (p. 50). The conflict in *A Manchester Strike* is presented as necessary and unavoidable. The verbs carry the burden of Martineau's Necessarian beliefs: the supply of labor "controls" wages, and reductions are "demanded" by the interests of capital; but natural laws also "order" workers' combinations, and workers "must" look after their own interests.

This inevitable opposition of interests over wages, however, is contained within a larger community of interests between masters and workers. In the novel, this belief in harmony is also expressed by Allen, who hopes there will not "need to be" a strike, because "both parties are necessary to each other" (p. 10). This other necessity—to maintain and increase the capital out of which the workers are paid—ensures the failure of the strike. At the outset, Wentworth explains that the strike demands cannot be met if the employers lose money during the work stoppage. The conflict and its resolution, therefore, are known from the novel's earliest chapters: the workers cannot win, but they must fight.

In addition to seeming tragically determined, Martineau's workers, especially her central character, are given heroic stature. This is an unprecedented characterization for workers in English literature, and it can also be traced to the influence of the political economists, who raised the category of labor to new heights in their theories, making it the very source of all value.[37] The theories of political economy made it possible to conceive of workers in tragic heroic terms, not just because it made them seem destined to suffer, but also because it made them seem important. Martineau emphasizes the power and importance of workers by embodying the enormous abstraction, labor, in a larger-than-life individual, her hero, William Allen. Combined with the story's pervasive determinism, the elevated stature of its principal sufferer indicates that tragedy is the tale's dominant generic model.

The details of Allen's story, moreover, show the appropriateness of tragedy to Martineau's didactic purposes. Allen is caught between the conflicting necessities of the marketplace; he is a sacrifice to relentless economic forces and the class antagonisms they create. Unlike Clack, a working-class demagogue provided for contrast, Allen is reasonable and self-effacing; he avoids all vituperative rhetoric and vengeful motives. He is, however, quietly sure that "something must be done" (p. 10) when wages are reduced.

Allen's heroic qualities, his strength, honesty, and unselfishness, are necessary to Martineau's economic point. She is trying to show that there is a real economic problem created by the pressure of population, that strikes are not simply the result of quick tempers or vanity, but are, rather, one of the disastrous consequences of an overloaded labor market. Allen's complete integrity is vital to the illustration of this economic causality. In addition to expressing a new valuation of labor, therefore, his elevated stature also reinforces the tale's economic determinism by preventing the reader from attributing the strike to work-ing-class irresponsibility.

The dramatic form in which Allen's story is presented, moreover, sharpens its tragic outlines. The chief events of the story take place on improvised stages before large audiences: a table in the courtyard of an inn, a cart in the middle of a field. These are the platforms from which Allen, figuratively and literally elevated above the other workers, soli-loquizes, in plain but elegant English, about the relationship between his personal destiny and public events. On a stage, Allen accepts the role of strike leader and representative, and on a stage he is later turned into a sacrificial victim by the strikers themselves. The events and their dramatic form clearly place Allen in the tradition of tragic stage heroes.

However, the means by which Allen is ennobled license the tone of contented acceptance in which his tragedy is narrated. The author stresses, for example, that Allen is not ignorant of the personal con-sequences of his actions. The author gives Allen complete foreknowl-edge. Like the strike plot, Allen's personal story is narrated as a *fait accompli*. Its outcome is known from the beginning, for when he is drafted to lead the strike, Allen knows the consequences of such leadership: "he bore in mind. . . that the sin of taking a prominent part in a combination of workmen, is apt to be remembered against the sinner when the days of trouble are over" (p. 45). Nevertheless, he feels duty-bound to lead the strike, because he also knows that he is the steadiest and most intelligent man in the union: he "did not, therefore, dally with his duty; but it cost him a bitter pang" (p. 45).

Our knowledge of Allen's future is further expanded by a speech in which he forecasts his treatment at the hands of both masters and men:

> "It is certainly an evil to a man of independent mind to be placed under the feet of any former enemy, to receive his weekly subsis-tence from the hands of his equals, and to fancy that the whisper is going round—'This is he who lives upon our gathered pence,'—Such evils await, as you know, him who comes forward to lead a combination; but they belong to the state of affairs; and since they can neither be helped, nor be allowed to weigh against the advantages of union, they should be, not only patiently, but silently borne." (P. 47)

Allen's language and ideas here are obviously Necessarian, but there is a more important, formal characteristic to notice: the speech makes the order of the narrative itself deterministic by moving the end of the story to the beginning and allowing the effect to appear simultaneously with the cause. Other possible resolutions of the story's conflict are ruled out by this narrative device.

Once Allen predicts and accepts the course of his future, he seeks consolation in the idea of his stoical heroism: "Well is it for the victim if he can say to himself that now is the time for him to practise the heroism which in grander scenes has often made his bosom throb" (p. 47). And he consciously ennobles himself by comparing his future situation "with that of venerated statesmen who have returned to the plough to be forgotten in their own age, and remembered in another,—with that of generals who have held out the decrepit hand with a petition to the gay passers by to give a halfpenny to the deliverer of their country" (p. 47). The transition from victim to hero recommended here is accomplished by the character's conscious acquiescence in his own predetermined destiny. This acquiescence gives Allen the only kind of heroic self-determination that Martineau's Necessarianism will allow; it gives the author an opportunity both to express her determinism and to provide an exemplary response to it. Lest we still miss Allen's heroism and mistakenly regard him as a pitiable victim of circumstances, the narrator records his reply to his wife, who feared that he might have been "drawn in to join against the masters": "Allen answered that he was not the man to be *drawn in* to do what his wife knew he disliked as much as she could do; but he might of his own free choice determine to do what she feared" (p. 54). Allen's heroic freedom consists in determining to do what he both dislikes and accepts as inevitable.

Since the ending is contained in the beginning, the reader cannot be drawn into a suspenseful account of Allen's history. Indeed, the mode of narration divides Allen himself into a character who suffers and one who divines and interprets his own suffering. Allen becomes the hero, the audience, and the chorus. As a result, he seems above any particular emotions, rendered affectively neutral, and the reader experiences a similar emotional blankness and distance from the represented suffering.

We are further distanced from Allen's suffering by a second kind of narrative determinism, the determinism that resides in the very form of "illustrations" of abstract principles. Martineau's belief that universal laws were the primary reality and that daily experience was merely a manifestation of these laws led her to equate the ideas of didactic tale and realistic narrative.[36] The priority of the law transforms itself into the priority of her didactic purpose, which exerts its own kind of necessity. The author never fears that she may be distorting reality to illustrate an abstraction: the abstraction *is* the reality. In her tales it is almost impossible to differentiate between the determinism of the laws she is illustrating and the determinism of her didactic purpose.[39] This separation between the two emerges, however, when the course of events is obviously not economically determined but is still narrated as necessary. In these cases we can perceive that the pressure of her illustrative form shapes the course of events and justifies their deterministic mode of presentation. The Manchester strike must lead to disaster in order to illustrate that strikes in general lead to disaster. Thus the didacticism of the story, which is generated by the author's uncritical belief in universal laws, generates its own determinism, removing us still further from the emotions of particular characters.

For example, some of the strikers, led by Clack, are responsible for heading off a happy ending: they make unreasonable demands that strain the bargaining process, and they reject the settlement that Allen proposes. The suffering that results is not, strictly speaking, necessary, not ordained by the laws of the marketplace. Indeed, Martineau wishes us to understand that the workers could have avoided suffering by compromise. Still, she presents the superfluous suffering as inescapable; and, indeed, it is necessary to the illustrative purpose of this tale. Her style consequently assures us that disaster is part of the natural, predictable course of the strike. The following series of poignant vignettes, for example, is marked by the repetition of such preliminary clauses as "now was the time," "these were the days," and "these were the times":

> Now was the time to see the young woman, with the babe in her arms, pushing at the curtained door of the dram-shop, while her husband held it against her,—he saying,—"Well, I tell you I'm coming in five minutes; I shan't be five minutes." . . .Now was the time to see the good son pacing slowly to the pawnbroker's to pledge his aged mother's last blanket to buy her bread. These were the days when the important men under the three balls civilly declared, or insolently swore, that they could and would take no more goods in pawn. . . a mother shewing that her winter shawl or her child's frock would take very little room,—or a young girl urging that if a pawnbroker did not want her grandmother's old bible he could get more for it at a book-stall than she could. These were the times for poor landlords to look after their rents and for hard landlords to press for them. (Pp. 112–13)

The introductory clauses make each particular event seem inevitable in its typicality. Our pity is solicited by the details: babes in arms, aged mothers' blankets, children's frocks, and grandmothers' old Bibles are the stock stuff of pathos. The emotion, however, is blunted by the opening clauses, which are not only the first but also the main clauses of the sentences. The "young woman, with the babe in her arms, pushing at the curtained door of the dram-shop" is grammatically and emotionally subordinated in the clause that creates her as an illustration of typical, expected suffering to be observed by narrator and reader: "Now was the time to see the young woman. . . ."

The didactic determinism of the novel, therefore, like its providential-economic determinism, creates a narrative style that flattens the tale's emotional course. These two kinds of determinism are obviously connected: Martineau's belief in the providential scheme of universal laws underlies her choice of the schematic, illustrative form. Together they diminish the plot's tragic impact. The content of the plot remains both intrinsically and conventionally painful, and yet the form of the narrative combines with the optimistic confidence of the narrative voice to urge acceptance of the determinism depicted, insisting not only on its inevitability, but also on its ultimate rightness. The result is a wide discrepancy between the events of the plot and the tone of the narrative, between the content of the tale and its emotional quality.

The discrepancy, moreover, is never overcome: Martineau's belief in the ultimate progressiveness of the laws she illustrates, her belief in Providence, is never justified by the plot. The classes are more completely alienated at the end of the story than they were at the beginning: "[Allen] no longer touched his hat to the masters, or appeared to see them as they passed" (p. 299). And no one seems to have gained an education in the "administration of labor": despite the fact that Allen was repeatedly advised to apprentice his children to other trades, we are told on the last page that they "grew up one after another to be employed in factories" (p. 299). The story does not support Martineau's providential belief, for it has no optimistic harmonious conclusion.

But the idea of a benevolent, providential order was not a conclusion of classical political economy. It was, rather, an assumption held by some political economists in paradoxical combination with the more pessimistic elements of the "science" and rejected by others as an unnecessary metaphysical foundation. The optimistic, providential perspective was held very firmly by two thinkers who influenced Martineau, Joseph Priestley and John McCulloch.[40] But the *Illustrations* are a potpourri of various economic doctrines, and it is not surprising that the ideas illustrated in *A Manchester Strike*, taken as they are from Malthus and from Ricardo (via James Mill), fail to fit into a long-range, providential perspective that predicts ultimate harmony.

The only hint of the author's awareness of any discrepancy between the story's implications and her providential beliefs is contained in the tale's very last paragraph. This is one of the rare places where the narrator expresses something other than bland acceptance. Seemingly exasperated by the short-sightedness of most workers and masters, she asks, "When will masters and men work cheerfully together for their common good, respect instead of proscribing [blacklisting] each other, and be equally proud to have such men as Wentworth and William Allen of their fellowship?" (p. 133). Both the tone and the content of the question are jarring, for until this very last moment Martineau's narrative methods have implied that the story could not have turned out differently. Although there are instances of self-destructive stubbornness on the part of both employers and workers in the tale, and even though Martineau's avowed purpose is to illustrate what workers' combinations ought not to do, the sense of overriding necessity conveyed by the narrative makes even the wrong-headed action seem foreordained. The sudden introduction, then, of an impatient protest against Allen's fate and of an exasperated appeal to a future state of "cheerful" harmony are both unexpected. They seem to express the author's bafflement at her inability to connect her sanguine assumptions about the marketplace with anything that actually happens in the story, and they jar the reader into a full realization of the discrepancy between the tale's content and its tone.

This very discrepancy may account for the wide scope of Harriet Martineau's influence. On the one hand, her optimistic belief in progress, with its explicit laissez-faire basis, gained her the admiration of industrialists and liberal legislators and theorists. On the other hand, her tragic vision, semiobscured as it was, won her the approval of many critics of industrialism, even, for a time, the qualified praise of some working-class radicals.[41] She left the writers of subsequent industrial fiction an ambiguous legacy, for she had at once ennobled workers and bound them in chains of necessity, depicted their suffering and advised acceptance.

Her working-class characters are not the permanently deformed, infantile creatures of the Ten Hours Movement propaganda who later found their way into *Helen Fleetwood*. Martineau shows us workers who are credible free agents in the technical economic sense, and although she eschewed the idea of free will, her characters do have heroic possibilities denied to the moral cripples in Tonna's fiction. But as we have seen, the plots that frame these dissimilar characterizations of workers are both meant to mirror God's benign Providence. And in both cases they fail: Tonna's born-and-bred industrial workers seem to be loose threads in the Divine Weaver's carpet; similarly, there appears to be a great gap between the little wheels, the workers' personal histories, and the great wheel of Martineau's providential Watch.

3

Causality versus Conscience:
The Problem of Form in
Mary Barton

As in the *Religion of Causation,* Man seemed to be crushed into a
mere creature, so was it on his behalf that remonstrance broke
forth, and, at the bidding of Channing, the *Religion of Conscience*
sprang to its feet. However fascinating the precision and simplicity of the Necessarian theory in its advance through the fields of
physical and biological law, it meets with vehement resistence in
its attempt to annex human nature, and put it under the same
code with the tides and trees and reptiles. Our personality . . . is
sure to recover from the most ingenious philosophy, and to
re-assert its power over the alternatives before it . . . ; and the
second period of our theology is marked by this recovered sense
of Moral Freedom.

James Martineau
"Three Stages of Unitarian Theology"

No one seems to see my idea of a tragic poem; so I, in reality,
mourn over my failure.

Elizabeth Gaskell
Letter to Edward Chapman

When Elizabeth Gaskell wrote *Mary Barton* (1845–47), many Unitarians were revising their theories about free will. In those years James
Martineau was trying to start what he later called the "second period of
Unitarian theology," the period in which "moral freedom" was emphasized. James Martineau, Harriet's younger brother, was the most influential English Unitarian theologian of the nineteenth century.[1] In
their early childhood he and his sister Harriet established a profound
emotional and intellectual bond that remained unbroken throughout
their youth.

It was James who suggested she read Priestley, but once Harriet had
arrived at her "grand conviction"[2] of Necessarianism, she took every
possible opportunity to impress the doctrine on her brother. According to James, Harriet dominated him intellectually throughout their
adolescence and early adulthood. Describing their conversation while
on a walking tour of Scotland in 1824, he reminisced:

> My sister's acute, rapid, and incisive advance to a conclusion upon every point pleasantly relieved my slower judgement and gave me courage to dismiss suspense. I was at that time, and for several years after, an enthusiastic disciple of the determinist philosophy . . . yet not without such inward reserves and misgivings as to render welcome my sister's more firm and ready verdict.[3]

Harriet managed to suppress James's "inward reservations and misgivings" until after she had become a well-known writer. R. K. Webb reports that in 1832 James still shared her views, and Harriet expressed the hope that James might also share her work of improving mankind: he by "lofty appeals to the guides of [Society], I by being the annalist of the poor."[4]

As this proposed division of labor indicates, Harriet was conscious of certain intellectual and temperamental differences between herself and her brother, even while they espoused the same philosophy. She thought her own talent lay in logical cause-and-effect analysis, while his consisted of eloquence and intuition. In time the differences Harriet perceived in their modes of thinking developed into a philosophical disagreement that separated the intellectually intense siblings for life. As James recalled:

> While she remained faithful through life to that early mode of thought, with me those "reserves and misgivings," suppressed for a while, recovered from the shock and gained the ascendancy. The divergence led to this result,—that while my sister changed her conclusions, and I my basis, we both cleared ourselves from incompatible admixtures, and paid the deference due to logical consistency and completeness.[5]

Harriet's Necessarianism finally led her to accept "free thought"; all organized religious practice came to seem incompatible with the logic of her determinism. James, on the other hand, rejected Harriet's basis, her "Religion of Causality," and reached down to "the springs of a sleeping enthusiasm" for a religion that could carry him "from the outer temple of devout science" to an inner conviction of the "greatness of human capacity, not so much for intellectual training, as for voluntary righteousness, for victory over temptation."[6]

The change in James both symbolized and helped to bring about a vast transformation in the Unitarian Church. William Ellery Channing, the American Transcendentalist, converted James to the doctrine of a "free ideal life . . . which we know is in subjection to nothing inflexible."[7] Channing's idea of the human will had been inspired by the writings of Coleridge,[8] and James, in his turn, set about transforming English Unitarianism from a "Religion of Causality" to a "Religion of Conscience," emphasizing voluntary righteousness. He was not the first English Unitarian to believe in free will; Priestley's determinism had been modified and even opposed by many Unitarian theologians of the early nineteenth century. Indeed, Harriet Martineau's extreme Necessarianism was somewhat anachronistic in the 1830's, for by that decade most Unitarians either ignored the issue or settled for a moderate determinism. James Martineau's version of Transcendentalism, however, strongly insisted on the idea of free will, giving it a new emphasis within Unitarianism. Although James was not the acknowledged leader of English Unitarians until later in the century, during the 1840s and 1850s his thought was a powerful intellectual stimulus that led to the de-emphasis of "scientific" explanations of behavior and a new stress on the other side of Unitarianism—its exhortations to moral exertion.

Although Elizabeth Gaskell and her husband, William, stayed within the old school of Unitarianism on most issues and made no decided moves toward Transcendentalism,[9] they were well acquainted with James Martineau. William Gaskell was a Unitarian minister and a colleague of Martineau's at Manchester New College in the 1840s, and their exposure to Martineau's brand of Unitarianism might easily have served to strengthen Elizabeth Gaskell's interest in the issue of moral responsibility.[10] Moreover, in 1845, at the very time when she first began writing *Mary Barton*, she was deeply influenced by a close friend of Martineau's. Although not himself a Unitarian, Francis Newman, brother of John Henry Newman, associated almost exclusively with Unitarians in the 1840s, and on many issues his thinking closely resembled James Martineau's. Like James Martineau, Newman made much of man's "higher nature," his free moral life. Rejecting the psychological materialism of Priestley and Harriet Martineau, he argued that "human intelligence is a result of other intelligence higher than itself— is not a source, or a result, of what is unintelligent."[11]

To Elizabeth Gaskell in the mid-1840s, Francis Newman seemed a living saint. She claimed to have hung on his every word,[12] and it is quite probable that an 1844 booklet of his, *Catholic Union*, was an important source of inspiration for *Mary Barton*. This booklet, together with a series of lectures given in 1846, clearly reveals Newman's belief in a transcendent "moral energy."[13] These works also, however, contain reminders of Unitarianism's earlier determinism, for in them Newman paradoxically insisted that morality does not exist in a realm apart from social and economic necessity. Thus he believed economic and spiritual issues interpenetrated one another, and like Gaskell in *Mary Barton*, he treated radical working-class movements sympathetically: Communism is called "one mode in which human nature is crying out for a new and better union than has yet been achieved."[14] Although he strove to affirm the independence of the human spirit, he continually reversed himself and implied that spirit is chained to matter, that it does not exist in a separate realm of freedom: "to the support of moral energies," he wrote, "certain material conditions are required."[15]

Elizabeth Gaskell absorbed this ambivalence about moral freedom not only from the works and conversation of Francis Newman, but also from the whole context of Unitarian intellectualism that surrounded her. The Unitarianism that shaped her perceptions was thus a different religion in several important respects from that which nurtured Harriet Martineau. Of course, because Gaskell's social experience also differed markedly from Martineau's, the dissimilarities in the two women's outlooks cannot be attributed solely to their religious beliefs. Nevertheless, important differences in their fiction can be traced to their disparate attitudes toward causality and free will. Martineau believed that Providence worked through natural laws that precluded human free will, whereas Gaskell, without abandoning the idea of Providence, tried to make room in her fiction for moral freedom. Gaskell's use of causality, like that of many other thoughtful Unitarians of the 1840s, was less consistent than Martineau's. It was, however, her very inconsistency, her refusal to be tied down to a single explanatory mode, that marked Elizabeth Gaskell's advance over Harriet Martineau in the craft of novel writing.

To move from the *Illustrations* to *Mary Barton* is to leave behind the narrowness of a unicausal interpretive scheme. The wider range of explanations available to Gaskell partly accounts for our sense that she is a more realistic novelist than Harriet Martineau. As James Martineau wrote, breaking away from the Necessarian doctrine constituted "an escape from a logical cage into the open air."[16] And as he further pointed out, the escape entailed perceptual and stylistic changes: "I could mingle with the world and believe in what I saw and felt, without refracting it through a glass, which construed it into something else. I could use the language of men—of their love and hate, of remorse and resolve, of repentance and prayer— in its simplicity."[17] The firm reliance on what is vividly seen and felt and an expanded use of the simple "language of men" are the hallmarks of Gaskell's realism. The "real" reality for her does not lie behind human behavior in a set of scientific laws; it is on the very surface of life, and although it is often obscured by conventional modes of perception, it can be adequately represented in common language. Indeed, Gaskell specifically objected to the kind of abstract language used by Harriet Martineau: she believed that presenting people as embodiments of labor and capital could only hide their true natures and the underlying motives of their actions.[18]

In one important respect, however, Elizabeth Gaskell must be considered Harriet Martineau's heir: she intended John Barton's story, the story of a working man, to be a tragedy. "I had so long felt," she wrote in a letter, "that the bewildered life of an ignorant thoughtful man of strong power of sympathy, dwelling in a town so full of striking contrasts as this is, was a tragic poem, that in writing he was my 'hero.' "[19] In several ways John Barton is a more successful working-class character than Martineau's William Allen, for many of Allen's characteristics seem inappropriate to a worker. His heroism relies, for example, on an elevated style of speaking, while Barton's tragic heroism gains poignancy from his working-class dialect. Adhering closely to classical models, Martineau presents Allen as far superior to other members of his class: she stresses how unusual his forbearance and intelligence are, and even makes him the victim of the striking workers. Barton, on the other hand, is presented as a typical worker. Indeed, his typicality is precisely what makes his story an important one to tell: "There are many such whose lives are tragic poems," Gaskell wrote, "which cannot take formal language."[20] Moreover, Gaskell did not adopt the reversed chronology of Martineau's fiction, her tendency to reveal the ending at the beginning of the story, destroying suspense and precluding catharsis. In fact, Gaskell believed that the ordering of events was a major flaw in Martineau's work; she complained about one of Martineau's books that "The *story* is too like a history—one knows all along how it must end."[21] Gaskell's own story, although it makes John Barton's decline seem inevitable, is not "like a history": she maintains suspense and seeks an intense emotional reaction from the reader. Barton has neither of Allen's defenses against suffering; he lacks both foreknowledge and stoicism. Barton thus seems more unequivocally victimized than did Allen.

Yet when the book came out, Gaskell complained that no one seemed to see her idea of a tragedy.[22] She concluded that she had failed but could not identify the source of her failure. Her confusion is not surprising, for there are many ways in which Gaskell undercut her own intended tragic effects. One of these, a relatively minor one, reminds us again of the religious kinship between Gaskell and Harriet Martineau: the providential resolution of John Barton's story partly mitigates his tragedy. Although moral freedom was an increasingly important idea in Unitarian theology in the 1840s, Gaskell was still writing within a teleological tradition. John Barton feels responsible for his crime, but in the end the very intensity of his remorse leads to both his own and his enemy's spiritual regeneration.[23] There is not even a hint of possible damnation in the novel; evil is eventually self-effacing and productive of good, although sin is not explicitly ordained by God.[24] The close of Barton's life, therefore, hardly appears to be tragic; his life veers from its tragic course in the final episode, and readers are apt to agree with an early reviewer who complained that the ending was a religious homily, "twisted out of shape, to serve the didactic purpose of the author."[25]

Long before the story's close, however, Gaskell's ambivalence about the tragedy she was writing manifests itself in the book's formal eclecticism,[26] an eclecticism that cannot be traced simply to the contradiction between tragic and providential perspectives. For tragedy and theodicy both contain explanatory systems; both trace cause and effect. A dominant impulse in *Mary Barton*, however, is to escape altogether from causality, to transcend explanation. *Mary Barton* expresses both stages of the Unitarianism of the 1840s; it was inspired by both the "Religion of Causality" that Harriet Martineau advocated and the "Religion of Conscience" that her brother eloquently preached. It contains, therefore, an ambivalence about causality that finds its way into Gaskell's tragedy and creates an irresolvable paradox there: Barton's political radicalism is presented both as proof that he is incapable of making moral choices and as an emblem of his moral responsibility. The author consequently seeks refuge from the contradictions of her tragedy in other narrative forms, primarily melodrama and domestic fiction. The resulting formal multiplicity is most apparent in the first half of the book. Only in the second half, after the tragic action is complete, does she temporarily achieve a kind of generic consistency by retreating into the domestic mentality of her heroine. However, because the major action of these chapters is the suppression of the tragic narrative, the book seems to divide into not merely separate but mutually exclusive stories. In the conclusion, when the narrator must return to the subject of John Barton, she seems to have abandoned any attempt to give a consistent explanation of his development. Instead, we are given several stories that mix social criticism with religious homily, and we are then assured that, after all, causal interpretations are irrelevant to the story's meaning.

Gaskell's inability to commit herself to a causal scheme leads, therefore, to formal inconsistencies, but it also leads to a high degree of formal self-consciousness. Although she does not find a narrative form that satisfactorily reveals the reality of working-class life, she does identify several conventional genres that hide the reality. Her attempt to render the truth is beset by irresolvable difficulties, but some relief, some certainty, is secured in attacking what is obviously false. Thus *Mary Barton* is partly about the ways in which narrative conventions mask and distort reality; form becomes content by this process. But the criticism of false conventions does not succeed in deflecting attention from the absence of a stable, self-assured narrative posture. Rather, it makes us more acutely aware of that absence simply by emphasizing the issue of genre. Thus, in the very act of trying to evade certain narrative responsibilities, the book becomes peculiarly self-regarding.

Gaskell's use of contrasting narrative forms is one of the most interesting and overlooked features of *Mary Barton*. In a sense, the first half of the novel is about the dangers inherent in various conventional ways of organizing reality. The two most obviously false and destructive conventional perspectives on the novel's action are the sentimentally romantic and the farcical. The narrator herself never adopts these modes; rather, they enter the narrative as the distorted literary viewpoints of a few characters. Esther and young Mary hold the sentimental perspective; Sally Leadbitter and Harry Carson hold the complementary viewpoint of farce. Gaskell is careful to point out that the sentimental perspective originates in literature; Mary's "foolish, unworldly ideas" come not only from her Aunt Esther's talk about "making a lady" of her, but also from "the romances which Miss Simmonds' young ladies were in the habit of recommending to each other."[27] And although the narrator excuses both Esther and Mary on the grounds of their youth, she indicates that their conventional literary delusions are truly pernicious. Esther's elopement ruins her and apparently also contributes to the death of Mary's mother, and Mary's desire to marry a gentleman brings her and almost all of the other characters in the book "bitter woe" (p. 80).

The complement to these sentimental notions, the convention that they play into and that makes them dangerous, is farce. Both Sally Leadbitter and Harry Carson see their lives and the lives of others as farce. Sally becomes a *farceuse* because she cannot be a sentimental heroine. Being "but a plain, red-haired, freckled, girl," she tries to make up for her lack of beauty "by a kind of witty boldness, which gave her, what her betters would have called piquancy" (p. 132). Sally is a working-class version of the witty female rogue: "Considerations of modesty or propriety never checked her utterance of a good thing" (p. 132). Her vision is entirely comic; it excludes any serious thought about the consequences of Mary's flirtation with young Carson at the same time that it denies the very possibility that Mary's romantic fantasies might be sincerely held: "Sally Leadbitter laughed in her sleeve at them both, and wondered how it would all end,—whether Mary would gain her point of marriage, with her sly affectation of believing such to be Mr. Carson's intention in courting her" (p. 180). Harry Carson, of course, shares this farcical perspective on Mary's actions. Both he and Sally imagine her to be a character in their own farcical world—a "sweet little coquette" (p. 181), "a darling little rascal" (p. 181) with an "ambitious heart" (p. 183). For Sally and Harry Carson, this characterization gives a conventional authorization, indeed a conventional imperative, to Mary's seduction.

Moreover, Mary's is not the only reality that the farcical perspective distorts: everything that enters Sally's or young Carson's purview becomes comic material. Sally is always "ready to recount the events of the day, to turn them into ridicule, and to mimic, with admirable fidelity, any person gifted with an absurdity who had fallen under her keen eye" (p. 133). The ability to mimic "with admirable fidelity" is also a talent, indeed a fatal talent, of Harry Carson. Young Carson's farcical vision leads him to caricature not only Mary, but the whole of the working class as well, and as Gaskell points out, these comic caricatures both mask and perpetuate working-class suffering. In her exposition of the dangers inherent in farcical distortions, the author brings together the sexual and social themes of the novel: both Mary and the delegation of striking workers are victimized by Harry Carson's conventional blindness.

If working-class women are seducible "little rascals" for Harry Carson, working-class men are clowns. Young Carson exhibits his blindness to the human reality of working-class men on several occasions (for instance, in his treatment of Mr. Wilson, in his interview with Jem, and in his obstinate behavior at the negotiating table), but the conventional attitude that motivates his behavior is most clearly expressed in the action that precipitates his murder. He is killed for making a joke, for attempting to transform a workers' delegation into a troop of Shakespearean clowns:

> Mr. Harry Carson had taken out his silver pencil, and had drawn an admirable caricature of them—lank, ragged, dispirited, and famine-stricken. Underneath he wrote a hasty quotation from the fat knight's well-known speech in Henry IV. He passed it to one of his neighbours, who acknowledged the likeness instantly, and by him it was set round to others, who all smiled and nodded their heads. (P. 235)

The caricature, tossed away by Carson but retrieved by a curious member of the workers' delegation, so enrages John Barton that he conspires with the ridiculed workers to kill the caricaturist. It is significant that the fatal joke is as much Shakespeare's as it is Carson's: that fact emphasizes the unreal, literary nature of Carson's perception. It also stresses how deeply entrenched the farcical distortion of working-class life is in English culture. Carson's destructive use of Shakespeare reminds Gaskell's readers that although they have the best precedents for laughing at rags and tatters, they must now free themselves from the conventional association between "low" characters and comedy.

But the whole incident raises another question: what new associations should replace the old? It is quite clear that Gaskell intends to expose the dangerous falseness of both sentimental romance and farce; but the ground of her exposition, the narrative mode that she adopted because she believed that it did reflect working-class reality, is difficult to identify. Most literary practices calling themselves realistic rely on contrasts with other, presumably false and outdated narrative perspectives.[28] In *Mary Barton* Gaskell purposely sets up false conventions for contrast, thereby calling attention to her own narrative method as the "true" perspective. The problem is that she then has trouble fixing on any one narrative mode; the ground of the contrast continually shifts in the first half of the book while the author searches for a mode of realism adequate to her subject matter. Thus, in her attempt to juxtapose reality and these false conventions, Gaskell employs several alternative narrative modes: tragedy, melodrama, domestic fiction, and finally religious homily.

The most obvious realistic contrast to both the sentimentality of Esther and Mary and the farce of Sally Leadbitter and Harry Carson is the tragedy of John Barton. Barton is the most active and outspoken adversary of both of these false conventions. It is from his perspective that we first see Esther's romantic folly; the story of the girl's elopement is completely contained within John Barton's gloomy interpretation of it: "bad's come over her, one way or another" (p. 46), he tells his friend Wilson. And his interpretation, of course, immediately undercuts all the story's romance. Moreover, his version of Esther's story makes it merely a part of a larger social tragedy. It includes the girl's social determinism: factory work, he is convinced, led to Esther's downfall by making her recklessly independent and giving her the means to buy finery. As Barton tells Esther's story, he reveals his perspective on the relationship between the classes, a perspective that is itself tragic and productive of tragedy. He opposes Esther's romantic dreams not only because they are dangerous, but also because he hates the class she wishes to join. Barton's is a completely polarized view of social reality: only rich and poor seem to exist, and the rich are the constant oppressors of the poor. The ubiquitous slavery metaphor makes its appearance here, attesting to Barton's radicalism, his polarized social vision, and the determinism that informs his thinking.

"We are their slaves as long as we can work; we pile up their fortunes with the sweat of our brows; and yet we are to live as separate as if we were in two worlds; ay, as separate as Dives and Lazarus, with a great gulf betwixt us: but I know who was best off then," and he wound up his speech with a low chuckle that had no mirth in it. (P. 45)

Even this closing reference to heavenly justice is a gloomy prophecy of revenge, not a joyful anticipation of saintly rewards.

Barton's tragic perspective, therefore, contrasts sharply with Esther's and, later, with Mary's romantic fantasies. Moreover, his interpretation is corroborated by the plot itself; he is correct to note that Esther's romantic dreamworld is really a disguised stage for tragedy. Barton's relationship to the farcical viewpoint is similar: again he opposes it energetically, and again in his opposition he speaks the truth. In fact, in the most decisive moment of his own tragedy, Barton contrasts Harry Carson's caricature, his fixed, farcical representation, with the tragic reality that lies behind the conventionally ludicrous appearance:

"it makes my heart burn within me, to see that folk can make a jest of earnest men; of chaps, who comed to ask for a bit o' fire for th' old granny, as shivers in the cold; for a bit o' bedding, and some warm clothing to the poor wife as lies in labour on th' damp flags; and for victuals for the childer, whose little voices are getting too faint and weak to cry aloud wi' hunger." (P. 238)

Through Barton's eyes we see behind the cartoon images of the ragged men to the suffering of thousands of helpless people. The delegates caricatured by Harry Carson are tragic; they are compelled to strike by their noblest characteristics: their sympathy with and sense of responsibility to their hungry dependents. But Carson's Shakespearean joke attempts to freeze the imagination at the level of appearances, where the workmen become a troop of clowns. In Falstaff's speech, alluded to but not quoted, they are "good enough to toss; food for powder, food for powder; they'll fill a pit as well as better. Tush, man, mortal men, mortal men."[29] Such dehumanization obscures the tragedy, making it perfectly appropriate that the story's central tragic action should be the destruction of this *farceur*, the murder of Harry Carson. Thus farce, the mask of tragedy, becomes its stuff, just as Falstaff's callous speech trails off into a sad and even leveling refrain: "Tush, man, mortal men, mortal men."

Tragedy, then, is the immediate realistic ground against which both romance and farce are contrasted. But the narrative method of this novel cannot be called tragic. As we will see, tragedy is forced to compete with other realistic forms in the book's first half, and in the last half it is present only as a suppressed reality. By examining the part of the story that Gaskell specifically intended as tragic—John Barton's own story—we can see why the author continually shifted to other modes of narration. For John Barton's tragedy is self-contradictory. Because she draws both on traditional ideas of heroic character and on determinist, Owenite ideas of character formation, the author encounters a paradox as she attempts to trace a continuous line of tragic development.

The causality Gaskell attempts to trace follows a traditional tragic pattern; it is the result of the interaction between the character's heroic qualities and external circumstances. As Gaskell told a correspondent after the book's publication, her original intention was to show the operations of inner and outer causes in the destiny of a Manchester weaver:

> I can remember now that the prevailing thought in my mind at the time . . . was the seeming injustice of the inequalities of fortune. Now, if they occasionally appeared unjust to the more fortunate, they must bewilder an ignorant man full of rude, illogical thought, and full also of sympathy for suffering which appealed to him through his senses. I fancied I saw how all this might lead to a course of action which might appear right for a time to the bewildered mind of such a one.[30]

This was, she said, her original "design": the very qualities that made Barton a hero, his thoughtfulness and sympathy, were to combine with external circumstances to produce a tragic action.

This tragic design is certainly apparent in John Barton's story. We are often reminded by both Barton's speeches and the narrator's characterizations of him that his love for his family and his sympathy for the suffering poor cause his hatred of the rich. His unselfishness is emphasized repeatedly; he feels angry not on his own behalf, but on behalf of those who are weaker and poorer. The need to stress Barton's heroic unselfishness determines many of the plot's details; it is significant, for example, that he is not one of the workers caricatured by Harry Carson. His rude thoughtfulness, his desire to understand the suffering he sees, is a second admirable trait contributing to his downfall. Barton is the only character who consistently seeks causes for the world's phenomena, but his analyses are marred by his ignorance, by the fact that his understanding is circumscribed by his limited experience.

Gaskell carefully shows how these qualities of mind are impressed with a tragic stamp by external circumstances, by what comes to Barton "through is senses." The links in the tragic chain are clearly identified and labeled: his parents' poverty, his son's death, his wife's death, the trade depression and the consequent suffering of neighbors, his trip to London, his hunger, his opium addiction. Each of these incidents or circumstances is noted by the narrator as yet another cause of Barton's bitterness. The account of his wife's death, for example, concludes with the gloss: "One of the good influences over John Barton's life had departed that night. One of the ties which bound him down to the gentle humanities of earth was loosened, and henceforward the neighbors all remarked he was a changed man" (p. 58). The story of his son's illness and death also ends with emphasis on its consequences: "You can fancy, now, the hoards of vengeance in his heart against the employers" (p. 61).

Even the narrator's disavowals of Barton's ideas and feelings are intended to contribute to his story's tragedy. Remarks such as "I know that this is not really the case [that the workers alone suffer from trade depressions]; and I know what is the truth in such matters: but what I wish to impress is what the workman feels and thinks" (p. 60) may seem annoying intrusions to twentieth-century readers, but they were designed to keep the nineteenth-century readers' own opinions from interfering with their ability to follow Barton's tragedy. The disavowals are there to prevent the reader from becoming distracted by the issue of whether or not Barton's ideas are objectively true; Barton, we are told in these asides, reached the wrong conclusions, but the circumstances of his life did not allow him to reach any other.

Their very inevitability, however, creates a problem for the author. Unlike Harriet Martineau, Gaskell is not able to rest comfortably with the determinism she traces. Two obstacles present themselves: first, her idea of heroism entails moral freedom; and second, Gaskell's and Martineau's determinisms are of very different kinds. Martineau's does not explain the development of the protagonist's character. William Allen is a fully formed hero at the story's outset; the development of his character is unexplored and irrelevant to the story. He is a heroic, working-class *homo economicus* whose actions may be explained by his character, but whose character is not itself tragically determined. Gaskell's tragic vision, on the other hand, encompasses the formation and deformation of John Barton's character. Her social determinism is, in this sense, closer to Charlotte Elizabeth Tonna's than to Harriet Martineau's. Both use Robert Owen's brand of social theory, showing how the worker's environment and experiences shape his moral being. But unlike Tonna, Gaskell wishes to show us a worker who is a hero, not a monster; she wishes to give us a tragedy, not a freak show. As she traces Barton's inescapable decline, a decline that entails moral degeneration, she risks reducing him to a character without a will. In the words James Martineau used to describe the effects of Necessarianism, she almost "crushes" him "into a mere creature"[31] with her causation.

Gaskell, then, was writing partly in the determinist tradition as it had been adapted by critics of industrialism, but her writing was also infused with the new Unitarian emphasis on free will. Consequently, a tension developed in her portrayal of John Barton, a tension between his social determinism and his tragic heroism. This tension increases as his crisis approaches until it finally emerges as an observable contradiction when the narrator directly confronts the political model of freedom Barton has come to advocate. His radical ambition to become a shaper of society, to cast off the role of a passive creature, acts as a magnet that draws both poles of the author's ambivalence about freedom toward one paradoxical center. The paradox is most clearly visible in the narrator's very last expository attempt to explain the causality of John Barton's story:

> No education had given him wisdom; and without wisdom, even love, with all its effects, too often works but harm. He acted to the best of his judgment but it was a widely-erring judgement.
>
> The actions of the uneducated seem to me typified in those of Frankenstein, that monster of many human qualities, ungifted with a soul, a knowledge of the difference between good and evil.
>
> The people rise up to life; they irritate us, they terrify us, and we become their enemies. Then, in the sorrowful moment of our triumphant power, their eyes gaze on us with a mute reproach. Why have we made them what they are; a powerful monster, yet without the inner means for peace and happiness?
>
> John Barton became a Chartist, a Communist, all that is commonly called wild and visionary. Ay! but being visionary is something. It shows a soul, a being not altogether sensual; a creature who looks forward for others, if not for himself. (Pp. 219–20)

All the elements of the tragedy are present in these metaphoric exchanges. Barton represents the uneducated, who are collected into the image of Frankenstein's tragically determined, larger-than-life monster. Then the monster, defeated and gazing at us, shrinks back to the dimensions of John Barton, the unselfish visionary. But these smooth metaphoric transitions do not quite cover the passage's central paradox: the "actions of the uneducated" grow out of their soullessness, their incapacity to make moral choices. Barton became a "Chartist, a Communist," a visionary in consequence of this soullessness. But the metaphor is too harsh, too denigrating to the hero, and the narrator pulls back and reverses herself: "But being visionary is something. It shows a soul." Suddenly John Barton's rebellious actions, instead of showing him to be a creature "ungifted with a soul," become the proof that he has a soul, the emblem of his humanity and this moral freedom. His heroism is saved, but only at the expense of the causality implied by the Frankenstein metaphor, a causality that traces Barton's crime to "us."

We can argue, therefore, that the paradoxical nature of Gaskell's tragic vision forces her to abandon it in the novel's second half. Even in the first half of the book, though, the narrator never confines her own view to this tragic dynamic, dangerous as it was to the very idea of moral freedom. Instead, she juxtaposes three "realistic" narrative modes in the book's early chapters: tragedy, melodrama, and a working-class domestic tale. The presence, indeed the competition, of the melodrama and the domestic tale allows two things. First, the author is able to avoid her tragic responsibilities, which are too contradictory to fulfill successfully; these other modes distract attention from and obscure the problematic causality of John Barton's story. Second, the presence of the melodrama, in particular, allows Gaskell to extend her critical exploration of conventional ways of interpreting reality.

Gaskell's use of melodrama is skillful: she first invites us into a melodramatic narrative, sets up melodramatic expectations, and then reveals that melodrama is a mere conventional distortion, a genre inappropriate to modern reality. Critics have claimed that *Mary Barton* becomes melodramatic with the murder of Harry Carson, [32] but this formulation is backwards. The first half of the book is much more seriously melodramatic than the second because in the first half there is a melodrama just offstage, in the wings, as it were, which threatens to take over the drama entirely. Indeed, the reader cannot initially tell whether the early chapters are part of a melodrama or of some other kind of narrative. They contain many melodramatic characteristics.[33] We view Esther's elopement not only from Barton's tragic perspective, but also through the unarticulated, excessive grief of her sister Mary, young Mary's mother. Her grief is so excessive that it kills her, suddenly and surprisingly. It is the kind of parabolical death that abounded in nineteenth-century melodramas, and it leads into young Mary's potential melodrama—the threat of her seduction by the rakish Harry Carson. The narrator, in true melodramatic manner, continually suspends any resolution of Mary's fate and makes dark prognostications about it: "Mary hoped to meet him every day in her walks, blushed when she heard his name, and tried to think of him as her future husband, and above all, tried to think of herself as his future wife. Alas! poor Mary! Bitter woe did thy weakness work thee" (p. 80). The wholly conventional language here ("Alas! poor Mary!") leads us to expect, mistakenly, that Mary's "bitter woe" will also be of the conventional melodramatic kind.

Although romance and farce finally do turn into tragedy in *Mary Barton*, they threaten repeatedly in the first half to turn into melodrama. Mary's renunciation of Harry Carson, her abandonment of romance, brings the melodrama even closer; for it is after his rejection that Harry Carson becomes truly villainous, indeed a potential rapist: "From blandishments he had even gone to threats—threats that whether she would or not she should be his" (p. 224). It is only after she has awakened from her romantic dream that Mary is in danger of becoming a true melodramatic heroine: an innocent girl sexually persecuted by a villain. Indeed, Mary registers the change linguistically. As soon as she understands her true position she declares: "if I had loved you before, I don't think I should have loved you now you have told me you meant to ruin me; for that's the plain English of not meaning to marry me till just this minute. . . . Now I scorn you, sir, for plotting to ruin a poor girl" (pp. 183–84). This is not "plain English," the language Mary usually speaks. It is popular stage English, [34] and it temporarily throws a melodramatic light across Mary's features. Harry Carson's murder, instead of beginning the novel's melodrama, effectively terminates it. In fact, as we will see, in the second half of the book melodrama joins romance and farce as an overtly discredited convention.

In the first half, however, Mary's potential melodrama competes for our attention with her father's tragedy. Through the melodramatic mode of presentation, our concern is solicited for Mary in a way that it never is for John. Indeed, Gaskell so arranges her narrative that we end up looking for the catastrophic event in the wrong plot. The melodrama of Mary's story, therefore, makes us inattentive to the threatening nature of John's career. The careful tracing of his decline does not have the interest of Mary's melodrama because we are not expecting John's story to culminate in some disastrous event. Our sense of impending catastrophe, which is essential to a tragic narrative, is misplaced in *Mary Barton*. It is attached not only to the wrong plot but also to the wrong set of narrative conventions. We mistakenly expect a melodramatic catastrophe, one arising from a simple confrontation between good and evil, but we are given a tragic catastrophe, a complexly and carefully motivated revenge murder, the outcome of an inner as well as an outer struggle. The presence of the melodrama in the book's first half, therefore, prevents us from clearly seeing John Barton's decline as the successive complications of a tragedy, and his story, with its unresolved contradictions, tends to fade into the background.

In the book's second half, most of the characters repeat our mistake. They continue to interpret the plot according to a preconceived melodramatic pattern, assuming that Jem killed Harry Carson. It then becomes Mary's job to discredit their conventional assumptions. To save Jem is to disprove the melodramatic interpretation of the murder. Melodrama is, therefore, explicitly consigned to the category of false conventions. It is associated with other kinds of sensation-seeking, and Sally Leadbitter is its most determined spokeswoman. Because her cliché-ridden mind is only able to perceive situations in terms of popular stage conventions, after Carson's murder she moves with ease from a farcical to a melodramatic interpretation of the plot. She holds to her melodramatic version of the story even after Jem's acquittal. In explaining why Jem was dismissed from his job, she reveals the source of her opinions: "Decent men were not going to work with a—no! I suppose I musn't say it, seeing you went to such trouble to get up an *alibi*; not that I should think much the worse of a spirited young fellow for falling foul of a rival,—they always do *at the theatre*" (p. 427; latter emphasis added). Mary, who is concerned for Jem, gasps, "Tell me all about it," and Sally continues, "Why, you see, they've always swords quite handy at them plays" (p. 427).

At this point in the story, Sally's melodramatic viewpoint is relatively harmless—the basis of a joke. But the same viewpoint predominates among the spectators at Jem's trial, almost costing him his life. It is Mary's hard task to disabuse the court of the notion that Jem was a "young fellow" who had "fallen foul of a rival." However, the courtroom, like Sally Leadbitter, seems receptive only to melodrama; even Mary's struggle to save Jem must be rendered melodramatically before it can be admitted: "The barrister, who defended Jem, took new heart when he was put in possession of these striking points to be adduced . . . because he saw the opportunities for a display of forensic eloquence which were presented by the facts; 'a gallant tar brought back from the pathless ocean by a girl's noble daring' " (p. 395). This bit of parody points up the difference between the narrative we have just read and the same facts couched in melodramatic language.

Far from being melodramatic, therefore, the last half of the book takes melodrama as its specific point of contrast. The fact that we ourselves formerly shared the melodramatic assumption, however, allows us to understand what a natural reading of the events it is and how difficult it will be to overcome. Because Mary must overthrow the assumptions not only of the other characters, but also of one of the major narrative conventions of the book's first half, we feel that her task is almost overwhelming. The drama of Mary's plight, therefore, is heightened by the narrative reversal, and the reader's interest in Mary's story intensifies.

By discrediting melodrama however, the later chapters raise the question of realistic narrative form even more insistently than do the earlier chapters. For the narrator's reversed attitude toward melodrama broadens her criticism of the conventional, a criticism that depends on a contrastingly realistic narrative ground. Again, the obvious candidate for such a ground is tragedy; the tragic interpretation of the murder is, after all, the truth that the melodramatic interpretation hides. But the tragic reality is precisely what all the actions of the book's second half are designed to conceal. The very causality that the narrator meticulously traced through the first half is hidden in the second. The events of the second half are more than an escape, an avoidance, of the tragic problem; they represent the problem's deliberate suppression.

In the second half of the book, Mary knows the truth, but she refuses to probe it, to ascertain its meaning. Instead, all her energies go into suppressing both public knowledge of her father's crime and her own consciousness of it. The "why" of the crime, the very substance of the tragedy is not even a subject for speculation in the later chapters: "[Mary] felt it was of no use to conjecture his motives. His actions had become so wild and irregular of late, that she could not reason upon them" (p. 301). In the chapters that are largely confined to Mary's consciousness, therefore, those that take place between the murder and Mary's return to Manchester after the trial, the narrator imposes a moratorium on reasoning about John Barton's life, on thinking about tragic causation. Mary's truth-concealing action takes the place of reason; finding an alibi substitutes for seeking the truth. Tragedy is still present as a narrative ground, but is increasingly shadowy; like melodrama, it is a genre Mary struggles against inhabiting. Thus, at precisely the moment when a stable, realistic narrative form is most needed, tragedy becomes unavailable and another genre emerges into prominence as Mary's special domain. Restricted almost entirely to Mary's viewpoint, the narrative becomes a working-class domestic tale that formally authorizes the suppression of tragic causality.

Elizabeth Gaskell was a pioneer of the working-class domestic tale. In 1837 she and her husband published a sketch of working-class life, "*rather* in the manner of Crabbe,"[35] which tried to illustrate that the "poetry of humble life" exists "even in a town."[36] Three short stories she published in *Howitt's Journal* share the intention of the sketch and are characterized by a wealth of domestic detail, illustrations of the charitable affection that the poor have for one another, and an emphasis on the trials and learning experiences of young women. All the women learn one thing: to do their duty, the duty obviously and immediately before them. These stories are also marked by some conspicuous absences: factories and other workplaces are alluded to but never shown, and people from other classes are almost entirely missing. The working-class domestic tales written by Gaskell combined the genres of homily and urban idyll; they were both exclusively domestic and exclusively working-class.

Much of *Mary Barton* is written in this same genre. The documentary realism for which Gaskell is often praised grows out of the impulse to compile domestic details. Thus she gives us elaborate and affectionate descriptions of working-class homes, clothes, and traditions, as well as careful transcriptions of working-class Lancashire dialect. Domesticity dominates the narratives told by old Alice and Job Leigh, narratives that are moving in the matter-of-fact spareness of their language and in the unobtrusiveness of their message: friends and family are all; duty is clear. Even Sally Leadbitter's farcical outlook is inspired by filial affection (pp. 132-33). Most of the working-class characters in the book share this domestic mentality: they think very little about the masters, they endure bad times, and they seek their satisfaction in the love of family and close friends. Margaret, Job Leigh, the Wilsons, and old Alice all belong to the domestic mode. This is the circle of duty and affection that Mary struggles to maintain.

But Mary is firmly established as a domestic heroine only after her interview with Esther, which reveals the truth about Harry Carson's murder, disabusing Mary of her melodramatic ideas. While the heroine glimpses the tragic abyss (a glimpse that speeds her on to the mental reality of a thoroughly domestic character), the narrator contrasts Mary's lot with Esther's. The contrast is explicitly between the domestic nature of Mary's working-class world and the territories of melodrama and tragedy that Esther inhabits. Just moments before, Mary believed she had driven Jem to murder; she is turned out of the Wilsons' home into the "busy, desolate, crowded street," and her own home seems to her "only the hiding place of four walls . . . where no welcome, no love, no sympathising tears awaited her" (p. 284). She thinks of herself melodramatically as an abandoned waif and longs for her mother, the absent center of a lost domestic idyll. She remembers "long-past times . . . when her father was a cheery-hearted man, rich in the love of his wife, and the companionship of his friend;—when (for it still worked round to that), when mother was alive" (p. 286). And while Mary longs, her mother actually seems to appear in the form of Esther, who had hidden her own melodrama *cum* tragedy behind the costume of a working-class wife. From Esther we get an entirely different perspective on Mary's reality: Mary, who a minute before fancied herself a pathetic creature in a comfortless room, is seen by Esther as the lucky inhabitant of "that home of her early innocence" (p. 293). The house is Esther's "old dwelling-place, whose very walls, and flags, dingy and sordid as they were, had a charm for her" (p. 297), and Mary now seems to be a potential mother, the woman with power to heal: "For [Esther] longed to open her wretched, wretched heart, so hopeless, so abandoned by all living things, to one who had loved her once; and yet she refrained, from dread of the averted eye, the altered voice, the internal loathing, which she feared such disclosure might create" (pp. 294–95). The poignant and ironic contrast firmly situates Mary in the narrative space between the distortions of melodrama and the abyss of tragedy. It identifies her as a domestic heroine, one still capable of becoming "the wife of a working-man" and thereby joining "that happy class to which [Esther] could never, never more belong" (p. 292).

The interview makes Mary a domestic heroine at the same time that it reveals the extent to which both her future and her present domestic worlds are threatened by the novel's other forms: the melodramatic lie that might condemn Jem and the tragic truth that might condemn her father. She emerges as a domestic heroine just in time to lock up her little house and embark on her mission to save these two men and rescue her personal life. For this reason, the events and settings of the book's second half are neither particularly domestic nor particularly working-class. We should not, however, let the public and adventurous events obscure the narrative mentality that pervades this part of the novel. As Kathleen Tillotsen has pointed out, the thickness of domestic detail in *Mary Barton* makes its " 'big scenes'—the chase down the Mersey, the murder trial . . . seem simply emergencies that must occasionally arise in ordinary life."[37]

Mary's existence is "ordinary," but it is also seriously threatened by the emergency she faces. A flawed social order has allowed melodrama and tragedy to break into Mary's world, and she must reestablish its domestic boundaries. Her task involves travel, public notoriety, and extraordinary events of all kinds, but these are necessary to combat melodrama, suppress tragedy, and save what little remains of her family. Mary's homelessness in the later chapters is symptomatic of the social evils the author is trying to illustrate. Mary's struggle to remain a domestic heroine is itself a social criticism with an ideal image of family life at its center. The domestic keynote of these later chapters sounds again and again: in Mary's relationship to Mrs. Wilson; in the minute but emotionally constrained accounts of Mary's tentative and fearful actions and reactions; in the descriptions of the lives and homes she encounters in Liverpool; and in the idyllic, domestic dreamworld that old Alice inhabits throughout the book's second half. Alice's reverie is both a vision of her own past and of Mary's future; Alice imagines the domestic world Mary's actions are retrieving.

For most of the book's second half, then, the domestic tale pre-dominates and suppresses the tragedy, although the two genres are complexly interrelated throughout the novel. Barton's tragedy is itself fundamentally domestic. The loss of his son is the most decisive blow against him. Domestic also is the tragic reality behind the clownish appearance of the workers' delegation, the barren rooms and the sickly wives and children that *Mary Barton* tries to expose. The book was inspired by scenes of blighted domestic life in the working class,[38] and John Barton's narrative sketches the disastrous course that such suffer-ing might initiate.

Although reality is always domestic in *Mary Barton*, it is by no means always tragic. Tragedy may grow out of working-class domestic life, but it ultimately excludes that life. For the most part, *Mary Barton* is a domestic tale, not a domestic tragedy, and the two genres present mutually exclusive kinds of reality in this novel.[39] Barton's tragic career, we are repeatedly told, increasingly takes him away from home; fur-thermore, most of the working-class characters, drawn in the domestic mode, are uninterested in Barton's talk about social injustice. In fact, the book's first dialogue, between Barton and Wilson, typifies the interaction between the hero and most of the working-class characters. Barton rails on for half a page against the "gentlefolk," but Wilson cuts him short: "Well, neighbour, . . . all that may be very true, but what I want to know now is about Esther" (p. 45). This kind of exchange is repeated on other occasions with Jem Wilson and with Job Leigh; the other men all express the assumptions that are built into Gaskell's domestic convention: being too aware of social injustice only distracts one from the principal realities of family and home; conversely, home and family can protect one from the tragedy that attends class conflict.

His respondents never try to refute Barton's social analyses in these exchanges. Rather, the other men quietly recur to their private preoc-cupations. Thus, after John Barton tells the sad story of his London journey and concludes that "as long as I live I shall curse them as so cruelly refused to hear us" (p. 145), Job Leigh tells his own London story, which includes his daughter's death and his retrieval of his granddaughter Margaret.[40] The narrator confides that Job chose the domestic subject matter because it was "neither sufficiently dissonant from the last to jar on the full heart, nor too much the same to cherish the continuance of the gloomy train of thought" (p. 145). The domestic tale suppresses the tragedy not by explicitly denying it, but rather by eluding its causality. John Barton's tragedy, as we have seen, is primarily concerned with cause and effect, with showing how and why the hero became "a Chartist, a Communist, all that is commonly called wild and visionary." Gaskell's domestic tales, on the other hand, aim at showing how to circumvent tragic cause-and-effect logic by simply acting, doing one's immediate duty, without stopping to ponder all of the consequences.

Inevitability, the solemn basis of tragedy, is thus obscured by a flurry of activity. On learning of her father's guilt, Mary first determines not to speculate about his motives and then wades into the myriad activities of the book's second half. The causal logic of this part of the book is explicitly and enthusiastically stated by the narrator in the first person:

> Oh! I do think that the necessity for exertion, for some kind of action . . . in time of distress, is a most infinite blessing. . . . Something to be done implies that there is yet hope of some good thing to be accomplished, or some additional evil that may be avoided; and by degrees the hope absorbs much of the sorrow. (P. 301)

Thus action itself disproves inevitability: it gradually absorbs the tragic causality at the same time that it keeps that causality from emerging into conscious, public view. John Barton dies, but he dies, as Mary wished, at home.

The domestic tale, therefore, is to tragedy in *Mary Barton* as the "Religion of Moral Freedom" was to the "Religion of Causality" in Unitarian theology in the 1840s. Gaskell could not sustain Barton's tragedy, because in doing so she risked denying his freedom, his heroism, even his humanity. But, as the narrator points out, action implies freedom without overtly denying the tragic causality, without providing an alternate interpretation. The action in the book's second half is specifically anti-interpretative; it is designed to establish an alibi for Jem, not to set up a competing version of the truth. Similarly, the transcendental element in Unitarianism was not so much a competing causality as it was a suspension of the older deterministic causality.

Throughout the Liverpool chapters, however, the narrator reminds us that the suspension is merely temporary, that John Barton's terrible guilt is in no way affected by Mary's adventures. We know that once the alibi is established, there will be nothing left to do but confront the awful truth. Thus Will Wilson's arrival in the courtroom produces Mary's collapse. She breaks under the pressure of the suppressed truth, the truth to which the novel must recur once the melodramatic lie is overthrown. Mary's illness gives some reprieve from the inevitable confrontation with John Barton, as do old Alice's death and the settlements of numerous domestic details between Mary and the Wilsons. Each of these in its own way, however, conjures up the "phantom likeness of John Barton" (p. 414) and the problematic causality that attends his story.

Causation once again becomes an explicit theme in the book, one that haunts and perplexes the narrator. Indeed, at one point she attacks the reader for demanding causal explanations. After giving a somewhat unconvincing account of Jem's reasons for prolonging Mary's (and by extension, the novel's) separation from John Barton, she impatiently asserts that reality is not always amenable to clear cause-and-effect analysis: "If you think this account of mine confused, of the half-feelings, half-reasons, which passed through Jem's mind, . . . if you are perplexed to disentangle the real motives, I do assure you it was from such an involved set of thoughts that Jem drew the resolution to act" (pp. 413–14). It is not, however, the reader, the threatening, skeptical, and ultimately guilty "you" of the novel, who demands cause-and-effect logic; it is the narrative itself. In the sentence quoted above, the narrator turns the novel inward by addressing the expectations that the book itself created and declaring both her inability and her unwillingness to meet them. It is a prominently placed sentence, standing at the end of the chapter between the courtroom scene and Mary's return to Manchester; it is an expression of failure, of liberation, and of formal self-consciousness that might well be taken as a motto for the chapters that follow.

The concluding chapters of *Mary Barton* return us to the story of John; Mary continues in the domestic mode, specifically refusing to think about causes. Indeed, where her father's story should be, there is nothing but a blank in Mary's mind: "He was her father! her own dear father! and in his sufferings, whatever their cause, more dearly loved than ever before. His crime was a thing apart, never more to be considered by her" (p. 422). The narrator, however, cannot so easily refuse to consider the causes of John Barton's suffering. Having returned to the subject, she must try to conclude it, but she faces the same bind she encountered earlier: she must indict society as the source of Barton's crime and still grant Barton his free will. Whereas her strategy in the Liverpool chapters was to suppress John Barton's story, her strategy in the concluding chapters is to tell different versions of the story. Since she has declared herself free from the necessity to "disentangle the real motives," she allows herself the luxury of presenting an "involved set" of interpretations without really striving after consistency. Thus the recapitulations contain elements of both social determinism and voluntarism. Finally, however, salvation comes in this novel not through retelling John Barton's story, but through making it irrelevant. All John Barton's and the narrator's explanations are for naught; his story is redeemed through the intervention of another story that makes all talk of causality superfluous.

In the terms of James Martineau's dichotomy, "conscience" is the key word in John Barton's development after the murder, just as "causality" had been before. The issue of John Barton's moral responsibility is partly settled by the mere description of the state in which Mary finds him on her return home: "He had taken the accustomed seat from mere force of habit, which ruled his automaton-body. For all energy, both physical and mental, seemed to have retreated inwards to some of the great citadels of life, there to do battle against the Destroyer, Conscience" (p. 422). John Barton now has no will; he acts from "mere force of habit." But the intensity of his remorse implies that in the past he was free. He takes full responsibility for his crime during his interview with Henry Carson, and his remorse intensifies in the course of conversation. So that remorse might appear a completely appropriate emotion, the narrator gives an account of the murder that makes it seem almost a voluntary political act rather than a desperate crime forced by the convergence of uncontrollable indignation and intolerable suffering. The version of Barton's crime given during his interview with Carson contains a causality compatible with freedom. It contains nothing of the intense suffering of the strikers or of Harry Carson's maddening arrogance: "To intimidate a class of men, known only to those below them as desirous to obtain the greatest quantity of work for the lowest wages,—at most to remove an overbearing partner from an obnoxious firm . . . this was the light in which John Barton had viewed his deed" (pp. 435–36). The very word "cause" takes on a new meaning in this account of Barton's story: instead of implying a set of circumstances that led up to the fatal action, it comes to denote the partisan purpose of the trade unionists, the "cause he had so blindly espoused" (p. 436).

This description of the murder as a wholly political, indeed almost unemotional, act contains a social criticism, but one that increases our sense of Barton's guilty freedom. The account allows the narrator once again to argue that domesticity is the ultimate ground of reality. John Barton's reasoning had produced the distortion of human reality that always occurs when men are severed from their domestic contexts: "he had no more imagined to himself the blighted home, and the miserable parents, than does the soldier, who discharges his musket, picture to himself the desolation of the wife, and the pitiful cries of the helpless little ones, who are in an instant to be made widowed, and fatherless" (p. 435). The analogy links Barton's failing to Harry Carson's insensitivity: each in his own way was deaf to "the pitiful cries" of helpless relations. This plea for a more highly developed domestic consciousness is itself a species of social criticism, albeit a vague one. Barton's sin of abstracting Harry Carson from his domestic context is presented as the characteristic error of industrial society. By substituting this kind of broad criticism of an abstract and abstracting mentality for the careful descriptions of social relationships and experiences contained in earlier chapters, the author unites the classes on the basis of a shared human reality, the universal reality of family life. The account of Barton's story that emerges from the interview with Mr. Carson, therefore, makes a critical point, but the point does not relieve the hero of any guilt. Indeed, it increases Barton's crimes by adding to his faults of resentment and murder the crime of insensitivity to human suffering, which was previously attributed to the masters. In this account, the murder is no longer the result but the cause of suffering:

> The sympathy for suffering, formerly so prevalent a feeling with him, again filled John Barton's heart, and almost impelled him to speak . . . some earnest, tender words to the stern man, shaking in his agony.
> But who was he, that he should utter sympathy, or consolation? The cause of all this woe. (P. 435)

This version of Barton's story is concerned with causation, but not the kind of causation that the earlier chapters traced. In this retelling, "cause" comes to mean political purpose, and Barton himself becomes the cause of another's suffering. Causation in this version, therefore, is compatible with conscience and its corollary, free will.

Those circumstances formerly presented as the sources of Barton's action, however, are not completely ignored in the resolution of his story. After the unforgiving Mr. Carson leaves him, Barton gives an account of his own tragedy, an account which contains a heavy dose of the social determinism of earlier chapters. From him we hear once more about the moral effects of poverty and ignorance: "You see I've so often been hankering after the right way; and it's a hard one for a poor man to find. . . . No one learned me, and no one told me" (p. 440). Ignorance and poverty are two determining circumstances, and the hypocrisy of the upper classes is a third: "I would fain have gone after the Bible rules if I'd seen folk credit it; they all spoke up for it, and went and did clean contrary" (p. 440). And we hear again about the hatred inspired by his son's death from want of medicine and proper food: "wife, and children never spoke, but their helplessnesss cried aloud, and I was driven to do as others did,—and then Tom died" (p. 440).

The image of Barton as a driven man, however, competes in this deathbed account with yet another characterization, one quite new to the novel. Barton acknowledges that he is creating a new self in his story-telling; he describes the act of narration as "wrestling with my soul for a character to take into the other world" (p. 434). Although Barton's characterization of himself has elements of social determinism, it is not completely dominated by that model of causation. Even as he recapitulates the familiar circumstances, he subtly undermines their explanatory power by prefacing them: "It's not much I can say for myself in t'other world. God forgive me: but I can say this . . . " (p. 440). This preface reminds us that John Barton's acknowledged guilt, his full moral responsibility, is the given context of his narrative; he is not rehearsing his story as a defense, as a proof of innocence. Instead, he is describing, somewhat inconsistently, the extenuating circumstances of a crime to which he has already pleaded guilty.

Accordingly, the focus of his narrative is not on the familiar circumstances of his decline, but on a new set of facts about his life, facts implying that he could have avoided his tragic course. We learn for the first time that the hero was once very devout, that he studied the Bible and tried to follow its precepts, that he even had a special comradeship with old Alice, who had tried to "strengthen" him. His faith, however, was not strong enough to survive the corrosive bitterness of his experience; the loss of his faith, we are told, was the turning point of his career: "At last I gave it up in despair, trying to make folks' actions square wi' th' Bible; and I thought I'd no longer labour at following th' Bible myself. I've said all this afore; may be. But from that time I've dropped down, down,—down" (p. 441). Despair, itself a sin, becomes the decisive factor in this religious account of Barton's life. The character that Barton creates "to take into the other world" is thus a cross between the tragically determined John Barton we know and a John Barton we have never seen before, the free but erring subject of a religious homily.

The writer seems to have felt some uneasiness about introducing a completely new version of the story at such a late hour, especially one that fits imperfectly with the older deterministic version, for she has Barton suggest that "I've said all this afore; may be." If the sentence is meant to make the new facts seem less strange, it defeats its own purpose, for it conveys the self-conscious uneasiness of the writer by reminding us that in fact *no one* has "said all this afore," that we are being given a new story, one that is not easy to reconcile with the old. The sentence therefore increases our awareness of the discontinuities of these last chapters.

The issues tangled in the summaries of Barton's life and crime (whether he is fully responsible or not, free or determined) are never finally sorted out. We must accept this "involved set" of accounts, but we are also reassured that ultimately it does not matter how we interpret Barton's story. For the novel we have been reading is finally resolved by the introduction of a different book, the Bible. The narrator finds relief from the multiple reinterpretations of John Barton's story by superimposing the ending as well as the meaning of the Gospel onto her novel, and the meaning of the Gospel is that we need not choose among the several versions of John Barton's story.

While John Barton is recounting his failure to live "Gospel-wise," Henry J. Carson recreates himself (in both senses of the phrase) through the other story: "He fell to the narrative now, afresh, with all the interest of a little child. He began at the beginning, and read on almost greedily, understanding for the first time the full meaning of the story" (pp. 439–40). The "full meaning" of the story turns out to be that John Barton should be forgiven, no matter what the sources or consequences of his crime. Henry Carson comes to forgive John Barton not because he has been told the hero's own story, but because Barton's words "I did not know what I was doing" (p. 435) referred him to the Gospel story.[41] Forgiveness is mandated by the other narrative, and all versions of John Barton's life thus become irrelevant to the novel's concluding and redeeming action: Carson's forgiveness, which is a foretaste of the Christian spirit that the narrator assures us will allow Carson to effect industrial social change.

Thus the conclusion of John Barton's story points to narrative as an instrument of God's Providence without having to sort out the tangle of its own narrative threads. In the few episodes that remain, the characters settle in Canada, and the domestic tale is finally protected by distance from the tragedy caused by industrial vicissitudes. But the final episodes fail to settle the question that the novel repeatedly raises: the question of an appropriate narrative form. It is not surprising that, in Gaskell's words, no one "saw" her "idea of a tragic poem," for the tragedy is even more obscured by antagonistic interpretations at the end of the novel than in the early chapters. We must therefore agree with the author's judgment that she failed to express perfectly her tragic intentions. But we must also remember that her tragic purpose contained its own contradiction, which had definite historical roots in the Unitarianism of the 1840s and in certain features of the tradition of industrial social criticism that Gaskell inherited. We should also remember that her failure is the foundation of the book's formal significance, for its very generic eclecticism points toward the formal self-consciousness of later British realism.

4

The Tailor Unraveled:
The Unaccountable "I" In Kingsley's
Alton Locke: Tailor and Poet

From Locke's time downwards, our whole Metaphysics have been
physical; not a spiritual Philosophy, but a material one. The
singular estimation in which his Essay was so long held as a
scientific work (for the character of the man entitled all he said to
veneration), will one day be thought a curious indication of the
spirit of these times. His whole doctrine is mechanical, in its aim
and origin, in its method and its results. It is a mere discussion
concerning the origin of our consciousness, or ideas, or whatever
else they are called; a genetic history of what we see in the mind.
But the grand secrets of Necessity and Freewill, of the mind's vital
or non-vital dependence on matter, of our mysterious relations to
Time and Space, to God, to the universe, are not, in the faintest
degree, touched on in their enquiries; and seem not to have the
smallest connexion with them.

Thomas Carlyle
"Signs of the Times"

A Familiar Contradiction, a Peculiar Form

Charles Kingsley embodied the contradictions in the critique of industrial capitalism more fully than any other Victorian writer. As a "broad
church" Anglican minister, he opposed the Calvinist idea of Predestination, and his sectarian commitment to the doctrine of free will was
reinforced by his association with the English Romantics and their
intellectual heirs. Because he was educated by S. T. Coleridge's son, the
Reverend Derwent Coleridge, and was influenced early in his manhood by Carlyle and by the Coleridgean F. D. Maurice, Kingsley's ideas
about human nature had a firmly romantic foundation.[1] Like his
religious and philosophical mentors, he opposed all deterministic explanations of human action and asserted that God's Providence was
mysteriously reconciled with man's free will.[2] His social criticism
evinces the same antideterminism; he often wrote in the spirit of
Carlyle's "Signs of the Times," opposing the mechanical model of
human nature and society.

Kingsley, however, was also an amateur naturalist and sanitary reformer, and his scientific interests often led him to deterministic explanations of human behavior.[3] Indeed, many of his writings emphasize the importance of those very circumstances that Carlyle insisted should be deemphasized. Kingsley's belief in the dependence of mind and the spirit on material sensation led him toward that very philosophical empiricism, the tradition of John Locke, that Carlyle abused.[4] Containing both major traditions of nineteenth-century social criticism (the Romantic tradition associated with Coleridge and the materialist tradition associated with determinists like Robert Owen), Kingsley's writings often contradict themselves on the issue of free will.

Moreover, the ambivalence about human freedom in Kingsley's work was increased by his contacts with Chartists in 1848, the year F. D. Maurice's group of Christian Socialists held meetings with working-class London radicals. Kingsley's frequent exposure to Chartist rhetoric about liberty during this period made him cautious about delivering unqualified endorsements of the principle of freedom. In his first written appeal to Chartists, Kingsley takes up the word "freedom" and echoes both Owen and Coleridge, insisting that freedom entails rationality and obedience to God's laws. He also uses the slavery metaphor, consciously imitating and inverting the Chartists' use of it, to reinforce his point that political liberty alone cannot free the working class: "That, I guess, is real slavery; to be a slave to one's own stomach, one's own pocket, one's own temper. Will the Charter cure *that*?"[5] Human freedom, Kingsley implies here, is a much more complicated matter than the Chartists realize.

Kingsley's industrial novel, *Alton Locke: Tailor and Poet* (1849), demonstrates just how complicated the issue of freedom is. An ambivalence about causality marks it more deeply than any other industrial novel. For Kingsley chose a form that expressed his Romantic faith in a free will benevolently reconciled with God-given circumstances; however, his reforming purpose led him to add incongruous elements, suggestions of negative environmental determinism, to that form. The resulting contradiction is neither avoided nor suppressed nor resolved in the narrative, for Kingsley's form encourages the narrator to review the free will/determinism controversy obsessively throughout the book. Indeed, the narrator is so indecisive about causality that he is simply unable to create a defined central character, and *Alton Locke* becomes, quite unintentionally, a novel that questions the reality of individual identity and undermines faith in the possibility of referential, realistic fiction.

Kingsley's form both expresses and nurtures his ambivalence about the relationship between character and circumstances, between free will and necessity. He tells the story of the tailor-poet Alton Locke in a form that presupposes the reconcilability of material circumstances and spiritual life: the fictional autobiography of a writer.[6] Kingsley associated the form with Carlyle's *Sartor Resartus*, a book that, like many Romantic autobiographies, records a journey in which a poet's "soul" emerges out of his encounter with the world.[7] In writing the first-person account of the life of a *tailor*-poet, in strewing it liberally with explicit references to Carlyle and allusions to *Sartor Resartus*, Kingsley repeatedly conjures the ghostly presence of that other fictional autobiography. He also resurrects Carlyle's preoccupation with the conflict between self and the world, "Freewill" and "Necessity," and *Sartor Resartus'* resolution of that conflict. Carlyle's hero does not rise above circumstances: rather, he transcends the previous limits of his selfhood by moving into the world and acknowledging it as his God-given home. The conflict between free will and necessity is for Teufelsdröckh the universal condition of human life, a condition that mars our happiness even in childhood: "Thus already Freewill often came in painful collision with Necessity; so that my tears flowed, and at seasons the Child itself might taste that root of bitterness, wherewith the whole fruitage of our life is mingled and tempered."[8] Only after he has reconciled himself with Nature can Teufelsdröckh transcend the "warfare" produced by the fact that "Our Life is compassed round with Necessity; yet is the meaning of Life itself no other than Freedom" (p. 126). Although *Sartor Resartus* is enough of a post-Romantic[9] work to scoff at mere "view-hunting," when Teufelsdröckh awakes from his healing sleep, he finds himself in a conventionally Romantic landscape. It is symbolic but nevertheless natural, and the hero is able to learn from it the lesson that "The Universe is not dead and demoniacal, a charnel-house with spectres; but godlike, and my Father's!" (p. 130). This insight gives him a third term with which he can transcend the primary opposites. "Duty" reconciles the demands of freedom and necessity: "The Situation that has not its Duty, its Ideal, was never yet occupied by man. Yes here, in this poor, miserable, hampered, despicable Actual, wherein thou even now standest, here or nowhere is thy Ideal: work it out therefrom; and working, believe, live, be free" (p. 135).

Although *Alton Locke* also preaches Teufelsdröckh's gospel of Duty, his version of the relationship between man and circumstances is essentially inappropriate to Alton's story. Kingsley was aware of the incongruity; he knew that such Romantic reconciliations came about because the world confronted by the hero was the world of Nature, a world of circumstances fitted by God for union with the mind of man. Kingsley, however, wrote *Alton Locke* about a real tailor in order to expose the sweating system of the London clothing industry.[10] Such a hero and such a purpose made the Romantic reconciliation of self and circumstances impossible. Alton's surroundings are necessarily portrayed as "dead and demoniacal"; his world is indeed "a charnel-house with spectres." His cannot be the enabling, life-enhancing world that Teufelsdröckh sees on his awakening: Nature, the "Living Garment of God." Indeed, the very inappropriateness to working-class life of the *Sartor Resartus* resolution inspired the composition of *Alton Locke*. In 1849 Kingsley walked through the West Country, trying to recover from the fatigue brought about by his work for the Christian Socialists and by the burdens of a cholera epidemic in his parish. Apparently, though, he could not forget the scenes he had recently quitted. His biographer tells us that while Kingsley strode across Dartmoor, invigorated by the rugged landscape, "he thought of those who never saw such sights, the Chartists and their families who lived in the evil, reeking alleys of London."[11] Directly he began composing one of the poems attributed to the hero in *Alton Locke*.

In writing *Alton Locke*, therefore, Kingsley chose a preeminently Romantic form that was, he knew, incongruous with his working-class subject. His choice of an inappropriate form, however, was strategic. In writing a poet's autobiography, Kingsley was able to validate the Romantic tenets that he had inherited from his mentors and that were consonant with his broad Church beliefs. The form assumes that the human will is free, that man's spirit emerges out of his encounter with his God-given surroundings, and that such spiritual births are momentous events. In writing a working-class poet's autobiography, moreover, Kingsley was able to point out, through the incongruities between form and content, what he as a Christian Socialist considered the faults of the Romantic tradition: its apparent blindness to the facts that some people are less free than others; that some circumstances prevent the birth of the spirit; and that, even when a poet's spirit does emerge, its existence is not an end in itself.

Kingsley, therefore, wanted both to use the form of the poet's fictional autobiography and to enlarge it by adding elements he thought it lacked: a social dimension and a religious perspective in which the poet appears as a tool of God's will. In *Alton Locke* these added elements are tightly bound together. The book breaks with its form by making the poet's emergence not an end in itself, but merely one means to a more important end: the realignment of social organization with Christian values. Kingsley consciously dissociated himself from Romantic writers on this issue of the poet's ultimate purpose. In an exchange of letters with F. D. Maurice, the Christian Socialist leader, the two clergymen agreed that Wordsworth, Byron, and Goethe were all engaged in a "self-building process . . . in which God . . .

was still the agent only in fitting them to be world-wise, men of genius, artists."[12] *Alton Locke* was composed on a different plan: God is the agent in making Alton a poet, but Alton is in turn the agent of God's willed social regeneration. Here, as in other poets' stories, God's hand directs the poet's destiny, but in *Alton Locke* the poetry itself is not the reigning *telos*. It is, rather, merely an instrument for social reform.

The necessity for social reform, however, implied that some circumstances were not willed by God and were, indeed, disabling. The elements Kingsley added to his fictional writer's autobiography were thus antithetical to those given in the form. A familiar contradiction, therefore, marks this narrative. Like Charlotte Elizabeth Tonna and Elizabeth Gaskell, Kingsley is torn between two models of causality: a providential vision that justifies suffering as a necessary soul-making process, and a view of suffering, especially the suffering of the poor, as a socially determined evil. But this narrator is more threatened by both kinds of determinism than were the narrators of *Helen Fleetwood* and *Mary Barton*; hence, he insists more frequently and strenuously than they on man's ultimate responsibility for his own physical and moral state. Social conditions may be determining, but they are also the result of the sinful actions of men.

The providential making of the poet is a given of Kingsley's form. He emphasizes this aspect of the story in the book's first paragraphs. However, these paragraphs also undercut the narrator's providential explanations. Accounting for his development, Alton begins by telling us that he is a "Cockney among Cockneys," with a knowledge of the world "bounded by the horizon which encircles Richmond Hill."[13] The closeness and ugliness of Alton's world are emphasized repeatedly in these early paragraphs, but we are also told that this imprisonment in a London slum was "God's gift":

> He made me [a Cockney], that I might learn to feel for poor wretches who sit stifled in reeking garrets and workrooms, drinking in disease with every breath—bound in their prisonhouse of bricks and iron, with their own funeral pall hanging over them, in that canopy of fog and poisonous smoke, from their cradle to their grave. . . . And so I have learned . . . to be a poet—a poet of the people. (P. 2)

A tension is felt in this passage between the enabling function of the described circumstances (their role in developing Alton's sympathies, making him a poet of the people) and their disabling function (the slow death that they represent for the "poor wretches" who share Alton's prisonhouse). A few lines further on, the contradiction is more palpable:

> I used . . . to call it the curse of circumstances that I was a sickly,
> decrepit Cockney. My mother used to tell me that it was the cross
> which God had given me to bear. I know now that she was right
> there. She used to say that my disease was God's will. I do not
> think, though, that she spoke right there also. I think that it was
> the will of the world and of the devil, of man's avarice and laziness
> and ignorance. (P. 2)

There is no reason for the reversal that takes place here. The two
propositions (that Alton's sickness was the cross God gave him and that
it was God's will) are not sufficiently different to make Alton's assent to
one and his denial of the other seem consistent. Because the providential account of the poet's development is beginning to shade into
providential justification of the very conditions Kingsley wants to condemn, the narrator trades one causal scheme for another halfway
through the passage.

In the next sentence, the antiprovidential perspective on Alton's
childhood is developed, and the narrator's ambivalence about causes is
schematized as a debate between his Calvinist mother and an unspec-
ified reformer:

> A sanitary reformer would not be long in guessing the cause of
> my unhealthiness. He would not rebuke me—nor would [my
> mother] now that she is at rest in bliss—for my wild longings to
> escape, for my envying the very flies and sparrows their wings,
> that I might flee miles away into the country, and breathe the air
> of heaven once, and die. (P. 3)

Mrs. Locke's religious determinism and the sanitary reformer's environmental determinism contain antagonistic valuations of the circumstances of Alton's life, antagonistic valuations that remain unresolved throughout the narrative.

Kingsley's choice of form both expresses this irresolution about the
kind of causation that operates in workers' lives and provides a context
in which the irresolution can be sustained. In writing a fictional poet's
autobiography, a form that normally assumed the providential interdependence of the realms of freedom and necessity, Kingsley denies
that working-class life is tragically determined. But in trying to include
the viewpoint of the sanitary reformer—and, as we noted, Kingsley was
himself a sanitary reformer—he constantly introduces ideas that
undercut the assumptions of the form. Workers, we are repeatedly
told, are not free, and God does not shape their lives. This ambivalence
about causal schemes is, as we have seen, one of the definitive characteristics of industrial novels. What is unique to *Alton Locke* is its strategy

for handling the formal problem. I say "handle" rather than "solve" because Kingsley's strategy does not even attempt a solution. It consists in simply allowing the issue of freedom versus determinism to become the narrator's irresolvable obsession.

One element of the form, in particular, its first-person point of view, authorizes this treatment. Alton is able to carry on long discussions of causality but then to claim his incapacity to come to a conclusion on the subject. No third-person narrator with omniscient pretentions could indulge such irresolution. Furthermore, like Teufelsdroeckh, Alton makes the Romantic claim that we are all mysteries to ourselves. In the following typical passage, it is the reader, the novel's "you," who demands clear causal lines and analyses, but the novel's "I," protected by the partiality of the viewpoint contained in that pronoun, refuses to explain its own development:

> So our god, or gods rather, till we were twelve years old, were hell, the rod, the ten commandments, and public opinion. Yet under them, not they, but something deeper far, both in her and us, preserved us pure. Call it natural character, conformation of the spirit—conformation of the brain, if you like, if you are a scientific man and a phrenologist. I never yet could dissect and map out my own being, or my neighbour's, as you analysts do. To me, I myself, ay, and each person round me, seem one inexplicable whole. (P. 5)

Here an essential question raised by the story, the question of how Alton, his sister, and his mother remain spiritually uncontaminated by their sordid surroundings, is acknowledged, explored, and then left unanswered in the name of Romantic integrity. This loyalty to the mystery is sanctioned by the first-person point of view that the passage stresses: "I never could dissect . . . as you analysts do": "To me, I myself, ay, and each person round me . . ." The narrator uses the ignorance allowed by the first person to protect himself, and he also invokes the immunity from logical rebuttal that the pronoun provides in much the same way that people in normal conversation erect hedges of self-referential phrases—"I, myself, personally believe, etc."—to buttress otherwise insupportable assertions.

First-person narration, therefore, licenses Alton to suggest numerous causes for his own development without ever settling on any one explanation; thus he need never resolve, control, or even avoid the issue of causality. As a result, the book contains dozens of assertions and counterassertions about causes, circumstances, and free will. Indeed, one chapter, "An Emersonian Sermon," is nothing more than a survey of several deterministic schemes and a concluding diatribe against them all. The diatribe is delivered by Alton's mentor, Sandy Mackaye, but Mackaye's is not the book's authoritative opinion on the issue; the narrator had previously made a confused attack on what he called the Scotsman's "undefined Unitarianism." Mackaye equates God with an unbending, righteous Providence; his faith is summed up in the sentence, "God is great; who hath resisted His Will?" But the young Alton finds this idea of God insufficient. Like Mrs. Locke's Calvinist idea, Mackaye's notion seems to make God the author of evil, to exclude the possibility of Special Providence, and to condemn the masses of men to misery. Thus the narrator's dissatisfaction:

> Did He indeed care for men at all?—was what I longed to know; was all this misery and misrule around us His will—His stern and necessary law—His lazy connivance? And were we to free ourselves from it by any frantic means that came to hand? or had He ever interfered Himself? Was there a chance, a hope, of His interfering now, in our own time, to take the matter into His own hand, and come out of His place to judge the earth in righteousness? . . . poor Mackaye could give no comfort there. "God was great—the wicked would be turned into hell." Ay—the few willful, triumphant wicked; but the millions of suffering, starving wicked, the victims of society and circumstance—what hope for them? (P. 193)

The narrator here obviously believes God may interfere and overthrow the prevailing "misrule." From this belief we might infer that the misery to which Alton refers is somehow outside of God's Providence; but, characteristically, he leaves the relationship between God's will and human suffering undefined. The relationship between man's spiritual state and his material circumstances is also left unclear by the passage: "the millions" are apparently both wicked and innocent, both responsible agents and passive victims.

In passages such as this, Alton seems obsessed with a great contradictory truth, one Kingsley claimed was beyond human comprehension: man is free and yet determined.[14] Because the narrator insists that he is very much a creature (rather than a creator) of the world he describes, because he never aspires to the godlike omniscience of the third person, he is free to ponder the mystery of causality whenever explanations are in order.

The first-person, moreover, licenses inconsistencies in all aspects of the narrative. Alton need not detail motives or trace a coherent plot. If a character seems inconsistent, the narrator justifies the characterization by claiming a necessarily limited knowledge of others: "I draw men as I have found them—inconsistent, piecemeal" (p. 191). The same excuse is used to explain inexplicable turns of plot. We never find out, for example, how the Chartists learned that Alton expurgated his poems to please his wealthy patrons. The scandal the Chartist press creates out of the incident is the turning point of Alton's career, but the original informer is never identified. Thus the whole incident goes unexplained: "Mackaye and Crossthwaite, I had thought, were the only souls to whom I had ever breathed the secret, and they denied indignantly the having ever betrayed my weakness. How it came out, I say again, I cannot conceive" (pp. 247–48).

The first-person point of view thus covers a number of narrative lapses in *Alton Locke*; it gives the narator freedom from causal explanations, indeed from cause-and-effect plotting, that no omniscient third-person narrator could legitimately claim. Finally, it gives the narrator too much latitude. His uncertainty about causation ultimately prevents him from fulfilling the essential responsibility of a first-person narrator: the creation of himself as a character. Alton Locke literally does not know what to make of himself.

First Person Null; First Person Plural

Alton's inability to explain himself leaves both referents of the "I" (character and narrator) undefined.[15] Alton never does assume a shape. He is meant to represent the universal mystery of personality, but he is so ineffable that his personality never emerges. As a narrator, he is characterized by his indeterminate obsessing about possible explanations; as a character, by mysteriousness and incoherence. In short, he is characterized by his lack of character. And yet Alton's lack of character is appropriate to the author's intention, an intention probably inspired by his inability to choose a causal scheme. Kingsley's intention was to write a history of Alton's obstructed development, a history in which the character's growth is prevented and his minimal identity disintegrates. The character Alton does not gradually merge with the narrator; rather, he becomes the narrator by gradually dissolving and being reborn. The plan of the book makes normal characterization obsolete, for it generates a narrative about the near impossibility of becoming a self.

By not creating himself, however, the narrator does not entirely avoid the need for explanations, for he must try to account for his own lack of identity. At times, therefore, so that we periodically receive a coherent account of the dissolution of Alton's self, the narrator weaves the failure of characterization into the social theme of the novel. Alton often attributes his failure to achieve selfhood to the disabling conditions of working-class life.[16] And as the small store of identity he accumulates in the book's first chapters begins to disappear, the narrator sometimes traces the loss to Alton's earlier social and cultural deprivation. Because Alton's appetite for beauty and grace had been starved, for example, he idolizes the wealthy and beautiful Lillian. In turn, his idolatry leads him "to emasculate" his poems by blunting their political message: "The poor man," the narrator remarks, "will understand [my weakness], and surely pardon it also" (p. 182).

The words that directly follow these, however, undercut the social analysis of Alton's self-betrayal: the poor man will pardon Alton's weakness, "seeing that he himself is Man" (p. 182). The phrase cuts away the social context and therefore the social explanation, and Alton becomes again that inscrutable being, Man. The narrator is as incapable of accounting for Alton's failure to become a character as he is incapable of creating him as a character. Alton "tears himself in pieces" (p. 340) for reasons the narrator can never quite formulate. It is for the love of Lillian, but what is the love of Lillian? Only the book's deepest mystery: "I could have fallen down, fool that I was! and worshipped—what? I could not tell then, for I cannot tell even now" (p. 149). To "explain" Alton's disintegration as the result of his love for Lillian, therefore, is merely to trace it to a source beyond the reach of explanation.

The narrator cannot account for either Alton's development or his lack of development. This general explanatory failure leads to the book's insistent questioning of the concept of identity. Alton is never exactly a character, never anything so strongly defined that we might call it by that name; nor does he simply exemplify the stultification of the self by working-class life. He is rather, a consciousness of disintegration and plurality that attests to the fictional nature of all identities. At various moments of crisis, Alton experiences himself as plural and begins to wonder if all ideas of continuous, singular personality are not simply convenient fabrications.

Alton's trial for inciting a riot is a case in point. The riot itself is partly caused by Alton's characterlessness, his "loss of self-possession" (pp. 269, 275). In an outburst that has no single, clear motive, Alton unintentionally inspires a group of country laborers to loot and burn a nearby farm: " 'Go, then,' I cried, losing my self-possession between disappointment and the maddening desire of influence—and, indeed, who could hear their story, or even look upon their faces, and not feel some indignation stir in him . . . —'go,' I cried, 'and get bread.' " (pp. 269–70). The narrator squeezes a number of motivations for Alton's outburst between the fateful words "go, then," and "get bread." The motivations are syntactically incidental, and there is simply no room to expand on them. However, it is clear that Alton's words contravene his intention in addressing the crowd; he addresses the crowd in the first place in order to dampen "the spirit of mad aimless riot" (p. 269). Alton is then borne along to the riot both by feelings he cannot master and by a crowd he cannot control. As he watches the ricks burn, he is unable to define himself in relation to the action: "Was it my doing? Was it not?" (p. 272).

Given this initial confusion, it is not surprising that Alton's trial for inciting the riot further unsettles his sense of who he is and what he has done. In a scene that reminds the modern reader of Camus's *L'Étranger*, we watch the prosecutor and the defense counsel construct other Alton Lockes—characters who come to seem as probable as any we have encountered in the book. As the story is told, untold, and retold, the narrator remarks, "there seemed no truth anywhere, and no falsehood either . . .; till I began to have doubts whether the riot had ever occurred at all—and indeed, doubts of my own identity also" (p. 279).[17] As the prosecutor details a seditious plot that Alton is alleged to have hatched, even to himself the hero becomes not just one but all seditious plotters:

> I really began to question whether the man might not be right after all. The whole theory seemed so horribly coherent—possible, natural. I might have done it, under possession of the devil, and forgotten it in excitement—I might—perhaps I did. And if there, why not elsewhere? Perhaps I had helped Jourdan Coupetête at Lyons, and been king of the Munster Anabaptists—why not? (P. 280)

Here the relationship between causal indeterminacy and characterlessness reveals itself. In Alton's near-madness as he loses his sense of himself, any fiction seems plausible. Kingsley, by expanding the narrative question from "why?" to "why not?"—that is, by allowing a number of merely possible explanations—creates a plurality of coexisting "characters."

The trial is not the only episode in which Alton is unable to recall the scattered fragments of himself and to differentiate between what he is and what others make of him. When O'Flynn's *Weekly Warwhoop* retails Alton's life story as the history of a weak-spirited turncoat, Alton is enraged, claims that the story is slanted, and yet admits, "my conscience told me that I had nothing to answer" (p. 250). The facts of the accusation are all true, and Alton has no clear alternative version of his life with which to defend himself. The Alton Locke of the *Weekly*

Warwhoop takes his place alongside the hero of the autobiography as one of his indeterminate selves.

"Alton" becomes a name given to a bundle of incompatible characteristics: he is rationalism; he is physical-force Chartism; he is unbridled envy and frustrated desire. In fact, in an attempt to give Alton some definite content, the narrator turns to actual events of recent history, but grounding Alton in such a "reality" only speeds the process of dissolution. As that climactic day for Chartists, April 10, 1849, approaches, Alton's story ostensibly becomes increasingly realistic, increasingly rooted in history. Simultaneously, however, Alton becomes less and less of an individual. He even stops using the first-person pronoun in his efforts to explain his actions. He claims that the Chartists' passions were "insane and wicked," but then asks, "were there no excuses for us? I do not say for myself. . . . But were there no excuses for the mass?" (p. 300). Alton has substituted the mass for himself, and when he returns to the first person, he does so explicitly as a representative of that mass: "My story may be instructive, as a type of the feelings of thousands beside me" (p. 304). One Alton becomes thousands, thousands who are themselves "insane," "torn apart by passions." The historical solution to the problem of Alton's identity, therefore, is a solution only in the sense that the character is further dissolved in it.

As the dissolution of Alton Locke proceeds, it takes us far beyond the boundaries of both Romantic autobiography and realistic fiction. When he ultimately enters a dream world in which the conventional Romantic reconciliation with circumstance—the reconciliation with nature—takes place in an unconventional way, Alton becomes nothing more than a visionary experience of plurality itself. His waking life merges with his dream so imperceptibly that it is difficult to define the precise moment when the narrative leaves the realm of realistic fiction. "Torn in pieces" by passion (p. 340), Alton, the aggregate Chartist, finds himself in the den of a former fellow tailor, Jemmy Downes. There, in one of the book's "documentary" passages, a nightmare begins:

> There was [Jemmy Downes'] little Irish wife—dead—and naked; the wasted white limbs gleamed in the lurid light; the unclosed eyes stared, as if reproachfully, at the husband whose drunkenness had brought her there to kill her with the pestilence; and on each side of her a little, shrivelled, impish child-corpse—the wretched man had laid their arms round the dead mother's neck . . . ; the rats had been busy already with them—but what matter to them now? (P. 335)

The scene is created by Downes' bizarre, diseased mind, but the room itself has done its part in driving the tailor insane. Through cracks in the floor, a pestilent backwater of the Thames gleams, and Downes fancies that "Day after day I saw the devils come up through the cracks, like little maggots and beetles . . . creeping down their throats" (p. 335). "It was too true," writes the narrator; "the poisonous exhalations had killed them. The wretched man's delirium tremens had given that horrible substantiality to the poisonous fever gases" (p. 335). Alton is literally locked into this room, "the very mouth of hell" (p. 337), by Jemmy Downes, and his incarceration simultaneously recapitulates the book's references to the prisonhouse of working-class life and transforms them into the material of a nightmare phantasm.

The episode completes Alton's dissolution; his fever and dream grow directly out of it. The continuity between the dream narrative and the earlier episode makes the reader aware of how unrealistic the story has grown and how undifferentiated Alton has become. That the sentence "I was a soft crab, under a stone on the sea-shore" (p. 340) does not jar us proves how diffuse the "I" of the novel has become; the "I" is dispersed far beyond the boundaries of the novel's form. The explicit purpose of the dream is first to realize fully and then to overcome this diffusion, this characterlessness, in Alton:

> And I was at the lowest point of created life: a madrepore rooted to the rock . . . ; and, worst of all, my individuality was gone. I was not one thing, but many things—a crowd of innumerable polypi; and I grew and grew, and the more I grew the more I divided, and multiplied thousand and ten thousand-fold. (P. 340)

Eleanor, Alton's future savior, explains the healing purpose of the dream and the significance of all this division:

> "He who tears himself in pieces by his lusts, ages only can make him one again. The madrepore shall become a shell, and the shell a fish, and the fish a bird, and the bird a beast; and then he shall become a man again, and see the glory of the latter days." (P. 340)

Alton is thus sentenced to recapitulate man's evolution. Like other Romantic heroes, therefore, he is restored through Nature; unlike those heroes, however, Alton *becomes* Nature instead of encountering it, and then only in a vision. Once again, the novel's deviation from the norm is significant. Kingsley wants to bring Alton into contact with the healing powers of Nature, but Alton's "circumstances" do not allow for such a solution. His healing merger with Nature thus reminds us of the

Romantic faith that circumstances are ultimately benign, but it also denies that faith. Alton can only be made whole again by experiences that remove him from his surroundings.

During the dream, we are again faced with Kingsley's ambivalence about the relationship between mind and circumstances, freedom and necessity, and again the narrator articulates the dilemma but leaves it unresolved:

> Where I had picked up the sensation which my dreams realized for me, I know not; my waking life, alas! had never given me experience of it. Has the mind power of creating sensations for itself? Surely it does so, in those delicious dreams about flying which haunt us poor wingless mortals, which would seem to give my namesake's philosophy the lie. (Pp. 341–42)

The thesis that material experience creates mental phenomena is associated here with John Locke, but in the book's opening pages the same epistemology was assumed by that latter-day Locke, the narrator. This passage questions the empiricist thesis and appears to be stating its opposite ("Has the mind power of creating sensations for itself? Surely it does so."). However, the passage ends tentatively: the "delicious dreams . . . *would seem* [emphasis added] to give my namesake's philosophy the lie."

The narrator, then, does not directly contradict earlier Lockean assertions about the dependence of man's mental life on his surroundings, and yet that dependence is denied when the novelist must resort to a dream in order to cure Alton. Circumstances, it turns out, did not shape Alton Locke; rather, they helped prevent his creation. Only when he is cut off from his surroundings, in the isolation of his feverish imagination, does he have the opportunity to become whole and singular.

The same fever that gives him his individuated manhood, however, takes away his life. Alton regains consciousness long enough to be converted, write his autobiography (which is published posthumously) while on a voyage to America, and die. Alton, the narrator alleges, has finally become a character, but since his story is over, the narrator has no way of proving it.

The Voiceless Narrator: Writing as Solvent and Writing as Source

If we judge him as a narrator, however, the reborn Alton also seems to lack a defined character. As we saw in the last sections, Alton is unable to create himself as a single, coherent character because he holds contradictory ideas about the sources of his own being. For related reasons, he is unable to project a distinctive, believable character, or voice, as a narrator. Alton's essence is not that of a character at all, but rather that of a writer—a writer, furthermore, who is so generalized that he might more precisely be called writing.

The characterlessness of Alton's narrative must be blamed in part on Kingsley's inability to disguise himself as a Cockney; Alton does not have an authentic working-class voice. This fact is partly the result of Kingsley's failure to fulfill the promise made by his use of the first-person pronoun, the promise to provide an intimate and authoritative account of a working-class life. The inauthenticity of the narrator's voice is not only a function of Alton's "proper" English. One would not, after all, expect a well-read London artisan to write or speak in Cockney dialect, although Alton's language is often comical in its excessive formality: " 'Pardon me, my dear fellow,' I said. 'I cannot bear the thought of being mixed up in conspiracy—perhaps in revolt and bloodshed' " (p. 105). The problem of Alton's voice, however, does not proceed simply from its lack of conformity to the stylistic expectations the reader brings to the work. It is also the result of unfulfilled prom-ises made by the narrator himself: "I am a Cockney among Cockneys" is the first thing we read; "I have drunk of the cup of which [the poor] drink. And so I have learned—if, indeed, I have learned—to be a poet—a poet of the people" (p. 2). We readers believe we are about to hear an intimate account of working-class life from the poet God chose to record it. We are, however, soon disappointed. Alton's early life is described, but the descriptions hardly seem to be from Alton's point of view. For example, the hero's introduction to the tailor's workroom provides a frame for a set piece on the moral and physical degradation of London's tailors. The description is effectively done; much of it is given in the desperate, ribald speeches of the tailors themselves. But Alton is a mere spectator in this scene, as he is of numerous other scenes of poverty and vice. Only when the drunken journeyman Jemmy Downes has finished his description of a tailor's life and death does the narrator seem to recall that his own young self is supposed to be a part of the action. A perfunctory reference is then made to the young hero's emotions: "I, shocked and bewildered, let my tears fall fast upon my knees" (p. 22). Neither shock nor bewilderment, how-ever, can be found in the tone of the description just given. In this, as in the novel's other London episodes, Alton's is neither a participating nor a shaping consciousness through which we might get a new, inti-mate understanding of working-class life.

Indeed, instead of making us understand a poor Cockney's life, the narrator continually turns to his readers and orders us to understand or attacks us for not understanding, thereby abdicating narrative responsibility. He also continually interrupts the narrative to remind us that *Alton Locke* is only a book. After a detailed but external description of the shivering young Alton studying through the night, for example, the narrator commands:

> Look at the picture awhile, ye comfortable folks, who take down from your shelves what books you like best at the moment, and then lie back, amid prints and statuettes, to grow wise in an easy-chair, with a blazing fire and camphine lamp. The lower classes uneducated! Perhaps you would be too, if learning cost you the privation which it costs some of them. (P. 34)

Here the narrator demands that we do *his* work, the work of imaginative recreation, or stand accused of insensitivity. However, even as we are being told to contemplate Alton's image, we are prevented from doing so by the narrator, who thrusts another image at us, a picture of ourselves reading. The one image not only displaces the other, but also creates in us a self-consciousness about the act of reading, a self-consciousness that raises us out of the text and shatters whatever illusion it had managed to create. The privations of the lower classes are a distant reality by the end of the passage; Alton and the class he supposedly represents have become "them." Such passages of direct address to the reader are meant to cover what they in fact reveal: that Alton is the merely literary invention of a writer who cannot convince us he lived the events he relates.

The inauthenticity of the book's "I" should not, however, be traced only to Kingsley's lack of imagination, for it is also a function of his ambivalence about causation. As I noted earlier, a full and intimate account of Alton's development would entail some causal explanations, explanations Kingsley could not formulate. The author, moreover, evidently realized that his narrative was insufficiently intimate, for he has Alton excuse his own objectivity. The following passage is inserted into the middle of a schematic account of Alton's poetic development: "I tell my story, not as I saw it then, but as I see it now. A long and lonely voyage . . . has given me opportunities for analysing my past history which were impossible then, amid the ceaseless inrush of new images" (pp. 78–79). Had the narrator carried out this program of objective analysis, he might have achieved a distinctive presence, but his refusal to settle on a causal scheme makes analysis impossible. He toys with various explanations for two pages following his announcement, and then completely changes his narrative principles: "I had much better simply tell my story, and leave my readers to judge of the facts" (p. 81).

Thus he drops the burden of analysis (judgment) where he repeatedly places the burden of imaginative realization: on the reader.

Kingsley's fear of causal consistency, therefore, compounds the problems generated by his lack of imagination; the narrator's voice turns out to be neither intimate nor authoritative. Indeed, compared to most of the characters in the book, Alton has the least distinct voice. Relative voicelessness is not always a remarkable failing in a character; creating voices is not the only way of creating characters. But in *Alton Locke*, character and voice are practically synonymous, so that Alton's lack of voice is the emblem of his characterlessness. However, it is also the feature that brings him close to his creator, proves Alton's freedom, and turns the narrative into a work preeminently about writing. For Alton is a creature and a representative of the written word; as such he is not so much characterized by his language as he is disseminated in it.

In contrast, Sandy Mackaye, the most fully realized character in the book, is distinguished by the fact that his dialogue is almost unreadable unless the reader imagines a speaking voice. The phonetic transcription of Mackaye's speech forces the reader to "hear" a strongly accented Scottish dialect. Sentences like the following cannot simply be read; to comprehend them the reader must mentally say them to himself:

> "Why maun ilk a one the noo steal his nebor's barnacles, before he glints out o'windows? Mak' a style for yoursel', laddie; ye're no mair Scots hind then ye are Lincolnshire laird: sae gang yer ain gate and leave them to gang theirs; and just mak' a gran', brode, simple Saxon style for yoursel'." (P. 97)

In this passage about the relationship between self-expression and identity, Mackaye not only argues for the perfect confluence of the two, but also embodies it. The fact that Mackaye and his voice are identical is proved by his writing. Although he is perhaps the best-read man in the book, with an extensive knowledge of both ancient and modern literature, he makes his written language a phonetic transcription of his speech. In what the narrator calls a "characteristic" letter, Mackaye writes, "Gowk, Telemachus, hearken! Item I. Ye're fou wi' the Circean cup, aneath the shade o' shovel hats and steeple houses" (p. 183). Even if we are aware that Mackaye's spelling is a literary convention deriving from Robert Burns, it manages to convince us that the Scotsman cannot be separated from his voice.

Alton's own dialogue is in marked contrast to Mackaye's: we need never imagine a voice for Alton when we read his dialogue. Indeed, the style of these passages often prevents us from imagining any voice.

Alton's speech is represented in the same periodic prose style that characterizes the book's narrative, descriptive, and discursive passages:

> "Surely, Crossthwaite, if matters were properly represented to the Government, they would not, for their own existence' sake, to put conscience out of the question, allow such a system to continue growing." (P. 104)

Such suspended syntax is a style of composing, not of conversing. Of all the working-class characters in *Alton Locke*, only the hero uses this formal syntax. Even Crossthwaite, who is nicknamed "the Orator" and lacks, like Alton, a regional or class dialect, speaks in syntactically loose sentences. Indeed, Crossthwaite's language is often so paratactic that one can only connect the syntactically autonomous elements by imagining that they are uttered in a voice charged with intense emotion:

> "Ay," he muttered to himself, "be slaves—what you are worthy to be, that you will be! You dare not combine—you dare not starve—you dare not die—and therefore you dare not be free!" (P. 104)

When Crossthwaite speaks, the narrator calls attention to the physical act of his articulation; Crossthwaite's tongue is several times referred to as a powerful weapon. "I'll give you such a taste of my tongue as shall turn you blue," he says to Jemmy Downe (p. 23), and a fellow tailor warns that Crossthwaite's tongue can "slang you up the chimney." On such occasions, Crossthwaite's power is associated closely with the physical fact of speech, literally with his tongue, which hurls the worker-slave metaphor at the workers themselves, removing Crossthwaite from his fellows and freeing him from the condition he names.

Alton's words, unlike Crossthwaite's, often defy any attempt at imagining their utterance; they are obviously, like the rest of the narrative, written words. Alton's relative voicelessness is appropriate, for he is, after all, a writer. By stylistically emphasizing this fact, Kingsley almost overcomes both his imaginative shortcomings and his ambivalence about Alton's free will: the "I" of the narrator is most believable when describing Alton's problems as a writer. His first imitative efforts, his fear of exposure and censure, his difficulty in finding a style, his artistic compromises, his battle with his publisher, and his slavery to the public taste are all narrated with an intimacy and imaginative completeness that the more exclusively working-class parts of the story lack. If Kingsley cannot quite become Alton, occasionally he can, through the character's writing, turn Alton into Kingsley.

When he does so, moreover, he temporarily raises his hero, like

Crossthwaite, into a realm of relative freedom. By recording his own imaginings and narrating his own story, Alton displays his free agency. The "I" itself is antideterministic; the narrator tells us as much while commenting on his patrons' use of the third person. Alton is present while the wealthy Dean and his beautiful daughter discuss the tailor-poet's future career, referring to him as "he": "that very '*he*' bespoke ... the gulf between us. I was not a man—an equal; but a thing—a subject, who was to be talked over, and examined, and made into something" (p. 150). The third person, according to Alton, puts the subject in a passive relation to destiny; he is "*to be talked* over" and "*to be made* into something" (emphasis added). The first-person point of view, on the other hand, asserts Alton's manhood and makes him literally the author of his own story. Despite the way Kingsley indulges his ambivalence about free will and necessity, therefore, Alton's occupation and the novel's narrative point of view are standing correctives to his various suggestions of determinism.

Alton the writer achieves some semblance of actuality and freedom, then, that is denied to Alton the worker. It is precisely as a writer, however, that he is most protean, least able to achieve and maintain an identity. In writing, instead of expressing himself, Alton denies, disguises, and disperses himself until there seems to be nothing personal about his own words. At the beginning of his career, Alton merely imitates the style and subject matter of other poets. Mackaye must recommend a style ("a gran', brode, simple, Saxon style") and insist on a subject matter close to Alton's experience:

> "Ay, Shelley's gran'; always gran'; but Fact is grander. . . . All around ye, in every gin-shop and costermonger's cellar, are God and Satan at death grips; every garret is a haill Paradise Lost or Paradise Regained; and will ye think it beneath ye to be the 'People's Poet'?" (P. 91)

Under Mackaye's tutelage, Alton does, we are told, manage to turn "Fact" into songs, if not into the epics the Scotsman suggested. But the narrator skims over his short period of "honest" self-expression; indeed, the four pages that describe it hardly mention the writing (called "astonishing" in its variety and quantity). Instead, they dwell almost exclusively on Alton's reading during that period, so that the chapter takes us not closer to the particularity of Alton's poetry but further away. We read first of other London poets (Hood and Charles Mackay) and then of writers like Carlyle, who have deeply influenced the working class. Next we are told of "democratic" art ("the revelation of the poetry which lies in common things") that is produced by "all authors who have really seized the nation's mind, from Crabbe and Burns and Wordsworth to Hood and Dickens, the great tide sets ever onward, outward, towards that which is common to the many, not that which is exclusive to the few" (p. 96). In the course of this passage on his songs, Alton's poetry is absorbed into ever larger categories of writing, until it is finally lost in a tide of literature that is no longer specifically about anything.

In the only glimpses we get of Alton's "true" self-expression, then, his particular writing quickly blurs into writing in general. The remainder of Alton's writing career, moreover, is a succession of disguises. For love he writes enervated, "insincere" verses and "emasculates" his earlier songs; for money he first turns out radical invective, to which his editor adds fire, and then produces "light fictions" and "scraps of showy rose-pink morality" for the "Howitt and Eliza Cook school" of popular journalism (p. 221). These failures of self-expression are both sources and proofs of Alton's lack of identity: they prevent Alton from playing his God-given role and also bespeak his characterlessness. Apparently there is no self behind Alton's writings; his freedom as a writer is the freedom to escape identity. Thus Alton's writing, his form of freedom and the activity out of which his identity might have emerged, is another medium for the dissolution of his self.

Just as the book's multiple versions of Alton's personality lead to reflections on the fictional nature of singular identity, the dissolution of Alton's self in the medium of words creates a high degree of self-referentiality in the text. By making us aware of the fictional nature of Alton's writing, the narrator repeatedly reminds us of the fabricated nature of *Alton Locke* itself. When we are told, for example, that Alton composed an "Autobiography of an Engine-Boiler in the Vauxhall Road," we cannot help reflecting on the fact that we are reading just such a fictional working-class autobiography. And when Mackaye calls that other autobiography "trash" (p. 183), we are amused at Kingsley's self-effacing joke. The point is not simply that Alton characterizes himself as an unreliable narrator, nor that the book, like most autobiographies and fictional autobiographies, often makes references to its own composition; in themselves these facts do distance us from the narrative and make us conscious of its fictional and "made" nature. But *Alton Locke* goes even further, for it locates its sources, especially the sources of its hero, in other writings; the book emphasizes not only that Alton is "made," but also that he is made out of the very substance he is made into: written words.

Like Alton's multiple identities, his literary essence is rooted in Kingsley's inconsistency about ultimate causes. Although the author hesitates to identify the sources of Alton's character in the fictional world of *Alton Locke*, he insists that Alton *be* explained. One way out of this plight is to locate Alton's sources in other books, so the narrator continually refers the reader to the literary context of his story. Some of these references are worked into the plot as Alton's models. *The Life and Poems of J. Bethune*, for example, presents a somewhat daunting but still inspirational portrait of a laborer-poet, one model after which Alton tries to fashion himself. But at other times, Kingsley identifies his literary sources without finding much pretext for doing so in the plot. In some cases such allusions are clearly documentary: a snippet of plot about an *agent provocateur* ends with the sentence, "I entreat all those who disbelieve . . . to read the evidence given on the trial of the John Street conspirators, and judge for themselves" (p. 314). Another episode actually contains a footnote to the *Morning Chronicle* articles about tailors.[18] On other occasions the narrator appeals to various social theorists to gain authority for his opinions, sometimes even suggesting that we interrupt our reading of Alton's story to inform ourselves on theoretical points. J. S. Mill's *Political Economy*, for example, is urgently pressed on us: "Have you perused therein the priceless chapter 'On the Probable Futurity of the Labouring Classes'? If not, let me give you the reference—vol. ii, p. 315, of the Second Edition" (p. 303).

In still other cases Kingsley seems unable to refrain from pointing out similarities between his plot and other plots. It is Mackaye who makes most of these connections, usually in asides, but in one particularly derivative segment of the story the Scotsman gets out the source, Bulwer Lytton's novel *Ernest Maltravers*, for the young hero to read. On the one hand, the reading episode integrates the source into the book, thereby preempting the criticism of a reader who recognizes the similarity between the plots; on the other hand, it identifies the source as a novel ("What!" says Alton, "Are you a novel reader, Mr. Mackaye?"), thereby calling attention to the fact that Alton is cut out from a pattern drawn in another fiction.

These are only a few instances of a practice that dominates the novel, suppressing the need for cause-and-effect narration. If in avoiding causal explanations the narrator cannot convincingly account for Alton's poetry, for example, he brings in Thomas Cooper's poetry as evidence that Alton's can exist. The narrator repeatedly tries to give the story sense and authority by resting it on a supporting network of other writings. The written words of Burns, Goethe, Carlyle, Novalis, J. S. Mill, Coleridge, Hood, Bethune, Charles Mackay, Ebenezer Elliott, Thomas Cooper, Bulwer Lytton, Byron, Tennyson, Chadwick, Dickens, Gaskell, Eliza Cook, the Howitts, Harriet Martineau—these are the ultimate sources of Alton Locke's being. They are sources, moreover, that can be named without committing the namer to any particular causal analysis.

Their naming, however, keeps continually before us the image of the author making his book out of other books.[19] The book's sources have varying degrees of authority and claim different relationships to an actual world. But they are books, nevertheless, and Kingsley's method makes us highly conscious of their "bookness": the narrator does not give us Mill's ideas; instead, he gives us the volume, chapter, and edition in which they can be found, calling attention to the fact that *Alton Locke* is one more book made out of books about the condition of England. References to social problems in *Alton Locke* thus often become statements about the problems of creating character or realizing identity, or become allusions to other books. In short, such references to an outside world ultimately become self-referential.

Because Kingsley was deeply influenced by both the Romantic and the materialist critiques of industrial capitalism, he was more ambivalent about the nature of freedom than were the other writers discussed in these chapters. His form, moreover, provided an environment in which his ambivalence grew, generating those features of his narrative that seem anachronistically modern. We must remember, however, that Kingsley did not intend to produce such a self-referential book. His is not the sly playfulness of an eighteenth-century novelist ironically pointing to his own skill in creating illusions, nor is it the ruthless frankness of the twentieth-century novelist compelled to self-exposure. Like the other writers discussed in these chapters, Kingsley had a naive faith in the ability of fictions to present reality (however romantically conceived) in a straightforward manner. Once the project was begun, however, the structure of reality itself (in this case, the body of industrial social criticism) proved to be contradictory, and the writer was forced to reconsider the very bases of his storytelling. How is character formed? What are the causes of people's actions? Are actions free? Can they be explained? The definitely early-Victorian quality of this novel arises from both its failure to answer these questions and its inability to suppress them.

In the industrial novels of the next decade, writers found that they could avoid such disruptive questions by deemphasizing adult male workers in their fictions and by searching out private solutions for social conflicts. We have already noted a similar shift of emphasis in *Mary Barton*, but, as we will see, the novels of the 1850s, which are much more intent on making the distinction between public and private that *Mary Barton* simply took for granted, dissolve the private in the very act of constituting it. The next three chapters will identify the major historical sources of this change in literary practice and analyze its consequences. The contradiction between free will and necessity did become less pronounced in the industrial fiction of the 1850s, but a new conflict arose in its place: an inability to reconcile the ethics of public and private life.

Part Two
THE FAMILY VERSUS SOCIETY

5

Family and Society:
The Rhetoric of Reconciliation
in the Debate over Industrialism

The man, in his rough work in the open world, must encounter all peril and trial:—to him, therefore, must be the failure, the offence, the inevitable error: often he must be wounded, or subdued; often misled; and *always* hardened. But he guards the woman from all this; within his house, as ruled by her, unless she herself has sought it, need enter no danger, no temptation, no cause of error or offence. This is the true nature of home—it is the place of Peace; the shelter, not only from all injury, but from all terror, doubt, and division. In so far as it is not this, it is not home; so far as the anxieties of the outer life penetrate into it, and the inconsistently-minded, unknown, unloved, or hostile society of the outer world is allowed by either husband or wife to cross the threshold, it ceases to be home.

There is not a war in the world, no, nor an injustice, but you women are answerable for it; not in that you have provided, but in that you have not hindered. . . . There is no suffering, no injustice, no misery, in the earth, but the guilt of it lies with you. Men can bear the sight of it, but you should not be able to bear it. Men may tread it down without sympathy in their own struggle; but men are feeble in sympathy, and contracted in hope; it is you only who can feel the depths of pain, and conceive the way of its healing. Instead of trying to do this, you turn away from it; you shut yourselves within your park walls and garden gates; and you are content to know that there is beyond them a whole world in wilderness.

The whole country is but a little garden, not more than enough for your children to run on the lawns of, if you would let them *all* run there.

John Ruskin
Sesame and Lilies

Many industrial novelists tried to overcome the discontinuity between freedom and determinism in their work by shifting the location of the novel's action from the public, social world to the private world of the family. Even though it was finally inconsistent for the critics of industrial capitalism to imagine a voluntary will operating against the material and psychological constraints of modern society, the family circle seemed a place potentially exempt from those restrictions, a sphere in which an individual will could prevail. Consequently, the novelists tended to turn, often with reluctance but also with relief, from an examination of public conduct to an examination of private conduct.

The movement from public to private themes and issues is common in English fiction; some critics have claimed that it defines realistic fiction in general. These critics point out that realism is a particular mode of interrelating the public and private realms by transforming social issues into personal issues. This method of interconnecting public and private concerns is celebrated by Raymond Williams in *The Long Revolution*:

> The society [in realistic fiction] is not a background against which the personal relationships are studied, nor are the individuals merely illustrations of aspects of the way of life. Every aspect of personal life is radically affected by the quality of the general life, yet the general life is seen at its most important in completely personal terms.[1]

Williams rightly points out in this passage that realism suffuses the social throughout the personal, strongly associating the two realms of experience. But Williams fails to note that the association of public and private in realist novels depends on an underlying assumption that the two are separate: because private problems are unlike public problems, because they seem responsive to individual efforts of will, whereas public problems do not, novelists often "solve" social conflicts by first translating them into private conflicts.[2] There would be no need for such displaced resolutions if the private and the public were not utterly distinct worlds. The private world in English novels is often a territory set aside for the alleviation of antagonisms that cannot be resolved in the social world. The very way in which realistic novels connect public and private fields of action, consequently, indicates the deep rift between the two; these novels, indeed, often display a structural tension created by the simultaneous impulses to associate and to dissociate the public and private realms of experience.

Industrial novels, especially those of the 1850s, display this normal tension in an exaggerated form. They make the connection between the family and society one of their main themes and primary organizing devices, but they simultaneously emphasize that the family must be isolated and protected from the larger social world. The family in these novels is often presented as society's primary reforming institution: it is portrayed either as a model or as a school of social reform. Bringing the public and private realms of life into greater proximity is thus crucial to the novels' reforming programs. However, if the family is to function as either a model or a school of social reform, it must, paradoxically, be separated from and purged of the ills infecting the public realm. While trying to obliterate the separation of public and private life, therefore, these novels reinforce that separation.

To understand why this contradiction emerges with such prominence in the industrial novels of the 1850s, we must briefly survey the roles assigned to the family by English social theorists generally and by industrial reformers in particular.

Metonymy, Metaphor, and the Paradox of the Family as an Instrument of Social Reform

In the first decade of Victoria's reign, Sarah Stickney Ellis published one of England's most widely read manuals on the duties of women, and Sir Arthur Helps published a very popular treatise on the responsibilities of employers. At first glance, the books seem to have little in common: Sarah Ellis's *Women of England* (1839) is a guide to domestic felicity, whereas Arthur Helps's *Claims of Labour* (1844) is a proposal for ending the class struggle; the former was addressed to women, the latter primarily to men. Yet these two books form a natural pair, for a common premise underlies the argument of each. Both authors take as their starting point the relationship between the family and the larger society, and both affirm that the cooperative relations of family life are the best antidote to the competitive strife of human relationships in society at large. Each author advocates spanning the distance between public and private ethics by infusing society with the harmonious spirit of family life. From this shared beginning, however, the authors diverge and follow separate paths, one depicting the kind of family that would be necessary to bring about social regeneration, the other imagining the kind of society that would result. Moreover, their proposed methods for reconnecting the public and private spheres of existence are quite distinct, although interrelated. Considered together, the two books illuminate the similarities and differences between two contemporaneous ideological developments: the idealization of domesticity and the popular revival of social and economic paternalism.

Arthur Helps and Sarah Ellis were both attempting to reintegrate what they perceived as the newly dissevered realms of public and private life; they make identical diagnoses of Victorian society's ills.

Both complain that the world has been separated into two unrelated spheres, each with its own principle of human interaction: the family, based on the cohesive principle of cooperation, and the larger society, based on the disintegrative principle of competition. The authors express their belief in a lost social harmony and their fear that the competitive principle of the marketplace has taken over the whole of the public world, driving the cooperative principle into the narrow sphere of the family. In each book, "society" comes to mean the world of commerce and production; "family" has a more ambiguous meaning, but it normally designates an enclave in which the virtues of benevolence, cooperation, and selflessness take refuge and survive. Sarah Ellis describes the world of commerce and production as an antifamily, a battlefield on which brother destroys brother:

> there is no union in the great field of action in which he is engaged; but envy, and hatred, and opposition, to the close of the day—every man's hand against his brother, and each struggling to exalt himself, not merely by trampling upon his fallen foe, but by usurping the place of his weaker brother, who faints by his side, from not having brought an equal portion of strength into the conflict, and who is consequently borne down by numbers, hurried over, and forgotten.[3]

Arthur Helps, in fact, begins his book with a statement about the specifically antifamilial principle of contemporary society:

> The tendency of modern society is to draw the family circle within narrower and narrower limits. Those amusements which used to be shared by all classes are becoming less frequent: the great lord has put away his crowd of retainers: the farmer, in most cases, does not live with his labouring men: and the master has less sympathy and social intercourse with his domestics.[4]

Both writers also claim that the family has a mission to reverse these tendencies in modern society, to break down the barrier separating public and private ethics. Thus Ellis argues that the family's function is "to win [the man] away from this warfare" and to ameliorate the system by reminding him of "his social duty, and his God."[5] while Helps calls for the renewal of paternalistic attitudes and practices: "There is the same need for protection and countenance on the one side, and for reverence and attachment on the other, that there ever has been."[6]

Although these two books are similar in invoking the familial virtues, they actually contain very different ideas of how, precisely, such virtues would overcome the public-private disjunction and thereby regenerate society. Helps's notion is essentially metaphoric, or analogical. Because, he reasons, industrialism has loosened the "old bonds" that used to tie the classes together in virtual kinship, employers must now invent ways of "strengthening the social intercourse" between the classes. Industrial relations, he recommends, should be modeled on the relationship between father and child:

> I believe that the parental relation will be found the best model on which to form the duties of the employer to the employed; calling, as it does, for active exertion, requiring the most watchful tenderness, and yet limited by the strictest rules of prudence from intrenching on that freedom of thought and action which is necessary for all spontaneous development.[7]

According to Helps and other nineteenth-century social paternalists,[8] society could be regenerated by duplicating the family's benevolent hierarchy: by acting out the roles assigned in a metaphoric equation between society and the family, masters and workers could bring themselves into a harmonious productive relationship. If employers would act like wise fathers and workers like dutiful children, antagonistic class interests would disappear, along with the extreme poverty and the class separation that accompanied early industrialism.

As a spokesman for the belief that society should be a large family, Arthur Helps can be placed in a tradition of English social paternalism dating back at least to the seventeenth century.[9] This tradition gained strength during the Restoration, when Stuart partisans used Robert Filmer's *Patriarcha* (written c. 1636) to advance the divine-right-of-kings theory.[10] Filmer's was an identity theory of family and society; he argued that the nation was a veritable family of which the king was actual father, the direct descendant of Adam. Fatherhood for Filmer implied absolute power over the persons and lives of his entire family. It also implied the king's ownership of literally everything; the king-father's power rested on the fact that God gave the world to Adam to be passed on by the laws of primogeniture through eldest sons. This royalist identity theory of family and society did not long survive the Glorious Revolution, but it had many modified descendants in the metaphoric patriarchal and paternalist social ideologies of the nineteenth century.

Arthur Helps's book promotes one of those ideologies. It is neither royalist nor extremely authoritarian; indeed, it is not, strictly speaking, political, for Helps concentrates exclusively on the relationship between employers and their employees, leaving the larger question of the organization of the state untouched. However, *Claims of Labour* shares an important underlying assumption with *Patriarcha*: the most natural, harmonious, and productive society is that which comes closest to duplicating the structure of the family. To be sure, Helps and Filmer mean very different things by the word "family." Helps means by it an enclave of cooperation, affectionate suasion, and limited freedom, whereas Filmer uses it to denote a small, absolutely despotic kingdom. Significant as these differences are, however, they should not obscure the two writers' shared method: both hold up the hierarchical organization of the family as a model for society, identifying the father's power as the most natural and traditional form of authority. Unlike Filmer, Helps realizes that the family and society are not literally identical, but he argues that the family is the best model on which to reorganize society and make it organic once more.

The method of social regeneration described by Sarah Ellis and by most spokesmen of the domestic cult, on the other hand, is metonymic.[11] The family and society are viewed as contiguous entities, families forming a series of enclaves that are at once a part of and separate from the larger society. Families exert a salutary moral influence on the public realm by spiritually regenerating individual men. Nothing in *Women of England* hints at the possible remaking of society in the hierarchical image of the family; indeed, the world in which men act is decidedly nonhierarchical. It is presented alternately as a battlefield and a marketplace composed of isolated individuals, but it is nonetheless capable of moral progress through the influence of family life, particularly through the influence of morally superior women. Because men who associate with such women at home assimilate their qualities, such men are inclined to treat their "brothers" more justly and charitably:

> so potent may have become this secret influence, that he may have borne it about with him like a kind of second conscience, for mental reference, and spritual counsel, in moments of trial; and when the snares of the world were around him, and temptations from within and without have bribed over the witness in his own bosom, he has thought of the humble monitress who sat alone, guarding the fireside comforts of his distant home; and the remembrance of her character, clothed in moral beauty, has scattered the clouds before his mental vision, and sent him back to that beloved home, a wiser and a better man.[12]

The family, therefore, becomes essential to society's moral well-being, and Sarah Ellis is consequently able to locate her social concern in the sphere of domestic life, having established that a moral and peaceful home life will contribute to social harmony. Thus, "family," the term often contrasted with "society," at length becomes its surrogate. Writing about the family becomes a way of writing about society, although the writer assumes no actual or ideal structural similarity between the two.

Each ideology, therefore, has a specific process by which it connects the familial and social spheres, and as we shall see, both processes have corresponding formal patterns in the industrial novels. Each ideology, however, also has a tendency to reproduce the very disjunction it tries to overcome. The disassociative tendency is most obvious in the domestic ideology, which was founded on the liberal premise that the family and society are structurally dissimilar. If Helps's metaphoric idea of the right relationship between the family and society can be related to Filmer's thought, Ellis's metonymic idea can be traced to a tradition of social thought founded by Filmer's chief antagonist, John Locke. Locke wrote his *Two Treatises on Government* (1690) partly to refute *Patriarcha*. In the *Second Treatise*, Locke argues that the family and the polity are neither equivalent nor similar institutions. Locke admits that both are based on voluntary compacts, but he sharply distinguishes between political and familial societies, arguing that they have different ends and therefore different rules of association.[13] He thus lays the groundwork for those nineteenth-century thinkers who believed the public and private realms operated on dissimilar, even antagonistic, principles.

Sarah Ellis wanted to reduce the dissimilarity between the ethics of public and private life, but she did not indicate that the differences could or should be completely erased. Moreover, she strongly advocated maintaining a strict separation of the domestic and social spheres, arguing that women develop their moral superiority only by their exclusion from the marketplace. Her writings consequently reinforced the assumption of an opposition between the family and society, and they spread the notion that domestic life should compensate for the unavoidably hardening and unsatisfying struggles of social existence. The ideology of domesticity was thus somewhat paradoxical: it was a scheme of social reform, but it was also used to preach acceptance of public strife. The ideology must simply be accepted as a contradictory system, at once associating and disassociating the spheres of private and public life.

A similar, although more submerged, ambiguity marks the ideology of social paternalism; indeed, it is through this shared characteristic that the logical and historical links between the two ideologies become apparent. The idealization of the family as an isolated enclave of harmony and hierarchical order is a necessary moment in the ideology of social paternalism, for if the family were to function as a normative model of industrial society, it had to be both hierarchical and harmonious. It had to be uncontaminated by the competitive spirit of the as yet unregenerated society. In short, it had to be a protected enclave where women and children gave voluntary and loving submission to a benign patriarch. Since women set the tone of family relations, they had to embody the soft virtues of acceptance and resignation. They could not, therefore, be allowed to participate in the toughening encounters of the marketplace. Agitation for equal rights within the family, moreover, was threatening because it rested on an assumption of disparate interests,[14] for if the family itself were divided by a consciousness of separate and antagonistic interests, it could not serve as a model for countering the competitive ethos in the sphere of production and commerce. The ideologists of social paternalism, then, in seeking to overcome the disjunction between the public and private spheres, reconstituted that very disjunction by insisting that the family be an ideal model, removed from social strife. Only when the work of remaking society in the image of the family was complete, presumably, could the rupture be healed. Until that time, paternalist thinkers necessarily relied on and contributed to the idea of the family as a sheltered enclave.

Tradition and Ethics: The Paradox Compounded

Both the metaphoric social paternalism and the metonymic domestic ideology, therefore, contain a paradox: society can be made similar to the family only if the family is rigorously isolated from society. Association, both claim, can only be brought about through dissociation. This paradox has important formal consequences for the industrial novels of the 1850s that are infused with these ideologies. Moreover, the novels, particularly *Hard Times* and *North and South*, are shaped by a further complication within the two ideologies: the term "family" itself contains ambiguity, ambiguity that can be observed alike in the novels of Dickens and Gaskell and the reformist proposals of Helps and Ellis. None of these writers is certain about the family's underlying principle of cohesion. On the one hand, they present it as a repository of traditional practices, a place dominated by spontaneous emotional and often irrational responses, a place where people are accepted and loved simply because they are family members. On the other hand, they present it as a moral shelter, a place where conscience is developed, behavior scrutinized, and universal ethics absorbed. Thus, in both Ellis and Helps, we find that the family itself is a paradoxical formation, combining prerational, wholly traditional, and particularizing tendencies with rational, ethical, and universalizing tendencies. The family, in short, is presented as everything capitalist society is not. For social paternalists and domestic ideologues alike, it serves as a residual category that includes incompatible elements.

The incompatibilities are even more visible in the industrial novels of the 1850s than they are in the expository works of Ellis and Helps, for the novels convert the ideological disjunctions into formal disjunctions. In later chapters we will see that when social problems are either metaphorically or metonymically displaced onto the personal sphere in industrial novels, the form of their solution often destroys the very basis for that substitution. We will see that in *Hard Times*, for example, the novel's solution is not only private, it is actually antisocial: when they begin to act like a family, the Gradgrinds become a clan whose interests oppose those of the society at large. The family-society metaphor is thus completely subverted in the novel's closing episode. In *North and South*, as we will see, the displacement is less disruptive, but Gaskell's private solution is also problematic: despite the narrator's attempt to make personal ethics the foundation of industrial reform, the heroine actually brings about the social change through her sexual, not her moral, power. The ideological contradictions of both *North and South* and *Hard Times*, therefore, take the form of an incompatibility between the novels' moral and social preoccupations and the resolutions of their plots.

The Family and Society in the Debate over Factory Reform

Although social paternalism and the ideology of domesticity descended from rival traditions of social thought and had separate methods of connecting the family and society, the two systems of thought displayed similar contradictions and produced related discontinuities in industrial narratives. Before discussing the narratives, however, we will survey the specific uses of the family-society tropes in the arguments of industrial reformers. Social paternalism and domestic ideology became closely intertwined in the mid-nineteenth-century rhetoric of these reformers, who were responsible for linking the subject of industrialism to that of family life.

As we saw in an earlier chapter, the proponents of factory reform between 1816 and 1842 directed their campaign only at shortening the working hours of children, a tactic they hoped would obviate the charge that they were interfering between employers and free laborers. Their legislation, however, would have indirectly shortened the hours of adult labor as well, and the cry of interference went up from a majority of manufacturers and a few political economists. The reformers then took the offensive against free-labor doctrine, arguing that even adult workers could not really be considered free agents. In their arguments, they extended their claims about child laborers to cover the condition of all factory workers. Workers need both protection and moral guidance, they insisted. For example, in response to a direct challenge from a foe of factory legislation, Richard Oastler forthrightly claimed that even adult male workers needed to be shielded from the consequences of an unregulated labor market: "Yes, the poor Factory Child *does* want a Friend . . . and her Father too, although a 'free-born' Briton . . . *he* wants a 'Protector' to find him work that *he* may toil, and let his children rest."[15] To many reformers, free labor was not only a myth but also a dangerous ideal, for it implied a society in which the classes were connected only through the "cash nexus."

The primarily Tory factory reformers cast the national government in the role of the British laborers' protector. Although they recognized, as their Parliamentary spokesman Lord Anthony Ashley remarked in 1844, that some employers took "parental care"[16] of their workers, they pressed the need for the government to act *in loco parentis* in the majority of cases. Robert Southey expressed the sentiments of these reformers in 1829 when he wrote that "whatever be the origins of government, its duties are patriarchal, that is to say, parental: superintendence [of the treatment of workers] is one of those duties."[17] The social paternalism of the factory reformers was thus not hidden by the fact that their legislation pertained only to children. Indeed, that fact gave them license to use flagrantly paternalistic language: it was an effortless rhetorical move to shift from descriptions of child workers to descriptions of childlike workers.

The language of social paternalism, therefore, always formed a part of factory reform propaganda, but it was not until the 1840s that reformers actually proposed protective legislation for adult workers.[18] When they did so, their speeches and publications began combining social paternalism with sentimental idealizations of family life in general and the role of mothers in particular. For the first adults singled out for protection were, predictably, women.[19]

As early as 1817, critics of industrialism had charged that factory labor made working-class domestic life all but impossible in the cotton trade. In the 1830s these charges were repeated; polemicists like Richard Oastler looked back nostalgically to their younger days when "the villages about Leeds and Huddersfield were occupied by respectable little clothiers, who . . . had their family at home; and they could at that time make a good profit by what they sold; there were filial affection and parental feeling and not over-labour." But since the introduction of the factories, Oastler continued, "it is almost the general system for the little children in these manufacturing villages to know nothing of their parents at all." These quotations are typical of factory reform arguments prior to 1842 in that they trace the desolation of working-class family life to the excessive labor of children. The relationship between parent and child was called unnatural because the child worked to support the parents. In this process, the children were supposedly exhausted and corrupted, the parents demoralized. Moreover, the reformers charged, in adolescence the children rebelled against their parents, deserted them, and set up households of their own.[20] Their financial independence allowed them to make early and careless marriages, thereby hastening the arrival of a new generation of insupportable infant workers.

In the early 1840s the portrait of working-class family life became even darker, for in addition to detailing the horrors of child labor, the reformers began to describe the suffering and poverty that resulted from female employment. The publication of a government report on the employment of children and young women in mines and manufactories in 1842 caused great concern, and reformers of the textile industry drew fresh ammunition from that report and from the independent testimony of medical men. Employing women in factories for periods exceeding ten hours a day, they argued, destroyed family life in two ways. First, it made women unfit for motherhood by keeping them ignorant of domestic skills and by making both parturition and nursing difficult. In an 1844 speech, Ashley claimed that "Many anatomical reasons are assigned by surgeons of the manufacturing towns, that 'the peculiar structure of the female form is not so well adapted to long-continued labour, and especially labour which is endured standing.' " Ashley described this "long-continued labour" by summarizing the testimony of a factory inspector:

> There are . . . among them, females who have been employed for some weeks, with an interval only of a few days, from six o'clock in the morning until twelve o'clock at night, less than two hours for meals, thus giving them for five nights in the week, six hours out of its twenty-four to go to and from their homes, and to obtain rest in bed.

"Where, Sir," exclaimed Ashley, "under this condition, are the possibilities of domestic life? . . . Regard the woman as wife or mother, how can she accomplish any portion of her calling?"[21] The suffering of the women themselves and of their neglected families, then, was the first reason given for limiting the hours of female labor in textile mills.

In this same speech, Ashley gives a second argument against female employment. Women, he claims, become too independent when they support their families. As women are hired to replace men in the factories, Ashley claimed, "they are forming various clubs and associations, and gradually acquiring all those privileges which are held to be the proper portion of the male sex." Ashley quotes the superintendent of police of Manchester to illustrate the social consequences of this "unnatural" behavior:

> Women . . . by being employed in a factory, lose the station ordained them by Providence, and become similar to the female followers of an army, wearing the garb of women, but actuated by the worst passions of men. The women are the leaders and exciters of the young men to violence in every riot and outbreak in the manufacturing districts, and the language they indulge in is of a horrid description. While they are themselves demoralized, they contaminate all that comes within their reach.

Limiting the hours of labor for women in factories, he concludes, will restore the domestic peace of the working class, a peace on which the future of England rests.[22]

In this and earlier speeches, Ashley uses the language of the domestic ideologues. He concludes his speech with an idea that recurs frequently in Sarah Ellis's *Mothers of England* (1843):

> Search the records, examine the opening years of those who have been distinguished for ability and virtue, and you will ascribe, with but few exceptions, the early cuture of their minds, and above all, the first discipline of the heart, to the intelligence and affection of the mother, or at least of some pious woman, who, with the self-denial and tenderness of her sex, has entered, as a substitute, on the sacred office. No, Sir, these sources of mischief [female factory employment] must be dried up. . . . I never will believe that there can be found in this house one individual man who will deliberately and conscientiously inflict, on the women of England, such a burthen of insufferable toil.[23]

Thus Ashley couples social paternalism and domestic ideology in a plea for "chivalrous" protection.[24]

This speech, moreover, clearly displays the dual use to which the factory reformers put the ideology of domesticity. It served as a polemic against both the cruel exploitation of women (their increasing helplessness) and the "unnatural" economic power of women (their growing independence). These two uses produced absolutely irreconcilable images of working women. In Ashley's speech, they are first described as martyrs, oppressed victims, lacking both time and energy to nurse their own babies. A few paragraphs later, they have meta-morphosed into mannish monsters, with time to form clubs and energy to lead insurrections. By insisting that women be restored to their domestic duties, Ashley thus uses domestic ideology to reinforce two pledges of the Tory social paternalists: their promises both to protect and to control the working class.[25] The ideology of domesticity, there-fore, was wedded to social paternalism in the 1840s partly through the rhetoric of factory reformers, who used metaphoric and metonymic tropes indiscriminately to define the relationship between the family and society.

The Family-Society Tropes and Industrial Relations in the Mid-Victorian Period

Important as the rhetorical strategy of the Tory reformers was in popularizing the family-society metaphor, that metaphor was by no means their exclusive property in the late 1840s, 1850s, and 1860s. According to some historians, nearly all of the parties to the ideological combat over industrialism used the family-society metaphor in the mid-Victorian period. Classical political economy was undergoing a theoretical crisis;[26] the threat of Chartism required an emotionally effective ideological alternative to Utilitarian individualism; changes in industrial equipment and organization required that workers be en-couraged to identify strongly with their employers' enterprises;[27] the repeal of the Corn Laws made the manufacturing middle classes more secure, and other economic conditions gave them a sense of greater prosperity than they had had in the early 1840s.[28] In short, the manu-facturing middle class was itself beginning to assume a father's per-spective. It was resolving what might be seen as its Oedipal struggle with the landed classes[29] and was simultaneously threatened by its own rebellious male offspring in the form of the Chartists. Thus, some historians have claimed, new, modified justifications of fatherly au-thority were both possible and necessary.

Arthur Helps's *Claims of Labour* should be read in this context. It does not, like Ashley's speeches, propose an interventionist state; nor does it, like Oastler's writings, posit an irreconcilable antagonism between factory production and a familial community. Rather, Helps uses the family metaphor as a recipe for industrial peace without government intervention. He points to the initiative taken by factory owners to improve the physical and moral conditions of their workers. Indeed, he conceives of industrial enterprises as vast productive households. His ideal of the relationship between worker and employer is similar to that encoded in the Elizabethan apprenticeship laws. Helps, then, represents a renaissance of paternalist rhetoric that was used by manufacturers themselves.

This more liberal paternalism, like the Tory variety, blended easily with domestic ideology. Helps, for example, recommended keeping all classes of women at home to protect them from the vicissitudes of the marketplace. He realized that workers' wives often had to contribute to the family income, but insisted that they should work in their houses and practice "different pursuits to call out the differences of the sexes."[30] These cloistered women, with their finely tuned moral sensibilities, could then temper their husbands' rashness. Indeed, all varieties of social paternalism nurtured the cult of domesticity in the middle decades of the century, the two ideologies finding perhaps their most complete joint expression in John Ruskin's *Sesame and Lilies* (1865). We can get a sense of how widely accepted the merger of the two ideologies had become if we recall that the lectures comprising that volume ("Of Kings' Treasures" and "Of Queens' Gardens") were first delivered by an heir of the Tory Radical tradition to an audience of Manchester manufacturers and their wives.

The two ideologies also occasionally appear alongside one another in industrial tales and novels of the 1840s and 1850s. The popular magazine tales of the period, however, are usually dominated by one ideology or the other, and they employ effective formal devices for overcoming the contradiction between private and public realms, which underlies both metaphoric and metonymic associations of the family and society. That contradiction, though, produces acute formal dislocations in the two novels of the 1850s that focus on the connection between middle-class family life and industrial relations, Dicken's *Hard Times* and Gaskell's *North and South*. *Hard Times* has a strongly metaphoric organization, whereas *North and South* posits a metonymic link between the family and society. As we will see in the following chapters, the self-conscious use of both tropes exerts pressures on the novel form, pressures that ultimately help reshape the genre itself.

6

Family and Society:
The Tropes of Reconciliation
in Popular Industrial Narratives

The justice we do not execute, we mimic in the novel and on the stage.

John Ruskin
Sesame and Lilies

The widespread use in the debate over industrialism of the family-society tropes, as we saw in the last chapter, derived partly from the fact that factory reformers took children and women for the objects of their legislation. Many writers of industrial fiction, following the lead of these reformers, centered their stories on the suffering of women and children. One of the earliest industrial novels, Frances Trollope's *Life and Adventures of Michael Armstrong, the Factory Boy* (1839–40), was a deliberately shocking piece of propaganda for the Ten Hours Movement; it gives the impression that almost all factory hands were children.[1] The factory where Michael works, the hellish Deep Valley Mill, is one of the most persistent early Victorian images of industrialism; it is a pestilent, disease-ridden establishment apparently worked solely by exhausted children, and containing only two adults—greedy, nightmarish distortions of a mother and father. Given such a presentation of the "facts," factory reform could only be seen as a natural extension of parental feelings.

Michael Armstrong, though, is an unusual fictional factory child in one respect: he is male. Most of the pathetic little cotton spinners depicted in the literature of the 1830s and 1840s were girls. Here again the fiction writers followed the lead of the Ten Hours Movement, whose publications abounded with sentimental portrayals of little girls. Poems entitled "Poor Hannah," "Little Nell," and "The Factory Child's Last Day" all purport to tell true stories of the sufferings of these little heroines. One little girl, we are told, "died of consumption, induced by protracted factory labour. With the last breath upon her lips, she cried out, 'Father, is it time?' and so died."[2] This sentimental emphasis on female children led Charlotte Elizabeth Tonna, in *Helen Fleetwood*, to illustrate in her portrayals of young girls what she considered to be the most debilitating physical and moral effects of the factory system. Even Harriet Martineau's *Manchester Strike*, which is primarily a story about adult male workers, includes a poignant account of a factory girl, William Allen's daughter Martha. Martineau burdens this little cripple with the "inevitable" (but not unbearable) afflictions of early industrialism. In doing so, she admits that the reformers' claims are partly accurate, although she denies that Martha's suffering can be legislated away.

For the factory reformers, one obvious propagandistic advantage of focusing on the suffering of little girls was that, because girls were generally assumed to be weaker, more passive, and more helpless than boys, they seemed indisputably in need of legislative protection. In contrast, there was a long and popular tradition in which working-class boys were portrayed as relatively self-sufficient, active, and capable of getting ahead in the world. Since the sixteenth century the apprentice boys of numerous tales had triumphed over evil and married their masters' daughters. Indeed, *Michael Armstrong* is written partly in this popular tradition of apprentice tales. And although it purposely departs from its model in order to show that industrial capitalism had made a mockery of the apprenticeship system, it returns to its model when brave little Michael escapes from Deep Valley Mill. However, his diminutive girlfriend, Fanny Fletcher, has to be rescued. She is never expected to make her own escape. Even in *Michael Armstrong*, the truly helpless sufferer, the factory worker who can only be delivered by the intervention of others, is a little girl.

There was a second advantage to the prolonged attention in factory reform literature of the 1830s to female suffering and impotence. The feminization of the factory child's image made industrial workers appear to be not only defenseless children but also permanent children, rendering the family metaphor for society quite consistent, for when workers were thought of as daughters rather than as sons, they seemed permanently in need of protection. They appeared constitutionally unable to grow up and challenge the father's authority. Thus, the "little factory slaves" could be "emancipated" without becoming dangerous. Even their passage to adulthood was not believed to constitute independence; it was seen rather, as the onset of a new kind of dependence.

As we saw in the last chapter, in the early 1840s factory reformers began calling attention to the helplessness of factory women, and at that time women workers began to be used to symbolize all suffering industrial laborers, just as young girls had stood as the pathetic representatives of that class a decade earlier. This change is strikingly illustrated in the differences between Charlotte Tonna's two industrial novels. *Helen Fleetwood* depicts the migration of a family from the country to a factory town, where the young girls become the family's chief supports; in *The Wrongs of Women*, published just five years later,[3] another country family arrives in the factory town, but only the mother can find work. Her misery and death and the consequent suffering of her children are the later novel's primary subjects. The message of the book is clear: like children, women must be protected from the long hours of labor demanded by unregulated factory production. The legislators, acting in their self-appointed roles as benevolent fathers, were duty-bound to protect the helpless factory women and children.

The feminization of the image of the working class in industrial fiction, therefore, both arose from and contributed to the paternalist rhetoric of the factory reformers. If workers were thought of as permanently dependent women, then society could easily be visualized as a large family, a family temporarily divided but capable of reunification. The idea of paternalistic reconciliation was reassuring at a time when Chartist agitation was growing louder. As we saw in previous chapters, writers such a Harriet Martineau, Elizabeth Gaskell, and Charles Kingsley confronted the fact of growing working-class independence in their fiction. But many others preferred to follow the rhetorical lead of the factory reformers. While Gaskell and Kingsley were struggling with the thorny issues of freedom and determinism in the lives of male workers, a host of lesser writers, often writing for workers themselves and publishing in cheap magazines, were describing the tribulations of a less threatening segment of the working class.

This focus on women, however, introduced a new kind of rhetoric to the debate over industrialism, a rhetoric that in some ways disrupted the pattern of the social paternalists' arguments: the rhetoric of domestic ideology, in which the family and society are metonymically, rather than metaphorically, related. To illustrate the need for protective legislation, factory reformers claimed that women's labor led to the degradation of the entire working class, for factory women could not properly care for and train their children. Deprived of the moral influences of their mother, working-class children became increasingly degenerate. The reformers argued that working-class morality could only be improved if working-class women were given the time and the skills to fulfill their primary roles, their domestic roles. Thus, a contradiction appeared in the reformers' arguments: women were thrust forward, by the rhetoric of social paternalism, as representative workers and yet were simultaneously told by domestic ideologists that the roles of worker and woman were antagonistic.

The contraction between the two closely affiliated ideologies is clearer in the fiction of the 1840s and 1850s than in the nonfictional reformist propaganda. In the speeches of industrial reformers, social paternalism and domestic ideology coexist, but most writers of popular magazine fiction about women workers adhered to one ideology or the other. Their stories consequently provide good examples of the formal patterns appropriate to the simplest versions of these ideologies. Stories that do mix the ideologies have greater difficulty, as we will see, in reconciling the formal tension between public and private concerns.

The most popular cheap magazine[4] stories about women workers were seamstress tales.[5] The distress of London's seamstresses came to light in 1843 through the same Parliamentary inquiries that revealed the extent of female exploitation in mining and manufacturing. According to the commissioners' report,[6] the London clothing industry became increasingly dependent on subcontractors and subsubcontractors as it tried to keep up with the demand for quickly produced clothes. The "sweating system" thus replaced production in dressmakers' and tailors' shops, and in many cases, wages fell below the subsistence level. These dismal facts were common knowledge in the late 1840s. Beginning in 1842, periodicals published excerpts from the Parliamentary reports on the working and living conditions of seamstresses, and newspapers carried dozens of stories of exploitation throughout the decade.[7] The London clothing industry was thus exposed repeatedly to public scrutiny, and seamstresses became, like factory and mine women, symbols of the poor, oppressed British worker.

Indeed, seamstresses were even more appealing sufferers than other working women because their trade was unmistakably feminine. Women who worked in mines or factories, as we saw in the last chapter, were often imagined to be mannish or even brutish. But upper-class and middle-class readers could easily identify themselves, their wives, or their daughters with the starving seamstresses they read about. The appeal of Thomas Hood's famous poem "The Song of the Shirt," for example, lay in lines like the following, which associate the image of the suffering worker with the reader's relatives:

> O, men, with sisters dear!
> O, men, with mothers and wives!
> It is not linen you're wearing out,
> But human creatures' lives![8]

Because almost all women sewed, the seamstress seemed at least as much woman as worker. She was, therefore, a perfect working-class symbol for writers who wished to see class relations entirely in terms of family relations.

J. M. Rymer and G. W. M. Reynolds were two such writers.[9] In 1844 Rymer published *The White Slave: A Romance for the Nineteenth Century*. After a decent interval of six years, Reynolds serialized a strikingly similar tale under the title *The Slaves of England: No. 1, The Seamstress*. Both were written primarily for male working-class readers. Unlike Hood's audience, Rymer's and Reynolds' readers were in a position to identify closely with seamstresses as workers; consequently, both authors stated their intentions to make their seamstress heroines stand for the most exploited sections of the working class. Rymer, in fact, in both his title and his preface, used the rhetoric of the factory and Parliamentary reformers—specifically, the worker-slave metaphor—to describe London's seamstresses. The purpose of his tale, he writes, is "to convince the public that there were white slaves in London a great deal worse off than the black slaves in Africa."[10] If the word "London" were changed to "Yorkshire," this sentence would be almost a direct quotation from Richard Oastler's 1830 "Yorkshire Slavery" letter. Reynolds, too, used the worker-slave metaphor to place his tale in the tradition of radical anticapitalist and anti-industrial literature. *The Seamstress* was to be only the first in a series of tales about London's exploited workers.

However, no other Slaves of England stories followed *The Seamstress* in the pages of *Reynolds's Miscellany*, for despite his radical rhetoric, Reynolds found that a melodramatic seamstress tale provided a highly popular mixture of social criticism and escapist romance, a mixture that would be difficult to achieve if the heroine were in a less womanly profession. The melodramatic seamstress stories of both Reynolds and Rymer envisioned an ultimate, although personal and fantastic, solution to class conflict.

The White Slave and *The Seamstress* are almost identical in form and plot. Both are self-consciously melodramatic; we are invited to imagine that each work takes place on a stage. The narrators frequently call their descriptions "scene setting," and exposition as well as narration is often given in dialogue. Thus, the heroine's alleged father recites the family's history at the opening of *The White Slave*:

> "A year since, and we were surrounded with life's luxuries; then we found, one by one, its necessaries flying from us; we wanted money, clothing—we wanted fire to warm our chilled limbs; but now, my Millicent, we have come to want food—aye, my child, food. You are weeping. . . .
>
> "Hush—hush! you will awaken poor Harry. . . . But, as I was saying, your mother—"
>
> "My mother! you did not mention her before, father."
>
> "Did I not, my child? How old are you—how old is Harry?"
> (P. 1)

This unintentionally comical and highly improbable dialogue is typical of melodrama. Reynolds's dialogue is somewhat subtler, but by using such dialogue, both authors designate the popular stage as their formal reference point.

In addition, both authors use conventional melodramatic plots to arrive at a gesture of social reconciliation; it is this gesture, given in each story's climactic tableau, that crystallizes the narratives' social meaning. The authors' stock plots can be summarized in a few phrases: villains, aided by the evil representatives of the sweating system, pursue and persecute pure young seamstresses, who are finally rescued by rich young men and restored to their true, aristocratic parents. These plots are chosen because they terminate in an image of familial solidarity between the working and upper classes. In the final conciliatory gestures, the ending tableaux of both stories, society's permanent children, its daughters, are reunited with their long-lost upper-class fathers, and the villains (jealous uncles and brothers who connive with "greedy Jews" and other foreigners) are punished. In Reynolds's story, the seamstress dies at the scene of the reconciliation; in Rymer's, she gets married. But the formal solutions of the social problem are identical: each writer recasts social conflicts as family conflicts and then resolves them in scenes of recognition and reunion. The stories move circuitously but ineluctably toward the revelation of the seamstresses' true parentage and their reunion with their families.

As the narrator of Reynolds's *The Seamstress* repeatedly points out, the story's climactic scene nearly dispenses with dialogue. The scene is depicted through descriptions of static gestures. Thus, the heroine's relatives group and regroup themselves around her deathbed in myriad postures of sorrowful reconciliation. These metaphoric ensembles are described for several pages, even though the narrator exclaims at the outset:

> Oh! who can imagine—for assuredly none can describe—the emotions of joy, and gratitude, and amazement which flowed up, wave upon wave, from the deep fountains of Virginia's heart? And it is because earth knows no language and tongue has no words capable of doing justice to the intensity—the melting tenderness and the thrilling fervour—of those feelings, that we do but glance over that scene which excited them.[11]

And, indeed, the reconciliation scene of *The Seamstress* does not consist of descriptions of inner states or of recorded dialogue. Rather, it is quintessentially melodramatic because it is made up of gestures,[12] gestures that convey, in a static pictorial form, remorse, atonement, re-union, protection.

This typically melodramatic tableau presentation, coupled with the standard melodramatic plot, is an ideal form for literalizing the family-society metaphor. The social and economic gap between the seamstress and her true parents is stressed at the beginning of the reconciliation scene in *The Seamstress*: "The scene is changed from the ducal mansion to the humble cottage—from the fashionable regions of Grosvenor Square to the quiet district of Camden Town" (p. 43). This is the distance that the family reunion spans.

To object that once the seamstress is recognized as the daughter of the aristocracy she is no longer a representative worker is to overlook the peculiar logic of melodrama and its affinity with the peculiar logic of social paternalism. Melodramas typically strain away from the literal facts of their narratives toward some more universal significance; they are a kind of modern morality play and are thus essentially metaphoric.[13] The conventional melodramatic gesture, the embrace of father and daughter, that fixes the seamstress and her family in their tableau of reconciliation, allows us to see these heroines, Millicent and Virginia, as simultaneously children of the upper classes and repre-sentatives of the poor and exploited. That, of course, is precisely the double vision recommended by the social paternalists. In short, melo-drama allows the social-paternalist metaphor to be literalized without being destroyed.

Moreover, in the ways these two melodramas sustain the social significance of their family dramas even after the reconciliation scenes, we can see how versatile an ideology social paternalism was. Rymer's *The White Slave* has a hopeful conclusion for the seamstress, her family, and English society in general. Its heroine, Millicent, is reunited with her real father, the Earl of Daubigny, and then marries the steadfast young gentleman who has tried to protect her from the outset, but who has been outsmarted by a lecherous villain, Colonel Savage, and his accomplices. In this tale, as in *The Seamstress* and numerous other stories of sweated labor, the villain is aided by the evil system of production, which is depicted as owned and operated by people out-side of society's family, primarily by Jews. The "foreignness" of the system allows reform to take place in *The White Slave* without hurting any legitimate member of society's family. Millicent's exploiters are exposed by her father to the righteous outrage of Christian public opinion:

"I tell you," said the earl, "what I will do. In all those cases where the keepers of workrooms have pursued a line of cruel policy towards my darling child, *as part of their system*, I will get my solicitor to draw up the circumstances as briefly and distinctly as possible, and such cases, so drawn up, shall be inserted in every newspaper of the kingdom." (P. 253)

The Christian subjects of the kingdom, it is assumed, will unite behind the responsible aristocracy against the strangers' system. The reader himself is thereby given the opportunity to participate in the story's happy ending by refusing to buy the products of sweated labor.

In this optimistic mood, Rymer ends his story with a plea that the reader not allow Millicent's good fortune to "obliterate the recollection that she suffered much," and that many young women continue to suffer. "Join up," he invites, "in a more glorious cry of emancipation than ever issued from the lips of would-be philanthropists, and let us insist upon looking at home, and dong something for the liberation from bondage of our own *White Slaves*" (p. 254). Rymer often refers to England as home, thus reinforcing his familial metaphor for society and making the rescue of the daughters of England seem a pressing but also a relatively simple matter.

Reynolds, on the other hand, gives the family metaphor a much darker significance. To maintain his reputation as a political radical and to please an enormous sensation-loving readership, Reynolds chose not to end his story with a scene of perfect social harmony. Virginia's rescue comes too late; she dies, and her death destroys not only the aristocratic relatives who had earlier denied her kinship but also her rescuers. In the bloody conclusion of *The Seamstress*, Reynolds makes the same catastrophic use of the familial metaphor that Carlyle makes in *Past and Present*, when the outcast pauper woman dies and her corpse infects the very men who have denied her aid: "She proves her sisterhood, her typhus-fever kills *them*; they actually were her brothers, though denying it."[14] Every bit as much a prophet of social dissolution as Carlyle, Reynolds first imagines the scene of social reconciliation tirely in familial terms and then claims that the family roles were adopted too late: the enraged and remorseful survivors kill one another. Thus he is able to present both the familial form of the needed reconciliation and the catastrophic punishment that awaits those who put off protecting the poor, exploited daughters of society.

The last paragraph of Reynolds's *The Seamstress* is strikingly similar to the last paragraph of *The White Slave*, but the former has a much more pessimistic tone. We are asked not to forget that countless young women are still in the clutches of un-Christian exploiters. However,

Reynolds's paragraph hints at a much less likely and more disastrous end to the shameful bondage of England's daughters:

> With regard to the establishment of Mssrs. Aaron and Sons, would to heaven we could announce that the earth had opened and swallowed it up, or that the red right arm of Jehovah had hurled the avenging thunder-bolt upon its roof! But it is not so. That establishment still exists and the system whereon it is based flourishes more than ever;—and while poor Virginia, one of the countless victims of that diabolical system, sleeps in the silent grave, the toils of the *White Slaves* whom she has left behind her are still contributing to the colossal wealth accumulated within the walls of that Palace of Infamy. (P. 46)

The sweating system is presented here as entrenched, powerful, and apparently invulnerable to negative public opinion, for it is already a "Palace of Infamy." When the system's end does come, it will be a violent one.

The family metaphor for society, therefore, helped shape both Rymer's optimistic vision of social harmony and Reynolds's double fantasy of class reconciliation and revenge. Their melodramatic forms allowed both authors to exploit fully the ideology of social paternalism. Their plots are only a means of literalizing the family-society metaphor—of allowing workers and aristocrats to come together in veritable families and form tableaux of remorse and reconciliation. Melodrama highlights such static, particular gestures, investing them with general significance; it is, therefore, a highly appropriate form for an ideology that is itself based on a metaphor.

Not all seamstress tales of the 1840s and 1850s were melodramas in which the heroines await upper-class paternal rescue. Indeed, most were domestic fictions[15] in which the heroines were viewed in their relationship to members of their own class. Typically, the stories were about young women who migrated to London from the country, expecting to support themselves and other members of their families by their needlework.[16] The women invariably became sick from overwork and lack of food and exercise. Some then became prostitutes; others were rescued by uncles and brothers returned unexpectedly from the colonies; still others died. Only a few rose through their own industry and the inspiration of other women.

Almost all of these narratives claimed that the London clothing industry not only produced misery in the lives of individual seamstresses but also created a grave social danger by making scores of working-class women unfit for motherhood. "How can we look for intellectual advancement among this numerous but suffering class of our fellow-creatures," asks the author of the pamphlet *The Slaves of the Needle*, "and, still more, what are we to expect at their hands, when they assume, as many of them in after-life do, the important position of *mothers*."[17] Most seamstress stories reproduce this emphasis on motherhood. They stress, in ways wholly ignored by Rymer and Reynolds, that the sweating system obstructs their heroines' domestic missions. The relationship between public and private in these stories is not, therefore, a primarily metaphoric one, as it was in the melodramas of Rymer and Reynolds. Here, private life is shown to be metonymically connected to the social world; domestic ideology permeates these tales and defines the seamstress not only as a representative worker but also as the possessor of maternal "Influence," the primary engine of social progress.

In these tales, the seamstress' two roles are in clear opposition: the more the seamstress works, the less capable she is of being a mother; the more she is identified as a mother, the less representative she becomes as a worker. Because her metonymic significance is thus in tension with her metaphoric significance, the stories are always resolved at the expense of one of her two roles. Sad stories end with the death of an infant or the permanent spinsterhood of the seamstress, who then continues to represent the poor and exploited. Happier tales end when the seamstress ceases to be a seamstress and goes on to fulfill "woman's mission" through maternity. Such endings do not reduce the heroines to social insignificance, however, for according to domestic ideology, motherhood is the most important of all social tasks. Indeed, in many of these tales, the good working-class wife is seen primarily as a social missionary.

Lucy Dean; the Noble Needlewoman is an example of didactic domestic fiction. It was written in 1850 by Eliza Meteyard (Silverpen) and published in *Eliza Cook's Journal*, one of the several "improving" cheap periodicals that appeared in the late 1840s and early 1850s and were intended to reach working-class women.[18] *Lucy Dean* is a good example of the ways in which domestic ideology affects popular fictional form. The story allows us to see how the ideology, in its simplest versions, connects the public and private realms by putting the latter completely at the service of the former. Paradoxically, this lavish narrative celebration of domesticity is almost devoid of truly private concerns. Whereas the social paternalists' narratives had translated social problems into familial problems in order to resolve them, Meteyard's narrative identifies family problems as social problems and accepts only those solutions that can be imitated by large numbers of working women.

Lucy Dean is a story with a thesis. It is a domestic tale both in the sense that domestic ideology pervades it and in the sense that its subject matter is ostensibly the domestic life of its heroine. Like much domestic fiction written for the working class, however, it is explicitly didactic. Its purpose, like that of Elizabeth Gaskell's early domestic stories, is not only to describe how the working class lives, but also to dictate how it should live. The narrator of *Lucy Dean* begins by quoting the text she intends to illustrate, very much as Hannah More had quoted passages from the Bible at the beginning of her tracts and as Harriet Martineau had listed the "principles" of her *Illustrations* at the end of each story. Meteyard's text is from Wakefield's *Art of Colonization*; using arguments borrowed from domestic writers, it urges female emigration to the colonies:

> You might persuade religious men to emigrate, and yet, in time, have a colony of which the morals and manners would be detestable; but, if you persuade religious women to emigrate, the whole colony will be comparatively virtuous and polite. As respects morals and manners, it is of little importance what colonial fathers are in comparison with what the mothers are.[19]

Lucy Dean's domestic trials and triumphs are intended to illustrate this general point; in its very form, then, the didactic domestic tale is characterized by the preeminence of the public over the private, the general over the particular. Its accounts of private life serve a social purpose, just as ideologists of domesticity justified their attention to home life on essentially social grounds. Both the arguments of the domestic ideologists and the form of the didactic domestic tale subordinate the personal to the social. Indeed, their very manner of constituting and exalting the personal turns it into a mere subcategory of the social.

Lucy's private life becomes significant only through its social repercussions, and the theme of colonization allows those repercussions to take enormous proportions. When we first see Lucy, she is the recognizable seamstress of dozens of tales, starving and stitching through the cold night. She wears mourning clothes and is about to part with her last friend and possession, the little songbird Sweet. Sweet is her only reminder of her family, and when she takes him to the bird-seller's shop, she consciously gives up her last vestige of domesticity: "it is destitution—the last stage of destitution—which forces me to part with it," she tells the bird-seller, Mr. Twiddlesing. She then goes on to explain: "Though it is only five years since I came up a healthy girl, with a mother, three sisters and a brother, from a distant part of Cornwall to London . . . , and now all that is left of us is me" (p. 313).

Lucy is not even allowed to complete her personal history, though, for neither her listeners nor her storyteller is very interested in yet another account of a seamstress' private grief. "The old tale, the old tale," interjects Twiddlesing's friend O'Flanagan, and the two "old men," as the narrator calls them, begin expounding on the evils of "individual charity" and the necessity of coming up with a general plan for permanently improving the lot of London's seamstresses. O'Flanagan's master, Robert Fortesque, we learn, always refuses to relieve individual cases of poverty, but would give money "to build ships with, to send these human women to lands where they are needed, where they might become mothers" (p. 313). Through these two old men, Lucy is put in touch with a woman writer, Mary Austen, who advocates female emigration.

Mary Austen, a public figure, lifts Lucy out of her obscure, private suffering by converting Lucy to the cult of domesticity; for in this story the ideology of domesticity occupies the place of religion, and Mary Austen is its high priestess. Her "Influence" is everywhere. She is ludicrously admired by the men in the story, who possess an astonishing capacity for reverence. But she is not, of course, an imposing or "unfeminine" woman. At their first meeting, Lucy is surprised to find that Mary is "but a little woman, years younger than herself, in whose face you saw the fervent, pitying, noble heart . . . ; and the written thoughts of whose heart, hundreds of Twiddlesings and O'Flanagans wrapped up carefully in silk paper" (p. 329). Mary Austen is thus a version of the saving Victorian child-woman, and her thoughts are grand idealizations of domesticity. She speaks so fervently of a housewife's daily tasks that they seem to be sacramental acts. "Could you wash, cook, bake, do you know how to provide a comfortable dinner, and nurse a child?" Mary asks Lucy. "To show you my own strong sense of duties like these I speak of," she continues,

> "look at me, and at my hands! Could you fancy that these can brew and bake, wash and iron, cook a dinner from an Irish stew to a cod's head and oyster sauce?"
> "I should hardly think so Madam—these hands look so frail and delicate."
> "They *can*," and the writer spoke with an emphasis which startled Lucy." (P. 329)

That emphasis, however, soon becomes Lucy's own, and the two women form a pact to liberate their "sister women" from "needle slavery" and ship them to the colonies, where they might become wives and mothers. Mary explains: "if men, who need, and ask for, good chaste, and useful wives, would help towards what is so priceless, a permanent and yearly fund might be raised for the purpose of female emigration, on such a plan, as would ensure fitting candidates here, and a fitting and moral reception for them in the colonies" (p. 330).

Thus inspired by Mary to help other seamstresses become colonial wives and mothers, Lucy saves enough money to help buy her passage to Australia. There, through contacts of Mary's, she becomes the "house-keeper" of an entire mining settlement. Eschewing marriage for herself at this stage, Lucy thus becomes a kind of public mother; together, her housekeeping and her "stern, moral nature" civilize the mining community, and the men become like children to her:

> The clear, fresh-smelling dormitory, their excellent comfortable meals, their clean and tidy shirts and stockings were productive of hourly fruit . . . and it was a touching, sacred thing, as their rude nature visibly softened under the pure and blessed influence of this noble woman . . . to see them alone or in bands go to the neat room after the day's labour was over, to beg a book, to ask advice, to talk with her, or to take her some little offering. (P. 378)

The mixture of domestic detail and quasireligious fervor in this passage is typical of the didactic domestic tale: the style has an unintentionally comical literalness—as in the image of clean stockings bearing fruit hourly—that flows from the ideology's metonymic structure. According to the domestic myth, clean stockings not only represent the progress of civilization, they also cause it; and both stockings and civilization depend on the housewife-priestess. Indeed, in this passage, Lucy is more than a priestess; she is a veritable demigoddess of nutrition and sanitation to whom the working men bring "offerings" and pray for further infantilization.

Lucy, however, cannot rest content with this role of virgin mother-goddess. She remembers her promise to Mary Austen ("a nobler influence still" [p. 378]) and sets off as a missionary of domesticity to collect money for female emigration. The money is spent not only on the women's passage but also on their training in the duties of housewifery and child care. In England, Mary Austen sets up schools for this purpose. The first batch of former seamstresses is married off within a month of its arrival in Australia, and thus Mary and Lucy fulfill their dream of mass-producing wives from the coarse material of seamstresses. By their associated efforts, Lucy and Mary become the mothers of mothers: they are mothers to the second power.

All this public domesticity naturally keeps both Mary and Lucy from having families of their own, and we are told that Mary, especially, feels this deprivation keenly. She can hardly remain calm when she contemplates her lack of opportunity to use her housewifely skills: "I know I should be serviceable, I know I should be happier—but then—(she stopped here for her voice was choked—) friends say, that my usefulness would be circumscribed" (p. 392). Even in this elaborate fantasy of public domesticity, then, a version of the public/private discontinuity does appear momentarily. It is ultimately overcome, though, when both heroines marry; and even in the above passage, Mary's desire to be a wife and mother is presented as part of her need to be socially serviceable. She does not want to marry anyone in particular; her desire for a private life is subsidiary to her desire to promote the public good.

Furthermore, when Mary and Lucy finally do marry, at the story's conclusion, they do so only out of a sense of duty. There is no mention of romance or of any private feeling or motive in their marriages; there is not the slightest hint that the women feel either desire or affection for their husbands. Lucy and the mine overseer, Mr. Elliott, agree to marry one another in an exchange that contains no emotion on either side. Elliott proposes by stating that Lucy is as good a woman as his mother was:

> "so let the image of a pure and earnest mother fade somewhat in the light of one, who of all others, will make a pure and earnest wife. We want no courtship . . . we will get married, Lucy, at Adelaide."
> "I answer as frankly," said Lucy, "that I will be your wife."
> (P. 394)

Mary's marriage is arranged in an even more no-nonsense fashion. The wealthy Mr. Fortesque instructs her:

> "Return with Lucy to her adopted country, Mary Austen, and marry Mr. Minwaring [a gentleman colonizer]; he says he has loved you from the hour he first saw you in my old study, and therefore to you both I leave my entire fortune . . . as a perpetual fund for female emigration." (P. 394–95)

Obediently, and for the good of the cause, Mary marries Mr. Minwaring, but we are never given even a glimpse of the two together.

This domestic tale, then, is devoid of truly private ground: it contains no courtships, no scenes of family life. Indeed, the only relationship that resembles a romance is that between Lucy and Mary. Before she leaves London, Lucy spends her Sundays lingering near Mary's house, and while she is in Australia she longs to see Mary's face and hear Mary's voice. Indeed, the narrator dwells so exclusively on the relationship between Mary and Lucy that all other relationships seem unimportant. This narrative focus sometimes has comic effects, as in this announcement that Lucy and Mary have become wives: "Two months after landing, Mary Austen and Lucy Dean were married in Sydney by the colonial bishop, amidst the greatest festivity and rejoicing" (p. 395). The implication here that Lucy and Mary married one another is no mere isolated effect of ambiguous phrasing, for the ending paragraph extends it by giving us the story's only vision of a happy couple:

> Lucy . . . took the coast-voyage to Camden to see Mrs. Minwaring; and there one evening, sitting hand in hand on the broad sands, against which swept the mighty ocean, their infants couched upon one shawl beside them, the spiritual faith of both seemed to have a voice and say,—"Flow on thou mighty ocean, and tell the myriad oceans of myriad worlds, that what is boundless in them, what is deep, or what is pure, has prototype and likeness in the Soul of Woman!" (P. 395)

This concluding image of the union of two perfectly self-sufficient, indeed "boundless," women is one extreme extension of domestic ideology: mothers are so sacred and noble that they are the only proper objects of love for other mothers. The primacy of the relationship between Mary and Lucy is thus another example of the subordination of the private to the public in *Lucy Dean*. Only that relationship which has most directly promoted the public good, which has united the classes in maternal harmony, only that relationship deserves and receives an emotional dimension.

Lucy Dean, then, is an extremely simple version of domestic ideology, one in which social concerns determine the shape of domestic existence precisely because domesticity is considered the foundation of social progress. The story's form, the didactic domestic tale, is characterized by this subordination of personal to social interests. In the very act of idealizing domesticity and giving it social significance, these tales colonize private territory for public use. Just as the social paternalists' seamstress melodramas personalize all social issues, the didactic seamstress tales refashion personal questions into questions of social morality.

It is no accident that these two extremes are reached in seamstress tales. The exclusive focus on women workers allowed these stories to seek solutions for class conflict in one of the two dominant images of feminity: the daughter and the mother. In the seamstress melodramas, workers are represented by women who are thought of as daughters; social issues are thereby personalized. In the didactic domestic tales, women often undergo a series of transformations in which they become workers and then working-class mothers, the bearers of social progress; their private lives are thereby given social importance. Popular domestic tales that deal more extensively with male workers and with the working-class family as a whole, however, present a more complicated, indeed contradictory, relationship between public and private concerns.

In the 1850s numerous stories were published that depicted the development of working-class boys and young men. Most of these were didactic tales—temperance and self-help fictions—and many were published in cheap periodicals intended for family instruction. Like the domestic seamstress tales, these tales were heavily influenced by domestic ideology and have a tendency to examine domestic life primarily in terms of its social significance. In these tales, however, public and private territories are much less easily merged than they are in *Lucy Dean*. Eliza Meteyard, considering only the relationship between women's social and domestic roles, had no difficulty in conflating the two; but writers who considered the relationship between men's social and domestic roles faced a more difficult subject. Domestic ideology was not all-sufficient for them because it tended to end just where the topic of men's roles began. Writers like Sarah Ellis give detailed instructions about how mothers and wives might "humanize" men, but they were very vague in describing just how these humanized men should go about changing the larger society. The subject of how working-class men might bring about social change was even more problematic, since changes from below often had radically democratic implications. Thus, in the magazine fiction, working-class male characters often must choose among competing models of social action, and social action in general often seems to conflict with their domestic duties.

This dimension of alternative social actions is encoded in the tales' formal conventions: many of them present contrasting examples of conduct.[20] *The Three Homes: A Tale of the Cotton Spinners* (1850), by "one who has been among the spindles," is typical in its form. The story was published in *The Working-Man's Friend and Family Advisor*, a periodical devoted to spreading domesticity among working-class men.[21] Workers were supposed to read issues of *The Working Man's Friend* aloud to their families, and the issues are full of stories that contrast drunken, lazy men with honest, heroic working-class fathers. *The Three Homes* depicts social progress in Manchester by ostensibly describing the home lives of three related families. The improvement in domestic life is shown to be one cause of improved working conditions, sanitation, and public morality. The three homes are sequentially related in order to give this sense of historical progress: the home of the spinner, Harry Sparkes, is described as it was in 1810; that of his daughter, Mary, is said to be a representative working-class home of the 1820s and 1830s; that of Sparkes's son, Charley, is established in 1850 just as the tale closes. As one home passes away and another comes into being, their similarities and differences are pointed out, so that the tale is structured something like a triptych that depicts a chronological sequence and also presents its three panels simultaneously for purposes of contrast.

If we accept the tale as it presents itself in this schematic fashion, its point is straightforward and clear. The employment of women for long hours in the factories led to misery inside the home: Mrs. Sparkes's infant son dies from an overdose of cordial because she was not home to nurse him. It also led to public disorder: Mary Sparkes's untidy and uneconomical housekeeping drives her husband out of the house and into the arms of the radicals. Young Charley's experience, on the other hand, is supposed to prove that by taking family responsibilities seriously, working men can promote both social progress and domestic prosperity. The story's thesis is thus the standard one used by factory reformers to pass legislation limiting the hours women could work. Its assumptions about the metonymic relationship between the family and society are drawn from domestic ideology.

The narrative, however, cannot be reduced to this schematic structure, for it contains much that is not consonant with domestic ideology. The most noticeable departure is in the description of Charley's own development. The best parts of Charley's character are induced by his parents, but in a negative sense: he is so horrified by his little brother's death and by his father's intemperance that he resolves to be responsible and sober. The people who then strengthen these resolves in him are not members of Charley's family, nor are they virtuous women. They are, rather, two middle-class men associated with "public" institutions: one is Charley's schoolmaster; the other is his employer, Mr. Davidson. There are, in fact, no positive female or familial influences in Charley's life. When he is young, his home life is something he must continually overcome, and when he matures it becomes nonexistent until the very end of the tale.

With its positive emphasis on public fathers (the schoolmaster, Mr. Davidson, and finally Charley himself) and its negative emphasis on incompetent mothers (Mrs. Sparkes and Mary Sparkes), the story is an ideological hybrid combining a liberal brand of social paternalism with domestic ideology. As we noted in the previous chapter, this ideological combination was not at all unusual in reformist literature of the late

1840s and 1850s. However, *The Three Homes* displays the underlying tension between the two ideologies by its inability to maintain its parallel structure and simultaneously illustrate its thesis.

Charley's marriage, which takes place when he is well over forty, ends the story, and we never see his home. The story is thus misnamed, unless we allow for the possibility that the third home of the title is Davidson's mill, which Charley eventually manages in a clearly paternalistic way. But if the mill is the third home, then the last panel of this narrative triptych is not formally parallel to the first two panels: it establishes a metaphoric rather than a metonymic relationship between the family and society.

There is, however, another way of interpreting the story, one which preserves its parallel structure but also reveals its contradictions. The story can be said to contrast not three homes but three kinds of male social behavior, two of which are opposed to family life and one of which is allegedly in harmony with it. Charley's father is a drunken spinner who spends his leisure time in a pub; Charley's brother-in-law, good-natured but weak-willed, becomes a radical activist during the strike and riots of 1842. But Charley himself works hard to support his destitute parents, becomes a manager of Davidson's mill, and then devotes himself to being a public father. Charley's social action thus appears to be consonant with all the values of family life. A somewhat closer look at the story, however, reveals that the appearance of public-private continuity in Charley's life is an illusion.

The nonexistence of his home life enables Charley to improve the living and working conditions of his class. Like Lucy Dean, Charley Sparkes becomes a public parent in lieu of having his own family: he organizes "day nurseries for the manufacturing poor," establishes night schools for adult workers, builds baths, washhouses, and dining-rooms near the factory, and begins "schools for the children . . . at which all the little workers at the mill were freely taught; and . . . playgrounds were set apart for their amusement and exercise during the intermissions of labour; and thus good healthy children grew up into good well-disciplined men and women."[22] Thus, as in *Lucy Dean* formerly private functions—child care, recreation, meals, and even personal cleanliness—are socialized. Lucy Dean's public mothering, however, was only a temporary arrangement that lasted until the miners' brides arrived from London; then, although the event is never described, the couples were supposed to have dispersed to their various cottages. The movement in *The Three Homes* is from makeshift, squalid, dark cottages to permanent, clean, luminous public buildings.

Thus, although the tale is intended to present two modes of social action that are not consonant with domestic life and one that is, it actually depicts three kinds of social action that exclude real domesticity. For, although Charley is an exemplary son and brother throughout the story, he does not simultaneously effect social change and become an actual father. His public fatherhood and his private fatherhood are in tension, a tension particularly evident in the story's closing paragraphs. Here, in his advice to workers, Charley tries to conflate the working-man's public and private responsibilities:

> "The industrious poor man," said he, "best serves his country by doing his duty to his family at home. He best amends his country by giving it good children. . . . He best governs by obeying the laws, and by ruling in love and mercy his own little kingdom at home. His best reform is that which corrects the irregularities of his own fireside." (P. 93)

In this passage, all public duties—serving one's country, governing, and reforming—are equated with being a parent; the speech thus follows the pattern established in domestic ideology. The reader must notice, however, that Charley's advice runs counter to his actions. The previous paragraphs present him doing his duty, not just to his family but to his fellow workers; they depict him governing other men, holding public meetings, and reforming a whole community. Instead of establishing his own "little kingdom at home," Charley repeatedly becomes a father by displacing other fathers: he first takes over the role of father in his parents' home, then in his brother-in-law's home, and finally at Davidson's mill.

The story itself, then, does not corroborate Charley's speech, for it does not present social improvement as the spontaneous outgrowth of being a good private parent; that is, it does not posit a purely metonymic relationship between public and private existence. Rather, it illustrates the necessity of remaking society as a large family in which some working men may rise to the position of public fathers, but only at the expense of their private lives. *The Three Homes*, therefore, depicts two roads to social progress, one domestic and one social, but it presents them as mutually exclusive.

In these four tales, then, we have seen three ways in which popular industrial fiction writers interrelated their social and familial concerns. Rymer and Reynolds wrote melodramas in which the social paternalists' metaphor could be realized while still remaining a metaphor. Their form and their ideology both called for the complete transformation of social problems into family problems, but the double vision encouraged by melodrama allows the reader to look through the family's gestures to their metaphoric social significance. The metonymic assumption of the didactic domestic tale, on the other hand, led to a more literal-minded, one-dimensional view of the connection between social and personal concerns. In *Lucy Dean*, personal problems are seen as social problems, and the tale systematically excludes truly private areas. In these serialized stories, the contradictions within social paternalism and domestic ideology are not prominent; the tales' ideological simplicity produces extreme but relatively unproblematic solutions to the question of how the public and private realms should be related. *The Three Homes*, on the other hand, includes elements of both social paternalism and domestic ideology; consequently, it presents a less consistent view of the connection between public and private issues. Although the tale explicitly states that the social and personal must be reconciled, the two spheres remain stubbornly distinct.

7

"Relationship Remembered against Relationship Forgot": Family and Society in *Hard Times* and *North and South*

And yet, in my opinion, the world is but one great family. Originally it was so. What then is this narrow [family] selfishness that reigns in us, but relationship remembered against relationship forgot?

Samuel Richardson
Clarissa Harlowe

Never before did I hear of an Irish Widow reduced to "prove her sisterhood by dying of typhus-fever and infecting seventeen persons,"—saying in such undeniable way, "You *see*, I was your sister!" Sisterhood, brotherhood, was often forgotten; but not till the rise of these ultimate Mammon and Shotbelt Gospels did I ever see it so expressly denied.

Thomas Carlyle
Past and Present

By 1854 Chartism was moribund, but militant trade unionism lived on in the north of England, producing some of the most prolonged strikes and lockouts of the century. The strike and lockout at Preston in 1853–54, for example, lasted more than eight months,[1] convincing many observers that, although Chartism no longer flourished in factory towns, the classes there were still mightily and dangerously opposed. Charles Dickens and Elizabeth Gaskell were two such observers; in their respective novels, *Hard Times* (1854) and *North and South* (1855), they attempted to describe industrial society and present solutions to the problems of class antagonism.

Like the magazine narratives discussed in the previous chapter, *Hard Times* and *North and South* ostensibly propose that social cohesion can be achieved by changing the relationship between family and society, by introducing cooperative behavior, presumably preserved in private life, into the public realm. These two novels, moreover, use the same metaphoric and metonymic tropes the magazine stories employed to connect public and private realms. Like J. M. Rymer and G. W. M. Reynolds, Dickens uses the social paternalists' metaphor[2] and concomitant melodramatic conventions, whereas Gaskell explores the metonymic relationship between the family and society, incorporating elements from didactic domestic fiction into her novel.

Hard Times and *North and South* reveal, however, in a way that the magazine fiction does not, the contradictions latent in social paternalism and domestic ideology. Despite their attempts to make social relations personal, to advocate that the relations between classes become like the cooperative associations of family life, both novels ultimately propose the isolation of families from the larger society. Critics have complained that these novels finally retreat into the private, familial areas of the plot, apparently leaving their social concerns behind; the endings have, therefore, been seen as false solutions, and their falseness has been traced either to their authors' fears of working-class revolt or to some inherent incompatibility between the presentation of social problems and the novel form.[3]

We have seen, however, that the tendency to dissociate the family from society is prevalent in both social paternalism and domestic ideology. Both assume the separation of the public and private spheres they attempt to integrate. The novels, unlike the magazine stories, parallel the ideologies by initially establishing definite boundaries between their social and private plots. In the seamstress melodramas, as we saw, the metaphoric children of the aristocrats were also revealed to be their actual children; thus, the mere discovery of the seamstresses' identities integrated the social and familial plots. But in *Hard Times* the children are not actual workers; although family relations are compared to class relations, the two are not identical. In *North and South*, too, there is an initial disconnection between the family under consideration and the society needing reformation. Here the domestic heroine, the woman whose influence advances social progress, is the daughter of a clergyman, but unlike many heroines of didactic domestic tales, she is not a member of the working class, nor is she at the outset related to either of the classes involved in industrial conflict. In both novels, then, as in both ideologies, there is at first a distance that is never completely overcome between the public and private spheres, for although their ostensible purpose is to connect the two realms, both ideologies ultimately advocate the continued isolation of the family from society. Social paternalists argued that only through such isolation could the family be preserved as a model, benign hierarchy. The domestic ideologists, too, insisted that the family remain a separate sphere, one untouched by competition and strife, because the home would have no power to heal if it were itself contaminated by society's ills. The final retreats into personal, familial concerns that critics have noticed in the novels, therefore, have analogies in both social paternalism and domestic ideology. By advocating the integration of public and private life and then dissociating the two, the novels reproduce the paradox of the ideologies that inform them.

Unlike the magazine stories, moreover, *Hard Times* and *North and South* belong to a genre that mandates both the integration and the separation of public and personal themes. As we saw in chapter 5, nineteenth-century English novels are characterized by a structural tension between impulses to associate and to dissociate public and private realms of experience. The tension, however, is unusually noticeable in these two industrial novels because they emphasize thematically the very thing they cannot achieve structurally: the integration of public and private life. A confluence of ideological and formal factors, therefore, caused the contradictions and reversals that critics of these novels have remarked.

The novels consequently not only lay bare the contradictions of two Victorian ideologies, but also magnify a paradox at the heart of the novel form. Just as the industrial novels of the 1840s exaggerated the novelistic tension between free will and determinism, the industrial novels of the 1850s highlight the novels' unstable relation between public and private realms. Like the earlier novels, the industrial novels of the 1850s focus attention on one of the genre's most problematic *données*. In *Hard Times* and *North and South*, therefore, Dickens and Gaskell explore the very foundations of their art, exposing its structural inconsistencies. In fact, both of these realistic novels become, as we will see, reflections on their narrative methods.

"Hard Times": The Unmaking of a Metaphor

Of these two reflections, Dickens's is the more fractured and discontinuous, for in *Hard Times* the impulse to dissociate the family and society is ultimately much stronger than the impulse to connect the two. The strength of the dissociative tendency is partly due to the fact that Dickens uses metaphor to connect his plots: metaphors separate even as they interrelate the things they compare. But the impulse toward separation is further strengthened by Dickens's special use of the family-society metaphor, a use that, as we will see, gives family reform priority over social reform and tries to substitute family solidarity for social cohesion. Finally, the novel questions the very enterprise of making metaphors in a world where connections, when they are possible, are almost always destructive.

However, before we analyze the ways in which *Hard Times* subverts
the family-society metaphor, we must outline the ways in which the
narrative first establishes its comparison between the Gradgrind family
and industrial society. The situation of the Gradgrind children is both
explicitly and implicitly likened to the situation of the Coketown workers, and the relationship between Louisa and her father is paralleled by
the relationship between Stephen Blackpool and his employer, Mr.
Bounderby. The first two chapters of the novel, where the ideas of
children and industrial workers are merged in the figures of working-
class children, lay the groundwork for the family-society metaphor. In
these chapters, we observe the overpowering presence of Gradgrind
and his philosophy, pacifying and repressing the school children. But
in the third and fourth chapters, the idea of oppressed children is split
off from the image of working-class children and embodied in the
figures of Tom and Louisa. This separation is so subtle that the reader
is at first only vaguely aware of the class difference between the little
Gradgrinds and the school children of the first chapter. In fact, in our
first view of Tom and Louisa, which is, significantly, through Mr.
Gradgrind's eyes, they are indistinguishable from a group of "young
rabble from a model school."[4] Moreover, once they are clearly identified by their father and separated from the larger group, they are
taken home to an establishment so like the model school that class
differences between the two groups of children still appear irrelevant
to their oppression.

Chapter five introduces another victim of the Gradgrind philosophy: the adult working population of Coketown. At this point, working-class children all but disappear from the novel; Sissy and Bitzer
become members of the Gradgrind and Bounderby establishments.
Having separated children and the working class from one another,
the narrative reconnects them through metaphor. Their original association in the composite figures of the opening chapters lingers, but the
narrator now adopts a new mode of connection: explicit analogy. In
one of those Carlylean questions that can only be answered affirmatively, the narrator asks, "Is it possible, I wonder, that there was any
analogy between the case of the Coketown population and the case of
the little Gradgrinds?"(p. 19). The story that follows answers this
question affirmatively and illustrates the proposed analogy in parallels
between Louisa and Stephen Blackpool. Still, for the first half of the
novel, Stephen's and Louisa's stories intersect only through their common inclusion of Mr. Bounderby; otherwise the stories proceed on
independent but parallel courses, the parallels constructed in such a
way as to maintain the metaphoric connection between the middle-

class family and the larger society: Stephen is to Mr. Bounderby as Louisa is to her father.

The parallels are implicitly developed in the interviews between Stephen and Bounderby in chapter eleven and between Louisa and Gradgrind in chapter fifteen. In each interview, the topic is marriage; in each the "father" is called on to give advice to the "child," and in each the former fails to give the proper advice, leaving the latter with a diminished sense of life's possibilities. Both Gradgrind and Bounderby discount the emotional reality of marriage. Bounderby maintains that Stephen's miserable marriage is a fact that he must continue to live with: "You didn't take your wife for fast and for loose; but for better for worse. If she has turned out worse—why all we have got to say is, she might have turned out better" (p. 58). In Bounderby's opinion, Stephen has taken a calculated risk—and lost. Mr. Bounderby stands behind the divorce law that condemns Stephen to suffer perpetually for his wife's intemperance. The employer's dismissal of his workman's problem clearly represents Bounderby's failure, and the failure of others like him, to recognize the human needs of the working class. "Show me the law to help me!" Stephen demands, and Bounderby's reply emphasizes the class injustice built into English law: "There *is* such a law. . . . But it's not for you at all. It costs money. It costs a mint of money" (pp. 57–58).[5]

Bounderby and the laws he upholds keep Stephen in his unhappy marriage, and Gradgrind, through a similar sort of blindness, leads Louisa into an equally miserable liaison, her loveless marriage to Bounderby. Like Bounderby, Gradgrind refuses to consider the emotional dimension of marriage. His advice to Louisa is significant in what it leaves out:

> I would advise you (since you ask me) to consider this question, as you have been accustomed to consider every other question, simply as one of tangible Fact. The ignorant and the giddy may embarrass such subjects with irrelevant fancies, and other absurdities that have no existence, properly viewed— . . . you know better. (P. 75)

Louisa's requests for help are understated compared to Stephen's, but they are repeated and insistent, and Gradgrind's failure to answer them is glaring. Gradgrind refuses to recognize his daughter's emotional needs, just as Bounderby has refused to recognize Stephen's.

The two interviews have similar effects on Stephen and Louisa. The first reaction of each is despondency. Stephen's desperate "Tis just a muddle a'toogether, an' the sooner I am dead, the better" echoes in Louisa's quieter reply, "What does it matter?" Both Stephen and Louisa then embrace the consolation to be found in chaste and self-sacrificing attachments outside their marriages, but for both such love is also self-destructive. Because of Stephen's dedication to Rachael, he refuses to take part in the strike, and Louisa's love for Tom impels her to marry Mr. Bounderby. Having been denied the paternal guidance they sought, the worker and the child find emotional transcendence in self-sacrifice. Stephen combines his loyalty to Rachael with his religious sentiments, seeing her as an angel and promising "t' trust 't th' time, when thou and me at last shall walk together far awa', beyond the deep gulf, in th' country where thy little sister is [heaven]" (p. 69). Louisa's hope is secular, but it reveals a similar devaluation of her present life. She believes herself unfitted by her education to do those things that according to the popular ideas of femininity might have saved Tom: "I don't know what other girls know. I can't play to you or sing to you. I can't talk to you so as to lighten your mind, for I never see any amusing sights or read any amusing books that it would be a pleasure or a relief to you to talk about, when you are tired" (p. 39). But because Tom has been her only love, she resolves to dedicate her otherwise useless life to his service by marrying Bounderby: "While it [life] lasts, I would wish to do the little I can, and the little I am fit for" (p. 77).

Indeed, when Stephen and Louisa meet, they feel an immediate sympathy for one another. In his second interview at the Bounderby home, Stephen "instinctively" addresses himself to Louisa, finding his "natural refuge" in her face (p. 113), and Louisa rushes out to help Stephen as soon as she discovers he is fired. Later she will have an interview with her father that parallels Stephen's second conversation with Bounderby; in it she confronts her father with his failings, just as Stephen presents the grievances of the working class to his employer.

In the second half of the novel, however, where Dickens joins his plots together, the family-society metaphor disintegrates. The contact between Stephen and Louisa begins the process of disintegration. Because the point of a metaphor is to find likeness in difference, and because its terms normally replace one another, introducing the two terms literally into the same scene destroys the necessary distance between the metaphor's levels. The metaphoric connection is then attenuated by this literal proximity, for the differences between the terms become more evident than the similarities. Integrating Louisa's and Stephen's stories, therefore, gradually destroys their metaphoric link: the difference between Gradgrind's daughter and Bounderby's workman become clearer than the likenesses.

The differences between Stephen and Louisa were always, of course, one dimension of their metaphoric connection. While Dickens paralleled Louisa's and Stephen's stories, he kept them distinct. The principle of metaphoric integration, therefore, led to a separation of the plots. Conversely, the train of events set off by Louisa's and Tom's visit to Stephen's house destroys the point of the metaphor: the idea that middle-class children and workers share a common oppression and hence a community of interests. That is to say, the family-society metaphor breaks down because Louisa and Tom grow up and have their own roles to play in the larger society, roles that are, moreover, opposed to Stephen's well-being. Certainly, Tom's interests are more directly antagonistic to Stephen's than are Louisa's; indeed, part of the reason for comparing workers to daughters was that both were believed to be perpetual children who never develop completely separate interests. Nevertheless, to the extent that Louisa's primary loyalty is to Tom, she does grow up to have interests opposed to Stephen's. The metaphoric connection between the worker and child—the connection that depends on separation—might have been potentially healing, but their literal connection is destructive.

Indeed, most literal relationships in this novel are destructive; *Hard Times* uses the family-society metaphor in a way that exaggerates its tendency toward separation. In developing the idea of a common oppression for workers and children, Dickens initially uses the metaphor in the pessimistic way that G. W. M. Reynolds and Thomas Carlyle used it,[6] to describe an extreme state of social crisis. As do Reynolds and Carlyle, Dickens reverses the usual direction of the paternalist metaphor. Instead of presenting us with an ideal family on which society should model itself, he depicts a family that is itself no more than a mirror of an exploitative society. At the outset, the Gradgrind family does not represent potential relations of social harmony, but actual relations of domination, denial, and oppression. The Gradgrinds embody none of the positive values normally associated with the family; Coketown is remarkably homogeneous publicly and privately. In fact, the narrator, in his descriptions of Coketown and the Gradgrind establishment, emphasizes the consistency of this oppression: the entire environment is "severely workful" (p. 17). The workers and the children suffer not from simple neglect, not from a lack of connection with their employers and parents, but from actively destructive connections. The relationships in the novel are like the "serpents of smoke" that coiled themselves around the town "and never got uncoiled": they suffocate the inhabitants. Louisa's relationships to her father, to Tom, and to Bounderby, are too close. Stephen is also caught in a destructive relationship, the continuance of which is enforced by legal coils, laws that only hinder and never help him. All of Bounderby's relationships are seen to be exploitative as well: he ends his connections with his mother, Mrs. Sparsit, Louisa, and Stephen only when he can no longer profit from them.

Hard Times, therefore, does not present industrial society as disconnected, nor does it initially display the family as a model of cohesive, nonexploitative relationships. Dickens's inverted use of the family-society metaphor gives the first part of the novel a definite structural symmetry, but it also makes social reform the second item on the novel's agenda. In order for paternalist reform to proceed here, for society to be reorganized as a harmonious extended family, the family itself must first be reformed. However, the process of bringing about family reform, of making the Gradgrind family cooperative and nurturing, creates disconnections: it divorces the family from the rest of society, and it separates family members from one another.

The first of these disconnections, the divorce of the Gradgrind family from the rest of society, can be seen as a characteristic discontinuity within social paternalism, a discontinuity exaggerated by Dickens's pessimistic use of the family-society metaphor. In *Hard Times*, Dickens, like many social paternalists, seeks to connect the family and society through metaphor alone. An additional literal connection between the two not only destroys the distance necessary to the social paternalists' metaphor, but also makes the family vulnerable to society's corruptions. In this novel, where almost all literal connections are destructive, the only imaginable regeneration establishes a new kind of distance between the Gradgrind family and industrial society, the distance not of metaphoric difference but of actual antagonism.

The Gradgrind family becomes a model of harmony and security, a paradigm for proper social realtions, only by undergoing internal change. Gradgrind taught his children to act on what they rationally determine to be their own best interests, but Tom's crime exposes the failure of an education based on this principle. Through Louisa's crises and through Sissy Jupe's subtle influence, Gradgrind comes to realize his love for his children and his responsibility to guide and protect them. He no longer views them as young automatons but as children in need of his emotional attention. Gradgrind's conversion to this new mode of fatherhood is proved by his conduct toward young Tom at the book's conclusion. In this episode, Gradgrind sacrifices his old principles of reason and self-interest to his new belief in family loyalty. The confrontation between Gradgrind and Bitzer, for example, is designed to emphasize the former's conversion from extreme utilitarianism to paternalism. The Gradgrind family manifests its new solidarity by conspiring with that other model of cohesion, the circus, to help young Tom escape. Thus, the Gradgrind family ostensibly comes to embody the virtues of loyalty and compassion, and thereby takes a necessary step toward becoming an appropriate model for society.

But what significance does this Gradgrind solidarity finally have for the larger society? How does the familial metaphor work itself out? Paradoxically, the new Gradgrind family cooperativeness accomplishes the final dismantling of the novel's metaphoric organization. At the very moment Dickens restores the usual, optimistic direction of the paternalist metaphor—the ideal family as a model for society—the parallel between the Gradgrind children and the working class collapses. For the Gradgrinds become a model family only by symbolically betraying the working class and breaking society's laws: although young Tom is primarily responsible for Stephen's death, the Gradgrind family rallies to his defense. Later, Mr. Gradgrind does clear Stephen's name of Tom's crime, but his first effort is to save his own son from justice. Moreover, as both Bitzer and Sleary point out, the act that proves the triumph of the cohesive forces of the novel compounds Tom's felony. For the Gradgrinds, therefore, becoming a model family means cutting themselves off from larger social considerations and retreating into the morality of clannishness.

Hard Times, then, ultimately exposes a dilemma inherent in the proposal that society be modeled on the family. The advocates of paternalist reform often idealized the family as a bastion of harmony and order, isolating it in their thought from the as yet unregenerated society in order to make it worthy of imitation. By advocating the isolation of the family, however, social paternalists reconstituted the very disjunction between the public and private spheres they set out to overcome. This dilemma, which inheres in *Hard Times'* structuring metaphor, partly accounts for the seeming reversal at the end of the book. By ending the novel with a depiction of the family as a protective dominion, Dickens is not turning away from his social ideology to meet some formal demand; he is, rather, drawing out to an absurd extreme the ideology's own paradoxical logic. The same social beliefs that have led Dickens to maintain the family-society analogy throughout the novel have led him to retreat into the purely private sphere at the story's end.

In *Hard Times*, however, the retreat into the family circle is frought with ambiguities: a novel that advocates easier divorces, and one that in fact separates the heroine, Louisa, from her husband in order to achieve family solidarity, cannot be said to create unequivocal optimism about family relations. The establishment of truly cooperative family connections in *Hard Times* requires not only the reform of certain relationships but also the complete severance of others. Stephen might have had a happy family life with Rachael if he could have been divorced from his drunken wife. Louisa can find a father in Gradgrind and a sister in Sissy Jupe only if she leaves Bounderby.

The establishment of proper father-child relations between Gradgrind and his children, moreover, results in separations among the Gradgrinds themselves. Louisa's crisis, after all, does not immediately turn Gradgrind into a father capable of protecting and guiding her. Rather, it teaches him that he has already interfered too much in her life, and he decides to withdraw, allowing Sissy to become Louisa's savior. The resolution of the father-daughter relationship is, indeed, an interrupted melodrama, one that shades into a domestic tale. We watch, partially through Mrs. Sparsit's jealous eyes, as Louisa is apparently seduced by the diabolical dandy James Harthouse. Preyed upon by husband, brother, and lover, Louisa is seen descending a gothic staircase of dishonor in Mrs. Sparsit's imagination. At the last moment, however, in true melodramatic fashion, Louisa summons the strength to escape her seducer and seek her father's protection. But in the scene of recognition and reconciliation between father and daughter, *Hard Times* departs from the conventions of melodrama. Louisa does confront her father and reveal her "true self" to him, and Gradgrind does recognize his daughter at that moment for the first time. According to the conventions, this scene should close with a tableau: the new-found daughter firmly supported in her father's strong arms. Louisa, however, has never suffered from her father's neglect; rather, she has had too much attention from him, and it has been the wrong kind of attention; "If you had only neglected me," she tells him, "what a much better and much happier creature I should have been this day" (p. 165). Recognition is completed in this scene, but reconciliation does not follow automatically; the old destructive bond must be broken first. The scene's final tableau represents not union but separation:

> He tightened his hold in time to prevent her sinking on the floor, but she cried out in a terrible voice, "I shall die if you hold me! Let me fall upon the ground!" And he laid her down there, and saw the pride of his heart and the triumph of his system, lying, an insensible heap, at his feet. (P. 167)

Gradgrind helps save his daughter by letting go of her. In their next conversation, he explains to Louisa why he is delegating his parental responsibility to Sissy Jupe:

> "I am far from feeling convinced now . . . that I am fit for the trust you repose in me; that I know how to respond to the appeal you have come home to make to me; that I have the right instinct how to help you, and to set you right, my child." (P. 169)

Gradgrind turns Louisa over to someone with the "right instinct," and Louisa is reclaimed by the innocent child-woman. As in a domestic tale, Sissy becomes an object of adoration and a surrogate mother for Louisa:

> [Louisa] fell upon her knees, and clinging to this stroller's child looked up at her almost with veneration.
> "Forgive me, pity me, help me! Have compassion on my great need, and let me lay this head of mine upon a loving heart!"
> "O lay it here!" cried Sissy. "Lay it here, my dear." (P. 172)

Louisa sinks to her knees and rests her had on Sissy's bosom; they become the accepting mother and the penitent child.[7]

It is Sissy, therefore, not Gradgrind, who reclaims Louisa and later protects her from James Harthouse. In these actions, Sissy plays the role of a family member; but Dickens reminds us that "this stroller's child" is not really related to Louisa. Indeed, at the close of Sissy's interview with Harthouse, Dickens emphasizes that she is not a Gradgrind. "Pardon my curiosity at parting. Related to the family?" Harthouse asks.

> "I am only a poor girl," returned Sissy. "I was separated from my father—he was only a stroller—and taken pity on by Mr. Gradgrind. I have lived in the house ever since." (P. 179)

Louisa's real relatives are powerless to help her; Sissy, an abandoned child, must play the parent to Louisa.

Sissy plays a similar role in the relationship between Gradgrind and Tom: she sets up the conditions for Tom's escape, thereby providing an occasion for Gradgrind to demonstrate his loyalty to his son. But even this climactic act of cooperation—the conspiracy to help Tom escape—is really an act of expulsion accomplished amid the trappings of farce. Gradgrind, sitting "forlorn, on the clown's performing chair in the middle of the [circus] ring," confronts his erring son, who is disguised as a black servant, "with seams in his black face, where fear and heat had started through the greasy composition daubed all over it" (p. 215). Tom is "grimly, detestably, ridiculously shameful," and Gradgrind is thoroughly humiliated. Tom, moreover, is not at all contrite; he is sullen toward his father and denounces Louisa outright. His conduct prompts Gradgrind to ask Sleary how he can "get this deplorable object away." The whole demoralizing incident ends in a farcical animal act, with Bitzer, Tom's pursuer, pinned down between a dancing horse and a wrestling dog.

Indeed, family solidarity and personal fidelity are reduced to canine wonders, as Sleary attempts to broaden Gradgrind's moral horizons with an illustration of natural affection, the story of Sissy's father's dog, Merrylegs, who returned to the circus after his master's death, seeking his little mistress. Sleary concludes, "It theemth to prethent two thingth to a perthon, don't it, Thquire? . . . one, that there ith a love in the world, not all thelf-interetht after all . . . ; t'other, that it hath a way of ith own of calculating or not calculating, with thomehow or another ith at leatht ath hard to give a name to, ath the wayth of the dogth ith!" (p. 222). In this ending, exemplary family behavior and "the wayth of the dogth" are indistinguishable. Tom's escape does prove that the Gradgrinds have become a loyal clan, but it also disperses them and makes them sadly ridiculous. A close look at their pageant of solidarity thus shows it to be a grim farce culminating in separation.

The novel, therefore, contains a hopelessness about family relationships, a hopelessness that makes it impossible for the Gradgrinds to become an appropriate model for a regenerated society. In *Hard Times* social paternalism's innate tendency toward public-private discontinuity is exaggerated by the novel's implicit view of family relations. The novel seems to retreat into the private realm, but that realm is itself criss-crossed by barriers. It is, therefore, not surprising that even the reformed Gradgrainds are powerless to change Coketown. Since their family cohesion is itself fragile and ambiguous, it can hardly provide inspiration for social cohesion.

In the last chapter, which depicts the characters' futures, the Gradgrinds remain in melancholy isolation from one another and from the larger society, which goes unreformed. Louisa is never to have a family of her own, Tom is to die repentant but alone. Gradgrind's political role, we are told, will change because of his reformation as a father, but as a consequence of that reformation he will become powerless and isolated. Like most of Dickens's good fathers, Gradgrind seems to become unfit for leadership (p. 225). Bounderby, on the other hand, remains completely unreformed, but his power extends itself. Although he cuts himself off from Mrs. Sparsit and Louisa, he manages to turn himself into a small crowd. At the novel's close there are twenty-five Josiah Bounderbys instead of one, all produced celibately, through the legal cloning of Bounderby's "vain-glorious will," which stipulates that

> five-and-twenty Humbugs, past five-and-fifty years of age, each taking upon himself the name, Josiah Bounderby of Coketown, should for ever dine in Bounderby Hall, for ever lodge in Bounderby buildings, for ever attend a Boundery chapel, for ever go to sleep under a Bounderby chaplain, for ever be supported out of a

Bounderby estate, and for ever nauseate all healthy stomachs, with a vast amount of Bounderby balderdash and bluster. (P. 225)

Since the good father is impotent and the bad father unrepentant, the job of reforming society falls on Sissy's slight shoulders. Sissy's future, the last to be predicted, is the only one in which family harmony and social progress are linked. Sissy's future actions link the two metonymically, however, in the manner of domestic ideology; more-over, the connection does not seem powerful enough to bring about social change. Sissy, of course, does become a mother, "grown learned in childish lore," and she extends her maternal care to "her humbler fellow creatures," trying "to beautify their lives of machinery and reality." The narrator, though, does not suggest that Sissy's activity can materially change the harsh industrial town. The society itself is not transformed into a vast family. The final paragraph refers to "our two fields of action" (p. 227) and recommends that the reader do his duty in each, but the hope that the two might be connected in a metaphoric transformation has been abandoned. Indeed, the "two fields of action" are more widely divided at the end of the novel than they were at its beginning.

Despite the fact that *Hard Times* overtly celebrates family love and social cohesion, therefore, the novel actually presents a series of separations: separations between the family and society, and separations within the family itself. As we have seen, the book's tendency to sever connections arises from its use of the family-society metaphor, for separation is both implicit in the trope and exaggerated by Dickens's vision of the actively harmful relationships dominating both public and private life. Indeed, the book seems suffused with a fear of making connections in a world where relationships are almost without exception destructive.

This fear helps account for the book's metaphoric organization: metaphors, because they generally maintain the differences between the objects they compare, can be seen as a way of avoiding the destructive proximity of literal connections. Thus, the metaphoric connection between Louisa and Stephen is beneficial insofar as it allows us to sympathize more fully with the working class by forcing us to see their suffering in terms of the suffering of oppressed children. But when Stephen and Louisa come into actual contact, their relationship becomes mutually harmful. The author's preference for metaphor is manifested in several other aspects of the novel as well; the narrator of *Hard Times* explicitly recommends making metaphors as a regenerative activity, and provides them in abundance himself. Metaphors are a hallmark of Dickens's style in all his novels, but in *Hard Times* they become a thematic preoccupation, even an obsession. This novel can, indeed, be seen as a book *about* metaphors.

It is also, however, a book in which metaphors often break down or reveal themselves to be pure illusions, mere shows that conceal (and often ill-conceal) seamy actualities.[8] In *Hard Times* even metaphoric connections are ambivalently presented. Indeed, as we will see, if the novel can be said to endorse unequivocally any connections at all, it endorses the connections made not by the fanciful narrator but by the book's most literal-minded character—the single character incapable of seeing anything in terms of anything else—Sissy Jupe. The novel, therefore, actually exhibits a distrust of its own metaphors at the same time that it explicitly recommends them.

Metaphor is introduced as an explicit theme in *Hard Times* through the book's many discussions of "Fancy," a theme that fits neatly into the novel's paternalist scheme; Coketown's workers and Gradgrind's children are both denied "Fancy." They are comparable, then, because they suffer a common oppression. Moreover, the issue allows the narrator to argue explicitly in favor of making metaphors and to crowd such tropes into his own narration.[9] The book, therefore, has an excessively metaphoric style, as well as a metaphoric structure, and its style becomes one of its themes. We are told, for example, that if the little Gradgrinds had been allowed to develop metaphoric imaginations, they might have seen their teacher as a ogre (p. 7) or their schoolroom as a "dark cavern" (p. 40). Similarly, workers with imaginative faculties would be able to see their illuminated factories as "Fairy palaces" (p. 49). But the emphasis on fact in Coketown allows no such fanciful escapes for workers or children. The narrator, as if to compensate for the poverty of indigenous Coketown metaphors, supplies an abundance of his own. In a single paragraph, for example, Coketown's brick is compared to "the painted face of a savage"; the factory chimneys discharge "interminable serpents of smoke"; and the piston of the steam engine is the "head of an elephant in a state of melancholy madness" (p. 17). These separate metaphors and similes coalesce into a single image of Coketown as a jungle, an image that was used by advocates of "internal missions," and one that resonates with echoes of the worker-slave metaphor. Paragraphs like this one illustrate the narrator's metaphoric excesses and demonstrate his already explicitly stated commitment to that trope.

The narrator, moreover, is not the novel's only locus of fanciful activity. The circus embodies fancy, and its members dramatize the social paternalists' trope: the family-society metaphor. The unrelated individuals of the circus society come together and behave like a loyal family. Most comically and grotesquely emblematic of this sort of family role-playing is the relationship between E. W. B. Childers, the Wild Huntsman of the North American prairies, and Master Kidderminster, a dwarf who "assisted as his infant son: being carried upside down over his father's shoulder, by one foot, and held by the crown of his head, heels upward, in the palm of his father's hand, according to the violent paternal manner in which wild huntsmen may be observed to fondle their offspring" (p. 23). The more normal members of the company are also described as "sisters," "mothers," and "fathers," and the whole group interacts as an extended family. In the following description, for example, family roles are emphasized and the interlocking system of support between families is expressed in the image of the pyramid: "the father of one of the families was in the habit of balancing the father of another of the families on the top of a great pole; the father of a third family often made a pyramid of both those fathers, with Master Kidderminster for the apex, and himself the base" (p. 27). The familial nature of the circus is again stressed when Sleary explains to Sissy Jupe the advantages of staying with the troupe: "Emma Gordon in whothe lap you're a lying at prethent, would be a mother to you and Jothphine would be a thithter to you" (p. 29).

The circus, then, is both a metaphor in itself and the novel's major symbol of fancy, the metaphor-making faculty. The circus master, Sleary, is adept at turning one thing into another. In his most important act of transformation, he helps young Tom escape by turning him into a black servant and then into a country bumpkin. The transforming power of fancy literally saves the Gradgrinds in the end. However, as we have already seen, the Gradgrinds' salvation is full of ambiguity: it entails an illegal act that cuts them off from society, and it disperses and humiliates them. If we look closer at the circus and its illusions, we can see that they, too, are ambiguously presented.[10]

The narrator first describes the circus as a place of harmless but nevertheless ridiculous ostentation, emphasizing the puffery of the playbills:

> [Signor Jupe] was . . . to exhibit "his astounding feat of throwing seventy-five hundredweight in rapid succession backhanded over his head, thus forming a fountain of solid iron in mid-air, a feat never before attempted in this or any other country and which having elicited such rapturous plaudits from enthusiastic throngs it cannot be withdrawn." (P. 9)

Sleary himself is an icon of modern commercialism: "Sleary . . . a stout modern statue with a moneybox at its elbow, in an ecclesiastical niche of early Gothic architecture, took the money." The narrator delights in exposing the circus' illusions, in revealing the often shabby reality behind the fanciful show. Master Kidderminster, the dwarf, is unmasked as he is described:

> Made up with curls, wreaths, wings, white bismuth, and carmine, this hopeful young person soared into so pleasing a Cupid as to constitute the chief delight of the maternal part of the spectators; but in private, where his characteristics were a precocious cutaway coat and an extremely gruff voice, he became the Turf, turfy. (P. 23)

And Kidderminster, like Sleary, is an unabashed mercenary: "If you want to cheek us," he exclaims to Bounderby, "pay your ochre at the doors" (p. 23).

Indeed, the ostentatious puffery of Kidderminster and Sleary closely resembles Mr. Bounderby's boastful lies. When Bounderby and Gradgrind visit the circus people at the Pegasus's Arms, Bounderby repeatedly compares himself to them, and even though he tries to emphasize the differences, the likenesses emerge. In his false description of his own childhood, he declares, "There was no rope-dancing for me; I danced on the bare ground and was larruped with the rope" (p. 20). The image of Bounderby as a circus performer sharpens as the conversation continues, and Kidderminster and Bounderby begin trading insults and blustering at one another. The circus people, professional humbugs themselves, see through Bounderby's show. Bounderby describes himself as a self-made man several times during the scene; and he is, it turns out, a self-made man in the same sense that Kidderminster is a self-made Cupid, for Bounderby, too, makes himself up. There is even an inverted similarity in their most extreme pretenses: Kidderminster pretends to be Childer's son; Bounderby pretends not to be his mother's child.

In the circus, therefore, Fancy and its major mode, the metaphoric transformation, often produce showy illusions that are akin to the self-aggrandizing mendacity depicted in the novel. There are, moreover, other indications in the novel that metaphors, especially metaphors that attempt to disguise an ugly reality, are useless or even pernicious things. When the narrator first asserts that factories look like fairy castles, for example, he immediately casts an ironic reflection on the analogy, attributing it to "travellers by express-train" (p. 49) through the manufacturing districts. Only a distant observer who never stops to investigate the reality of a factory would make the fanciful comparison. It is an outsider's metaphor, a falsification that perpetuates ignorance of a reality that, according to the novel's own statements, needs confronting.

The narrator even creates ambivalence about the worker-child metaphor, implying that it, too, can be a pernicious falsification. He uses the metaphor and simultaneously abuses others for using it; he begins one paragraph:

> Now, besides very many babies just able to walk, there happened to be in Coketown a considerable population of babies who had been walking against time towards the infinite world, twenty, thirty, forty, fifty years and more. These portentous infants being alarming creatures to stalk about in any human society, the eighteen denominations incessantly scratched one another's faces and pulled one another's hair by way of agreeing on the steps to be taken for their improvement. (P. 38)

Even in these opening sentences, where the worker-infant metaphor is apparently the narrator's own, he makes it seem mildly ridiculous. And as the passage proceeds, the practice of seeing workers as babies comes to seem truly destructive, for it authorizes the arrogant pronouncements of Coketown's "eighteen denominations":

> Body number one said they must take everything on trust. Body number two, said they must take everything on political economy. Body number three, wrote leaden little books for them, showing how the good grown-up baby invariably got to the savings-bank, and the bad grown-up baby invariably got transported. (P. 38)

By thus satirizing the worker-infant metaphor, which is itself a *reductio ad absurdum* of the paternalists' worker-child analogy, the narrator ironically undercuts the metaphoric structure of the entire novel.

Although the narrator overtly recommends that the workers' "Lives of machinery and reality" can be "beautified" by the indulgence of "innocent and pretty" fantasies (p. 226), he also hints that "pretty" fantasies about industrial life are seldom really innocent. The metaphors the narrator uses most seriously are those which intensify descriptions of the bleakness and horror of both the workers' and the children's lives. Coketown is alternately a devouring monster with "smokey jaws" and a strangely monotonous jungle in which only two kinds of savage animals perform endlessly repetitive movements: the smokey snakes and the metallic elephants constantly coil and bob; it is, preeminently, the "citadel" of "an unnatural family" in which the very buildings are "shouldering, and trampling, and pressing one another to death" (p. 48). In that other citadel of an "unnatural family," Gradgrind's Stone Lodge, the inmates also torture one another; Gradgrind himself is a ogre, "a monster in a lecturing castle, with Heaven knows how many heads manipulated into one, taking childhood captive, and dragging it into gloomy statistical dens by the hair" (p. 7). "Reason" is the Gradgrinds' "grim Idol, cruel and cold, with its victims bound hand to foot, and its big dumb shape set up with a sightless stare, never to be moved by anything but so many calculated tons of leverage" (p. 151).

These are, indeed, metaphoric transformations, the works of Fancy, and they help uncover an additional, submerged meaning of the word. To fancy something is to desire it, and the narrator's fanciful descriptions of Coketown and the Gradgrinds often depict a world driven by rapacious desires, especially the desires of an incestuous, "unnatural" family. The would-be fathers in the book, the upper-class men, do not neglect their metaphoric children; they try, rather, to consume them. The sexual exploitation of Louisa exposes the sexual anxiety stimulated by the social paternalists' metaphor, for if society is one big family, then fancy and incest are practically inextricable. The metaphors used suggest such destructive connections do not contain the "imaginative graces" prescribed by the narrator to "beautify" reality (p. 226). The kinds of metaphors the narrator explicitly recommends, the fanciful "garden[s] in the stormy ways of this world" (p. 15), prove in practice to be either inappropriate or destructive falsifications. The metaphors that reveal the book's truths, however, reveal its fear of fancy.

Thus, in this novel, where metaphor is an explicit theme, metaphoric connections are actually ambiguously presented. The circus, the "travellers by express-train," and the "eighteen denominations of Coketown" all produce self-interested falsifications, whereas the narrator's own metaphors tend to darken his already gloomy vision of the literal connections among Coketown's inhabitants and to reveal the burden of illicit sexuality carried by the social paternalists' metaphor. In the novel's practice, metaphoric connection never becomes a way of escaping those destructive relationships or converting them into relationships of loving support.

Indeed, the one character in the novel who can bring about positive relationship is the completely literal-minded Sissy Jupe. Since Sissy has long been seen by critics as a mere remnant of the circus left behind in Coketown,[11] it is necessary to establish the fact that she acts as a literal-minded foil to the falsifications of both the circus and Gradgrind's school. Sissy refuses to see one thing in terms of another—not because she is totally unimaginative, but because she insists on the priority of literal relationships. When Sleary offers her the metaphoric family of the circus to replace her lost relationship with her father, she declines it. Preferring to carry out what she believes are her father's intentions, she gives herself instead to the Gradgrind household in the hope that her father will reclaim her there. She stubbornly holds onto the bottle of "nine oils" that her father sent her to buy just before he abandoned her, insisting that if he sent her for it, he must literally have needed it (p. 31). Later in the book, when Sissy discusses her past life, she explains that she alone saw through her father's clownish appearance to the truly shy and pathetic man. The other members of Sleary's circus were taken in by the clown's theatrical persona: "Sometimes they played tricks upon him; but they never knew how he felt them, and shrunk up, when he was alone with me. He was far, far timider than they thought!" (p. 45). Sissy, who is not herself a circus performer, instinctively penetrates the circus' illusions. She tries to cheer her father by reading him *The Arabian Nights*, but her own imagination is far from fantastic: her mind is filled with the literal and the mundane.

Her literal-mindedness, the quality that sets her apart from the circus company, also sets her apart from the products of the Gradgrind school. Sissy is too mired in literal particulars to be able to transform the events of life into generalizations. Her imagination is too literal, for example, to allow for the *figurative* representations of statistics, as we learn when she tells Louisa about her academic failure:

> "And I find (Mr. M'Choakumchild said) that in a given time a hundred thousand persons went to sea on long voyages, and only five hundred of them were drowned or burnt to death. What is the percentage? And I said, Miss"; here Sissy fairly sobbed as confessing with extreme contrition to her greatest error; "I said it was nothing."
> "Nothing, Sissy?"
> "Nothing, Miss—to the relations and friends of the people who were killed." (P. 44)

Sissy's attitude allows us to see that statistics resemble many of the book's other figurative operations which distance and disguise painful realities.[12]

Sissy, moreover, is able to save Louisa not by creating fanciful escapes, but by accepting the ugly reality of the young Mrs. Bounderby's life. Sissy's refusal to be repelled by the unembellished facts of Louisa's life constitutes the whole of the saving action:

> "First, Sissy, do you know what I am? I am so proud, so confused and troubled, so resentful and unjust to everyone and to myself, that everything is stormy, dark, and wicked to me. Does not that repel you?"
> "No!"
> "I am so unhappy, and all that should have made me otherwise is so laid waste, that if I had been bereft of sense this hour, and

instead of being so learned as you think me, had to begin to acquire the simplest truths, I could not want a guide to peace, contentment, honour, all the good of which I am quite devoid, more abjectly than I do. Does not that repel you?"

"No!" (P. 172)

The relationship between Sissy and Louisa is built on this foundation of explicitly stated and accepted facts.

Sissy also uses her literal-mindedness to protect Louisa from James Harthouse. Harthouse tries to evade Sissy's prohibition on his seeing Louisa, but Sissy simply repeats her message, "You may be sure, Sir, you will never see her again as long as you live" (p. 175). Harthouse, the narrator emphasizes, is vanquished by this simple matter-of-factness, by the "child-like ingenuousness with which his visitor spoke, her modest fearlessness, her truthfulness which put all artifice aside, her entire forgetfulness of herself in her earnest quiet holding to the object with which she had come" (pp. 175–76). Similarly, Sissy insists that Harthouse "leave [Coketown] immediately and finally" (p. 177), and none of his artful maneuvers sway her from a strict construction of those words. Harthouse finally follows her instructions to the letter.

For all its talk about fancy, and for all its own metaphors, *Hard Times* finally cannot be said to endorse metaphoric connections. The saving relationships are made by the literal-minded Sissy. Even though we are told on the last page that Sissy provides the workers with "imaginative graces and delights" (p. 226), nothing we know of her makes this a credible claim. We are told in the same sentence, moreover, that Sissy is "holding this course as part of no fantastic vow, or bond, or brotherhood, or sisterhood, or pledge, or covenant, or fancy dress, or fancy fair; but simply as a duty to be done" (pp. 226–27). This description of Sissy's charitable activities constitutes yet another covert negation of the metaphoric activities the book overtly endorses: she does not do them as a member of a metaphoric family (a "brotherhood" or "sisterhood") or as a participant in a fanciful pageant (a "fancy dress, or fancy fair"). Up to its very last page, *Hard Times* is a book that simultaneously flaunts and discredits its metaphoricality, calling into question both the possibility of paternalist reform and the validity of its own narrative practice.

North and South: The Paradoxes of Metonymy

On October 14, 1854, Dickens wrote to his managing editor at *Household Words*: "Mrs. Gaskell's story, so divided, is wearisome in the last degree. It would have scant attraction enough if the casting in Whitefriars had been correct; but thus wire-drawn it is a dreary business."[13] These ill-humored comments about *North and South*, which was then being published serially in *Household Words*, were apparently made after Dickens had read the novel's seventh installment. Since *Hard Times* was just then appearing in a single volume (its serialization in *Household Words* having been completed only two months earlier), it is not surprising that Dickens was unusually annoyed by this particular installment of *North and South*. For the part contains a prominent conversation in which the principal characters use, discuss, and ultimately discard the metaphor that Dickens had used, however ambiguously, at the center of his novel: the family-society analogy in which workers are likened to children and employers to fathers.

Gaskell's characters use the metaphor self-consciously, remarking on both its ambivalence and its limited usefulness. The heroine, Margaret Hale, introduces the analogy to describe the despotic insolence of the masters: "he—that is, my informant,—spoke as if the masters would like their hands to be merely tall, large children—living in the present moment—with a blind unreasoning kind of obedience."[14] With this use of the worker/child comparison, Mr. Thornton, the manufacturer, agrees: "In our infancy we require a wise despotism to govern us. . . . I agree with Miss Hale so far as to consider our people in the condition of children, while I deny that we, the masters, have anything to do with the making or keeping them so" (p. 167). When Margaret's father develops the guiding and nurturing implications of the mataphor, however, Mr. Thornton demurs, insisting that his relationship to his workers must end at the factory gates (p. 168). Margaret and her father are unwilling to allow the despotic authority licensed by the metaphor, while Mr. Thornton denies the social responsibility it entails.

The characters also repeatedly apologize for arguing analogically, and they blame one another for introducing the metaphor. Mr. Hale disclaims the simile even as he uses it: "If I get wrong in my reasoning, recollect, it is you who adopted the analogy" (p. 168). Mr. Thornton concedes his mistake in using the comparison, but he also disowns responsibility for it: "I used the comparison (suggested by Miss Hale) of the position of the master to that of a parent; so I ought not to complain of your turning the simile into a weapon against me" (p. 168). Finally, the characters reject metaphor as a mode of social analysis altogether: "Pray don't go into similes, Margaret," pleads her father at last, "you have led us off once already" (p. 170).

Thus Elizabeth Gaskell's characters consider and reject the metaphor of the social paternalists. The conversation identifies both the analogy's usefulness and its danger: it might make the masters more responsible for the well-being of their workpeople, but the comparison also degrades the workers and could justify arbitrary authority. Once the metaphor has been used to elicit these insights on both sides of the argument, it is discarded completely. The characters agree that the familial metaphor, one of limited usefulness, is too likely to "lead us off."

North and South, therefore, explicitly rejects metaphors in general and the family-society metaphor in particular. This novel connects the private and public spheres metonymically, following the recipe for social reform suggested by such domestic ideologues as Sarah Ellis. The one proposition that all participants in the conversation described above can agree to is Margaret's claim that "the most proudly independent man depends on those around him for their insensible influence on his character—his life" (p. 169). "Influence" is the key term in *North and South*, just as it is in Sarah Ellis's *Mothers of England* (1843), which is subtitled, *Their Influence and Responsibility*.[15] John Thornton agrees with Margaret that the topic under consideration should be how one is "influenced by others, and not by circumstances" (p. 170). This emphasis on the influence of others, as opposed to the influence of circumstances, is precisely what distinguishes *North and South* from Gaskell's earlier industrial novel *Mary Barton*. And in treating its topic, *North and South* follows Sarah Ellis's domestic treatise, trying to illustrate Thornton's contention that the strongest interpersonal influence is that which works "indirectly" (p. 170), through actions rather than words.[16]

In *North and South*, as in *Mothers of England*, the moral influence women indirectly exert on men is said to be the force connecting public and private life. The moral influence of an ethically scrupulous woman is at the center of Gaskell's novel. Margaret Hale is a woman who applies a single standard of behavior to both private relations and the relations between the classes. In *North and South* the spheres of the family and of trade and production are not connected through the kind of metaphoric structural symmetry that Dickens attempts in *Hard Times*, where fathers and children serve as analogues for employers and workers. In Gaskell's novel the private and public spheres are associated through their integration in Margaret Hale's life and through her influence over the manufacturer John Thornton.

The novel's emphasis on the moral influence of women leads to one of its most obvious points of contrast with *Hard Times*. The father-daughter relationship serves Dickens as a metaphor for the master-worker relationship; Gaskell, in contrast, uses the relationship between mothers and sons to illustrate the profound effect that women have on men's social behavior. Dickens' book emphasizes the role of fathers; Gaskell's stresses the role of mothers. Much of the plot of *North and*

South turns on the relationships Mrs. Hale and Mrs. Thornton have with their sons, and several of the characters' comments highlight the social importance of mothers. Indeed, on one occasion the familial metaphor is used to express a belief in social maternalism. Justifying her initial antagonism toward John Thornton, Margaret charges him with "professing to despise people for careless, wasteful improvidence, without ever seeming to think it his duty to try to make them different—to give them anything of the training which his mother gave him, and to which he evidently owes his position" (p. 128). The implication is clear: Margaret believes Mr. Thornton should be a mother to his workmen; he should give them the same kind of moral training his mother gave him. Moreover, although Margaret, a mere daughter, is the moral center of the book, her power is described as that of a mother. For example, when Mr. Thornton expresses his feelings of love and admiration for Margaret, he willfully transforms her into a second mother:

> I choose to believe that I owe my very life to you—ay—smile—, and think it an exaggeration if you will. I believe it, because it adds a value to that life to think . . . circumstances so wrought, that whenever I exult in existence henceforward, I may say to myself, "All this gladness in life, all honest pride in doing my work in the world, all this keen sense of being, I owe to her!" (P. 253)

Her ability to supplant Mr. Thornton's mother, like her ability to change roles with her own mother, is proof of Margaret's moral elevation.

We will see that this novel's emphasis on female influence also allows for a more cohesive industrial narrative than does *Hard Times*. *North and South*, however, is not perfectly coherent. Like Dickens's novel, Gaskell's displays the contradictions inherent in both its informing ideology and its genre. We will discover that this novel finally implies a break between the two spheres. Moreover, it creates uncertainty about the source of women's influence, casting doubt on the moral nature of that influence and thereby calling into question one of this novel's central precepts: social reform depends on private ethics. Finally, we will see that the novel questions the literary practice of metonymy itself, the normal method of signification in realistic fiction, by demonstrating that outward signs (one's actions and words as well as one's possessions) are indecipherable or even misleading during periods of rapid cultural change.

North and South, then, displays elisions and contradictions, but it displays them less prominently than does *Hard Times*. Superficially,

Gaskell's novel is more associative and also more coherent than that of Dickens, for the metonymic method of connecting the social and familial concerns of the novel allows Gaskell a greater freedom than that provided by Dickens's analogy to develop and integrate both social and familial themes. And because the author does not try to maintain an analogy between children and workers, she need not look for a common source of oppression. Instead of focusing on issues like the lack of fancy in industrial society, she can introduce specifically working-class issues, such as low wages, bad housing, and trade unionism. She need not describe the two spheres only in relation to one another, selecting details with an eye to the organizing metaphor. The families in the novel need not be either positive or negative models; they can be portrayed as mixtures of good and bad characteristics. Nor need workers themselves be infantilized; they can, indeed, be depicted as strong fathers. Similarly, northern manufacturers need not be simplistically portrayed as "bad fathers" but may be shown as men with the capacity to struggle and grow. In short, the industrial world need not seem a jungle of destructive relationships that must all be severed before the work of social reconstruction can begin. Finally, the author need not maintain a separation of her plots, developing each independently lest the interaction destroy the isomorphic structure implied in the family-society metaphor. Indeed, metonymy assumes the literal proximity of the things it connects; the plots of *North and South* are interwoven from the outset, and they remain interwoven at the end. Hence, the impulse toward separation is not as strong in *North and South* as it is in *Hard Times*. Gaskell's novel makes looser but also more flexible and lasting connections than those made in *Hard Times*.

Gaskell creates the impression of coherence in *North and South* and articulates the metonymic relationship between society and family through her use of Margaret Hale to control the novel's point of view, through comparing public and private plot episodes while concentrating on ethical dilemmas common to both spheres, and, finally, through making Margaret and John Thornton actual representatives of the English upper classes, thereby endowing their marriage with practical social consequences. These devices allow her to intertwine her social and familial themes and plots so thoroughly that the very conventional resolution of the novel's love plot appears to be a partial solution to industrial social problems.

We will see, however, that the novel provides its own counters to these associative techniques. We are repeatedly given other versions of the action as well, versions that are foreign to Margaret's point of view. Some of these other viewpoints, moreover, subvert the assumptions shared by Margaret and the narrator and undo the carefully constructed connections between the public good and ethically correct private behavior. Indeed, as we survey Gaskell's integrating techniques, we will see that the novel provides a running ironic commentary on its official ideas.

Gaskell integrates the social and familial issues by filtering both through the scrupulously ethical, if somewhat immature, mind of Margaret Hale. The point of view of the novel is only slightly distinct from Margaret's consciousness. The narrator has access to other minds, particularly to Mr. Thornton's, but Margaret's mental processes are the primary subject of the book. The narrator in *North and South* seldom tries to stand back and generalize, let alone to articulate such grand metaphoric syntheses as the narrator of *Hard Times* attempted. The connections made in *North and South* are those made by the characters themselves, primarily by Margaret. Social and familial issues, therefore, are first related associatively through their simultaneous presence in Margaret's mind.

In addition, the issues are integrated by Margaret's insistence on applying a single ethical standard to questions of both public and private behavior. In fact, Gaskell uses Margaret's origins in a southern rural parsonage to explain her critical distance from the two types of conventional urban morality she encounters in London and the industrial city Milton-Northern. As Margaret moves through the novel's social territories (Helstone, London, and Milton), she struggles to maintain her moral bearings. Her personal choices, particularly her choice of a husband, depend on her ability to confront the "foreign" social systems, to modify her own ethical code, and yet to maintain her moral integrity.

The implied author, by establishing her narrative vantage point in this heroine's mind, presents her social criticism as a natural byproduct of the working out of Margaret's personal destiny. Margaret's habit of ethical scrutiny is what ostensibly makes her an ideal woman. Her moral consciousness happened to be nurtured in her father's country parsonage, but it is precisely the kind of consciousness that domestic theorists encouraged all women to develop. It is supposed to give Margaret her peculiarly female influence over others, and links the public and private realms of existence in action as well as in consciousness. Margaret is full of the moral courage that Sarah Ellis described as women's most important attribute, "without which they are incapable of working out any lasting good by their influence over others."[17] Because Margaret insists on applying the moral standards of personal relations (charity, patience, sympathy, cooperation) to the relations between strangers and between classes, she supposedly becomes a paragon in the eyes of two representative Milton men, Higgins (the weaver and trade union leader) and Thornton (the rich manufacturer). In fact, it is partly through Margaret's influence that these two men are ultimately able to achieve a cooperative relationship.

In the world of *North and South*, however, it is not easy to achieve moral clarity. The story of Margaret's influence does not form a rectilinear narrative pointing directly to social harmony. Unlike Dickens's social solution—which finally is little more than the multiplication of havens of temporary emotional respite from industrial reality—Gaskell's ethical alternative, which might actually change that reality, requires the depiction of a morally complex world. Margaret can achieve and maintain her influence only if, first, she has a consistent and realistic set of beliefs about how people should interact and, second, she expresses those beliefs in words and actions intelligible to others. The action of the novel revolves around Margaret's difficulty in meeting both of these requirements.

By contrasting two major plot episodes, one public and the other private, Gaskell articulates the ethical dilemmas of modern society and tries to illustrate what Margaret firmly believes: that a single standard of conduct in both spheres will guarantee the exemplary action upon which woman's influence rests. The meaning of these episodes, however, is ambiguous, for Margaret's actions are not understood by Mr. Thornton, her most significant observer, and yet her influence over him continues to grow.

The first episode, in which Margaret is forced into public action by circumstances, climaxes in the riot at Thornton's mill and includes Margaret's attempts to keep peace, the misinterpretation of her actions, and Thornton's proposal of marriage. The second climaxes in the confrontation between Margaret's mutineer brother, Frederick Hale, and Leonards, a man who tries to capture Frederick and turn him over to the authorities. This episode includes Margaret's interview with the police inspector, in which she tells a lie to save her brother, and Mr. Thornton's discovery of her lie.

In the first episode, Margaret is personally disinterested, because in urging Thornton to face the rioters and then in braving them herself to save Thornton, she acts out of an abstract sense of justice. She is, consequently, deeply mortified when observers misinterpret her action as an expression of love for Mr. Thornton, but she is also consoled by the knowledge that she adhered to her own standards of justice and womanly conduct. "Oh how low I am fallen that they should say that of me!" soliloquizes Margaret when she realizes how her action had been misread:

> It was not fair . . . that he should stand there—sheltered, awaiting the soldiers, who might catch those poor maddened creatures as

in a trap—without an effort on his part, to bring them to reason. And it was worse than unfair for them to set on him as they threatened. I would do it again, let who will say what they like of me. If I saved one blow, one cruel, angry action that might otherwise have been committed, *I did woman's work.* Let them insult my maiden pride as they will—I walk pure before God! (P. 247; emphasis added)

Margaret's action on this occasion, both practical and exemplary, is intended to influence others, but its impact is blocked by the moral blindness of those who witness it. The private-public disjunction is so automatically accepted by Mrs. Thornton and her servants that they are incapable of associating a generous act with an impersonal motive. Their uncomprehending gaze haunts Margaret after the riot, causing "a sense of shame so acute that it seemed as if she would fain have burrowed into the earth to hide herself, and yet she could not escape out of that unwinking glare of many eyes" (p. 249).

This misunderstanding alone implies that in Milton it might be impossible for Margaret or any other women to exert her moral influence for the public good. Thornton's reaction to Margaret's behavior, moreover, further undercuts the novel's assumption that women sway men through their moral power. Thornton does not actually misinterpret Margaret's action; rather, he fails to interpret it altogether. He is not sure whether her embrace was motivated by some lofty ideal or by fondness for him. His feeling for her is the same in either case, and it has little to do with a correct apprehension of her moral character: "Everything seemed dim and vague beyond—behind—besides the touch of her arms around his neck—the soft clinging which made the dark colour come and go in his cheek as he thought of it" (p. 244).

This is the sensation that binds Thornton to Margaret, and ultimately binds the public and personal areas of the plot.[18] Margaret contemptuously repulses Thornton's proposal of marriage:

> You seem to fancy that my conduct of yesterday . . . was a personal act between you and me; and that you may come and thank me for it, instead of perceiving, as a gentleman would . . . that any woman, worthy of the name of woman, would come forward to shield, with her reverenced helplessness, a man in danger from the violence of numbers. (P. 253)

The revelation of this impersonal motive wounds Thornton, but it does not alter his feeling for Margaret.[19] He continues to love her, not because he has come to understand her, but because she remains mysterious:

> He could not . . . shake off the recollection that she had been
> there; that her arms had been round him, once—if never again.
> He only caught glimpses of her; he did not understand her
> altogether. At one time she was so brave, and at another so timid;
> now so tender, and then so haughty and regal-proud. (P. 268)

His love has immediate social repercussion—he refuses to press
charges against the rioters—but they cannot be attributed to Margaret's moral power.

Indeed, throughout the book we are given these two perspectives on
the relationship between the private and public realms. Margaret tends
to turn all issues, even the most personal, into questions of abstract
morality. This tendency is one that we saw fully realized in the domestic
magazine tales, where private territory was often completely colonized
by social considerations, and strictly personal or romantic motives were
abolished. In *North and South*, though, Thornton checks this tendency.
For him, personal relations are not ethical bonds but emotional ties. In
a sense, he represents an opposite tendency within domestic ideology,
one that stresses the nonjudgmental, all-accepting nature of family
love.[20] Until the end of the book, Margaret subjects her own behavior to
ethical scrutiny, afraid that she might lose Thornton's regard. Thornton's actual feelings about her, however, are an ironic comment on her
fears and their assumptions, for he continues to love her even when he
comes to doubt her moral purity.

The second of the book's two parallel plot episodes, that dealing with
Frederick Hale's visit and its aftermath, illustrates the distance between
Margaret's viewpoint and Thornton's. This part of the plot is narrated
primarily from Margaret's perspective, and the narrator apparently
shares the heroine's assumptions about the relationship between public
and private conduct. The incident at Thornton's mill and her brother's
mutiny involve similar ethical issues for Margaret. In the first incident,
she believes that Thornton is exercising his authority in an unreasonable and even brutal manner. While she does not condone the actions
of the rioting strikers, she sympathizes with their misery and understands their rebellion:

> "Mr. Thornton," said Margaret, shaking all over with her pas-
> sion, "go down this instant, if you are not a coward. Go down and
> face them like a man. . . . Speak to them kindly. Don't let the
> soldiers come in and cut down poor creatures who are driven
> made." (P. 232)

The same hatred of imperious authority leads her to justify her
brother's mutiny. Unlike Louisa Gradgrind, who supports her brother

simply because he is her brother, Margaret judges her brother and his captain by the same criteria she uses to judge the rioters and Mr. Thornton. Her brother's rebellion seems nobler than the strikers' riot, just as Captain Reid's rule was crueler than Mr. Thornton's, but the same issues of authority, justice, and mercy unite the two acts of defiance. In summing up her brother's case, Margaret declares, "Loyalty and obedience to wisdom and justice are fine; but it is still finer to defy arbitrary power, unjustly and cruelly used" (p. 154). This is not the novel's final word on the issues of authority and rebellion; no good comes of either the mutiny or the riot, and it is significant that Frederick must remain banished from England. Nevertheless, Margaret's protection of her brother, more than an act of sisterly solidarity, is an act of conscience. It is also another instance of her habit of attaching abstract ethical judgments to personal relationships.

In her interview with the police inspector, however, Margaret discovers that protecting Frederick entails a violation of another section of her ethical code. Her moral courage fails her, and she gives in to the temptation to lie, denying that she had been at the railway station the previous evening. This lie subsequently causes her immense mental suffering, and its discovery by Mr. Thornton increases her mortification. Once again her actions are misinterpreted, but she cannot console herself with self-righteousness. In justifying her action at Thornton's mill, she tells herself that she "did it because it was right, and simple, and true to save where she could save; even to try to save. 'Fais ce que dois, advienne que pourra'" (p. 257). But after her deceitful behavior, she can only condemn herself: "Where now was her proud motto, 'Fais ce que dois, advienne que pourra'? If she had but dared to tell the truth . . . how light of heart she would now have felt" (p. 358).

Margaret's lie assumes enormous significance in the novel; indeed, it is made into the central ethical problem. Margaret blames herself and is blamed by the narrator for failing to adhere in her private life to the same moral code that informed her public actions. The narrator drives the point of this inconsistency home repeatedly:

> She remembered—she then strong in her own untempted truth—asking [Thornton], if he did not think that buying in the cheapest and selling in the dearest market proved some want of the transparent justice which is so intimately connected with the idea of truth: and she had used the word chivalric—and her father had corrected her with the higher word, Christian . . . while she sat silently by with a slight feeling of contempt.
> No more contempt for her!—no more talk about the chivalric! Henceforward she must feel humiliated and disgraced in his sight. (P. 378)

The heroine and the narrator both seem to believe that Margaret has lost her right to question the ethics of industrial society because she has failed to maintain her private moral integrity. Therefore, by contrasting the two plot episodes, the novel tries to show that a woman's social influence depends upon her ability to maintain a consistent ethical code and to teach that code through her example.

In fact, however, the man who represents industrial society in this book does not really care whether or not Margaret has told a lie to save her brother. Indeed, he is relieved when he finds that she has, for he suspected her of a more serious fault, of secretly meeting a lover. He is tortured by this suspicion, moreover, not because it suggests that Margaret is immoral but because it implies she loves someone else. Thornton completely subordinates the ethical to the personal emotional issue:

> It was this that made the misery—that he passionately loved her, and thought her, even with all her faults, more lovely and more excellent than any other woman; yet he deemed her so attached to some other man, so led away by her affection for him, as to violate her truthful nature. The very falsehood that stained her, was proof how blindly she loved another. (P. 387)

Once again, Thornton's feelings for Margaret are not dependent on his moral judgment of her.

Social progress in this part of the novel proceeds, moreover, almost independently of Margaret's influence. It is Margaret who sends Higgins to Thornton for work, but Thornton is not at first aware of that fact. He hires the unemployed weaver because he finds Higgins to be generous and honest. Indeed, Thornton is annoyed when he learns that Margaret interfered: "he dreaded the admission of any thought of her, as a motive to what he was doing solely because it was right" (p. 404). Thus, the connections made by paralleling these two plot episodes—connections between a woman's private ethics, her moral influence, and the social actions of the men around her—are unmade by the revelation of Thronton's actual thoughts and motives. Contrary to one set of assumptions of the domestic ideologists, Thornton's love for Margaret, his moral judgment of her, and his treatment of his workmen are three disconnected phenomena.

But this undercurrent of private-public dissociation is subsequently obscured by the ending's successful integration of the love plot with the novel's social issues. Thornton's attitude toward his workmen undergoes a change that the narrator hints is due to Margaret's indirect effort: "He and they had led parallel lives—very close, but never touching—till the accident (or so it seemed) of his acquaintance with Higgins" (p. 511). And when the two lovers meet in London, Thornton reports his improved relations with his workmen to Margaret as if he had developed them, at least in part, with her opinion in mind (p. 526). To complete the circle of public-private reciprocity, Gaskell has Higgins redeem Margaret in Thornton's eyes, reopening the possibility of their marriage and further intertwining the love plot with Margaret's and Thornton's social roles.

The conventional "happy ending" of this novel is used to strengthen the metonymic connection between private and public life. Gaskell invests the marraige with both practical and symbolic social significance. It gives Thornton the financial independence to continue his experiments in industrial relations. Indeed, these experiments themselves are a further step toward the interpenetration of the private and public spheres, as Mr. Thornton explains:

> I have arrived at the conviction that no mere institutions, however wise, and however much thought may have been required to organize and arrange them, can attach class to class as they should be attached, unless the working out of such institutions bring the individuals of the different classes into actual personal contact. (P. 525)

Margaret's habit of taking a personal interest in individual members of the working class has become one of Thornton's management practices, a practice that Margaret's inheritance allows him to continue. In fact, unlike Dickens's idea of personal contact between the classes, which he largely restricts to leisure time, Gaskell's idea actually calls for cooperative industrial planning, a minor transformation of class relationships in the workplace itself.[21] The private solution in *North and South* does not entail a retreat from social responsibility; rather, it is a solution that clears away practical barriers to social harmony.

Finally, the marriage represents a new unity of purpose between the upper classes. Margaret and Thornton have respectively represented the aristocratic south and the manufacturing north from the outset of their acquaintance. In the course of their relationship, each loses the destructive element in his or her outlook: Margaret is chastened out of her prejudice against "shoppy" middle-class people, and Thornton outgrows the extreme individualism and willfulness that had blinded him to his social responsibilities. But both retain the positive aspects of their class and regional characteristics: Margaret remains the embodiment of such "chivalric" virtues as self-sacrifice and charity, while Thornton's integrity and industry are only increased by his new con-

cern for the well-being of his workers. At the end of the novel, however, Margaret represents the landed and Thornton the manufacturing interest in a new sense, for Margaret actually owns the land under
Thornton's mill.[22] Margaret and Thornton metonymically stand for
the English upper classes, with their two kinds of power; they represent the best of their respective classes, standing in their typical economic relationship to one another. Their marriage, therefore, is a
symbolic type of the solidarity that should exist between England's
upper classes, and it is the final instance of Elizabeth Gaskell's metonymic method of linking the social and familial spheres.

Gaskell combines her social and familial resolutions so successfully
that we almost forget that the whole structure is based on the initial and
enduring separation of the public and private spheres. The source and
nature of Margaret's power remain, as we have seen, mysterious, but
even if we accept Margaret's belief that her power is primarily moral, a
deep gulf remains between her own private world and the industrial
society she encounters. If Margaret's power derives from her moral
consciousness, it has developed in isolation from contemporary society.
Helstone, her home, represents not only the rural south, with its
mixture of quaintness and poverty, but also an enclave where all social
relationships are personal: a large, isolated family. The Margaret Hale
formed in this isolation, with her simple honesty and her quaint femininity, has a power to charm and to change John Thornton that no
woman created by his own social reality could possess. The Thorntons
repeatedly call Margaret a stranger (pp. 141, 214, 393), and indeed,
according to this novel and to the ideology that informs it, all women
must be strangers to the industrial society they seek to reform. The
principal authors of the domestic ideal all insisted that women maintain their moral superiority only by their confinement in the home,
their isolation from the marketplace; and this insistence on isolation
leads back toward the idea that society and the family are irrevocably
opposed. This metonymic method of connecting the public and private
spheres, like the social paternalists' metaphor, paradoxically depends
on their separation. The novel's solution hides but does not resolve this
basic dilemma.

The novel introduces a further complication within domestic ideology by presenting Thornton's view of Margaret's power. In fact, the
book does not consistently present the family as an ethical enclave, a
territory that can or should serve as a school for social reform. Personal
bonds in this book are not developed by the faculty of moral judgment;
rather, they are the products of chance emotional and sensual encounters. They are mysterious, irrational, and adventitious; consequently,

they are far too incalculable to be counted on as the basis of social reform. Thornton's feelings for Margaret are irreducibly personal phenomena, untouched by ethical or social considerations. His feelings may have social consequences, but such consequences are quite unpredictable.

In *North and South* the metonymic link between public and private twists and slackens as the novel contradicts itself about the nature of private life. At times the book holds out hope that the public and private spheres can be purposefully associated, as they are in didactic domestic tales; at other times, their association seems random and uncontrollable. Thus, this novel repeatedly questions both the logic and the value of the relationship it tries to illustrate.

Indeed, just as *Hard Times* suggests that metaphors are often inappropriate, useless, or even dangerous, *North and South* questions the logic and value of making metonymic connections. *North and South* is partly a book *about* metonymy because it is a book about the difficulty of interpreting the surfaces of reality, of finding the meaning of objects, words, and actions. The process of association by which characters in *North and South* make meaning is shown to be illogical, capricious, culturally biased, and at times dangerously erroneous. And yet, metonymic association is the very process by which the novel itself creates meanings.

Like most practitioners of realistic fiction, Gaskell delineates characters and situations by giving eloquent, superficial details of dress, gesture, stature, bearing, behavior. We know the details are significant because they are given; we know we are to read the description of a face as a description of character. In the opening chapters, for example, we know that Margaret's unconventional beauty expresses an unconventional spirit, that her height bespeaks heroism, and that her "rich red lips" are a token of passionate impulsiveness. We also know that she is active in the household and therefore virtuous and industrious. In these opening chapters we can determine most of what we need to know about characters from such descriptions of their faces, bodies, clothes, and occupations. As in most realistic fiction, all of the details fit together in a pattern of conventional associations that writer and reader share. The book begins with the assumption that a home, a dress, a feature, a profession can represent a character, that the surface of life is a system of comprehensible signs.

Very soon, however, the novel subtly begins to undermine these assumptions. When Margaret's father abruptly changes his occupation, the novel enters a world in which the meaning of life's surfaces is not always clear, in which objects are randomly and mistakenly associated with characteristics and emotions they do not represent. In a sense, then, the novel becomes a covert criticism of its own metonymic narrative mode.

The most subtle form of this criticism is contained in the novel's associative style, for Gaskell strives for a kind of psychological realism that exposes the arbitrariness of the way individuals find meaning in objects. She does so, moreover, at precisely the point in the narrative where Mr. Hale's decision to quit the parsonage calls agreed-upon social meanings into question. As Margaret prepares to enter an unfamiliar world, she clings to the old parsonage, gathering "associations"—private meanings—from object after object:

> Margaret went along the walk under the pear-tree wall. She had never been along it since she paced it at Henry Lennox's side. Here, at this bed of thyme, he began to speak of what she must not think of now. Her eyes were on that late-blowing rose as she was trying to answer: and she had caught the idea of the vivid beauty of the feathery leaves of the carrots in the very middle of his sentence. (P. 89)

The connections made here between the garden plants and Henry Lennox's proposal are neither prefabricated metonymic connections (like that between the occupation of clergyman and moral rectitude) that would be generally understood nor metaphoric connections that depend on some objective characteristic shared by the object and the idea it evokes. They are, rather, purely private associations based on happenstance, the coincidence of Margaret's perception of the plants and her perception of Lennox's proposal of marriage.

As the novel proceeds and social meanings become increasingly difficult to fix upon, the author relies more and more heavily on these private, arbitrary associations. Indeed, the novel hints, in a manner anticipating Proust, that these completely relative and accidental associations are the strongest and the most definitive. Mrs. Hale's maid, Dixon, is seen to be bound to her mistress by the association in the servant's mind between her mistress and a casual act of kindness; Dixon explains her affection for her employer in a digressive, associative sentence:

> "Ever since Lady Beresford's maid first took me in to see her dressed out in white crepe and corn-ears, and scarlet poppies, and I ran a needle down into my finger, and broke it in, and she tore up her worked pocket-handkershief, after they'd cut it out, and came in to wet the bandages again with lotion when she

returned from the ball—where she'd been the prettiest young
lady of all—I've never loved any one like her." (P. 178)

And in one of the book's most moving interchanges, Mrs. Thornton
agrees to befriend Margaret, not because she sympathizes with the
dying Mrs. Hale, but because her emotions are touched by an
accidental association of object and idea:

> And it was no thought of her son, or of her living daughter Fanny
> that stirred her heart at last; but a sudden remembrance, sug-
> gested by something in the arrangement of the room,—of a little
> daughter—dead in infancy—long years ago—that, like a sudden
> sunbeam, melted the icy crust, behind which there was a real
> tender woman. (P. 306)

These are the illogical and wholly subjective significances that actually motivate people in *North and South*. Like John Thornton's love, the
lasting metonymic associations in *North and South* are irrational and
capricious as well as indecipherable to others. The book thus suggests a
kind of anarchy of signification, and the sense of anarchy is reinforced
by the way the book dwells on the difficulties that northerners and
southerners have in understanding one another. We have already seen
that Margaret's most public action is misunderstood by Mrs. Thornton
and her servant; moreover, almost everything else about Margaret is
misinterpreted in Milton. Even her looks are now said to misrepresent
her character, or to distort it by exaggerating one aspect:

> Margaret could not help her looks; but the short curled upper lip,
> the round, massive up-turned chin, the manner of carrying her
> head, her movements, full of a soft feminine defiance, always
> gave strangers the impression of haughtiness. (P. 100)

And Mrs. Thornton reads negative, mistaken meanings into nearly
everything she encounters in the Hales' small establishment:

> Margaret was busy embroidering a small piece of cambric for
> some little article of dress for Edith's expected baby—"flimsy,
> useless work," as Mrs. Thornton observed to herself. She liked
> Mrs. Hale's double knitting far better; that was sensible of its
> kind. The room altogether was full of knick-knacks, which must
> take a long time to dust; and time to people of limited income was
> money. (P. 139)

Even Higgins, who can generally "read [Margaret's] proud bonny face like a book," initially fails to comprehend her friendly intentions. When Margaret asks his name, he gives it, but then wonders, "Whatten yo' asking for?"

> Margaret [the narrator continues] was surprised at this last question, for at Helstone it would have been an understood thing, after the inquiries she had made, that she intended to come and call upon any poor neighbor whose name and habitation she had asked for. (Pp. 112–13)

Now, in this new cultural context, she hardly understands her own behavior; "It seemed all at once to take the shape of an impertinence on her part; she read this meaning too in the man's eyes" (p. 113).

But just as the Hales are being misread in Milton, they are also misreading. The things that Mrs. Hale thinks are always tokens of old families and good breeding—old lace, for example, and sumptuous dinners—are merely tokens of wealth in Milton, where they can be bought by any rich manufacturer. Furthermore, because Margaret and her mother think of John Thornton as a "tradesman," they are very surprised to learn of his importance in the town. Margaret must unlearn the prefabricated association between trade and vulgarity before she can properly perceive Thornton for what he is. The point is emphasized during Frederick's visit, when the narrator juxtaposes Margaret's early impressions of Mr. Thornton with her later knowledge of him. Frederick, catching a glimpse of Thornton, wonders "Who could it have been? Some of the shopmen?" (p. 323). When Margaret finds out this "shopman" is Thornton, she is surprised but also unable to explain why Frederick is mistaken:

> "I fancied you meant some one of a different class, not a gentleman; somebody come on an errand."
>
> "He looked like some one of that kind," said Frederick, carelessly. I took him for a shopman, and he turns out a manufacturer."
>
> Margaret was silent. She remembered how at first, before she knew his character, she had spoken and thought of him just as Frederick was doing. It was but a natural impression that was made upon him, and yet she was a little annoyed by it. She was unwilling to speak; she wanted to make Frederick understand what kind of person Mr. Thornton was—but she was tongue-tied. (P. 324)

Margaret reflects that the impression is "natural," and yet the incident shows that Frederick's judgment of Thornton from the latter's appearance is culturally produced, not "natural" at all. Such socially sanctioned associations, the novel tells us, are culturally relative and untrustworthy, especially in times of rapid social change.[23]

The novel itself is supposed to provide an overview that transcends these partial, time-bound, and chaotic modes of signification by uniting north and south in the marriage of Thornton and Margaret. And yet, skepticism about the possibility of arriving at such an "objective" overview pervades the book, bringing with it a longing for constancy. Margaret, on her last visit to Helstone, continues to struggle with the conviction that she has lost Thornton's good opinion and cannot console herself with the idea that there is some static reality unchanged by the misinterpretations of others: "She tried to comfort herself with the idea, that what he imagined her to be, did not alter the fact of what she was. But it was a truism, a phantom, and broke down under the weight of her regret" (pp. 487–88). Linking the misinterpretation of her Milton behavior with the changes she sees all around her at Helstone, she begins to look beyond this life for an absolutely static and therefore meaningful world:

> A sense of change, of individual nothingness, of perplexity and disappointment, overpowered Margaret. Nothing had been the same; and this slight, all-pervading instability, had given her greater pain than if all had been too entirely changed for her to recognize it.
> "I begin to understand now what heaven must be—and, oh! the grandeur and repose of the words—"The same yesterday, today, and forever." (P. 488)

The narrator tells us, however, that such constancy, which would end all "perplexity and disappointment," is not for the living.

Indeed, *North and South* ends with the recognition that Margaret's marriage to Thornton will itself be incomprehensible in both the north and the south, the still wholly separate worlds of the novel. In the last lines of the book, Margaret asks Thornton:

> ". . . but what will [Aunt Shaw] say?"
> "I can guess. Her first exclamation will be, "That man!""
> "Hush!" said Margaret, "or I shall try and show you your mother's indignant tones as she says, "That woman!"" (P. 530)

At the very moment when the novel achieves its metonymic substitution of the family for society, it ironically implies that the meaning of the marriage will be lost on the observers, who are still blinded by conventional metonymic associations.

North and South, like *Hard Times*, is a novel that strains against its own narrative mode. It not only questions the ethical connection that Margaret believes in between the public and private realms, but also comments skeptically on the possibility of metonymic representation in a time of rapid cultural change. The novel creates a longing for a realm of absolute significance and unchanging values, the realm Margaret perpetually strives toward, but it repeatedly credits purely subjective, emotional, and preconscious meanings, meanings that are wholly fortuitous and involve their own kind of isolation. In fact, the meanings it most often discards are the conventional metonymic associations on which realism actually relies, the meanings sanctioned by tradition and usage. These are the connections that Aunt Shaw and Mrs. Thornton make, the connections the book tells us we must all learn to unmake so that some deeper bond between people might be discovered. The lesson that Clarissa Harlowe teaches in this chapter's first epigraph is, thus, illustrated in *North and South*, where "relationship remembered" always entails "relationship forgot."

The epigraph, in turn, reminds us that the question of how narrative should connect the public and private realms of experience is at least as old as the form of the novel itself. The debate over industrialism, however, caused the issue to be emphasized in the works of both social critics and fiction writers trying to point the way to social cohesion. The result is a group of fictions written expressly to illustrate the right relationship between the family and society, fictions which put that relationship prominently in the foreground of their concerns. The magazine stories among these fictions deal with the connection in conventional and superficial ways: they set out to be simple illustrations of popular ideologies, and they largely succeed by glancing over the contradictions in the systems of thought that inform them. *Hard Times* and *North and South*, however, examine the available connections between the public and private spheres in ways that expose contradictions in the ideologies they use as well as the tensions in their narrative methods.

Part Three
Facts Versus Values

8

The Politics of Representation and the Representation of Politics in the 1840s

The disjunction between the ethics of the marketplace and those of the family can be viewed as one manifestation of a discontinuity between facts and values. To both the social paternalists and the domestic ideologists, the market was the domain of facts (what is) and the family that of values (what ought to be). Both groups tended to equate the marketplace with the whole public world, thereby relegating nonmarket values to the private world of the family, which became a normative contrast to society.

Many other nineteenth-century thinkers, however, refused to relinquish the possibility of disinterested and self-sacrificing public action. Two of the most important industrial novels, Benjamin Disraeli's *Sybil* and George Eliot's *Felix Holt*, should be read within the context of these efforts to keep the idea of the public from being reduced to that of the marketplace. The novels are widely separated in time. Disraeli's was published during the Chartist agitation of the 1840s, and Eliot's was published just after the passage of the Second Reform Bill in 1867–68. However, they participate in one debate, the debate over the franchise, and they draw on a single tradition of thought about representation that persists throughout the nineteenth century. Even though it requires a departure from the chronological arrangement of this study, therefore, these two political novels will be analyzed here as parts of a continuous discourse.

Both novels rely upon a complicated tradition of philosophical-political thought that finds its earliest nineteenth-century articulation in the writings of S. T. Coleridge. Coleridge's writing can help us to understand two important characteristics of the general discourse surrounding industrialism. The first is the often-noted fact that industrial reform and political conservatism frequently went hand in hand. Because his philosophical system led him to hope for social regeneration through the agency of an autonomous government, a government that was not the simple reflection of social forces, Coleridge opposed both liberal and radical Parliamentary reformers. He believed that if the state were to become merely one more arena for competition among social and economic groups, the political marketplace recommended by liberal theorists, the idea of the public good would then become indistinguishable from the desires of the most numerous enfranchised group. Values would be equated with mere facts; "what is" would overcome "what ought to be." From this philosophical position, Coleridge opposed the First Reform Bill. He thought it would make Parliament a mirror image of the economic realm, a place where the representatives of each social class struggle to attain the upper hand. By eschewing this model of politics, Coleridge believed he was keeping channels open to that transcendent reality from which meaning flows. This seminal political thinker forged an important theoretical link, therefore, between antidemocratic ideas and visions of social regeneration, a link that is strong in those industrial novels that deal extensively with politics.

The second characteristic illuminated by Coleridge's political thought is less obvious than the first but perhaps more consequential for English literature. Coleridge articulated an internal connection between politics and those other activities that are preeminently concerned with making and recovering meaning: writing and reading. He assimilated the activities of statesmanship and literature into a single hermeneutic enterprise, which he unified by a concept of symbolic representation.

Coleridge was only one of a number of nineteenth-century writers concerned with the relationship between political and literary representation. Carlyle and Disraeli in the 1830s and 1840s and Matthew Arnold and George Eliot in the 1860s were all, in varying degrees, attracted to Coleridge's Idealist version of that relationship, his contention that true representation of any kind is always symbolic. This is not to say that all of the later thinkers accepted Coleridge's definition of symbolic representation or even that they always consciously attempted to subordinate both literary and political representation to some overarching idea of representation in general. But it is the case that they took representation as their subject matter and considered it in the light of a theory that encouraged them to seek homologies between political and literary representation.

Coleridge's Symbols of Eternity: Tautegorical Representation

In his battle to infuse the public realm with transcendent values, as in his battle to save the idea of free will, Coleridge identified the Utilitarians as his chief enemies. And rightly so, for Utilitarians did hold a particularly reductive view of the nature of value.[1] As empiricism became the ruling epistomology in England, the cognitive status of normative ideas became increasingly problematic. Some philosophers denied them the stature of real knowledge, reserving that term exclusively for ideas that could be tested experimentally or that were self-evident. However, Jeremy Bentham and his followers believed they had solved the problem of values by developing normative standards to evaluate facts according to the principles of empiricism itself. Bentham thought his most fundamental premise needed no empirical verification; the proposition that all humans seek pleasure and avoid pain seemed self-evident to him. Once his principle was established, Bentham believed, one could calculate the moral value of actions (although not the value of actors) by measuring their social utility (the greatest happiness for the greatest number). For Bentham, the fact that an action was self-interested did not detract from its moral efficacy; in fact, it guaranteed it, for the enlighted pursuit of one's self-interest would lead to the good of the whole community. This Utilitarian ethic was certainly not free from internal contradictions,[2] but it did establish a continuity between facts and values. The apparently morally neutral activity of pursuing one's own interests was itself the engine of social morality.

The Utilitarian theory of political representation conforms to the same model. It is most fully articulated in James Mill's *Essay on Government* (1820), which argues that the state should be, in the vocabulary of later political theorists, a descriptive microcosm of the population it governs.[3] Representation, according to this theory, should be descriptive in two related senses. First, a constituency's representative should resemble the constituency by sharing its economic and social interests. Second, through this form of representation, the whole realm of the political becomes a descriptive representation of the social-economic order. In the Utilitarian's view, political value, like economic value, would be created by the inclusion of and competition among as many interests as possible. Political value, in this model, thus emerges from an aggregation of social facts and describes the facts on which it is based.

Coleridge, however, whose opinions were typical of other anti-Utilitarian Romantics, believed this apparent facts-values continuity was actually spurious. In his view, the smooth, mechanical transition from neutral phenomena to moral meanings, or from social and economic facts to political values, was accomplished by collapsing the category of values into that of facts. Coleridge recognized that the Utilitarians had based their ethics and theories of representation on the model of political economy, equating exchange value with value in general, and he feared that this reductive equation might wipe the idea of transcendent values (God-given essential values, in his view) from human consciousness, thus obliterating the light that shines only for those who recognize a reality beyond mere appearances and observable facts. The perceivable world, he held, was unintelligible, a veritable chaos, when not illumined by the higher reality. Thus Coleridge directly contradicted Bentham: whereas the Utilitarian argued that an accumulation of facts would produce value and meaning, Coleridge held that facts cannot be interpreted or evaluated without prior insight into the meaning of the universe.

To his adversaries, therefore, Bentham's system, precisely because of its illegitimate facts-values continuity, actually threatened to produce an absolute rupture between facts and values, between the world and any knowledge of its ultimate meaning. Coleridge expresses this fear in 1817 when he writes,

> We are . . . a busy, enterprising, and commercial nation. The habits attached to this character must, if there exist no adequate counterpoise, inevitably lead us, under the specious names of utility, practical knowledge, and so forth, to look at all things thro' the medium of the market, and to estimate the Worth of all pursuits and attainments by their marketable value.[4]

Coleridge, trying to salvage this idea of essential worth, engaged in the apparently paradoxical project of establishing the existence of a separate realm of spiritual values in order to achieve a true confluence between those values and daily life.

In the second decade of the century, when Coleridge adopted his idea of the state from the German Idealists, he explicitly contrasted it to the marketplace, hypostatizing the opposed forces of the "Spirit of Commerce" (which he identified with industrialism and laissez-faire economics) and the "Spirit of the State."[5] Although the former operates according to fixed rules, it nevertheless works, Coleridge wrote, on principles "appropriate to the Mosaic Chaos, ere its brute tendencies had been enlightened by the WORD."[6] That is, the market place, even at its most orderly, represents the unintelligible, what Carlyle later called the inane. Commerce is an energetic but undirected source of change. In itself it is simply meaningless, a fact devoid of value. It can only be meaningfully directed by the state, which is the agent of the Word.

As the above quotation implies, Coleridge explicitly connected the activities of statescraft and textual interpretation, encircling both with what we might call an antidescriptive theory of representation, one that denies that a true representation is a reflection of empirical facts. This theory of representation, along with its implications for both political and literary theory, can best be seen in "The Statesman's Manual" (1816) and "A Lay Sermon" (1817). Although the former book ends in a passage (later paraphrased by Carlyle) asserting the standard Romantic belief that God is somehow contained in nature, it does not assert that nature represents God in any immediately comprehensible way. In this passage, the natural world provides a question about spiritual relaties, not an answer: "Are we struck with admiration at beholding the cope of heaven imaged in a Dew-drop? The least of the animalcula to which that drop would be an Ocean contains in itself an infinite problem of which God Omni-present is the only solution."[7] And when, in an appendix to the book, Coleridge returns to the subject of nature as a divinely revelatory fact, he once again stresses the difficulty of deciphering that fact: it must be read "in a figurative sense . . . to find therein correspondencies and symbols of the spiritual world."[8] An 1819 lecture makes the same point even more forcefully: "The other great Bible of God, the Book of Nature, [will] become transparent to us, when we regard the forms of matter as being the expression, an unrolled but yet glorious fragment, of the wisdom of the Supreme Being."[9] The book of nature reveals the truth only to those who already know it. It is not absolutely but only potentially a transparent expression of divinity.

The Bible, however, which always receives priority as a stable point of reference when Coleridge discusses the book of nature, seems a more transparent conduit of divinity. Coleridge fixes on the Bible in "The Statesman's Manual" as the one finite fact that bears infinite value, the one book that is consubstantial with its divine meaning: "The Bible alone contains a Science of Realities: and therefore each of its Elements is at the same time a living GERM, in which the Present involves the Future, and in the Finite the Infinite exists potentially."[10] Moreover, since "The Bible alone" articulates the divine intention, it is the readiest source of meaning and consequently must be the surest teacher of "the Elements of Political Science."[11] "Cabinets and Legislatures" that try to proceed by any other light, Coleridge writes, are meaninglessly, "impertinently busy."[12] Consequently, despite its residue of pantheism, we find in "The Statesman's Manual" a deep division between the world and its meaning, between facts and values. Those two facts, the Bible and the Bible-inspired state, that do directly represent realities are, in this sense, very unrepresentative.

In other writings, Coleridge admits more facts, mainly literary ones, into the circle of the eternally significant, but the circle remains very small. It is restricted by Coleridge's theory of representation, a theory that is designed to produce an unproblematic relationship between an appearance and the reality it represents. The eternal, he believed, expresses itself in the temporal through symbols, symbols that are never arbitrarily related to their meanings. The relationship between a symbol and what it represents is, in Coleridge's term, "tautegorical." As he explains in "The Statesman's Manual" while elaborating his famous distinction between symbols and allegories,

> a Symbol . . . is characterised by a translucence of the Special in the Individual or of the General in the Especial or of the Universal in the General. Above all by the translucence of the Eternal through and in the Temporal. It always partakes of the Reality which it renders intelligible, and while it enunciates the whole, abides itself as a living part in that Unity, of which it is the representative. The other [allegories] are but empty echoes which the fancy arbitrarily associates with apparitions of matter. [13]

Symbols, then, are a kind of synecdochal representation that is always and simultaneously what it is and what it represents. Consequently, although a product of the human mind, the symbol is never arbitrary; it accomplishes the confluence of signifier and signified, fact and value, through its natural and eternal relationship to its meaning. By limiting signification to this form of symbolic representation, Coleridge at once maintains the division between meaningful and meaningless facts and establishes an absolute continuity between meaningful facts and their eternal values.

This theory of exclusive and absolute representation permeates Coleridge's political thought in "A Lay Sermon," the companion piece to "The Statesman's Manual." As we have already seen, in this "sermon", meaningless facts, such as the entire sphere of commerce and production, are sharply distinguished from those facts that represent a higher reality, such as the state itself. Consequently it is not surprising that Coleridge argued to exclude the majority of people from participation in government, for the majority are animated by the spirit of trade. He thought the landed gentry and aristocracy, on the other hand, to be freer from commerce and thus potentially better governors.

In this regard, Coleridge's theory seems to resemble that of other political theorists who resisted Parliamentary reform or sought to minimize its scope. Indeed, Coleridge obviously imitated Burke in his mixed language of "interests" and "estates," his belief that M.P.s ought not to represent merely "local" or personal interests, and even his apparent approval of the concept of virtual representation.[14] But these are relatively superficial resemblances; underlying them is a radical difference in theories of representation. Although Burke and Coleridge both rejected the claims of reformers that Parliament should reflect the population of England in its composition and should carry out the will of the people, they reject these claims for different reasons. Burke believed that Parliament should represent the objective interests of the whole nation, interests that the people, even the electors, might not comprehend.[15] Only a small group of rational, well-educated men, each representing an objective interest (not the mere opinion or will of a particular constituency), could be expected to perceive the objective good of the nation as a whole, and consequently only members of a "natural aristocracy" should be elected to Parliament. The franchise, then, should be restricted to accomplish the elite representation of objective interests. Burke's argument is obviously antidemocratic, but it at least suggests how the people should be represented: by the representation of their long-range (and essentially harmonious) interests rather than by the representation of their transient (and often mutually antagonistic) wills and opinions.

In "A Lay Sermon," however, Coleridge departs from the terms of the debate, and adhering to his theory of symbolic representation, inverts the common notion of political representation: he does not argue that the state should represent any or all of the people's interests or opinions; rather, he argues that although the state must be distinguished from the church, it should nevertheless represent the will of God to the people. As Coleridge wrote in one of his notebooks, the state is not a social institution, not a mere empirical government. It is, rather, an eternal Platonic Idea that finds expression in particular governments and social groups.[16] Not all social groups, though, are equally proximate to the Idea. Although the energy of the commercial interests is necessary to the life of the nation, the state is naturally associated with the landed interests. But Coleridge does not argue that the state represents the objective interests of agriculture; instead he argues that agriculture represents the state.

It represents the state, moreover, in much the same way that any symbol represents an eternal verity, tautegorically:

> That Agriculture requires principles essentially different from those of Trade,—that a gentleman ought not to regard his estate as a merchant his cargo, or a shopkeeper his stock,—admits of an easy proof from the different tenure of Landed Property, and from the purposes of Agriculture itself, which ultimately are the same as those of the State of which it is the offspring.[17]

Here agriculture (a euphemism for the aristocracy) occupies a subordinate but tautegorical relationship to the state. It is the part of the whole that best represents the whole because its aims and the aims of the state coincide: "as the *specific* ends of Agriculture are the maintenance, strength, and security of the State, so (we repeat) must its *ultimate* ends be the same as those of the State: even as the ultimate end of the spring and wheels of a watch must be the same as that of the watch."[18] Political representation, then, is another version of symbolic representation. It proceeds from the higher ontological levels to the lower: the eternal, incorporeal realm of the transcendent reality, value, is represented, on the political plane, in the symbolic fact of the state, which is in turn represented on the social plane in the symbolic fact of agriculture.

Political meaning, like all meaning, descends from the higher and rarer, through representative symbols, to the lower and more numerous; it is not built up, as in the liberal model, from the facts, the political constituents representing themselves in the descriptive microcosm of Parliament. Nor is political meaning constructed in the deliberate process of an elite's attempt to define the objective interests of the nation, as in Burke's model. In Coleridge's theory, the state represents the long-range interests of the nation only because it symbolizes God's will, God's will and the nation's interests being necessarily identical. Apparently, however, Coleridge's statesman need not consider various interests, no matter how objective and harmoniously linked, in order to understand God's will. Indeed, many interests seem to require domination by, rather than reflection in, the state. The commercial interests, for example, must submit to be governed by another, for they are not at all consubstantial with the state, which is consubstantial with the Word. As we have seen, if commerce represents anything in itself, it represents chaos; it is raw energy devoid of form, signifying nonmeaning. Although Coleridge hoped that all citizens would internalize the idea of the state and thus submit to its governance, most citizens, he claimed, are incapable of independently interpreting and representing the Idea.

In attempting to explain the right relationship between facts and values, therefore, Coleridge comes up with a theory of political representation that is continuous with his theory of literary representation. In both cases, Coleridge severs the realms of value and society, claiming that symbols are not invested with meaning through some social process, whether a process of rational exchange or customary habit, but are, rather, *inherently* meaningful. Meaning flows to society from a realm of absolute value, but the descent is constricted within very narrow channels. Consequently, the net effect of Colerdige's theory of representation is to exclude the majority of facts and social processes from the realm of meaning and to limit the method of signification to the absolute authority of the representative symbol.

Carlyle's Signs of the Times: The Ironic Degradation of the Symbol

The internal coherence of Coleridge's theory of symbols has recently been challenged by critics claiming that, in discussing the distinctions between symbol and allegory, Coleridge inadvertently collapses the categories. He cannot, they argue, maintain his belief in the existence of eternal and transparent representations.[19] Indeed, it could be argued that Coleridge's later introduction of the idea of the clerisy also reveals his doubts about the existence of absolutely intelligible symbols. Why, after all, would a special group of interpreters be necessary to decipher such transparent representations? But even if one were to defend the consistency of Coleridge's own writings, it must be admitted that the next writer in the tradition we are tracing explicitly problematizes the concept of the symbol, introducing a gap between the symbol and its meaning as well as the possibility of the ironic degeneration of symbols.

Like those of Coleridge, Thomas Carlyle's ideas about political representation are inseparable from his theory of symbols. For Carlyle, however, the connection between symbols and government is a negative one: politics is primarily a realm where the ironic potentials of symbols actualize themselves. This instability of meaning in the political realm in turn motivates Carlyle to locate the "divine" nature of symbols in the heroic. As we will see, Carlyle's dualistic theory of symbols allows him to demote politics from the realm of values to that of facts and simultaneously to lift the politie onto a sacred foundation.

The section on symbols in *Sartor Resartus*, one of the first of Carlyle's works to speak of the "tragic" necessity of political involvement,[20] allows us to measure his distance from Coleridge on the issue of representation. Here we learn that symbols, like all other representations, have a partially oppositional relationship to the content they signify. Rather than being transparently expressive, they are always somewhat opaque, sometimes even stifling meaning. The relationship between language and thought is paradigmatic of this oppositional representation: "Speech is too often not, as the Frenchman defined it, the art of concealing Thought; but of quite stifling and suspending Thought, so that there is none to conceal."[21] Teufelsdröckh's discussion of symbols grows directly out of these remarks on the nonrepresentative, nonexpressive nature of language: "Of kin to the so incalculable influences of Concealment, and connected with still greater things, is the wondrous agency of *Symbols*. In a Symbol there is concealment and yet revelation: here therefore, by Silence and by Speech acting together, comes a double significance" (p. 151). This "double significance" defines the opacity of all symbols and admits a possibility that Coleridge could never have entertained: the possibility that symbols can have ironic significance.

This potential irony of the symbol is an outgrowth of its social origin. Unlike Coleridge, Carlyle insists on the social derivation of the symbol, and the difference between the two writers on this fundamental issue can be accounted for in several ways. First, *Sartor Resartus* was written just after the passage of the 1832 Reform Bill; at such a time the collective, social nature of signification was difficult to ignore. And although Carlyle never had any faith in the "machinery" of the ballot, he could nevertheless see that such machinery was inevitable and make adjustments in the theory of symbols that would accommodate the social determination of meaning. Coleridge's *Lay Sermons*, on the other hand, were written during a period of general political reaction, when antidemocratic forces seemed on the rise.

By the 1830s, moreover, the battle lines between the Utilitarians and their enemies had been slightly revised. Compared to Coleridge's, Carlyle's attacks are more insistently directed against the Benthamites' stress on the isolated individual. "Call ye that a Society," rants Teufelsdröckh, "where there is no longer any Social Idea extant; not so much as the Idea of a common Home, but only of a common over-crowded Lodging-house? Where each, isolated, regardless of his neighbour, turned against his neighbour, clutches what he can get, and cries 'mine!' and calls it Peace, because, in the cut-purse cum cut-throat Scramble, no steel knives, but only far cunninger sort, can be employed?" (p. 160) In contrast, Carlyle emphasizes and exalts the social nature of man, partly by locating the sources of value and meaning there. In his concept of society, meaning is produced collectively, not by the self-interested exchanges of competitive individuals, but by "sacred" combinations of men.

Even though Carlyle divides symbols into two categories, the extrinsically and the intrinsically valuable, both, it turns out, are at least partially socially determined, arbitrary and potentially ironic. Symbols with "merely extrinsic value" are the more obviously opaque and detachable from what they represent since they are mere "accidental Standards" that have "no intrinsic, necessary divineness, or even worth, but have acquired [through custom] an extrinsic one" (p. 154). These symbols are the opposite of the tautegorical, transparent representatives of the divine for which Coleridge tried to reserve the term "symbol." Indeed, they resemble Coleridge's allegories, which are also arbitrary signs for invisible truths. However, Carlyle insists on the worth of these customary signs, for he regards the arbitrariness of the extrinsically valuable symbols as a proof of their social origin, and their social origin guarantees their participation in the divine: these arbitrary signs can only take on meaning as the result of an agreement among "multitudes more or less sacredly uniting together; in which union . . . there is ever something mystical and borrowing of the Godlike" (p. 154). Most symbols, then, participate in the divine not because they are transparent or synecdochal representations of eternal truth, but because they acquire meaning through a process that, in its very social contingency, "borrows" God. For Carlyle, these extrinsically valuable symbols represent both the content assigned to them and the social, God-like process through which they acquire significance. Unlike Coleridge's Symbol, therefore, these symbols are both doubly representative and doubly opaque, requiring interpretation or customary knowledge because of their arbitrariness and reflecting back on themselves by representing the social process of representation.

In contrast, the intrinsically valuable symbols at first seem to be, like Coleridge's symbols, the synecdochal, natural representatives of eternal truth: "Another matter it is, however, when your Symbol has intrinsic meaning, and is of itself *fit* that men should unite round it. Let but the Godlike manifest itself to Sense; let but Eternity look, more or less visibly, through the Time-Figure (Zietbild)! Then is it fit that men unite there" (p. 154). Here the symbol initially seems to be transparent (eternity "looks through") and to take its meaning and value (words used synonymously by Teufelsdröckh) directly from the realm of the divine, not from the social process. But as Teufelsdröckh continues, these distinctions between extrinsically and intrinsically meaningful symbols begin to evaporate.

The transparency of the symbol is repeatedly qualified; indeed, the fact that these symbols have intrinsic value means that they are more than mere representations. They have a solid, independent existence that obscures the vision both of the eternal truth that looks through and of he who would behold the gaze of the eternal. In the sentences quoted above, for example, eternity looks through "more or less visibly," and in subsequent passages the symbol is said to emit intermittent "gleams" of the eternity it represents. Even the most lasting of symbols, Christianity itself, is not an open conduit of light, continuous with its meaning, but an opaque entity "whose significance will ever demand to be anew inquired into, and anew made manifest" (p. 155).

The social process of signification, therefore, extends even to intrinsically valuable symbols, which gain value through that process. However, the social origins of symbolic value entail not only the historical creation of the symbol but also its corruption. Since even the intrinsically valuable symbol has a component of arbitrary, customary meaning, which it takes on "from day to day, and from age to age" (p. 154), all symbols turn out to be partly divine, but also perishable, for "as Time adds much to the sacredness of Symbols, so likewise in his progress he at length defaces, even desecrates them; and Symbols, like all terrestrial Garments, wax old" (p. 155). Once a symbol of eternity has thus degenerated into a mere sign of the times, it can completely obscure the truth it once stood for and impair our vision of other truths as well: "move whithersoever you may, are not the tatters and rags of superannuated worn-out Symbols . . . dropping off everywhere to hoodwink, to halter, to tether you; nay, if you shake them not aside, threatening to accumulate, and perhaps produce suffocation?" (p. 156)

By insisting that the social process is an origin of symbolic meaning, Carlyle comes to admit that symbols may devolve into meaninglessness. One stage of that devolution is irony, the moment when a symbol comes to signify the opposite of its "normal" or original meaning. In *Sartor Resartus*, Carlyle associates the state itself with this phase of symbol degeneration. Teufelsdröckh illustrates how the corrupted symbol comes to mean the opposite of what it orginally meant with an anecdote revealing the ludicrous aspect a state takes on when it adheres to the chivalric ceremonies that once made it seem awesome: "When, as the last English Coronation was preparing I read in their Newspapers that the 'Champion of England,' he who has to offer battle to the universe for his new King, had brought it so far that he could now 'mount his horse with little assistance,' I said to myself: Here also we have a Symbol well-nigh superannuated" (p. 156). Through this process of degeneration, the state has become an emblem of the evaporation of meaning from society itself: "Once-sacred Symbols fluttering as empty Pageants, whereof men grudge even the expense; . . . the State shrunken into a Police-Office, straitened to get its pay' " (p. 161).

Carlyle unquestionably regrets this shrinkage of the "soul Politic" (p. 161), for it betokens the dimming of the "Social Idea" itself, but he expresses little faith in the state as an agent of social regeneration. For him, the state cannot be a simple synecdoche for God's translucent and ordering Word; the primacy of the social in Carlyle's system turns the state into a symbol that participates in the divine by virtue of its social nature, but that is also, in its degenerate condition, a barrier to eternal truth. In Teufelsdröckh's discourse, "State" often refers to a specific set of declining institutions, an actual government, rather than to an eternal idea. It is more easily equated with politics than is Coleridge's state; for Teufelsdröckh the whole realm of the political is stuck in the ironic stage of devolution, and the section of *Sartor Resartus* that treats it extensively treats it ironically. The editor purports to be shocked by Teufelsdröckh's radicalism as the latter questions the worth of political enterprises: "How, with our English love of Ministry and Opposition, and that generous conflict of Parties . . . how shall we domesticate ourselves in this spectral Necropolis, or rather City both of the Dead and of the Unborn, where the Present seems little other than an inconsiderable Film dividing the Past and the Future?' " (p. 173) The editor responds with "shuddering admiration" and also disbelief ("Is Teufelsdröckh acquainted with the British Constitution even slightly?") as Teufelsdröckh "makes little" of the "Representative Machine" (p. 173) and generally regards the province of "the Political" with "astonishment, hesitation, and even pain" (p. 172).

In *Sartor Resartus*, politics is a bundle of desecrated symbols that originally signified an eternal realm of values but now ironically represent the temporal sphere of facts. Once deciphered, the ironic symbol of the state turns out to be a mirror of the population. Hence, descriptive representation, Carlyle tells us in *Past and Present*, is inevitable, no matter what the form of government: "In the long-run every Government is the exact symbol of its People, with their wisdom and unwisdom." The government remains a symbol, but only a symbol of society, and that fact has both a positive and a negative value. On the one hand, whatever sacredness a government has is gathered from this social determination; but on the other hand, its social determination is precisely what prevents it from governing the social realm and from being a source of transcendence. *Past and Present*, like *Sartor Resartus*, emphasizes the negative consequences of the government's social origin. The dependence of the political on the social-economic is as marked in *Past and Present* as it is in the work of any liberal theorist: "But the Government cannot do, by all its signalling and commanding, what the Society is radically indisposed to do. . . . The main substance of this immense Problem of Organizing Labour, and first of all of Managing the Working Classes, will, it is very clear, have to be solved by those who stand practically in the middle of it; by those who themselves work and preside over work." Thus Carlyle demotes the political from a position above the social to a position below it, claiming that "A Human Chaos *in* which there is no light, you vainly attempt to irradiate by light shed *on* it: order never can arise there."[22]

The exaltation of the social in Carlyle's work, therefore, ultimately leads, via the redefinition of the symbol, to the devaluation of the political, its association with both ironic and descriptive representation. In what way, then, is Carlyle's theory of representation, especially his theory of political representation, descended from Coleridge's theory? The answer lies in the fact that Carlyle too considers neither the state nor society to be the ultimate foundation of what he calls the politie.

Although Carlyle purports to believe that every social act of representation is divine, in the last analysis, he, like Coleridge, longs to sever value from the time-bound, customary process of signification and root it in a nonsocial absolute. He thus allows the realm of the political to absorb and actualize the ironic potential of the symbol because he can then locate the purified remainder, the divine essence of the symbol, in a realm apart from politics but nevertheless underlying the politie: the realm of "Hero-worship."

This purified territory enables Carlyle to ironize politics, and at the same time, the irony of politics is the very thing that creates the need for the politie's separate symbolic foundation. The placement of the section on hero-worship in *Sartor Resartus* reveals this connection: it comes just after the section on politics in the chapter "Organic Filaments" and is introduced as a necessary antidote to Teufelsdröckh's "soul-confusing labyrinths of Speculative Radicalism" (p. 173). Hero-worship, we are told, is a "clearer region" (p. 173), a space illuminated by an "organic filament," a synecdochal representation of divinity: the hero himself. These "filaments" strongly resemble Coleridge's symbols; the social process verifies, but does not create them. Rather they are unambiguous facts that force their meaning on all who behold them: "Meanwhile, observe with joy, so cunningly has Nature ordered it, that whatsoever man ought to obey, he cannot but obey. Before no faintest revelation of the Godlike did he ever stand irreverent; least of all, when the Godlike showed itself revealed in his fellow-man" (p. 174). The resulting hero-worship, concludes Teufelsdröckh, is the "corner-stone of living rock, whereon all Polities for the remotest time may stand secure" (p. 174).

The ironic instability of politics is finally not really threatening, for the politie is grounded, through another foundation, in eternal verities. Carlyle manages, in his revision of the theory of symbols, to combat the Benthamite social model by insisting on the mystical divinity of society, its participation in the divine work of making value. Simultaneously, however, he escapes from the negative consequences of socially determined meaning by allowing politics to absorb them and then creating a purified region of heroic symbolism. He both undermines Coleridge's model of symbolic representation and reestablishes it in a symbiotic relationship with political irony.

The Politics of Irony: Representation by Opposition in Disraeli's *Sybil*

Disraeli's *Sybil, or the Two Nations* incorporates this Carlylean combination of ironic and synecdochal symbolic representation, for as we will see, Disraeli also needed at once to assert the primacy of the social, a primacy he associated with what he called England's "territorial constitution," and to escape from its ironic implications. *Sybil* illustrates the relationships among politics, literary irony, and symbolism in early Victorian novels, for it attempts to provide a homologous literary form for both actual and desired methods of political representation. Disraeli's ideas about political representation are a blend of Burke, the old Tories, and Romantic Idealists like Coleridge. In his *Vindication of the English Constitution*, which appeared ten years before *Sybil*, he follows Burke in stressing the balances within the English constitution and the need for the government to represent "the Nation" as a whole. However, in reaction to both Whig and radical parliamentary reformers, he insists, like Tory opponents of Burke, that the House of Commons in general, and individual M.P.s in particular, necessarily represent local and partial interests. In the *Vindication* he scoffs at the idea that they represent "the People."[23] The Commons, he claims, is a very small estate within the realm, and when members of the House represent anything beyond themselves, they represent that estate only. Expanding the franchise, he continues, would not make the House more representative of the people, for representativeness is not guaranteed by the elective process. Using a prescriptive argument, he insists that representation is an inherited privilege, not an abstract right. Indeed, the very idea of political rights is anathema to him. Politics, he argues in contradistinction to Hobbes (pp. 18–19), must be founded squarely on the already given, the inherited, instead of being derived from the abstract and "artificial" logic of mere words (pp. 20–21).

But the principle of prescription has a limited use for Disraeli; it helps him combat the representative model of the Utilitarians, but it is useless against his other enemies, the Whig Oligarchs, whose rule was already established. Consequently, in the *Vindication* Disraeli turns away from the issue of Parliamentary representation altogether, shifting his emphasis to the institution of the monarchy. Like Bolingbroke, he calls on the Tory party to end the tyranny of the Whig oligarchy by restoring the full power of the monarch. A strong sovereign, surrounded by his traditional friends, old Tory aristocratic families, would be both a representative of the nation as a whole and a symbolic representative, in Coleridge's sense, of divine authority.

In the *Vindication*, therefore, Disraeli eschews the model of descriptive representation and invokes Coleridge's symbolic model. His work recalls Carlyle's assurance, in *Sartor Resartus*, that of all titles, only "king" signifies eternity. Carlyle's passage on the word "king" immediately precedes the passages on politics and hero-worship, and provides their continuity: "The only Title wherein I, with confidence, trace eternity, is that of King. *Konig* (King), anciently *Konning*, means Ken-ning (Cunning), or which is the same thing, Can-ning. Ever must the Sovereign of Mankind be fitly entitled King' " (p. 171–72). Teufelsdröckh's rhapsody, it must be remembered, applies to the *title* king, to the essence represented by the word, not to any particular monarch. Typically, Carlyle judges the fitness of word and thing by tracing the pedigree of the word, by looking to the signifier for the essence of the signified. Carlyle even implies that sovereignty might precede the fitting title, as if "king" were a word independent of inheritance that could be bestowed on a man to name his essence. Although the signifier here is hardly arbitrary, its fitness depends not on royal descent but on the charismatic qualities of the signified.

For Disraeli, however, the actual monarch, whose legitimacy is unquestioned, is the perfect combination of word and inheritance only because of his royal descent. The king is thus the optimal symbol, an organic filament representing the nation as a whole and representing God's sovereignty to the nation, but his symbolic essence inheres in his inheritance. In *Sybil*, as we will see, Disraeli often uses this seemingly unproblematic mode of symbolic representation exemplified by the monarch. Synecdochal symbolism is both a political principle and a literary method in *Sybil*.

Sybil, however, is also a book about the subject the *Vindication* glances away from: the representation of the common people in Parliament. Faced with Chartist agitation for the extension of the franchise, Disraeli tried to fashion a theory of Parliamentary representation that would accord with his desire for royal hegemony. The resulting amalgamation came to be known as Tory Democracy. According to this ideology, the monarch's power would be restored by the very M.P.s who would best represent the mass of the people: Tories from old aristocratic families, like the members of Disraeli's coterie, Young England. In response to the Chartists' call for popular representation, therefore, *Sybil* suggests that the working class would best be represented, not by workers themselves (that is, not by descriptive representatives) but by their opposites on the social scale, the aristocracy. This newest industrial class, moreover, should not be represented by the new usurping aristocrats created since the Reformation, but by the old Norman or, better still, Saxon aristocracy.

Sybil, then, tells us there is an identity of interests between the extremes of the social and historical spectrum: the highest and oldest class should therefore represent its opposite, the lowest and newest class. The movement from facts to values in *Sybil* is thus a simultaneous leap, through representation, upward in society and backward in history. The simple device of making Walter and Sybil Gerard, the Chartist leader and his daughter, the descendants of Saxon aristocrats is the most obvious encoding of this ideology in the novel. It is, moreover, an instance of symbolic representation, and we will return to this device shortly. There is, however, another more subtle and problematic literary analogue to Tory democracy in *Sybil*.

In addition to formulating an antidescriptive theory of Parliamentary representation to combat that of the Chartists, Disraeli also wanted to delegitimize what he insisted was a new, usurping oligarchy of aristocratic families who claimed they were already representing the people. In other words, Disraeli's task is to legitimize one kind of representation through opposition while delegitimizing another. As we will see, however, the novel ultimately legitimizes both, revealing the interdependence of irony and symbolism in this antidescriptive tradition.

In *Sybil* illegitimate representation through opposition finds its appropriate literary form in irony. Consequently, the novel's main structural device is the ironic juxtaposition of the aristocracy, and the working class, the two "nations" of the subtitle.[24] Ostensibly, we are led to believe that, as the term "two nations" implies, there is a great gap between these two classes, "who," as Stephen Morely remarks, "are as ignorant of each other's habits, thoughts, and feelings, as if they were dwellers in different zones, or inhabitants of different planets."[25] And, indeed, the novel does display how little each class knows about the other. The binary structure of the book finally impresses us, however, not with the differences between the classes, but with their similarities. This is not to say that *Sybil* contains no descriptions of poverty and exploitation such as those found in other industrial novels. It does, but in this novel the workers presented as typical are neither poor nor exploited. Indeed, they seem to have been chosen not for their representativeness as workers but for their comic comparability to the aristocracy. In *Sybil* both typical aristocrats and workers are not so much representatives of their own classes as ironic representatives of the opposite class.

Chapters 10 and 11 of book 2 provide a case in point: a pair of dinner parties, one in the Temple of the Muses, a popular working-class club, and one in the sumptuous country house of Lord de Mowbray. Each party is ironically presented in itself. The very things Dandy Mick, the young weaver, and his party believe indicate their superiority actually indicate their ignorance: their approval of their surroundings, their haughtiness toward the waiters, their scorn of the "himmigrants" from the country. Similarly, almost all members of the de Mowbray party inadvertently reveal their folly, ignorance, or pretension in the act of trying to impress their dinner partners. But the largest irony is the effect of the juxtaposition itself, which allows us to see the resemblances between the two groups. Disraeli, indeed, carefully parallels the details of the parties. The conversations at both revolve around the protection and extension of class power and privilege. Each party includes two young women, is held in richly decorated surroundings, is served by obsequious waiters. These details underline the comic pretensions of the working-class establishment, where "waiters flew about with as much agility as if they were serving nobles" (p. 93). The factory people in this setting ape the aristocracy ("they mash their taters here very elegant"), and thus they become ludicrous. However, they also make the aristocracy appear ludicrous. The parallels show us that the behavior of the de Mowbrays is just as pretentious as that of Dandy Mick and the factory girls. The workers resent the encroachment of agricultural laborers, calling them slaves "sent down by Pickford's van into the labour market to bring down our wages" (p. 98). Lord de Mowbray, himself only two generations removed from a servant, similarly bemoans the encroachment of the railroad, which represents the "levelling spirit of the age" (p. 104) with its "dangerous tendency to equality" (p. 103). And de Mowbray's daughters reiterate the theme, reminding us of the family's real class origins when they insist on the ludicrousness of enobling members of the middle class (p. 107) or refer to their own spurious genealogy: "I never can forget I am a daughter of the first Crusaders" (p. 107). The de Mowbrays and the factory workers in these chapters become ironic mirrors of one another: the aristocrats ironically represent the workers by behaving like them and thus reminding us of their working-class origins, while the workers ironically reveal a truth about the aristocracy. In a sense, then, this juxtaposition assures us that the present aristocracy already represents the people. The claims of the Whig oligarchy are thus credited in a way that comically subverts them.

There are numerous other instances of such juxtapositions: The society of tramps in the park mirrors the party at Lady Delorane's. An evening at Lord Marney's, full of aristocratic complaints about being financially drained, is preceded by a colliers' public-house dinner, at which economic complaint is also the substance of the conversation and the miners are clearly presented as an aristocracy of labor who, like Lord Marney, enjoy "a presciptive right" (p. 143) in the house they inhabit. The Hatton twins display inverted images of the two nations' methods of creating illegitimate aristocrats. The Chartist congress is, in Stephen Morley's words, "a vulgar caricature of the bad passions and the low intrigues, the factions and the failures, of our oppressors" (pp. 289–90). A Parliamentary division, which is very vaguely represented, because "the mysteries of the Lobby are only for the initiated" (p. 215), is followed by a trade union initiation. Finally, when the mob led by

"Bishop" Hatton, the illegitimate leader of the people, burns down the Earl de Mowbray's house, the narrator once again draws an analogy between the two usurpers: "the flame that . . . announced to the startled country that in a short hour the splendid mimicry of Norman rule would cease to exist, told also the pitiless fate of the ruthless savage, who, with analogous pretentions, had presumed to style himself the Liberator of the People" (p. 425).

All of these and many other passages direct our attention to the underlying ways in which the classes indicate one another. This ironic form of representation through opposition, then, is morphologically similar to Disraeli's wished-for political system, where the working class would electorally indicate the aristocracy and the aristocracy would represent the working class. According to Tory Democracy, however, representation through opposition should bring out the best in both classes, natural deference and industry in the working class, responsibility and generosity in the aristocracy. Representation through opposition should be a way of moving from what is to what ought to be. The novel's ironic representations, on the other hand, bring out the worst in both classes: their common pretension, selfishness, and ignorance.

Despite its structural similarity to Disraeli's political ideal, therefore, irony is not a means of infusing facts with values in *Sybil*; rather, it is a means of devaluing what should be significant facts. *Sybil's* irony devalues the fact of aristocracy by relating the aristocrats' family histories, which gradually subtract all independent content from the aristocrats; they are revealed to be anything but real aristocrats. Their fictional genealogies, the creations of the inheritance lawyer known as Baptist Hatton, are belied by the narrator's true histories. History, therefore, collapses the class differences, showing the fact of an aristocratic title to be fictional and thus meaningless. This collapse is most apparent in the case of the de Mowbrays, whose name and title have the weakest historical basis. The narrator, like the malicious Lord Marney in the following passage, ironically emphasizes the gap between the de Mowbrays' aristocratic signifier and its signified:

> "And how do you find the people about you, Marney?" said Lord de Mowbray, seating himself on a sofa by his guest. "All very well, my lord," replied the earl, who ever treated Lord de Mowbray with a certain degree of ceremony, especially when the descendant of the Crusaders affected the familiar. . . . The old nobility of Spain delighted to address each other only by their names, when in the presence of a spic-and-span grandee; calling

> each other "Infantado," "Sidonia," "Ossuna," and then turning
> round with the most distinguished consideration, and appealing
> to the Most Noble Marquis of Ensenada. (P. 110)

Unlike the ironic juxtapositions that reveal the underlying similarities
between the aristocracy and the working class, this verbal irony reveals
the correlative difference: the difference between de Mobray's title
and what he is actually entitled to, between, in Disraeli's terms, words
and inheritance. The effects of both kinds of irony are the same,
however; both devalue the aristocrat by revealing the illegitimate
source of his title.

In itself, this one revelation of illegitimacy could hardly be said to
devalue the whole idea of aristocracy in the book. Indeed, one of the
functions of the irony surrounding de Mowbray is to create a desire for
the restoration of the legitimate heirs, for reattaching title and name to
their proper signifieds, Sybil and Walter Gerard. Confined to de Mowbray, then, this irony, like that of the Spanish aristocrats, might be said
to legitimize legitimacy. However, the irony is not so confined. After
all, Lord Marney himself, the wielder of the ironic weapon, is also
vulnerable to it; the Marney family, like the de Mowbrays, achieved its
name and titles through corruption, intrigue, and usurpation.
Although the Marney family is older than the de Mowbrays, in the
book's time scale it is an upstart family, the bearer of a displaced name.
Marney's words in the above passage, then, are only one level of irony;
the narrator's irony envelopes and destabilizes them.

This process of destabilization, moreover, occurs repeatedly as the
narrator deflates the pretensions of one aristocratic family after
another. Indeed, almost all aristocratic family histories in *Sybil* are
devaluations. They are explorations that lead from the fact of the
name back to its moment of acquisition, which turns out to be, not an
originary moment of meaning, but a moment when meaning is displaced through usurpation. Most importantly, as long as one inhabits
the realm of history, one encounters nothing but displacement and
usurpation; one never reaches the origins that confer legitimacy. In
Sybil history and displacement are synonymous.

The narrator sums up his view of the historical process in this
description of Egremont among the ruins of Marney Abbey:

> He stood among the ruins that . . . had seen many changes:
> changes of creeds, of dynasties, of laws, of manners. New orders
> of men had arisen in the country, new sources of wealth had
> opened, new dispositions of power to which that wealth had
> necessarily led. His own house, his own order, had established
> themselves on the ruins of that great body, the emblems of whose
> ancient magnificence and strength surrounded him. (P. 61)

There is a slight regret in this passage about the displacement of the monastery, which emanates from the fact that the monks were not themselves usurping aristocrats. But even this displacement is presented here as an inevitable by-product of historical progress. The conversation that follows this description of history draws heavily on Carlyle's *Past and Present*. But whereas that book simply juxtaposes the two terms, drawing in its turn on Pugin's *Contrasts*, *Sybil* concentrates on the process that leads from past to present, a process of necessary and continual displacement that wears away the absolute Puginesque distinctions: medieval-modern, sacred-profane. Thus, although Egremont regrets the passing of the monasteries, the narrator is normally neutral about the historical process. Indeed, as we will see when we analyze the relationship between politics and society in *Sybil*, Disraeli's political position is actually dependent on this vision of history as perpetual displacement, a realm without origins or stable values.

It is, therefore, Disraeli's vision of history that underlies his irony and collapses its terms. One consequence of this collapse is a disharmony between the book's major literary mode of representation, irony, and Disraeli's desired system of political representation, which necessitates, as we will see, the intervention of the symbolic mode. Instead of being homologous with Disraeli's politics, irony inverts it. Instead of bridging the gap between the actual and wished for, irony widens it. The very historical discoveries that delegitimize the aristocracy make it an appropriate ironic representative of the working class. The structural juxtapositions reinforce this historical identification, so that the ironic representation keeps pointing to an underlying literal identity in the past, when the aristocrats were their own opposites. History, then, which is supposed to legitimize aristocracies, delegitimizes this one and, at the same time, creates the basis of the book's irony. The meaningfulness of the literary irony, therefore, depends on the meaninglessness of history. The meaninglessness of history, however, which allows for the success of the literary representation, is precisely what makes the aristocracy an inappropriate political representative of the working class; the literary irony collapses the true class difference on which political representation should depend.

The Constitution of Irony: the Political versus the Social in *Sybil*

Irony, therefore, for Disraeli as for Carlyle, is a true representation of false representation. In *Sybil* as in *Sartor Resartus*, its natural haunt is that realm of unredeemed politics that cannot save itself from the corrosions of history, cannot become an autonomous realm of eternal value above the ephemeral social facts. However, Disraeli is even more ambivalent than Carlyle about the dependence of politics on society, for his antidescriptive scheme of political representation leads him, on the one hand, to approve of this dependence and, on the other, to hold out the possibility of an autonomous political realm.

Disraeli's statesmen, like Coleridge's, are primarily engaged in the activity of creating and interpreting representations; the representations of *Sybil*'s Lord Masque and Mr. Tadpole, however, are not symbols but lies: lies, moreover, that disguise themselves as the most intimate, secret truths. Lady Firebrace's activities typify political representations in Sybil:

> Lady Firebrace, a great stateswoman among the Tories, was proud of an admirer who was a member of the Whig Cabinet. She was rather an agreeable guest in a country-house, with her extensive correspondence, and her bulletins from both sides. Tadpole, flattered by her notice, and charmed with female society that talked his own slang, and entered with affected enthusiasm into all his petty plots and barren machinations, was vigilant in his communication; while her Whig Cavalier, an easy individual, who always made love by talking or writing politics, abandoned himself without reserve, and instructed Lady Firebrace regularly after every council. . . . The best of the joke was, that all this time Lord Masque and Tadpole were two old foxes, neither of whom conveyed to Lady Firebrace a single circumstance but with the wish, intention, and malice aforethought, that it should be communicated to his rival. (P. 105–6)

Politics here, as in most of *Sybil*, is the art of misrepresentation. Lord Masque and Mr. Tadpole knowingly produce counterfeit verbal currency; Lady Firebrace circulates it, and the exchange results in the devaluation of all information.

Similarly, the business of representing a constituency in Parliament is portrayed as a kind of nonrepresentation, which is often conducted through absence rather than presence. A Whig Lord, for example, is brought in to vote "in a wheeled chair; he was unconscious, but had heard as much of the debate as a good many" (p. 215). M. P.s on both sides spend most of the day, not deciding the merits of the issues, but finding ways of avoiding the debate. Each man's primary concern is to find a member of the opposite party who will agree to make an absent pair with him:

> "We want a brace of pairs," said Lord Milford. "Will you two fellows pair?"
> "I must go down," said Mr. Egerton; "but I will pair from half-past seven to eleven."
> "I just paired with Ormsby at White's," said Breners. (P. 207)

Simultaneously, the Tory Ladies plot to conjure up a ghostly vote from "Colonel Fantomme, who they think is dying; but Mr. Tadpole has got a mesmerist who has done wonders for him, and who has guaranteed that he shall vote" (p. 210).

These misrepresentations and nonrepresentations are the book's dominant instances of actual political representation. Disraeli contrasts them to mere suggestions of political forthrightness and presence; we never actually hear or see Mr. Tenchard, for example, or Egremont himself, in political action. But the narrator, often ironically through uncomprehending reports, makes a space for such true political representations in the novel. The fact that this space goes unfilled, however, is symptomatic of a fundamental contradiction in Disraeli's political vision: whenever he begins portraying true political representation, he starts sketching an autonomous political realm, but an autonomous political realm would threaten what Disraeli called the "territorial constitution," the very thing that Tory Democracy is designed to perpetuate. Only through history can Disraeli ground the aristocracy that should represent the nation; however, only by splitting off the realms of the political and the social-historical can he conceive of true political representation. The constitution he is committed to preserving necessarily makes the political an emanation of the social in order to preserve the overall hegemony of the aristocracy.

The relationships among Lady Firebrace, Mr. Tadpole, and Lord Masque illustrate one side of this bind. The above passage presents the relationship between politics and society as a relationship between political language and gossip. In the corrupt world of *Sybil*, the language of statecraft is inseparable from the language of gossip, but even their inseparability relies on a radical difference. Lady Firebrace's gossip, as we have seen, is the ironic opposite of the truth, but that only makes it typical of political language in *Sybil*. The significant difference between the language of the statesmen and Lady Firebrace's gossip is that the former is self-consciously false and the latter is not. Thus Disraeli seems to be placing even ironic political language (what Lord Masque tells Lady Firebrace) on a higher level than gossip (the same message related by Lady Firebrace to Mr. Tadpole). Despite the fact that the contents of the two are identical, Disraeli seems to be elevating even corrupt politics above the social by showing that gossip merely *aspires* to be political news. Far from depending on and representing the realm of the social, the realm of the political stands above and manipulates the social into ironically representing politics itself. Gossip is only political (ironically) by mistaking itself to be political (literally).

Thus it appears that Disraeli's use of irony here expresses his desire for an autonomous political realm, that it creates a real and stable difference between the political and social, establishing, albeit with a degraded content, the downward direction of representation recommended by Coleridge. However, Disraeli is unable to give any independent purpose or content to this allegedly superior political realm, for to do so would be to deny the premise that access to political office should depend upon social position. Disraeli, as a defender of the exclusive rights of inheritance, would then simply be undermining himself.

In the abstract discursiveness of the *Statesman's Manual*, Coleridge was able to maintain that agriculture tautegorically represents the state, and that both can be sources of value uncontaminated by the chaos of society and commerce. But in the concrete historicity of *Sybil*, Disraeli needs to describe the complete interpenetration of the commercial, social, and political, for the territorial constitution itself depends on that interpenetration. Only through such an interpenetration can all commercial, social, and intellectual energies be absorbed by agriculture, contained by aristocracy.

Thus the constitution, the narrator explicitly tells us, creates a politics that aims at aristocracy and an aristocracy that aims at politics. In the following passage, the narrator approvingly describes the normative direction of social and political exchange, in which money is traded for land, and land becomes political power, which is, in time, used to purchase a title:

> In a commercial country like England, every half century develops some new and vast source of public wealth, which brings into national notice a new and powerful class. A couple of centuries ago, a Turkey Merchant was the great creator of wealth; the West Indian Planter followed him. In the middle of the last century appeared the Nabob. These characters in their zenith in turn merged in the land, and became English aristocrats. . . . The expenditure of the revolutionary war produced the Loanmonger, who succeeded the Nabob; and the application of science to industry developed the Manufacturer, who in turn aspires to be "large-acred," and always will, as long as we have a territorial constitution; a better security for the preponderance of the landed interest than any corn-law, fixed or fluctuating. (P. 11)

Under such a constitution, the social and political are necessarily mirror images of one another. Consequently, Disraeli's desire for a transcending politics conflicts with his desire for a territorial constitution. But the two desires also imply one another. Disraeli follows Coleridge in believing that only the aristocracy has the possibility of representing, in a nondescriptive way, the state or the nation: hence the need to insure the ascendancy of agriculture (or aristocracy). But the means of securing that ascendancy, the territorial constitution, collapses the differences between the social and political, making autonomous politics threatening if not impossible.

Disraeli is unable to represent the true disinterested representation of the nation, for he is unable to find a content for an autonomous politics. Such a content fails to emerge in the interactions between Lady Firebrace and her friends. But it also fails to emerge in the "principled" politics of the M.P. Mr. Trenchard, who is even more unrepresentable than the other politicians because his politics are completely independent of social roots. Lady St. Julians interprets the motivations of Mr. Trenchard in a cynical speech that nevertheless echoes the narrator:

> "People get into Parliament to get on; their aims are indefinite. If they have indulged in hallucinations about place before they enter the House, they are soon freed from such distempered fancies; they find they have no more talent than other people, and if they had, they learn that power, patronage, and pay are reserved for us and our friends. . . . Well then, of course such people are entirely in one's power, if one only had time and inclination to notice them. . . . Ask them to a ball, and they will give you their votes." (P. 217)

Lady St. Julians here is simply filling in the details of the exchange demanded by the territorial constitution, and yet Egremont immediately arrives on the scene to reveal her folly. Mr. Trenchard, he claims, is one politician who, like Egremont, avoids society. But when Lady St. Julians, asks incredulously, "If Society is not his object, what is?" Egremont cannot really answer her question: "Aye! . . . there is a great question for you and Lady Firebrace to ponder over. This is a lesson for you fine ladies, who think you can govern the world by what you call your social influences" (p. 219). The lesson, though, remains a purely negative one. Mr. Trenchard's purpose is never identified, and his function in the narrative seems simply to open the possibility of a politics that is not a reflection of the social. Disraeli wishes to maintain the ascendancy of politics over society, but politics necessarily becomes a mere blank or, like Mr. Trenchard, a question mark when it no longer represents society.

Disraeli, therefore, cannot present the nonidentity of politics and society even as an ideal any more than he can present the ideal nonidentity of the aristocracy and the working-class. Politics and society, like the two nations themselves, are constantly juxtaposed only to reveal the identity between opposites that underlies the juxtaposition. In both cases the differences are effaced by the process of historical displacement, which constantly disrupts signification and readjusts values. The process that creates politics as a representation of the social, the process of increasing social value through a series of exchanges between the commercial-social and political realms, is the very process that, traced backward by the narrator, devalues the aristocracy. Thus history itself collapses the crucial distinctions of Tory Democracy (people-aristocrats, social-political, facts-values), resolving difference into sameness, irony into descriptive literalism.

The Vindication of the Constitution: Irony and Symbolism in *Sybil*

Ultimately, therefore, those sections of *Sybil* that represent the relations between the two nations and depict political representation itself, like the discussions of symbols and politics in *Sartor Resartus*, trace the historical degeneration of values to the level of meaningless facts. Like Carlyle, Disraeli keeps rehearsing the decline of extrinsically valuable symbols into ironic representations. His irony in turn twists itself into descriptive representation, so that the government in *Sybil* is also finally "the exact symbol of its People, with their wisdom and unwisdom."[26]

The final result of Disraeli's constant collapsing of oppositions also recalls Carlyle's ultimate solution to the problem of political irony: The "soul-confusing labyrinths" of ironic representation in both works create a need for tautegorical symbols on which stable oppositions might rest. The existence of tautegorical representation as the foundation of values insures the stability of the whole system, redeeming even the ironies of historical displacement.

Sybil and Walter Gerard are Disraeli's organic filaments of eternity, embodiments of the heroic. They represent, in as transparent a manner as possible, ahistorical values; they "body-forth" those values, to use Carlyle's word, by combining very incongruous social facts. That is why, considered as novelistic charactes, they have always seemed somewhat ridiculous.[27] But the very things that make them ludicrous as descriptive representatives of social facts make them meaningful as symbols of timeless values.

Walter Gerard stands for the ideal unity of the nation; he embodies the representation of the people through the aristocracy by being both a working-class leader and an aristocrat. According to the assumptions of descriptive representation, therefore, he is nonsense. In order to make him a transparent representation of the harmony of the people and the aristocracy, Disraeli lifts him out of the historical present and places him in a medieval past. We first see Gerard in the ruins of Marney Abbey, undecipherable in social terms, but symbolically pellucid: "His garments gave no clue to his position in life: they might have been worn by a squire or by his gamekeeper; a dark velveteen dress and leathern gaiters" (p. 61). Gerard's clothes resonate with Carlylean associations: in *Sartor Resartus* leather clothes signify both a stability of identity and a confluence of signifier and signified (pp. 143–47). His dress also, like his surroundings, clearly evokes a legendary medievalism curiously removed from the historical realm. When Gerard speaks, in his symbolically archaic English, of his surroundings, he turns the abbey, not into a part of history, but into an escape from it:

> "The Monastics could possess no private property; they could save no money; they could bequeath nothing. . . . The monastry, too, was a proprietor that never died and never wasted. The farmer had a deathless landlord then; not a harsh guardian, or a grinding mortgagee, or a dilatory master in chancery: all was certain; the manor had not to dread a change of lords or the oaks to tremble at the axe of the squandering heir. . . . The abbot was ever the same." (P. 63)

The middle ages in this book, as in so much Victorian literature, are not so much a historical period as a prehistorical one.

Gerard represents this prehistorical harmony between an ideal aristocracy and the people in every detail of his characterization, from his clothes and speech to the "preponderance of the animal man" in him (a sign, according to the narrator, of true aristocracy). Even his natural leadership of the people and his tendency toward violence symbolize a pastness noncontinuous with the present. Expelled from history at the moment when history (as a process of displacement) begins, the Gerard family is largely prehistorical, and its modern representatives represent their origins transparently. In Walter Gerard, there is very little distance between origin and being, signified and signifier. The distance that does emerge is produced by his involvement in politics, his inappropriate participation in the realm of history.

Sybil, however, has no real political involvement. Representing the dispossessed, she possesses only the legendary past that is frozen into value, noncontinuous with the present, and therefore pure, preserved in its pristine form. Indeed, Sybil is a conglomerate of noninheritors, of history's left-outs: female, Saxon, and Catholic. Through the Blessed Virgin, the "Hebrew Maiden," as the narrator calls her, Disraeli even manages to associate Sybil with his ultimate disinherited, aristocratic archtypes, the Jews. Like her father's, Sybil's symbolic value depends on her ahistoricity, but Sybil is much more clearly a symbol of the eternal and sacred itself than is her father.

Her establishment as a tautegorical symbol of the sacred is so obvious that it hardly needs rehearsing. One need only recall her first appearance in the book, amid the ruins of the abbey, in the garb of a religious, singing the evening hymn to the virgin, or the fact that the narrator calls her "the Religious," or that she is next seen in a posture meant to evoke visions of the Virgin, atop a small pony led by her father, or that she has lived all her life in a convent, is continually encountered in churches, and breaks into religious song at the slightest provocation:

> "if I ever gain [says Stephen Morley] the opportunity of fully carrying the principle of association into practice, I will sing *Nunc me dimittis*."
> "*Nunc me dimittis*," burst forth the Religious in a voice of thrilling melody, and she pursued for some minutes the divine canticle. (P. 84)

To her father's archaic English she adds Latin maxims. The obviousness of all this, however, is precisely what makes Sybil a tautegorical symbol of the sacred; Disraeli tries to make her mean nothing more nor less than she appears to mean.

There is no difference between facts and values in Sybil. All is transparent, obvious. Even her name signifies her essence and origin. It alludes to wisdom and deathlessness, and it is the same as that of her female ancestors. Her father's name, too, is identical with his forebears'. It is, indeed, that identity that revives Gerard's interest in tracing his ancestry: "When you came the other day, and showed me in the book that the last Abbot of Marney was a Walter Gerard, the old feeling stirred again" (p. 85). Tracing names in the Gerard family reveals the unity of name and thing. "Curious," muses Baptist Hatton, "how, even when peasants, the good blood keeps the good old family names" (p. 259). Sybil's given name really is a "given": unlike the book's false aristocrats, she need not be baptized by Hatton. There is no gap in her between origin and being, fact and value, for she has been displaced from the displacements of history.

Indeed, Sybil is utterly removed from all kinds of historical fact. As an embodiment of pure value, she remains completely uncontaminated by not only the political but also the social world, which is nevertheless depicted as a threat to her very existence. Sybil is often menaced by representatives of both nations, by working-class ruffians as well as by Lord Montchesney. Her dog, Harold, is both a fellow aristocrat[28] and a kind of portable cloister. In his absence she must rely for protection on Egremont, who rescues her twice. By making her seem unnaturally helpless and ignorant about society, the author thus emphasizes the incompatibility between Sybil and the actual social world. As a symbol of the sacred, she is identical with her separation from the profane: "holy walls," her father explains, "have made her what she is" (p. 85). Sybil thus represents a kind of value that is not socially produced, that is , indeed, produced by its removal from the social process of exchange.

Like Carlyle's heroic organic filaments, however, Sybil can only serve as foundation of the politie if she is brought into contact with the social world. Hence her marriage to Egremont, which represents the Coleridgean union of the sacred with its rightful representative, the state.[29] Through Sybil and Egremont, divinity is channeled into the politie, value transforms fact. Thus Egremont becomes the representative of a symbol; only in that way can he represent the nation. Through Egremont's union with the symbolic, politics is detached from social facts and political factions and fastened to the realm of values: "there was one voice that had sounded in that proud Parliament, that, free from the slang of faction, had dared to express immortal truths" (p. 296). Literary and desired political representation thus begin to coincide in the mode of the symbolic.

As we have already noted, however, Egremont's actual politics are unrepresented in the novel. The quotation above presents Egremont at two removes; Sybil is reading a newspaper account of Egremont's Parliamentary speech, but the actual contents of that speech are very briefly sketched. Moreover, it must be recalled that when Egremont marries Sybil he is no longer eligible to be a member of the House of Commons. He becomes a representative of a symbol, then, at the same moment when he leaves the contested public territory. The whole issue of Parliamentary representation and its relationship to transcendent politics is thereby quietly dropped. The confluence of political facts and values is achieved only through exclusion.

Sybil's restoration to the aristocracy, moreover, represents a similar confluence of values and facts. The issue of Sybil's restoration is complicated, for in order to regain her title, she must, it seems, enter history and society, the territories of irony, the milieux that corrode the symbol. Thus at least one critic, Patrick Brantlinger, has noted the seeming contradiction between Disraeli's satire of the aristocracy and his final "bestowal" of noble heridity on Sybil. The ending, he complains, "elevate[s] Sybil to a station of doubtful value."[30] The point would be a valid one if it were the case that Sybil ever represents any social class, but she never does. She does not represent first one class and then another, but neither. The method of her restoration, moreover, separates it from the pseudo-ennobling displacements in the book: she regains her title through the violence of a popular uprising, which merely reverses the original violence of her displacement from history. Instead of being another displacement, it is the reversal of a displacement, the undoing of history, In this sense, Sybil remains above history. There is no transformation of her into an aristocrat, no revelation about her. Like the queen to whom she is continually compared, she is one with her origins from the outset, the perfect and divine confluence of word and thing.

Consequently, Sybil is not elevated to aristocracy. As the embodiment of absolute value in the book, she cannot be elevated. Sybil's restoration, rather, is an elevation of the aristocracy. She bestows value on the title she takes, relegitimizing aristocracy in the novel and simultaneously realigning social facts and absolute values. We do not see Sybil after her restoration; all we see is this realignment. Lady St. Julians and Lady Bardolf (formerly Lady Firebrace) report that Lord Valentine "raves" about Sybil and that Egremont is one of the foremost peers of the Nation. Evaluation coincides with value, redeeming even Lady St. Julians, whose words are finally acknowledged truth. Representation in the social world is no longer misrepresentation.

But Sybil's restoration by no means puts an end to the book's irony and its source, the historical process of endless displacement. Indeed, her restoration reveals the ultimate symbiosis of ironic and symbolic representation in this novel. By relegitimizing the aristocracy, by making it once again a normative goal, Sybil reinforces the territorial constitution through which all energies are channeled toward aristocracy. Thus Sybil's restoration is shown to begin one of those series of displacements that underlie the book's irony:

> Dandy Mick was rewarded for all the dangers he had encountered in the service of Sybil, and what he conceived was the vindication of popular rights [Sybil's restoration]. Lord Marney established him in business, and Mick took Devilsdust for a partner. Devilsdust, having thus obtained a position in society, and become a capitalist, thought it but a due homage to the social decencies to assume a decorous appellation, and he called himself by the name of the town where he was born. The firm of Radley, Mowbray, and Co., is a rising one; and will probably furnish in time a crop of members of Parliament and peers of the realm. (P. 429)

Devilsdust, the nameless working-class orphan and political radical, has already in name replaced the late Earl de Mowbray, and his posterity are expected to purchase the title, once again creating the gap between signified and signifier that enables irony. Thus, paradoxically, symbolic representation (the unification of word and thing in Sybil) enters the historical process as the stable point out of which and toward which irony proceeds.

Instead of being quelled by symbolic representation, irony is, in a sense, enlivened by it. For the sought-after signifier, the aristocratic title, has received a transfusion of meaning from on high through Sybil's restoration, a transfusion that is the precondition of the symbol's future degeneration. Dandy Mick and Devilsdust, moreover, remain to absorb the ironic future that still accompanies all titles. Most importantly, although the triumph of symbolic representation does not exclude ironic representation, it does delay the moment of its collapse into descriptive representation. Dandy Mick and Devilsdust will ultimately represent their class, but only after they have established the appearance of difference from it. Their Chartist demands for direct representation are abandoned as they begin the circuitous journey to ironic representation demanded by the territorial constitution and legitimized by Sybil's restoration.

Disraeli is one of the few Victorian novelists to concentrate on the specifically political problem of the industrial revolution: its creation of a new class that demanded political representation. He is, thus, one of the few industrial novelists to take representation itself as his theme. In his attempt to discredit the model of descriptive political representation, the model adopted by both Utilitarians and Chartists, Disraeli took up the political position that provided the clearest alternative: the Romantic-Idealist position articulated by Coleridge and Carlyle. Inherent in this position, as we have seen, is the attempt to derive a theory of political representation from a larger theory of symbolic representation, which also subsumed a concept of literary representation. The theory that influenced Disraeli, therefore, entailed an isomorphic relationship between political and literary representation, between the ideology of his novel and his methods of representing that ideology.

We have also seen that by the 1840s the Romantic-Idealist position had lost its original exclusive commitment to symbolic, tautegorical representation. For a variety of historical reasons, an ironic potential had been discerned in the symbol itself and had then been located specifically in political symbols. Disraeli inherited a position that had already combined irony with tautegorical symbolism, and the exigencies of his own political situation reinforced that combination. Literary irony and symbolism thus become firmly associated with antidescriptive political theory, leading to a curious oxymoron: the political novel in which politics is always in the process of dissolving into a representation of something else—the social (ironically) or the sacred (symbolically)—and itself goes unrepresented.

What this industrial novel displays, then, is the exclusion of politics from the novel, even in the work of a writer who was above all a political man and who believed that politics, like literature, provided the best hope for reconciling facts and values. Disraeli cannot, finally, create a mode of representation for his desired politics. Politics and literature tend to exclude rather than complement each other, reminding us of Coningsby's earlier wish to replace the Parliament with the press: we ought to consider, the young hero tells us, a state consisting of "a free monarchy established on fundamental laws, itself the apex of a vast pile of municipal and local government ruling an educated people, represented by a free and an intelligent press." Here the place of the representative political institution is altogether usurped by the representative printed word.

The difficulty of reconciling political and literary representation, moreover, is not confined to novelists like Disraeli, who prefer ironic and symbolic methods. Indeed, as we will see in the next chapter, at least one later novelist, George Eliot, can be said to have based her early career on the assumption that descriptive fictional representation is in direct competition with descriptive political representation. As attempts to occupy the same space, realistic fictional representation of the populace and elective political representation of the populace excluded each other for Eliot. While considering the plight of the industrial working class in *Felix Holt*, she explicitly developed an alternative political model, one that permanently altered her methods of representation, exposing the contradictions within the realism which she espoused more explicitly and intelligently than any other Victorian novelist.

9

The Politics of Culture and the Debate over Representation in the 1860s

In a London art gallery in 1861, two middle-aged women stand before a painting of a stork killing a toad. The painting provokes a short, sharp argument. The older woman dislikes it intensely, calling it coarse and amoral; the younger woman admires it, explaining, somewhat condescendingly, that the purpose of art is the careful delineation of the actual. Good art, she insists, must show the world as it is. The older woman then pointedly asks whether it would be good art to delineate carefully men on a raft eating a comrade. According to the older woman's later report, the question silences her companion.[1]

In itself, the exchange is hardly remarkable. It seems still another iteration of a debate that was already wearing thin by 1861, the controversy between aesthetic idealists and realists. If the followers of the one orthodoxy required art to imbue reality with value, to show the world as it could be, followers of the other orthodoxy required art to record facts and show the world as it is. These two debaters, however, were more than followers of established orthodoxies. As an exchange between Harriet Martineau and George Eliot, women whose opinions had a profound effect on the theory and practice of literary representation, the dispute deserves closer attention.

George Eliot's naive belief, in 1861, in a totally unembellished rendering of reality might surprise not only those turn-of-the-century detractors who called her work tediously didactic, but also all those more recent critics who have rightly noted that even early works such as *Adam Bede* present a world at once probable and "shaped through and through by moral judgment and moral evaluation."[2] Martineau's remarks, too, might seem puzzling: certainly no early-Victorian writer seems more comfortable with unpleasant facts than the writer who— long before George Eliot professed to find "few sublimely beautiful women" and even fewer real "heroes"[3]—had introduced English readers to truly plebeian and unpicturesque protagonists, to dismal quotidian destinies, to an unflinching (at times even unfeeling) scrutiny of the harshest realities. Indeed, many of her contemporaries would have considered "men on a raft eating a comrade" an accurate emblem for Martineau's own social vision.[4]

The argument between the two women, then, was not, as it might have seemed to a casual eavesdropper, an argument between an aesthetic idealist and a realist, but rather a debate between two writers in a developing realist tradition who were eager to settle the relationship between facts and values. Both were bent on defending fictional practices developed explicitly to connect facts and values through representations of the "lower orders." Their argument helps illuminate the distance between those early industrial narratives with which this study opened, Martineau's *Illustrations of Political Economy*, and the narrative with which it will close, Eliot's *Felix Holt*. It reveals that the distance was in part created by a new insistence on representation for its own sake; but the distance was further enlarged in the 1860s by a widespread anxiety about the object of representation, an anxiety that, as we will see, led to new demands for an alliance between politics and literature that ultimately helped transform the procedures of English realism.

Theoretically at least, Harriet Martineau and George Eliot were equally dedicated to keeping facts and values continuous and inseparable. In the early stages of Eliot's career, the difference between the two writers resided in their disparate opinions about how fiction should render the continuity between facts and values. In a sense, Martineau was actually the more extreme realist since she seems to have believed not only that values can be easily induced from facts but also that facts can be even more easily deduced from values. Since she believed the world was a perfectly ordered Providential machine, she felt justified in deriving a set of particular facts, not from observation of the world, but from general principles about how things should work. One should therefore be able to read the *Illustrations* backward, beginning with the principles outlined at the end and deducing from them a narrative of particular facts. That, after all, is how Martineau describes their composition. And just as the descriptive particulars of the narrative are supposed to illustrate their values, that is, represent their values in such a transparent way that their values could also be said to represent them, those values are themselves facts illustrating still more inclusive values, for Martineau regarded political economy itself as an illustration of Providential necessity in general, a science that showed how facts derived from universal laws.[5] Realistic fiction, Martineau is claiming in her exchange with Eliot, must always show this connection; storks may indeed eat toads, but the reality of that fact lies in the manifestation of its connection to Providential design. "Mere delineation" is not dangerous in its accurate objectivity but in its inaccurate partiality, its willful obscuring of the links between facts and meaning, its deceitful suggestion that facts might be neutral. According to Martineau, a deductive, didactic method of fiction reaches the truth more efficiently than a random recording of perceived phenomena out of which one might try to tease a general law. Deducing facts from principles she knew to be true seemed to her the fastest and surest way to get the facts right.

George Eliot's narrative method purports to be inductive rather than deductive. Unable to share the older woman's belief in a benign Providential necessity, the younger adopts, as critics have shown, the methodology and diction of those who observe a more inscrutable process of evolution. Still, like Martineau, Eliot assumes a bond between facts and values. She clung to the hope that a detailed recording of everyday life might automatically lead to moral progress. This, at least, is the faith professed in the much-analyzed seventeenth chapter of *Adam Bede*, where the narrator defends herself against an imagined idealistic reader by claiming that realistic fiction could increase the world's stock of charity: "These fellow-mortals, every one, must be accepted as they are . . . it is these . . . you should tolerate, pity, and love: it is these more or less ugly, stupid, inconsistent people . . . for whom you should cherish all possible hopes, all possible patience." By recommending an acceptance of the obscure, the imperfect, and the commonplace, the narrator also recommends her own fictional practice as one of transformation. A better world will be created by George Eliot narrators, telling one another endless stories, struggling to include myriad details within the sphere of significance, and thereby gradually expanding the sympathetic imaginations of their hearers. Eliot assures us that we get from facts to values by the process of inclusion, equalization, and acceptance, by the slow-moving narrative method we now call metonymic realism.

Despite their shared assumptions, then, Martineau and Eliot developed very different models of realism. Neither could justify a hierarchy of facts; in theory, both believed that all facts are equally meaningful. But these beliefs led them to opposite conclusions about representation. Martineau reasoned that, since all facts are equally significant, the writer should simply select those most convenient for her purpose, for representation is always the illustration of general principles or it is not representation at all. In contrast, Eliot held that, since all facts are equally significant, the writer should include as many as possible, trusting general principles to emerge from the compilation. Although neither writer described her actual compositional practices in her theories, the theoretical dispute was clear-cut and fundamental.

And yet, if we are to trust Martineau's account of their 1861 conversation, George Eliot, so suddenly silenced, no longer seemed eager to argue that the artist need only multiply facts to arrive at values. Had Martineau hit on a difficulty that Eliot was herself beginning to find insistently perplexing? Even before 1861, the relationship between facts and values, the issue of representation itself, had been much more problematic for Eliot than for Martineau. Despite her explicit professions of faith in a readable universe, her very earliest fiction manifests a deep skepticism about the legibility of facts, the apprehendable significance of appearances.[6] Indeed, Eliot's early realism is so strongly marked by that skepticism that it seems its definitive trait, the trait that necessitates heaping sign upon sign and simultaneously guarantees that no accumulation of signs will ever speak for itself and thus render both narrator and narrative superfluous.

Even Eliot's early novels, then, evince an anxiety about representation that marked many nineteenth-century realist fictions. However, the discontinuity between facts and values, already apparent in her earlier work, became increasingly obtrusive in George Eliot's fiction during the 1860s. Why did this tension manifest itself so much more pronouncedly in her writing during that decade?[7] To answer this question, we must connect the artistic impasse that the novelist reached after *Silas Marner* with her growing desire to accommodate her literary methods of representation to her convictions about political representation. This desire, as we will see, is linked to a new emphasis on culture in the debate over representation, an emphasis that finally disrupts all the discursive patterns that had formerly composed the debate over the "Condition of England."

George Eliot's pre-1860s statements about literary representation reveal a close but paradoxical relationship to liberal, even Utilitarian, theories of value and political representation. Both assume that the accumulation of facts automatically produces value, and each asserts that the value of a representation is directly proportional to the amount of detail it includes about observable social reality.

For example, James Mill believed the best Parliament would be a detailed, proportional rendering of English society.[8] The fitness of a representative would largely be determined by his likeness to those he represents, his membership in certain social categories. The larger the franchise (the more individuals admitted to it without regard to property qualifications), the more the constituencies would return representatives who are socially allied with the majority of the total population of the district, that is, who are engaged in the same industry or otherwise share the economic interests of the majority. The more the representatives share these social traits with their constituencies, the more accurate and therefore the more valuable the whole representation—Parliament itself—becomes. The principle of representation here is jointly synecdochal and metonymic: Parliament would be a synecdochal miniature of society because each representative would be a part of what he represents; the representative's membership in his own constituency, however, is determined by his outward social relationship, his metonmyic manifestations of typicality. James Mill's project, then, could be called the effort to represent, synecdochally in the political realm, as many of the metonymic relationships of the social world as possible.

The similarity between James Mill's idea of Parliament as a representation of the social and Eliot's idea of the novel as a representation of the social is obvious. "Art is the next thing to life," Eliot claimed, and the task before the fiction writer was to represent the various classes through typical members, assuming (as James Mill did) that outward conditions create and signify inward states:

> The thing for mankind to know is, not what are the motives and influences which the moralist thinks ought to act on the laborer or the artisan, but what are the motives and influences which *do* act on him. We want to be taught to feel, not for the heroic artisan or the sentimental peasant, but for the peasant in all his coarse apathy, and the artisan in all his suspicious selfishness.[9]

In other words, the artist must represent not the "ought" but the "is." It was for this reason that Eliot saw the industrial novels, especially *Mary Barton* and *Alton Locke*, as important steps forward in the development of the novel. And it was also for this reason that she criticized Dickens in the article she wrote just before embarking on her own career as a novelist. In her review essay "The Natural History of German Life: Riehl," from which the above quotation is taken, she complains that Dickens fails to render typical and probable relationships between external and internal states when writing about the lower classes: "But for the precious salt of his humor, which compels him to reproduce external traits that serve, in some degree, as a corrective to his frequently false psychology, his preternaturally virtuous poor children and artisans, his melodramatic boatmen and courtesans, would be as noxious as Eugéne Sue's idealized proletaires" (p. 143). Dickens correctly reproduces signs but misses their significance; he fails to render the network of metonymic associations connecting social conditions, character, and its external signs. In contradistinction to this failure, George Eliot can be said to define her project in the literary realm as identical to James Mill's project in the political realm to represent as many of the metonymic relationships of the social world as possible.

In part because of the very analogy between them, however, there is an underlying antagonism between Eliot's claims for descriptive literary representation and James Mill's claims for descriptive political representation. As the above quotation from her essay on Riehl and the previous quotation from Adam Bede both indicate, Eliot saw her own literary practice as a primary mechanism for social reform. As such, it becomes an *alternative*, at least for the foreseeable future, to political representation. The working class, faulty and degenerate as it is, should be represented, not in Parliament, but in novels. Such novels would increase the classes' understanding of each other, but concentrating as they must (in Eliot's view) on the disabilities of the lower classes, they would also prevent premature moves toward the direct political representation of those classes. As Eliot explained in the essay on Riehl, the fiction she favors would disabuse people of the "miserable fallacy that high morality and refined sentiment can grow out of harsh social relations, ignorance, and want; or that the working classes are in a condition to enter at once into a millenial state of *altruism*" (p. 144). Because they are entirely lacking in altruism, Eliot claims, they are unfit to be brought into a representative political system. She uses the German peasant as a typical example of the lower-class political mentality: "His only notion of representation is that of a representation of ranks—of classes; his only notion of a deputy is of one who takes care, not of the national welfare, but of the interests of his own order" (p. 159). It is clear from this quotation that descriptive representation of the social world is precisely what Eliot wished to prevent in politics, and descriptive literary representation was her way of preventing it. In short, the literary representation of the people, as Eliot envisions it, takes the place of and forestalls their political representation.

In the 1860s Eliot began to have doubts even about the descriptive *literary* representation of the social. Her novels of the 1860s manifest a deep skepticism about the principle of mere aggregation in literature as well as politics. *Felix Holt* especially marks a turning point. In it Eliot attempts to represent not only the social, but also the political realm itself. Like *Sybil*, the novel attempts to become a representation of representation, in a sense absorbing the competition as well as offering an alternative to it. But *Felix Holt* does not entirely abandon the realistic representational mode. Just as *Sybil* was an ironic novel casting doubt on the efficacy of ironic representation, *Felix Holt* attempts to be a description of the evils of descriptive representation. Moreover, just as *Sybil* finally produces a wish for symbolic representation, *Felix Holt* also creates a yearning for an antidescriptive politics and an analogous literary form, a yearning that produces internal paradoxes and creates a new uneasiness about fictional form and about the relationship in general between facts and values. No longer does Eliot believe that the "ought" can grow out of the "is," in literature any more than in politics. As we will see, "is" and "ought" in *Felix Holt* are more than merely difficult to connect; they are purposely, programmatically disconnected by Eliot's politically inspired attempt to escape from the web of metonymic associations. Finally, in *Felix Holt*, because these connections must not be made, pure politics and literature, instead of representing a divine reality, as in *Sybil*, or a social reality, as in Eliot's earlier fiction, strive to represent merely one another.

Eliot's political inspiration came from several sources in the 1860s. She heard echoes on many sides of her own belief that politics should not be a descriptive representation of the social world. Those echoes were, of course, responses to a growing movement to enlarge the franchise and make Parliament more representative in James Mill's sense of the word. "Representation of the People" bills were continually before Parliament during the 1850s and 1860s. Radical M. P.s like John Bright and working-class reformers outside of Parliament appropriated the rhetoric of market-place accumulation to urge an extension of the franchise and to argue that including more classes in the political process would result in an improvement of the process. Opposed to this ideology of aggregation there stood, predictably, the defenders of elite representation on the Burkean model (Bagehot) and adherents of what we identified in the last chapter as the symbolic idea of representation (Disraeli). But in addition to these predictable opponents of reform, objectors to the bills arose also from within the camp of what had once been Utilitarianism itself. The Utilitarian principles of accumulation and description became less and less coherent, less and less a stable foundation on which to base a theory of representation.

In 1865–66 the Representation of the People Bill split the Liberal party wide open and even divided the inheritors of the Utilitarian tradition from each other. On one side, Radical M.P.s and their supporters adhered to the idea of proportional descriptive representation, a Parliament reproducing in miniature the relative class sizes of the whole population. Members like John Bright insisted on this numerical principle. Parliament was not, he reiterated endlessly, a "fair representation of the nation," for "only sixteen out of every hundred men are now on the electoral rolls, and . . . half the House of Commons . . . is elected by a number of electors not exceeding altogether three men out of every hundred in the United Kingdom."[10] Relying on the Utilitarian principle of individual representation, Bright reasoned that the larger the number of individual electors, the more valuable the representation. He did not ignore the fact that the principle of numerical inclusion would entirely change the class nature of Parliament. He accepted the working-class majority as a somewhat regrettable fact, which might, he hinted to a working-class audience in 1866, be changed by the very process of representing it politically:

> You cannot help being numerous; if you had had better government during the last hundred years—if the land had been more in the hands of the people and less in the hands of a small class—if you had had fewer wars, lighter taxes, better instruction, and freer trade, one-half of those in this country who are now called the working class, would have been, in comfort and position, equal to those whom we call the middle class.[11]

Good government, government by the working-class's own representatives, would transform the very social world it mirrors. Bright, like Eliot, believed that accurate representation finally transforms the reality described. But whereas Eliot held that faith for literary representation, Bright kept it for politics. Politically representing the working-class majority would lead to its absorption into the middle class. Thus, Bright was able to reconcile individualism, middle-class hegemony, and the accumulation principle of value by suggesting that, in the long run, accurate representation would create class mobility and class mobility would create a majority of middle-class electors. Thinking of the population as an aggregate of political individuals, all of whom should be included in the electorate, is thus the way to create value, both in the representation and ultimately in the thing represented.

Bright's major opponent among the Liberal M.P.s, Robert Lowe, was also a latter-day Benthamite.[12] However, his opinions on political representation differed markedly from Bright's. He openly feared the "mere working of numbers" on which Bright relied. Nevertheless, his residual Benthamism manifests itself in the fact that he played his own numbers game in speaking against extending the franchise. Like Bright, he seems to have been obsessed with finding a number that would define value in political representation, but whereas Bright concentrated on the ratio of electors to men in the general population, on a one-to-one correlation of citizens to votes, Lowe stressed the money value of the property qualification for the franchise. Lowe saw in Bright's favorite equation, one man equals one vote, a symbol of "uniformity and monotony of representation."[13] "I think," he told Parliament in 1866, "there is a danger that we may become too much like each other—that we may become merely the multiple of one number." Lowe did not abandon the idea that the political realm should be a mirror image of the social realm, but he claimed that only by maintaining the ten-pound franchise could the political be kept an accurate representation of the social;

> For, although it is quite true that a Bill for the Redistribution of Seats should aim at making Parliament a mirror of the country, it is also true that there can be nothing more inappropriate than the argument when applied to the enlargement of the franchise. For to pass a Bill which puts the power in a majority of the boroughs into the hands of the working classes, is not to make this House a faithful reflection of the country, but is to make it an inversion . . . by giving political power into the hands of those who have very little social power of any kind.[14]

On these grounds, grounds that reverse Bright by linking descriptive representation to an exclusive franchise, Lowe opposed any "devaluation" of the franchise. "Going down" by any amount from the ten-pound figure set in 1832 would, he insisted, begin a slide that could only stop at universal suffrage. Thus the only way to insure valuable (descriptively accurate) representation was to make sure the representative represented (property) value and therefore social power.

In the debate between Lowe and Bright over representation, there was agreement about the relationship between facts and values, for it was carried on within the confines of descriptive assumptions. Each man had a version of the numerical principle; each tried to find a ratio that would define the correct relationship between fact and value. For Bright, the larger the number of electors, the greater the value of the representation: there should be one hundred electors out of one hundred men in the population. He tried to make the formula one man equals one vote stand for individualism, accumulation, and unity; if the franchise had been sufficiently enlarged, he claimed, "we, the people in these islands, would have been no longer two nations. We should have felt more—that henceforth we are one people."[15] But the same formula stands in Lowe's rhetoric for the reduction of all values to the scale of individual pettiness, a politics of "that bare and level plain, where every ant's nest is a mountain and every thistle a forest tree."[16] For Lowe, the greater the amount of social power, measured by wealth, embodied in the individual electors, the more valuable their representation. Thus the formula £10 equals 1 vote, for Bright a symbol of exclusion and disunity, assured Lowe that value accumulated in the social realm will be accurately reflected in the political. Underlying both positions is an accumulation theory of value and a descriptive theory of political representation. Both men wanted to see the relationships of the social world reproduced in the political, but Bright wanted, by representing each individual, to represent the relative sizes of the classes and Lowe wanted to represent their relative power, which is itself represented by their property.

The debate among liberals inside Parliament, in its general outlines, then, did not probingly question older Utilitarian assumptions about facts and values or representation: the debate was over *which* social facts should be accumulated and described. But precisely by failing to challenge such assumptions, this debate indicates how little the principles of accumulation and description had come to mean in the 1860s. They no longer seemed to entail any single political program for liberals; they had lost their associations with political reform and social change. Indeed, Lowe uses the assumptions of the Utilitarians to arrive at a program of interest representation almost identical to that of the conservative Whigs of an earlier era.[17]

Since the principles had come to entail no single political program, it is not surprising that two writers who had inherited the best of the liberal tradition began looking for other bases on which to rest a theory of representation. John Stuart Mill and Matthew Arnold directly inspired George Eliot's political fiction of the 1860s, and *Felix Holt's* formal anomalies and achievements can only be understood with reference to their contributions to the theory of representation.

Matthew Arnold's series of short essays gathered in *Culture and Anarchy* and J. S. Mill's lengthy essay "On Representative Government" seem at first glance to have little in common. In the name of culture, Arnold refuses to identify specific remedies for the spiritual and social ills he describes. The exclusive concentration on "machinery," he claims, is England's problem and thus cannot be its cure. In contrast, "On Representative Government" is a detailed blueprint for an intricate piece of electoral machinery. Arnold trusts to the internal workings of culture; J. S. Mill, it seems, trusts to the external workings of an institution. Moreover, Mill's book, written in the relatively quiet first year of the 1860s, is very different in tone from *Culture and Anarchy*, which exudes, even after revisions, the atmosphere of crisis precipitated by the Hyde Park riots of 1866 that surrounded its original composition. Arnold's book, then, is often read as a reactionary statement, recommending a turn away from practical politics toward intellectual cultivation. Mill's, on the other hand, calls for increased active participation in the political realm by all classes and by both sexes.

Despite their fundamental differences, however, these two books have much in common. Indeed, to read *Culture and Anarchy* as a development of central themes in "On Representative Government" is to shed considerable light on both texts. For Arnold's book is then accurately placed on a continuum of liberal statements about representation in the 1860s, and Mill's book is identified as a text that radically undermines the Utilitarian principles of accumulation and description. Moreover, such a reading allows for a more precise definition of the political impulse of *Felix Holt* than has yet been made, for although it has long been recognized that Eliot's novel has an intimate relationship to *Culture and Anarchy*, the latter's connection to the larger liberal discourse on representation has not been completely understood, and consequently the curious intertwining of descriptive and antidescriptive elements in the novel has gone unremarked.

John Stuart Mill's "On Representative Government" has been read as an extension of the descriptive principle,[18] and this interpretation of the essay is perfectly understandable, for in addition to arguing for virtually universal suffrage (including female suffrage), Mill recommends Thomas Hare's elaborate scheme for the representation of minorities and thus often seems to advocate a correspondence theory of representation based on population.[19] Hare was a proportionalist, and Mill's essay at times seems to support his assumptions: "[Hare's system] secures a representation in proportion to numbers, of every division of the electoral body: not two great parties alone, with perhaps a few large sectional minorities in particular places, but every minority in the whole nation, consisting of a sufficiently large number to be, on principles of equal justice, entitled to a representative."[20] Passages such as this justify the conclusion that J. S. Mill, like his father and like John Bright, wanted the most accurate possible proportional correspondence between Parliament and the total population, a correspondence achieved through numerical inclusion and the representation of hitherto submerged constituencies.

J. S. Mill's reasons for supporting Hare's scheme, however, reveal a profound skepticism about both purely descriptive representation and the Utilitarian definition of value itself. The system of minority representation turns out to be a way of reorganizing the franchise to compensate for its extension, and thus in Mill we begin to see the connection between Utilitarian desires to extend the franchise and a new liberal attempt to redefine the nature of politics and split it off from civil society. Mill believed universal suffrage to be inevitable as well as desirable. He thought, as Bright did, that it would have an elevating and integrating effect on the working class. But in 1859, when it was suspected that working-class majorities would be neither deferential nor altruistic, he also feared the extension of the franchise and doubted the descriptive assumption underlying it, the assumption that the most valuable representation is the most accurate reflection of social facts:

> "The natural tendency of representative government, as of modern civilization, is towards collective mediocrity: and this tendency is increased by all reductions [of the property qualification] and extensions of the franchise, their effect being to place the principal power in the hands of classes more and more below the highest level of instruction in the community." (P. 259)

Here the accumulation of mere numbers leads to a devaluation of representation. Hare's system is seen by Mill as a way of reversing this trend and insuring some elite representation:

> In the false democracy which, instead of giving representation to all, gives it only to the local majorities, the voice of the instructed minority may have no organs at all in the representative body . . . Against this evil the system of personal representation proposed by Mr. Hare, is almost a specific. The minority of instructed minds scattered through the local constituencies, would unite to return a number, proportional to their own numbers, of the very ablest men the country contains. (P. 260)

If Mill had rested with this proposal, it might be argued that his assumptions remain descriptive and proportional, that he differs from Bright and Lowe only by coming up with yet another social fact to be described. Mill wishes the proportional representation of "instruction" just as Bright wants the proportional representation of class size and Lowe the proportional representation of property. But Mill did not rest here; he went on to advocate a system that is impossible to reconcile with those Utilitarian theories of value and representation that underlay his father's book.

The question of the representation of intellect is symptomatic of the degree of Mill's divergence from the older Utilitarian principles.[21] Although in the above passage he writes of "instructed minds" receiving representation "proportional to their own numbers," he quickly revises himself and supplements Hare's plan with a plan of his own to have votes "weighed as well as counted" (p. 261). This "plurality scheme," as he calls it, is designed to combat the twin evils of universal suffrage, "that of too low a standard of political intelligence, and that of class legislation" (p. 281), by giving plural votes to people with "mental superiority." "Mental superiority," Mill claims, could be ascertained by a number of signs: occupation, education, and voluntary examination "at which any person whatever . . . might prove that he came up to the standard of knowledge and ability laid down as sufficient, and be admitted, in consequence, to the plurality of votes" (286). Although the representatives of the instructed would not thus obtain a clear majority, they would have sufficient numbers to prevent the "class legislation" of the representatives of the uninstructed. Universal suffrage would, thus, not mean the proportional representation of various constituencies, but their disproportional representation, a reflection purposely distorted.

This proposed distortion differs from Lowe's in that Mill's is not designed simply to emphasize a discrete social fact, such as the possession of property. Mill has, actually, departed from all such descriptive intentions. His proposed Parliament would not correspond to any empirical social reality but would, rather, directly express, by distorting what is, that which ought to be. Mill, it turns out, wishes the state institution to represent value *to* the population. According to his essay, the state represents value, first, by so constructing its institutions that they teach the population what it should want instead of passively mirroring what it does want. By adopting Mill's plurality scheme, for example, the state would stand for no present social fact but for a normative value to be realized in the future:

> The national institutions should place all things that they are concerned with, before the mind of the citizen in the light in which it is good that he should regard them: and as it is for his good that he should think that every one is entitled to some influence, but the better and wiser to more than others, it is important that this conviction should be professed by the State, and embodied in the national institutions. (P. 283)

The state, then, in the very workings of its institutions, would not mirror the desires and ambitions of the population, but instruct the population about what its desires and ambitions should be. Value, in Mill's essay, thus becomes a set of normative propositions that are not arrived at by accumulating facts.

In addition to instructing rather than describing the population through its institutional structures, the state will also, Mill hopes, represent value divorced from fact by encouraging the electors to use the political process as a way of escaping from their ordinary, class-bound, personal selves. Indeed, Mill often sounds surprisingly like Coleridge and the other antidescriptive theorists who insisted that the very nature of the political was the suppression of those interested motivations that drive civil society. In exercising the franchise, Mill reasoned, the elector should not seek to represent himself, but to represent the public. Hence in "On Representative Government" he argues against the secret ballot, which both his father before him and he himself in an earlier, more orthodox Utilitarian phase, had warmly advocated: "The Spirit of the vote by ballot—the interpretation likely to be put on it in the mind of an elector—is that the suffrage is given to him for himself" (p. 301). This, of course, is precisely what descriptive theorists thought the suffrage should be given to people for.[22] But Mill, again concentrating on what the state represents to the people ("the interpretation likely to be put on it in the mind of an elector") through its institutions, wishes to see it make a sharp distinction between the empirical self, encumbered by personal and class interests, mere social facts, and the disinterested political self, laden with values. "In any political election," he continues, "the voter is under an absolute moral obligation to consider the interest of the public, not his private advantage, and give his vote to the best of his judgement, exactly as he would be bound to do if he were the sole voter, and the election depended upon him alone" (p. 304). The introduction of the ballot would introduce an aura of privacy that would encourage the voter to think of politics as simply another arena for expressing his private interests. The public realm of politics, he reasoned, had to be kept literally public, with electors declaring their votes vocally, to insure that the vox populi would not be replaced by a mere assortment of private scribblings.

Mill undermines both the accumulation theory of value and the descriptive theory of representation on which his father's position rested. The son, like the father, wanted to involve the largest possible number of people in the political process, but unlike the father, he did not conceive of that process as merely a representation of the accumulated and competing interests of the people. In Mill's scheme, politics is not a process of thousands of individuals representing themselves and thereby producing transformations (as in John Bright's vision); rather, it is a process of thousands transforming themselves directly, freeing themselves from their social determinations and entering a realm of disinterested reason or pure value. Indeed, Mill wanted to give plural votes to the "mentally superior" because he thought they were the least likely to vote their personal or class interest, or more precisely, he thought their selves were less likely to be determined by narrow, partial, or, to use his word, "sinister" interests. Thus the disproportionate representation of the mentally superior not only teaches the population to value learning and therefore, over time, transforms them, but also immediately insures that political discourse will be more than the mere reiteration of a social discourse; it will instead be the articulation of disinterested reason.

In some ways, "On Representative Government" seems to belong as much in the tradition of Coleridge as in that of James Mill, for although it makes an argument for universal suffrage, it makes it in conjunction with a radically antidescriptive account of representation. This conjunction is a peculiarity of liberal thought in the 1860s, and in "On Representative Government" we can clearly see its underlying logic, for here Mill puts the two previously antagonistic ideas into a system that makes them seem to depend upon one another. Universal suffrage creates the need for a politics that is no longer a reflection of the social world; the creation of politics as *the* realm of value suggests, in turn, an arena where all might eventually transcend their class interests. The creation of such an arena provides a new opportunity for class harmony that could only be realized if the working class were allowed to participate. Universal suffrage thus creates the need for an antidescriptive politics, and an antidescriptive politics allows and even justifies universal suffrage.

This new direction in liberal thought, moreover, helps explain why George Eliot took politics as her subject matter in the 1860s, for the new conjunction of antidescriptive and universalist elements imposed an unusual political burden on intellectuals, who, as we have seen, were expected to represent the new disinterested politics directly. Eliot, who attended very closely to the development of Mill's thought in the 1860s, and who was herself a primary promoter of the decade's discourse about intellectuals, could not escape becoming conscious of this burden. No longer could she offer her own descriptive representations of society as an alternative to political representation, for the intellectual's task had been redefined. She should no longer merely represent the totality of society as it is; she should also represent that realm of pure value in which what should be comes into being: the political.

If Mill forged a binding link between Eliot's duty to represent politics and her role as an intellectual, Matthew Arnold made an even tighter bond between that duty and her role as an artist. Many of Arnold's ideas in *Culture and Anarchy* were obviously anticipated by Mill in "On Representative Government," but Arnold develops those ideas in directions that exaggerate their anti-Benthamism and their antidemocratic implications. In Arnold's book, the liberal break with descriptive representation becomes explicit, and so does the connection between that break and universal suffrage. Additionally, however, Arnold turns his critique of descriptive representation into a general attack on British political institutions and then proposes a new ground for those institutions, a ground with particular significance for a writer like Eliot: culture.

Arnold's antipathy to the Utilitarian theory of value needs little demonstration. Even the most casual reader of *Culture and Anarchy* will recall the author's scorn for the idea that social order and value result from the aggregation and competition of atomized facts, individual wills and interests. But it should also be noted that Arnold sees the Utilitarian theory of value as a general fallacy underlying all the various descriptive approaches to political representation, all positions resting on the assumption that the political realm should be a reflection of the social. And it should also be noted that Arnold sees this descriptive bias at work everywhere in English politics. One whole chapter of *Culture and Anarchy*, "Doing as One Likes," is devoted to refuting the Utilitarian reliance on individual liberty as the producer of value and to showing how ubiquitous Utilitarian assumptions are in English political thought. Thus, the Hyde Park rioter for the franchise is merely extending the logic of his betters, not introducing a new principle of representation:

> He has no visionary schemes of revolution and transformation, though of course he would like his class to rule, as the aristocratic class like their class to rule, and the middle class theirs. . . . The rough has not yet quite found his groove and settled down to his work, and so he is just asserting his personal liberty a little, going where he likes, assembling where he likes, bawling as he likes, hustling as he likes. Just as the rest of us,—as the country squires in the aristocratic class, as the political dissenters in the middle class—he has no idea of a *State*. [23]

Arnold follows Mill arguing that, as long as the government is the mere reflection of social facts, the representation of "our ordinary selves, which do not carry us beyond the ideas and wishes of the class to which we happen to belong" (p. 94), no adequate idea of the state can develop. A government which is the mere description of a set of social relationships—no matter what those relationships are—will never develop an adequate ground of authority: "we are all afraid of giving to the State too much power, because we only conceive of the State as something equivalent to the class in occupation of the executive government, and are afraid of that class abusing power to its own purposes" (p. 95). At this point Arnold, in concluding his argument, stresses again that this disempowering fallacy about representation is at bottom a fallacy about the relation of facts to values:

> And [we will be afraid] with much justice; owing to the exaggerated notion which we English, as I have said, entertain of the right

and blessedness of the mere doing as one likes, of the affirming oneself, and oneself just as it is. People of the aristocratic class want to affirm their ordinary selves, their likings and dislikings; people of the middle class the same, people of the working class the same. By our every-day selves, however, we are separate, personal, at war; we are only safe from one another's tyranny when no one has any power; and this safety, in its turn, cannot save us from anarchy. And when, therefore, anarchy presents itself [in the form of working-class riots for the franchise] as a danger to us, we know not where to turn. (P. 95)

No accumulation or combination of mere social facts will add up to values. Like Mill, Arnold argues that if England is to be saved from anarchy, if it is to deal with working-class demands for the franchise without disintegrating through intensified class conflict, the state must become the representative of something other than social facts.

That something is, in Arnold's phrase, the "best self," by which "we are united, impersonal, at harmony" (p. 95). Certain individuals, Arnold assures us, have already managed to rise above their social and personal selves: "Therefore, when we speak of ourselves as divided into Barbarians [aristocrats], Philistines [middle class], and Populace [working class], we must be understood always to imply that within each of these classes there are a certain number of *aliens*, if we may so call them,—persons who are mainly led, not by their class spirit, but by a general *humane* spirit, by the love of human perfection" (p. 109). These "aliens," as their name indicates, are even more thoroughly defined by their asocial characteristics than Mill's intellectual elite, but they serve the same function in both men's political thought: they embody the things to which politics should be devoted but which are necessarily excluded from politics under descriptive systems of representation. "In other countries," Arnold argues, "the governors, not depending so immediately on the favour of the governed, have everything to urge them, if they know anything of right reason . . . to set it authoritatively before the community. But our whole scheme of government being *representative*, every one of our governors has all possible temptation, instead of setting up before the governed who elect him, and on whose favour he depends, a high standard of right reason, to accomodate himself as much as possible to their natural taste for the bathos" (p. 113–14). Thus even if a representative were himself an "alien," he would be forced to speak "a sort of conventional language, or what we call clap-trap, which is essential to the working of representative institutions" (p. 116). All classes are hence "left to believe that, not only in our own eyes, but in the eyes of our representative and ruling men, there is nothing more admirable than our ordinary self, whatever our ordinary self happens to be, Barbarian, Philistine, or Populace" (p. 117).

Arnold's way of pitting the best self against the ordinary self, then, and associating the former with the state is very close to Mill's method of opposing "public spirited," disinterested action to personal and class-bound action; and Arnold's elevation of the "aliens" closely parallels Mill's arguments for creating elite representation through his plurality scheme. Arnold is simply more aware of the sharp break with discriptive theories of representation implied in establishing these distinctions. Arnold's book, however, does not just recapitulate, on a higher level of self-awareness, ideas already articulated by Mill; rather, it uses Mill's ideas, then widespread in liberal, intellectual circles, as a foundation for a new argument about the content of political representation. Mill writes of "mental superiority" and the predominance of "right reason" in the intellectual elite who should be disproportionately represented in Parliament. Arnold also uses these terms when describing the "remnant" of aliens. But whereas Mill uses "education" in general to describe the process by which one rises above his personal, class-bound self, Arnold uses "culture," a word that gives a wholly different emphasis to Arnold's discussion. The two terms are, finally, equally vague; Mill leaves education completely undefined, and Arnold defines culture simply as "a pursuit of our total perfection by means of getting to know, on all the matters which most concern us, the best which has been thought and said in the world" (p. 6). Nevertheless, despite the common vagueness of their terms, Arnold associates culture with a timeless, transcendent body of texts and other works of art. Pursuing both "sweetness and light" without regard to practical considerations, culture is the process that scrapes away economic, sectional, and class identity (social identity itself), leaving the pure and disinterested kernel of the best self behind. It is this self that the state should represent. And what is this self? The knowledge of the best that has been thought and said. It follows that the state should represent culture.

Through this line of reasoning, culture, especially literary culture, a realm of values, becomes opposed to society, a realm of facts. Through this line of reasoning we are also returned to a theory of representation even more like Coleridge's than Mill's was, for Arnold, like Coleridge, explicitly links, in his theory of culture, literature and the state. Unlike Coleridge, however, he cannot link them by making them joint symbols of a higher reality, the Word of God, for he wants to justify an entirely secular culture, one distinct from religion. Consequently culture and the state become all the more exclusively interdependent. Indeed, it is almost impossible to differentiate the two, for in the lucid circularity of Arnold's argument they seem to indicate only each other: "We want an authority, and we find nothing but jealous classes, checks and a deadlock; culture suggests the idea of the *the State*. We find no basis for a firm State-power in our ordinary selves; culture suggests one to us in our *best self*" (p. 96). And this best self, required by the state that is required by culture, turns out to be "the very self which culture, or the study of perfection, seeks to develop in us" (p. 95). Thus pure politics and culture grasp one another in a tight embrace of mutual support, having cut themselves off from any dependence on a God above or a social world below. They end by representing one another.

The Politics of Culture and the Problem of Realism

This desire to have an exclusive representational link between politics and culture is at the heart of *Felix Holt*. *Romola* had earlier reflected the consequences for George Eliot's realism of the need for an alternative to descriptive representation, but *Felix Holt* is the first of Eliot's novels to acknowledge the contemporary political sources of this need. Whereas in *Romola* Eliot turned to a distant, foreign past, in *Felix Holt* she returns to the familiar recent history of England, examining the problems of facts and values as they emerge from the events of a provincial parliamentary election. In this novel she undertakes the task of the Arnoldian intellectual and attempts the direct representation of pure political value in the characterization of her protagonist. The consequences of this attempt are various, but the most startling and significant is the protagonist's outspoken opposition to the novelist's usual methods of representation. No longer able to squelch an imaginary idealist opponent, as in *Adam Bede*, the narrator now seems undermined by Felix's own cultured mode of beholding reality, a mode that unsettles the assumptions of descriptive representation by denying the interpretable significance of those signs that supposedly represent social facts.

Felix Holt is full of comments about the nature of signs. The first meeting between Felix and the Reverend Rufus Lyon explicitly introduces the subject of the problematic relationship between outward signs, or facts, and inner significance. In this conversation, the signs of the social, the representations of mere fact, are explicitly devalued. Felix and Mr. Lyon, the book's two moral arbiters, admit to one another that they scarcely see the conventional physical signs by which their fellows communicate their importance and priorities. When Felix enters the room, we are told what he does not see. He does not see the wax candle on the table that makes the dissenting minister feel uneasy:

> when, after seating himself, at the minister's invitation, near the little table which held the work-basket, he stared at the wax-candle opposite to him, he did so without any wonder or consciousness that the candle was not of tallow. But the minister's sensitiveness gave another interpretation to the gaze which he divined rather than saw; and in alarm lest this inconsistent extravagance should obstruct his usefulness, he hastened to say—
> "You are doubtless amazed to see me with a wax-light, my young friend; but this undue luxury is paid for with the earnings of my daughter, who is so delicately framed that the smell of tallow is loathsome to her."
> "I heeded not the candle, sir, I thank Heaven I am not a mouse to have a nose that takes note of wax or tallow."[24]

Mr. Lyon, who has not even actually seen Felix's gaze, replies that he is "equally indifferent."

The implied "mouse" who does have a nose for wax or tallow is the minister's unregenerate daughter, Esther. But we must note that the narrator also falls into this category of mouse, and so do all of us who are forced by the narrative method to read internal significances through a set of external, metonymic signs. Narrator and reader must make meaning out of the petty facts that Felix is too cultivated and "abstracted," as the narrator repeatedly tells us, to notice. It is through wax candles that we come to know Esther, and it is through the detail of Felix's inattention to such details that we come to know him. Our first introduction to Felix, then, reveals the wide discrepancy in this novel between the state of mind explicitly recommended in the cultured person of Felix and the mental practices actually encouraged by the method of Eliot's realism.

We soon learn, moreover, that Felix's inattention to metonymic signs contains a curious paradox; it is not just a casual abstraction but a programmatic denial of the meanings and values conventionally attached to signs. In his person, Felix is more than an escapee from realism (as the Reverend Rufus Lyon is); he represents an attack on conventional reading. This fact becomes clear when he discusses his own metonymic unreadability. Referring to himself, Felix says to Rufus,

> "You're thinking that you have a roughly-written page before you now."
> That was true. The minister, accustomed to the respectable air

of provincial townsmen, and especially to the sleek well-clipped gravity of his own male congregation, felt a slight shock as his glasses made perfectly clear to him the shaggy-headed, large-eyed, strong-limbed person of this questionable young man, without waistcoat or cravat. (P. 55)

Faced with this illegible creature, Rufus tries to suspend "interpretations." Nevertheless, he inadvertently gives a spiritual meaning to Felix's appearance:

"I myself have experienced that when the spirit is much exercised it is difficult to remember neckbands and strings and such small accidents of our vesture, which are nevertheless decent and needful so long as we sojourn in the flesh. And you too, my young friend . . . are undergoing some travail of mind."(P. 55)

But Rufus has misread these significant absences about Felix's person; they do not betoken the distractedness of an unquiet spirit. Felix is not simply inattentive to all conventional signs of respectable prosperity; he is, rather, actively hostile to them, for he sees them not as arbitrary signs but as material causes of spiritual degeneration. Rufus tries to bring him to a relatively settled Protestant view of the relationship between outward appearance and inward essence, a view that stresses the conventionality of signs: "The ring and the robe of Joseph were no objects for a good man's ambition, but they were the signs of that credit which he won by his divinely-inspired skill, and which enabled him to act as a saviour to his brethen" (p. 59). Felix, however, will have none of this talk about crediting such appearances. It is his avowed purpose to prove that these so-called signs are not signs at all, but actual promoters of inner corruption. He answers Rufus,

"O yes, your ringed and scented men of the people!—I won't be one of them. Let a man once throttle himself with a satin stock, and he'll get new wants and new motives. Metamorphosis will have begun at his neck-joint, and it will go on till it has changed his likings first and then his reasonings, which will follow his likings as the feet of a hungry dog follow his nose." (P. 59)

Oddly, Felix, who professes not to be interested in outward appearances, actually believes some of those appearances to be absolutely related to inner states. He reverses the normal causality of realism: instead of believing that meanings find expression in signs, he believes that signs cause their meanings. In Felix's image, the sign literally makes its own meaning.

Felix, therefore, first attributes too little and then too much to the world of appearances. He first pronounces them unworthy of his notice, arbitrary and thus insignificant phenomena; but he then reverses himself and pronounces them perniciously powerful representations that paradoxically determine the reality for which they stand. According to the first account, they are meaningless epiphenomena; according to the second, they are the primary reality; they have been reified into essences.

Before examining the logic underlying this paradox and its significance for the novel as a whole, we should note that Felix's second attitude toward material signs is as antithetical to Eliot's usual method of representation as was his earlier indifference, for it makes values too fixed and obvious in material facts. It turns signs into conspicuous symbols, leaving no room for the realist's project of interpretation, of accumulating and sifting appearances to discover the really real. Such a project relies on the arbitrariness of signs, thus on their independence, but it cannot tolerate their reification into entities so powerfully primary that they absorb all meaning into themselves and become one with their values.

Thus, perhaps feeling her *raison d'etre* threatened from two sides by the protagonist, the narrator of *Felix Holt* assures us that the real world is one in which signs can neither be ignored nor be perceived as obtruding and static meanings. For example, she criticizes the "little minister" for wanting a more fixed and obvious relationship between signs and their meanings than an ambiguous world permits:

> He cared intensely for his opinions, and would have liked events to speak for them in a sort of picture-writing that everybody could understand. The enthusiasms of the world are not to be stimulated by a commentary in small and subtle characters which alone can tell the whole truth. (P. 327)

The narrator, however, never explicitly criticizes Felix, who, after all, insists on "picture-writing" even more strenuously than Rufus does:

> It was a constant source of irritation to him that the public men on his side were, on the whole, not conspicuously better than the public men on the other side; that the spirit of innovation, which with him was a part of religion, was in many of its mouthpieces no more of a religion than the faith in rotten boroughs; and he was thus predisposed to distrust Harold Transome. (P. 169)

Here we have, once again, Felix, with the author's apparent complicity, complaining about the emptiness of conventional signs, only this time the political dimension of the complaint is explicit. We might say that Felix's simultaneous disdain for and fear of signs always had an implied political parallel in the joint contempt and alarm with which the book faces those new political phenomena, the workers; they are also at once empty of real political meaning and capable of usurping all meaning. The above passage, however, applies the critique of signs to the sphere of traditional Parliamentary politics. Harold Transome, the Radical political candidate, is a mere arbitrary sign. There is no conspicuous connection between Harold and the party he stands for, according to Felix. Moreover, the label radical names no inner essence of Harold that is conspicuous to Felix. Harold is an anomaly who outwardly seems to have become a radical simply by claiming to be one, and whose claim has apparently had no transforming effect on his inner self. It is this independence of the word from the thing it supposedly represents that Felix refuses, with the author's apparent approval, to accept.

The maligned separation of the word from its referent, however, a separation that here makes the word seem insignificant, is conceived by Felix as the consequence of the all-determining significance of other signs, for Harold and his election agents are those "ringed and scented men of the people" whose satin stocks determine their characters and cause their inability to be true representatives of radicalism. The emptiness of the independent, arbitrary word, it seems, results from the determinism of the reified sign, which draws all meaning toward itself. This latter is the perfectly consequential sign that Felix fears, but it is also, because it becomes one with its meaning, the sign for which Felix yearns.

Felix's longing, moreover, is at least partly shared by the narrator, for whom Felix himself becomes a piece of that "picture-writing" she elsewhere repudiates. In her descriptions of Felix, the narrator gives the same details repeatedly and always makes them stand for the same inner qualities, qualities that can be summed up in the word "culture":

> Felix Holt's face had the look of the habitual meditative abstraction from objects of mere personal vanity or desire, which is the peculiar stamp of culture, and makes a very roughly-cut face worthy to be called 'the human face divine.' Even lions and dogs know a distinction between men's glances; and doubtless those Duffield men, in the expectation with which they looked up at Felix, were unconsciously influenced by the grandeur of his full yet firm mouth, and the calm clearness of his grey eyes. (P. 272)

With his booming voice, his massive frame, his leonine head, and his perfect integrity, Felix has nothing small or subtle about him. His meaning is known unconsciously by those he encounters, and therefore he need not be perceived in detail and deciphered. In his character, appearance and essence seem pure and identical. We do not need to see much of Felix because what we do see is wholly expressive, a "picture-writing that everybody could understand."

Felix's status as picture-writing is never more apparent than during the episodes of the riot and trial, the very episodes that seem to separate explicitly his appearance from his reality. He appears to be guilty of leading a riot, actually kills a constable, and is accused of manslaughter. He is arrested and placed on trial, where the prosecution produces "picture-writing," the outline of appearances, against him. Indeed, this trial is the context for the narrator's disparaging remarks about oversimplifying the relationship between facts and values. Here at last, it seems, Felix can only be acquitted by a "commentary in small and subtle characters." The trial, one expects, will be a triumph of inductive realism in which truth is rendered by gathering and interpreting the details that completely change the picture.

This expectation, however, is disappointed, for instead of filling in the facts of Felix's case, the defense's most important witness, Esther, simply sweeps them aside: "His nature is very noble; he is tenderhearted; he could never have had any intention that was not brave and good" (p. 415). This testimony is hardly sufficient to exonerate Felix in the eyes of the law, yet everyone in the courtroom is willing to believe it. In marked contrast to both *Alton Locke* and *Mary Barton*, where trials were used to complicate and thematize certain narrative problems (the problems of causality and character formation), *Felix Holt* uses its trial to deny a problem of representation. The disjunction between facts and values is only a distant threat in this episode. No one who has the slightest contact with Felix ever doubts his innocence, and Esther's testimony convinces everyone else. He is finally delivered simply because he is obviously and indisputably good. The unmistakable marks of his "cultured nature" (p. 375), as Esther calls it, overwhelm the evidence, the facts, once again emphasizing that the meaning of Felix Holt cannot be reached by multiplying appearances, most of which are insignificant.

The appearances are made insignificant, however, by the emptying power of certain signs that apparently have a life of their own. In this case those signs are "the grandeur of [Felix's] full yet firm mouth, and the calm clearness of his grey eyes," which can create their own reality even in the dimmest beholder. Thus even the narrator sometimes comes under Felix's spell and abandons herself to the seeming certainties of picture-writing. And for the narrator, as for Felix, those certainties come to entail contradictory conceptions of signs: signs appear to be either contemptibly insignificant or awesomely all significant. In either case, they take on properties incommensurable with the narrator's official belief that the truth can be known only through a "commentary in small and subtle characters."

The Politics of Culture and the Problem of Representation; or, The Representable versus the Representative

Felix, then, contradicts the narrator's normal and explicitly articulated narrative practices, and this unremarked but nevertheless obvious contradiction strikingly manifests the disruptive power of the antidescriptive representational theories formulated by Eliot and her contemporaries. But *Felix Holt* does more than display the problems that the politics of culture created for the realist writer; it also elucidates the central problem within the discourse of culture itself, revealing the paradoxical relationship between the Arnoldian idea of culture and that of representation: on the one hand, culture disparages representation; on the other hand, it elevates representation onto a plane above the world represented, a plane on which it constitutes its own separate and determining reality without attaching itself to some higher realm of spiritual value, without, in other words, becoming symbolic. Felix's alternately scornful and awed responses to the devalued signs of the social point toward the novel's larger dilemma about representation in general: a descriptive representation of the social becomes a mere fact, but a representation cut off from the social seems to violate novelistic assumptions of referentiality in the process of empowering a realm composed completely of representations.

Although Felix is sometimes presented as a piece of picture-writing, a transparent representative of culture, he is just as often made the object of ludicrous misinterpretations. In this and in several other ways, the novel repeatedly stresses his nonrepresentativeness. Felix is in many ways a latter-day Sybil, but unlike his prototype, he is neither narratively nor symbolically explicable. As a disinherited aristocrat and a symbol of the divine, Sybil is at all times a piece of picture-writing. Her severance from the social world and its subtle system of conventional signs is referable to both her origins and her obvious symbolic significance. Indeed, the plot is so constructed that Sybil's very removal from the social realm is itself socially contingent and is, moreover, the direct cause of her spiritual elevation. The declassed member of the old Catholic nobility, sent to a convent and thus able to retain and represent the spiritual authority of her ancestors, Sybil is superficially overdetermined by Disraeli's adaptation of literary conventions to his political purpose.

Felix, however, presents immediate problems if we appeal either to his origins or to his status as a symbol. Like Sybil, Felix is supposed to represent a realm of pure value, but his separation from the social is neither socially contingent nor, strictly speaking, spiritually significant. Felix is the embodiment of the best self, the self absolutely unconditioned by mere social facts. He is, in short, Arnold's "alien," and hence there is not, nor can there be, any social explanation for his development, for any such explanation would make the best self the mere product of the very conditions that shape and constrain the ordinary self. Felix, feeling a strong sensation of revulsion, simply rejects his ordinary self after briefly giving in to his most sensual impulses. "I was converted," he tells Rufus Lyon, "by six weeks' debauchery" (p. 57). He goes on to explain:

> If I had not seen that I was making a hog of myself very fast, and that pig-wash, even if I could have got plenty of it, was a poor sort of thing,[25] I should never have looked life fairly in the face to see what was to be done with it. I laughed out loud at last to think of a poor devil like me, in a Scotch garret, with my stockings out at heel and a shilling or two to be dissipated upon, with a smell of raw haggis mounting from below, and old women breathing gin as they passed me on the stairs—wanting to turn my life into easy pleasure. Then I began to see what else it could be turned into. Not much, perhaps. This world is not a very fine place for a good many of the people in it. But I've made up my mind it shan't be the worse for me, if I can help it. . . . That's the upshot of my conversion, Mr. Lyon, if you want to know it." (P. 57)

With its concentration on physical decay—on raw entrails and sour breath—counterposed against physical desire, Felix's speech almost equates his conversion with the transcendence of the body that had formerly held him a prisoner of its contradictions. But this transcendence leads to the rejection of all of Felix's given social "conditions." He drops out of the lower-middle class, gives up his father's inheritance of quack medicines, and resolves to make his home among "people who don't follow the fashions" (p. 58). He does all this in the name of accepting his natural place in society, but Rufus Lyon rightly recognizes that Felix is practicing a kind of unwordliness that amounts, as we have already noted, to a simultaneous fear and attempted disregard of the social. The ascendancy of the best self over the ordinary self in Felix is proved by his ability to trade in one set of social conditions for another, because at the moment of the trade, social conditions themselves lose their conditioning power. In turn, Felix's ability to deter mine his determinants must itself remain undetermined, beyond the reach of social and historical, indeed of narrative explanations.

The inexplicability of the working-class hero's development, we should remember, is characteristic of the industrial novel. When we last encountered it, however, it constituted a contradictory moment within narratives preoccupied with problems of linear plot causality and character development. *Felix Holt* is simply unconcerned about these issues in the life of Felix himself. His freedom from social conditions is not stressed in order to prove his possession of a free will, but rather in order to prove his significance as the representative of the best self, the self that is left when the merely social is cut away. Hence, Felix, again, resembles Sybil more closely than he resembles the unaccountable working-class heroes of the 1840s, whose only claim to freedom from social determination was the incoherence of their stories or the disintegration of their characters. In contradistinction, the more political protagonists, Sybil and Felix, achieve coherence by transcending the social. As we saw in the last chapter, however, Sybil's transcendence is given not only in the plot but also in the very conventions of symbolism: meaning supposedly descends through Sybil from the realm of divine significance to that of social fact. What appear to be the social conditions of Sybil's life are not really conditions at all, but are rather the channels through which divinity enters the world and is at the same time kept separate from it.

No gothic ruins, Latin phrases, or medieval apparel, however, provide a ground of absolute value and intelligibility for Felix. He represents a realm that is not at all given, but is, rather, in the process of being created by books like *Felix Holt*. He represents a pure, disinterested politics and a pure, disinterested culture that ostensibly represent only one another, disregarding alike the worlds of absolute spirituality (the province of religion) and mere mundane self-interest (the province of civil society). Felix is, therefore, in all his coherence, cut off not only from social-historical (narrative) intelligibility but also from readily available symbolic intelligibility. The realm he is supposed to represent, moreover, is not only largely uncreated but also essentially antagonistic to the symbolism that confers intelligibility on characters like Sybil, for if a symbol is a "natural" or participating representative of a fixed and eternal truth, a supposed extension of referent into sign that asserts the identity of both signifier and signified, sign and referent, then the ideology of culture wipes out the possibility of symbolism by breaking the chains of representation that formerly linked realm to realm.

Felix Holt stresses these newly made discontinuities and the problems they create for conventional interpretation by introducing Felix to us through the misinterpretations of Rufus and Esther Lyon. As we have seen, Rufus registers our confusion over Felix's refusal to be socially readable, his obstinate rejection of conventional metonymic signs. Rufus is not long bothered by his side of Felix's character since he himself tends to ignore such signs. He is, however, lastingly bemused by Felix's refusal to take on religious significance. He is unsatisfied by Felix's spiritual autobiography and objects to the younger man's use of the word "conversion," which he at first considers "unseemly." For Rufus, there are only two dimensions of being: the social of self-interested and the religious or self-transcending. Felix's opposition to his father's medicines falls into neither of these categories, and hence Rufus can at first make no sense of it. Felix's unfamiliar language confuses Rufus, for, proceeding from a realm as yet uncreated for the minister, it fails to place Felix within either a mundane or a sacred context: "Notwithstanding his conscientiousness and a certain originality in his own mental disposition, [Rufus] was too little used to high principle quite dissociated from sectarian phraseology to be as immediately in sympathy with it as he would otherwise have been" (p. 56). As we have seen, Rufus and Felix both insist that values are detached from the social process of conventional signification, but they represent different forms of detachment. Rufus's detachment, like Sybil's, is long-established, given, marked out by its own gradually accumulated conventional signs. Felix's form of detachment from the social, the idea of the best-self, can only come into being by distinguishing itself from that of Rufus. Like Arnold in *Culture and Anarchy*, George Eliot in *Felix Holt* uses religion as the primary differential term against which culture is defined.

Hence Felix, relentlessly insisting not only on his distance from the merely social but also on his secularism, is an enigma to the simple, bipartite mind of Rufus Lyon. Rufus's confusion, however, is necessary to allow us to distinguish between this new kind of disinterestedness and the old, familiar religious kind. Esther's misunderstanding of Felix develops a similar definitive contrast: a contrast between what is conventionally thought to be cultured and what is authentically cultured in an Arnoldian sense. Felix's first conversation with Rufus merges into his first encounter with Esther, who, as we have seen, is predefined as a user of conventional codes. She despises the merely fashionable, a characteristic that gives her an initial, ironic likeness to Felix, who claims to be one of the "people who don't follow the fashions." But Esther's distaste for the ostentatiously fashionable itself rests on social considerations; brazen advertizers of their own fashionableness are, she declares, essentially vulgar: "[Miss Jermyn] considers herself a judge of what is ladylike, and she is vulgarity personified—with large feet, and the most odious scent on her handkerchief, and a bonnet that looks like 'The Fashion' printed in capital letters" (p. 65). Esther, like the narrator, purports to value subtle signs; indeed, subtlety is *the* sign of all she values. Again like Felix, Esther holds a system of values that demands a positive lack of certain obvious signs: "A real fine-lady does not wear clothes that flare in people's eyes, or use importunate scents, or make a noise as she moves: she is something refined, and graceful, and charming, and never obtrusive" (p. 65). Esther and Felix are both, in a sense, too cultured to follow the dictates of common conventionality.

Felix's culture, however, purports to be above all conventionality: "One sort of fine-ladyism is as good as another," he chides Esther (p. 65). Esther's culture, on the other hand, is merely the product of an uncommon conventionality. Through this contrast with Esther, we are supposed to see that Felix's disdain for conventionality proceeds from neither snobbishness nor misanthropy, the two most widely used accusations against those who prided themselves on their culture as a means of differentiating themselves from the common herd. To emphasize this difference between Felix's authentic culture and Esther's self-interested pretensions to culture, Eliot plants a volume of Byron's poems in Esther's work basket and has it tumble out just before tea. Felix is thus able to condemn the conventional kind of unconventionality associated with that poet, the reactionary unconventionality, in Felix's view, of a sneering, egotistical aristocrat. "He is a worldly and vain writer," comments Rufus; but Felix, as always, secularizes the judgment: "A misanthropic debauchee . . . whose notion of a hero was that he should disorder his stomach and despise mankind" (p. 64). The fine lady who reads Byron, according to Felix, is as shallow and conventional in her unconventional pretense as the common devotees of fashion: "And she reads Byron also, and admires Childe Harold—gentlemen of unspeakable woes, who employ a hairdresser, and look seriously at themselves in the glass" (p. 65). Between this conventional disdain for conventionality, a disdain developed merely to refine social distinctions, and Felix's authentic culture, *Felix Holt* would have us believe, there is no true connection.

Authentic culture thus defines itself, on the one hand, against religious transcendence, which it closely resembles; indeed, the narrator goes so far as to call Felix's beliefs about politics and culture his religion, implying both the similarities between the two forms of transcendence and the uneasiness of their coexistence. On the other hand, authentic culture defines itself against false culture, a combination of genteel refinement and Byronic misanthropy, which it unmasks as a deceiving semblance, a cultural imposter. Both reference points are necessary to place Felix, for this representative of the new politics of culture might too easily be assimilated to either alternative realm. The sphere inhabited by Felix, we learn from these distinctions, is independent of those inhabited by Rufus and Esther, neither of whom can make sense of Felix. Rufus only hopes, after Felix's first visit to the Lyon household, that the young man's "natural yearning towards the better" might lead him to some form of orthodox religious belief and make him satisfied with "the ordinary fruits of the Spirit" (p. 67), and Esther is only disappointed that the signs of Felix's mental superiority ("But he speaks better English than most of your visitors") do not indicate a corresponding social superiority. She only laments that he is not "something higher than that" (p. 68).

This lack of comprehension, however, which is supposed to signify Felix's independence from the alternative realms, paradoxically proves that Felix's significance is incomprehensible without reference to those realms. His independent sphere really exists only as a differential term that, within the novel, seems incapable of achieving a separate content, and this incapacity can be traced to the antirepresentational moment within the politics of culture. Felix represents a realm that proclaims itself independent of religious absolutes and social conventions alike. It is not an extension, instrument, reflection, or expression of any other realm. Indeed, it insists so strenuously on its difference from both the conventional-social and the divine that it denies its own nature as representation. Disinterested politics and culture are neither descriptive nor ironic representations of the social, drawing meaning from a realm below; and they are not symbols of the divine, participating in and passing down meaning from a realm above. Rather, Felix, as a representative Arnoldian best self, signifies a culture and a politics that exist on a single plane of differentiation, a plane on which, as we have already seen, politics and culture represent only one another. Felix's politics consist solely of the recommendation of culture, and the culture he recommends is one that develops, by teaching disinterested habits of mind, an autonomous political self in everyone, a self fit to serve as the basis for the state.

By embodying the politics of culture, therefore, Felix Holt in one sense embodies an aggressively nonrepresentational mode of being. His authenticity and purity depend on the independence of his politics and culture from the very things politics and culture had formerly been said to represent: the social and the divine. In another sense, however, the realm that Felix represents is composed of nothing but representations. Political power, Felix tells a group of working men on the eve of the Treby election, grows not out of the possession of things but out of the possession of mental images, ideas. At first Felix claims that these ideas must "agree with the nature of things" (p. 273). Political representation for working men will not bring them power unless they already have true representations of the world in their minds. They can, of course, improve and expand their small stock of notions only if they read,

> For suppose there's a poor voter named Jack, who has seven children, and twelve or fifteen shillings a-week wages, perhaps less. Jack can't read—I don't say whose fault that is—he never had the chance to learn; he knows so little that he perhaps thinks God made the poor-laws, and if anybody said the pattern of the workhouse was laid down in the Testament, he wouldn't be able to contradict him. (P. 274)

In its initial formulation, therefore, true politics for Felix Holt, like true culture for Matthew Arnold, is said to be the representation of the best self formed through an acquaintance with true representations of "the nature of things." This formulation, which relies on a correspondence theory of truth, appears to stress the ultimate grounding of politics and culture in nature and thus to deprive them of their autonomy as a separable realm of values.

Paradoxically, however, George Eliot manages to turn the very fact of the essentially representational nature of this realm into a condition of its independence. She does this in two ways, one of which is very common in nineteenth-century fiction. Any representation can achieve some autonomy from what it represents by calling attention to its status as representation. The strategy of insisting on the mere representationalism of the work is to some degree always a strategy of asserting relative autonomy. It is a way of advertising the work as epiphenomenon in order to refocus on the phenomenon of representation itself. Like all of Eliot's novels, *Felix Holt* has many such moments of self-reflectiveness: "A character is apt to look but indifferent written out this way. Reduced to a map, our premises seem insignificant, but they make, nevertheless, a very pretty freehold to live in and walk over" (p. 102). This passage refers not so much to Harold Transome as to the narrator's admittedly schematic way of representing him. It is a passage marking a transition from one kind of representation (the enumeration of general characteristics) to another more lifelike kind (detailed narration). Nevertheless, it serves to mark a distinction between life and representation in general that, even in this self-deprecatory way, sets representation free from its ostensible object.

Felix Holt, however, does more than merely call attention to a distinction between representation and life in order to achieve a certain (often depreciated) autonomy. It also tries to depict and recommend the independence of the whole realm of representation, and in this attempt it further exposes the paradox of the politics of culture, for although the novel seems to judge representations on the basis of their correspondence to facts, to "things as they are," the texts of cuture and true political discourse are actually valued as rational structures independent of "things as they are." Even in Felix's election-eve speech, the property of language found to be most important for the creation of the political self is not its correspondence to "the nature of things" but its ability to create a possible world of abstract values independent of current conditions. The point about the voter named Jack, after all, is not just that he lacks facts about the poor law and the workhouse, but that his ignorance traps him within current social conditions. It makes him credulous of claims that whatever exists is unchangeable; indeed, it traps him within discourses either of nature or of the divinely ordained. In a sense, Jack's inability to read incarcerates him within a world of mere facts and denies him access to a realm of strictly human potentialities. It is not, finally, facts that Jack needs, but a knowledge of their conditional nature, a knowledge that, for Felix, entails a realm beyond facts. It is only in this realm, a realm where abstract values (what Felix calls "ruling beliefs") are represented, that the truly political self can come into being.

The political self-representation of such a voter as Jack is an impossibility, Felix maintains, for Jack has no opinions, no representations of how the world should be; hence, he has no politics to be represented. Such a man would be constantly alienating his vote, selling it to the highest bidder, instead of developing a political self, a set of representable opinions. Moreover, the men who would buy his vote would also lack any authentic political selves, would be mere brokers of stolen words detached from thoughts, words that do not really represent what they claim to represent: "men who have no real opinions, but who pilfer the words of every opinion, and turn them into a cant which will serve their purpose at the moment" (p. 275). Once again, although the passage seems to express a loathing of independent words, words detached from the sentiments that engendered them, it actually promotes the independence of the realm of representation, for the real opinions that the political self is made of derive not from lived interests but from the written word, and that written word contains not what is but what should be. The language of authentic politics is part of a larger sphere of pure representation, a sphere supposedly representing no other sphere and yet curiously calling attention to its representational status.

True politics and culture thus constitute the realm of representation and nothing else in *Felix Holt*. It is precisely its independence of everything other than representation that sets this realm apart from the merely social, where men are driven not by ideas derived from language, but by material need or greed. The ordinary self cannot even be said to have ideas, that is, general principles that can be logically formulated and hence widely applied. The thoughts of the ordinary self are a mere reflex of egotistical striving, its political language a form of nonsense characterized by an inability to maintain distinctions between levels of abstraction. Eliot satirizes this so-called politics of the ordinary self through her depiction of Mr. Chubb, the proprietor of the Sugar Loaf public house, where the Sproxton miners do their drinking. Chubb's failure to particpate in a realm of representation blocks his development into an authentic political being. Chubb is unable to inhabit that sphere in which opinions about the world derive from each other and are formulated as general principles. Indeed, Chubb's language is the reverse of real political language because it reduces all ideas to his "idee," which is merely a naming of himself: "The coming election was a great opportunity for applying his political 'idee,' which was, that society existed for the sake of the individual, and that the name of that individual was Chubb" (p. 119). Mr. Chubb is disappointed in the Loamshire newspapers because they are so seldom relevant to his "idee," so he relies for pertinent political information on "a cousin in another country, also a publican, but in a larger way."

> He was now enlightened enough to know that there was a way of using voteless miners and navvies at nominations and elections. He approved of that; it entered into his political 'idee;' and indeed he would have been for extending the franchise to this class—at least in Sproxton. If any one had observed that you must draw a line somewhere, Mr. Chubb would have concurred at once, and would have given permission to draw it at a radius of two miles from his own tap.

Chubb humorously reduces all political abstractions to the concrete; here his misinterpretation of the word "line" indicates a failure to grasp that some words refer not to objects in the world but to logical propositions. This failure excludes him from the sphere in which the rules of principled discourse operate. Chubb, like Jack, will never be really representable, for the only self that can be truly represented is the self made out of representations, the self composed of formal determinants severed from material interests.

Felix, of course, is supposed to be just such a self, constructed of representations and hence utterly representable; but although Felix's political self is theoretically eminently representable, his vaunted autonomy, as we have just seen, makes him wholly unrepresentative and enigmatic within the context of the novel. The paradoxical combination of these characteristics uncovers a central tension inside the politics of culture that creates a realm in which representations are said to exist in and of and for themselves. They are emphatically representations, but they represent only each other. Despite Felix's disdain for conventional social signs, despite his longing for an accurately labeled world in which word and thing have some "plain" and obvious relationship, Felix actually stands for an independent sphere of representations, not a language of correspondences with things, but of differences from things. Viewed in this light, Felix's fear of the tyranny of signs begins to make more sense: it is the underside of his wish that the sphere of representations be dominant. The problem with the metonymic signs that inspire Felix's contempt is that, in one sense, they are not free enough of social reference. They are too much the mere indices of meaningless social distinctions. Felix seems to long for a truly independent realm of meanings, but that realm paradoxically constitutes itself as representation (rather than as, for example, a primary spiritual reality). The realm of meaning remains a realm of representational signs, but signs that are mysteriously ungrounded and hence for Eliot, at once powerfully independent and exceptionally vulnerable.

Cultural Currency and the Problem of Inheritance

> La civilisation, la *vie* est une chose apprise et inventée, qu'on le sache bien: '*Inventas aut qui vitam excoluere per artes.*' Les hommes après quelques années de paix oublient trop cette vérité: ils arrivent à croire que la *culture* est chose innée, qu' elle est la méme chose que la *nature*. La Sauvagerie est toujours là à deux pas, et, dès qu' on lâche pied, elle recommence.

George Eliot quotes this passage from Sainte-Beuve in one of her *Theophrastus Such* essays, "Debasing the Moral Currency." Both the essay and the above quotation seek to promote anxiety about the imminent collapse of civilization, which, they claim, is being undermined by a number of movements from below. The essay's main target is the burletta, a popular form of satiric theater, which had, from our perspective, an interesting history. At the beginning of the previous century, the burletta satirized contemporary political figures and events, but the Licensing Act of 1737 specifically outlawed political satire on the stage.[26] Hence the burletta began burlesquing the classics, and that which was to become known as culture took the place of politics as the object of ridicule. By the 1860s this satirization of the classics, which was originally intended to replace subversive theater, was itself perceived by Eliot as the ultimate in subversion, for not only had culture been politicized, it had also been conceived as the basis of the very social order it was supposed to transcend, albeit a basis oddly depending on its own fragility.

Following Saint-Beuve, Theophrastus Such argues that culture can be preserved only if it is sharply distinguished from nature, and yet it is precisely that distinction that produces the hysteria about culture in the first place, for its artificiality is the source of its fragility. If culture and civilization were natural, they would be dependable and would not require constant, vigilant protection. "Debasing the Moral Currency" thus uncovers yet another conundrum within the discourse of culture: the problem and its solution are one and the same. Keeping this in mind when we turn back to *Felix Holt*, we will be able to account for its often-remarked stasis.

Like Felix, the essayist of "Debasing the Moral Currency" imagines that the products of culture make up a realm of "sublimity"[27] independent of both nature and the social-economic order, a realm above the pursuit, in the essay's words, of "bread and ambition." But culture is also the foundation of the social-economic order in this essay, for it is presented as the source and stay of that comprehensive phenomenon, civilization. The essay uses these ideas to defend culture against the spirit of burlesque, but in doing so it reveals the threat implicit in its own formulations, for it insists that the independence of that realm of signs called culture is precisely the source of its vulnerability and the vulnerability of the entire civilization. Although the essay calls cultural artifacts "symbols" and briefly alludes to their "implicit ideal," its main purpose is to emphasize their lack of any intrinsic natural meaning or value. Psychological associationism combines with the politics of culture here, leading the essayist to claim that works of art have merely relative values. Even their content is unstable, for any cultural product can be transformed by ludicrous associations. Since the reality of culture is always "inward," to use Matthew Arnold's word, its products are constantly vulnerable to such transformations, even though this vulnerability is not widely recognized:

> But after all our psychological teaching, and in the midst of our zeal for education, we are still, most of us, at the stage of believing that mental powers and habits have somehow, not perhaps in the general statement, but in any particular case, a kind of spiritual glaze against conditions which we are continually applying to them. We soak our children in habits of contempt and exultant

gibing [by taking them to the burletta], and yet are confident that—as Clarissa one day said to me—"We can always teach them to be reverent in the right place, you know." And doubtless if she were to take her boys to see a burlesque Socrates, with swollen legs, dying in the utterance of cockney puns, and were to hang up a sketch of this comic scene among their bedroom prints, she would think this preparation not at all to the prejudice of their emotions on hearing their tutor read that narrative of the "Apology" which has been consecrated by the reverent gratitude of ages. (P. 88)

It is precisely because the "Apology" has a historical but not a natural and automatic connection to noble ideas and sensations that it can be infected and ruined by a burlesque seen in childhood. According to the essayist, this independence of the cultural object from any particular meaning makes all kinds of random and degrading associations possible.

The currency metaphor that dominates the essay also stresses the variability of the meaning and value of cultural objects, a variability that makes them capable of inflation and deflation:

This is what I call debasing the moral currency: lowering the value of every inspiring fact and tradition so that it will command less and less of the spiritual products, the generous motives which sustain the charm and elevation of our social existence—the something besides bread by which man saves his soul alive. The bread-winner of the family may demand more and more coppery shillings, or assignats, or greenbacks for his day's work, and so get the needful quantum of food; but let that moral currency be emptied of its value—let a greedy buffoonery debase all historic beauty, majesty, and pathos, and the more you heap up the desecrated symbols the greater will be the lack of the ennobling emotions which subdue the tyranny of suffering, and make ambition one with social virtue. (P. 87)

Here we confront the essential insubstantiality of cultural objects; the essayist turns them into tokens disconnected from any particular meanings and associated with "spiritual products" only by conventional assent. Significantly, this moral currency is compared not to gold or silver, not to any independently valuable medium of exchange, but to "coppery shillings, or assignats, or greenbacks," the mere *representations* of value.

This way of conceiving of culture would not necessarily be threatening if it implied the existence of a realm of enduring values beyond cultural representations. However, again like Felix, the essayist posits no independent sphere of spiritual values for these representations to represent. According to the above passage, moral currency differs from money in precisely this regard: cultural "symbols" are variable representations representing their own highly unstable and chaotic associations, whereas money is variable representation representing the stable realities of labor and bodily sustenance. The moral currency can be absolutely debased in a way that money cannot be, for the variable value of money simply leads to adjustments in exchange. Even if the currency is inflated, if more and more greenbacks are required to purchase the same amount of food, there is nevertheless a stable relationship between a day's work and its real rewards. The laborer simply demands more of the devalued currency to buy the same amount. Behind the variability of money value, of the representation of wealth, the essay posits a source of stable value, labor, and a stock of the products of that labor whose intrinsic value remains untouched by the fluctuations of currency values. But cultural currency, the essayist insists, has no such grounding: "the more you heap up the desecrated symbols," he warns, "the greater will be the lack of the ennobling emotions." As cultural signs lose their individual values, their multiplication and accumulation become mere signs of devaluation itself and hence sources of emotional emptiness. Their absolute independence produces their absolute relativity.

The only safeguard against such utter degradation is the enforcement of a stable set of references among works of art. Cultural representations must become their own sphere of value, creating an unresolvable, but by now familiar, contradiction. Cultural objects are, on the one hand, an endlessly degradable currency; but on the other hand, they themselves make up "our mental wealth" (p. 86). They are the "treasure" and sole inheritance of our children, who are in danger of being reduced to "the moral imbecility of an inward giggle at what might have stimulated their high emulation or fed the fountains of compassion, trust, and constancy." These infinitely debasable "symbols," the essayist paradoxically insists, contain all we have of value. Culture alone bears the values and meanings of which it can be so easily emptied: "One wonders where these parents have deposited that stock of morally educating stimuli which is to be independent of poetic tradition, and to subsist in spite of the finest images being degraded and the finest words of genius being poisoned as with some befooling drug" (p. 87). Clearly, the essayist believes that no such independent stock exists.

Having first deprived works of art of any intrinsic value and having then insisted on their unique status as bearers of value, the essayist can only conclude with a scheme to enforce the historical but nonetheless invented connections between these tokens and their conventional meanings and values, which are located in other tokens. Following Sainte-Beuve, Theophrastus Such finds salvation in stressing the very artificiality of culture, an artificiality whose failure to be recognized compounds the problem. The solution to the problems caused by the independence of the realm of culture is the recognition of and insistence on that independence. Because culture is ungrounded, it must continually be lifted above all soiling associations. Because it is not natural, it requires a "spiritual police" (p. 89); because it has no intrinsic meaning, its meaning must be enforced.

This "solution" permeates *Felix Holt*, where anxiety about the independence of culture and politics is both the seed and the issue of the demand for their independence. Like "Debasing the Moral Currency," *Felix Holt* converts its political and cultural concerns into issues of inheritance, apparently preparing the way for a traditional novelistic solution of the problem of inheritance, in which name and thing come together in the person of the legitimate inheritor. However, again in keeping with the ideological solution presented in the essay, the resolution of this novel's inheritance plot merely turns an extreme instance of the problem (the gap between representations and what they are supposed to represent) into its own solution. This resolution (which is simultaneously a reproblematizing) methodically severs the representational links between realms. In the end, the imperative to separate culture from nature leads to the severance of politics and culture from personal inheritance, which is in turn cut away from biological descent, from genealogy. As we will see, the very illegitimacy and arbitrariness of social conventions, especially those governing property relationships and familial identity, provide their own justification.

At the beginning of the novel, the topics of politics and inheritance seem closely intertwined. Indeed, a character's politics and his attitude toward his inheritance become almost identical in the first volume. Although they are dissociated in the initial contrast the narrator establishes between Harold Transome and Felix Holt, the ironic tone of the passage already foretells the underlying unity of the terms:

> Felix was heir to nothing better than a quack medicine; his mother lived up a back street in Treby Magna, and her sitting room was ornamented with her best tea tray and several framed testimonials to the virtues of Holt's Cathartic Lozenges and Holt's Restorative Elixir. There could hardly have been a lot less like Harold Transome's than this of the quack doctor's son, except in the superficial facts that he called himself a Radical, that he was the only son of his mother, and that he had lately returned to his

home with ideas and resolves not a little disturbing to that mother's mind. (Pp. 45–46)

Although the passage stresses the dissimilarity of the material inheritances, the real differences between Felix and Harold are hidden under the superficial similarities. The deep contrast between the two men lies not in the quantity or quality of their personal inheritances, but in their attitudes toward them, attitudes that give opposite meanings to their superficially similar, "disturbing" behavior and make them representatives of very different kinds of radicalism. Indeed, the radicalism of each is defined by his relationship to his heritage.

Felix gives up his father's legacy, the legacy of quack medicines, but this is not a gesture rejecting the past. It is, rather, a gesture rejecting the cant of the present. With its obvious Carlylean associations, it repudiates a fake cathartic and restorative so that true purgation and restoration can take place. Indeed, the act of renunciation itself is the cathartic that restores Felix to continuity with his familial past, as he explains to Rufus Lyon: "My father was a weaver first of all. It would have been better for him if he had remained a weaver. I came home through Lancashire and saw an uncle of mine who is a weaver still. I mean to stick to the class I belong to" (p. 58). Felix's radicalism is supposedly an extension of these sentiments. He is in favor of purging the social order of "privilege, monopoly, and oppression" (pp. 168–69) in order to achieve, through education, a more thorough continuity with the national past. Felix is not opposed to change as long as it is accompanied by continuity, and he sees the "increasing self-assertion of the majority" as an opportunity for the extension of that which best creates continuity: culture. Indeed, for Felix, as for the essayist of "Debasing the Moral Currency," culture and continuity are one and the same thing. Thus Felix apparently disobliges his mother and tarnishes his father's posthumous reputation, not out of any filial impiety, but out of a desire to restore a lost familial continuity. Similarly, he becomes a radical not out of rebellious or even innovative impulses, but out of a desire to recover, protect, and extend a national heritage.

In every one of these particulars, Harold Transome provides a contrast to Felix. Upon the death of his older brother, he accepts his position as heir to the family estate. He is, however, financially independent of this inheritance, for he has made a fortune in the Orient. The estate is important to him not because it is a source of income but because it insures his class privileges and social preeminence. It makes it possible, indeed, for him to stand as a Radical candidate for the House of Commons. Thus Harold uses his patrimony, his position as a landed gentleman, to undermine the position of the gentry as a whole. He is, in a sense, assuming and repudiating his legacy simultaneously. His attachment to his patrimony is like his attachment to his mother; he accepts both as components of what it means to be a gentleman, but he wishes that neither restrict or determine the course of his actions. His family's estate, his mother's elegant but archaic aristocratic imperiousness, even his family's Toryism, are all necessary background for a gentleman. "A woman ought to be a Tory," he tells his mother, "and graceful, and handsome, like you. I should hate a woman who took up my opinions, and talked for me. I'm an Oriental, you know. I say, mother, shall we have this room furnished with rose-colour? I notice it suits your bright grey hair" (pp. 99–100). The memory of his family's hereditary Toryism, like his mother's elegant head, is to be preserved, but emptied of its content; both are reduced to merely "bright" decorative trophies, part of the gentlemanly furniture against which Harold's independent Radicalism is set off all the more strikingly. Harold, like Felix, senses the artificiality of such tokens, but he believes their artificiality insures his independence from them; he does not yet realize the extent to which their very incongruity might enthrall him. By turning his patrimony and his mother into mere ornaments, Harold thinks he relieves himself of the necessity of responding to them: "Women, very properly, don't change their views, but keep to the notions in which they have been brought up. It doesn't signify what they think—they are not called upon to judge or to act. You must really leave me to take my own course in these matters" (p. 35).

In direct contrast to Felix, who rejected his patrimony partly in order to reestablish a broken family continuity, Harold accepts his patrimony partly in order to assert his predominance within the family and disrupt a continuity. He assigns the continuity to his mother, making her a sign of his stable background, and then transforms her into a silent relic, forbidden to signify about the present. Like those of Felix, Harold's national politics are an extension of his family politics, an extension of the love of predominance that has "nourished an inclination to as much opposition as would enable him to assert his own independence and power without throwing himself into that tabooed condition which robs power of its triumph" (p. 102). Harold wants change because, as a younger son, he had always regarded the world as "rather ill-arranged." Unlike that of Felix, his Radicalism conspicuously lacks large principles; it is, in the narrator's phrase, "not stringently consistent" (p. 102). It conspicuously excludes any altruistic desire to continue and enlarge a national cultural tradition. Indeed, Harold himself was never an avid seeker of knowledge, and he completely lacks the capacity to venerate, which is the emotional precondition for the politics of culture: "He was not sorry the money was wanting to send him to Oxford; he did not see the good of Oxford; he had been surrounded by many things during his short life, of which he had distinctly said to himself that he did not see the good, and he was not disposed to venerate on the strength of any good that others saw" (p. 101). Like his family politics, then, Harold's national politics are self-aggrandizing and demonstrate a complacent indifference to the preservation of a vital heritage.

By thus linking true Radicalism with unselfish responsibility to one's family heritage and false Radicalism with egotistical indifference, the novel at first seems to be working toward a solution that will combine true politics and legitimate inheritance, creating, as at the ending of *Sybil*, the illusion of an ideal confluence of word and thing. Felix seems another Sybil who can transparently represent his origins, whereas Harold only ironically represents both the working class and his family. Felix's reunification with his class of origin, like Sybil's, is simply another manifestation of his supposed transparency. His reentry into the working class, like his insistence on plain speech and his general hostility to conventional signs, seems to signify his desire for natural, truthful, signification. Felix attempts to become one with his origins. His father had started on the road to ironic representation, which had been trod by Dandy Mick and Devilsdust in *Sybil*, but Felix, the watch repairman, has turned back the clock to the "right" time, has restored himself to his family and his family to its natural, prior condition. In this regard too, Felix aspires to picture-writing, to the status of a natural sign, who has recovered and merged with his real origins and natural inheritance. He consequently seems to present the solution to the problems of ironic representation raised in the course of Harold's career.

This solution, however, which was unstable even in *Sybil*, is a theoretical impossibility in *Felix Holt*, for the later novel is designed to convince us of the necessary and everlasting unnaturalness of representation. Felix's little history of restoration is wholly incidental to the novel's preeminent inheritance plot, which reveals and articulates the embroiled hereditary connections between Harold and Esther Lyon. Even as an incidental *motif*, Felix's story contains many problematic elements that prevent us from reading it as a verification of the natural sign.

First and most obviously, Felix's inheritance, like his character and his destiny in general, is precisely what is not given in his circumstances. Sybil's inheritance was also not immediately available; it, too, had to be retrieved. However, Sybil never *wills* her inheritance on the basis of some abstract ethical consideration. Her inheritance, like everything else that makes her a symbol, comes to her through the reversals of history. The inheritance could not be symbolic if it did not appear in the world in this given, unwilled fashion. But Felix chooses to renounce one inheritance and embrace another. His accepted inheritance, like all of his other characteristics, is artificial, willed. It is willed, moreover, against his given social circumstances in order to emphasize that it does not represent them.

Only by making such an underdetermined ethical choice can Felix come to represent an undetermined culture. In addition to being oxymoronic simply by being an ungiven heritage, Felix's inheritance remains elusive even after he has chosen it, for it does not consist of things but of the lack of things. This is emphasized at the outset: "Felix was heir to nothing better than a quack medicine." And when he renounces that, he is heir to nothing at all. Like his costume, Felix's inheritance implicitly indicts conventional signs, but it fixes on no natural signs as their opposites. Like the costume, the inheritance emphasizes absences that are supposed to be significant, that we must be schooled to read, and that turn out to signify the gap between facts and values, between the realms of social experience and ultimate significance.

It is precisely this nothingness of inheritance, this willed space in the world of privately owned objects, that allows Felix to receive the national heritage, culture. That heritage, however, somehow depends on the preservation of the institution of private property and on the maintenance of clear class distinctions, although it is not itself supposed to be anyone's private property or the distinctive mark of any class. In Eliot's 1870 essay "The Address of Felix Holt to the Working Men," this simultaneous dependence and independence of culture and society becomes explicit, but the novel's plot lets us feel the full contradictory force of the idea. Only by dedicating himself to working-class life, to the absence (structurally provided by the class system) of private property, can he escape his ordinary (class-determined) self. The less Felix cares for personal inheritance, the freer he is to receive the national inheritance. That inheritance may be technically owned by the likes of the Transomes, but it is not really theirs, precisely because their concentration on cultural objects as personal possessions blinds them to the real meaning and value of what they possess. Someone must take responsibility for the material conditions of the production and preservation of culture; hence men like Harold collect and preserve to enhance their positions as gentlemen, but their indifference to the intrinsic worth of such objects frees the objects from them, allowing their spiritual appropriation by men like Felix, men who have foresworn material appropriation. The maintenance of the class relationship between Felix and Harold is thus absolutely necessary to the process of overcoming that relationship through culture.

This is, moreover, the view attained from the perspective of the novel's dominant inheritance plot, the plot in which Esther Lyon and Harold Transome are embroiled. Like the short history of Felix's restoration to the working class, the stories of Esther's renunciation and Harold's succession emphasize the necessary gap between culture and society. Whereas Felix's story reveals the paradoxical relationship that separates culture from society, however, Harold's and Esther's stories show that the gap created is really a magnetic field across which culture and society hold one another in a state of static tension precisely because neither can claim any grounding in nature. They also reveal that the exposure of the artificiality of both realms of signs (the social and the cultural), their distinctness from and lack of dependence on nature, at once discredits signs and serves as the motivation for protecting them.

In *Sybil* the illegitimate title-holder was displaced by the true heir, whose natural genealogical roots attached her to the Mowbray estate. Nature thus provided the solution to the problem of signs. The "solution" of *Felix Holt*, however, is exactly the opposite. The unnaturalness of representation must be fully brought to consciousness and accepted. As in *Sybil*, the estate is held by an illegitimate heir. Indeed, Harold Transome is doubly illegitimate; the mismatch between name and thing is compound, for the Transomes of Transome Court hold the name and estate as a family only by a legal fiction which bars the claim of another family that could inherit under the terms of a vastly complicated entailment. The only real Transome in the novel is a half-witted laborer named Tommy Trounsem, on whose continued existence the settlement of entail rests. So long as Tommy remains alive, Harold's family has a legal claim to the name and estate, but their claim has never rested on genealogy. They are not blood relations of the original Transomes. As Harold learns at the end of the book, and as the reader and half of Treby have known all along, Harold is not even a legitimate member of this already somewhat illegitimate family. He is, rather, the issue of an adulterous relationship between his mother and the despised lawyer Jermyn, who has been able to keep the family at Transome Court but has made them pay handsomely for the privilege. Harold owns his name and estate, then, only by a pair of legal fictions; the pure conventionality and unnaturalness of his connection to his name and estate are thus emphasized and reemphasized.

As in *Sybil*, also, a riot becomes the occasion for the restoration of a rightful heir to the estate. Tommy Trounsem dies in the riot, and the estate reverts to the Bycliffes, of whom Esther is the living descendent.

Once again Eliot avoids a simple genealogical claim for Esther. Indeed, Frederic Harrison, who advised Eliot on the legal intricacies of the plot, implored her to make Esther a real Transome so that her claim would carry the weight of nature as well as that of legality, but Eliot insisted on grounding Esther's claim also in legal conventions.[28] Thus, although *Felix Holt* resembles *Sybil* in that a young woman is discovered, in the aftermath of a popular uprising, to be the heir to an estate, it reverses *Sybil* by making that young woman no more the natural heir to the estate than is the family she has the power to dispossess.

Despite first impressions, then, genealogy and inheritance in the world of *Felix Holt*, have very little to do with one another at the outset and even less to do with one another in the end. The book explodes the illusion that inheritance is grounded in nature. Name, property, and person are arbitrarily or merely conventionally attached. Indeed, the book could be read as a double assault on the legitimacy of inheritance, both stages of which are conducted by women. First, Mrs. Transome's adultery asserts the primacy of maternity over paternity, revealing that Harold's legally inherited link to the gentry is a mere fiction. Mrs. Transome, we are told by the narrator, lovingly traced the genealogy of her family (the Lingons) for Esther: "genealogies entered into her stock of ideas, and her talk on such subjects was as necessary as the notes of the linnet or the blackbird. She had no ultimate analysis of things that went beyond blood and family—the Herons of Fenshore or the Badgers of Hillbury" (p. 350). Even here, within the assumptions of aristocratic legitimacy, Mrs. Transome's association with genealogy limits her to the sphere of nature, blood and biological kinship, where she lives as unconsciously as a bird or a badger, and when, through the instrument of her own body, biological kinship and official aristocratic lineage become radically distinct, Mrs. Transome seems to represent nature all the more clearly as opposed to civilization. Indeed, the power she finally achieves comes precisely through the splitting off of genealogy from inheritance. Although the revelation of Harold's paternity humiliates her, it also serves as a kind of revenge against her imperious son, for his link to the gentry is now entirely through her. All claims based on male descent, including the claims of property, are shown to be groundless.

Property inheritance is then further discredited by Esther's renunciation of both Harold and the estate. If Esther were to accept Harold and her inheritance, or for that matter, her inheritance alone, she, like Sybil but more tentatively, might legitimize the social process. Instead she exposes the emptiness and meaninglessness of social conventions by disclaiming the importance of personal, material wealth. She seems, therefore, to withhold the kind of legitimation Sybil bestowed, but the two cases are not perfectly comparable. In a significant reversal of the conventions of the domestic novel, Felix, not Esther, is the real locus of value in this book; Esther does not have an independent value that could simply be added to the estate she inherits. The legitimacy she withholds is not really hers to bestow, for to accept her estate would be to lose Felix and hence to exchange value for wealth. Only in choosing Felix does Esther come to represent the cultural over the social, just as Mrs. Transome, despite herself, comes to represent the natural over the social.

In a sense, then, nature and culture combine to expose and discredit the social at the end of *Felix Holt*. Nothing changes because of this discrediting, however. Indeed, *because* of this discrediting, nothing changes. The Transomes seem so vulnerable and exposed in their illegitimacy that we are finally relieved when they are able to retain their name and estate. The novel carefully solicits our sympathy for the impropriety of their position, until we are willing to see the very arbitrariness of their property settlement as a rationale for its continuance. We learn along with Esther the appropriate response to the delegitimized upper classes. The revelation of Harold's true parentage renders him pathetic, and it would seem excessively punitive to appropriate his property when he has just lost his legitimacy. Deprived of a ground either in nature or in a divine order, the Transomes occupy a situation so vertiginous that it drives Esther away but also forces her to withdraw any claim on her own behalf.

In the end, it is not just the privileged signs of an autonomous culture that must be preserved in their independence, but all conventional, customary signs as well, especially those that have been discredited, those that have been exposed as purely arbitrary, for as we saw in "Debasing the Moral Currency," the very artificiality of a sign system is a reason for sustaining it. It seems to be the job of culture, as it is the job of *Felix Holt*, to expose the illegitimacy of the social as a precondition for its maintenance. Thus the politics of culture first advocates the independence of the realm of representation from mere descriptive functions, insisting nevertheless on its representativeness; it then identifies the independence of representative signs as the source of the problem of civilization, its fragility; finally, it recommends a solution in the consciousness of the independence of the representational sphere. Once all misguided naturalist or transcendental attempts to ground a legitimate social order are abandoned, the order that exists can be preserved only by owning its arbitrariness. By this process, the politics of culture empties out the social in an attempt to leave it intact.

Conclusion

This last point has led many commentators to assume that the politics of culture was all along an accommodation to industrial society. The whole project has been called merely a way of rescuing the same social realm it pretended to despise. The rescue, moreover, has been said to disable an entire tradition of anti-industrial social criticism by appropriating and disarming it, and then putting it to the uses of its adversaries. According to this analysis, the politics of culture preserves the economic and social dynamics of industrialism by giving them up as sources of meaning and gratification. Its whole mission is thus seen as one of diffusing frustration by deflecting attention from the social and redirecting it toward a separate realm: the transcendent realm occupied by the state and high culture.

Even if we were to accept this account of the ultimate function of the politics of culture (and, as we will see, there are reasons why we should not), it would not be an adequate description of the paradoxical complexity that gives the ideology much of its power. Moreover, the functionalist explanation tells us virtually nothing about how the politics of culture affected the novel. By approaching the politics of culture differently and placing it within a larger debate about representation and the relationship between facts and values, we have been able to draw out the contradictory entailments of the ideology and simultaneously examine its literary consequences.

From this wider perspective, we have seen that, when they insisted on the independence of a realm of representation and justified artificiality per se, the framers of the discourse of culture did ultimately deny themselves a ground from which to criticize industrial society, but their thought cannot be reduced to this denial. Admittedly, the politics of culture disarmed a whole tradition of social criticism and brought the Condition of England Debate to an end. To understand how it played that role, however, we must fully credit its desire for an independent realm of representation. It is indeed true that this desire corroded the foundations on which earlier critiques of industrial society had rested. But the politics of culture does not deflect attention from social criticism; rather, it turns a withering eye on the assumptions of that criticism, for if one were to accept the full consequences of this thought, industrial society could no longer be condemned for its unnatural determinism, or chaotic arbitrariness, or for its failure to protect or resemble the natural organizational structure of the family. Nor could one object to its interference with the workings of Providence or its obstructions of the downward flow of divinely originated meaning, for all of these arguments, the arguments that gave rise to the novelistic subgenre examined in this book, depend on natural or divine sanctions. The new need to secularize the realm of meaning and simultaneously stress its independence of nature leads finally to a devaluation not only of industrial society, but also of the whole earlier discourse about industrialism, the very discourse that prepared the way for the politics of culture.

The politics of culture, then, can be said to have ended what we call the Condition of England Debate. It certainly did not put an end to social criticism, but it drastically altered its terms. Similarly, *Felix Holt* did not put an end to the social-problem novel, but it did end that specific manifestation of it we call the industrial novel. The effects of this ideology on literary form, however, reverberate far beyond the industrial novel itself. *Felix Holt* shows us that, just as the politics of culture emptied out the social but attempted to preserve it as a set of independent representations, it emptied out a certain kind of realism, too, not by calling attention to the sign's nonreferentiality, but by emphasizing its being *as representation*. This emphasis resulted in the separation of the representative (according to the conventions of realism) from the representable (according to the precepts of the ideology). Eliot was still committed to the kind of realism she defended against Harriet Martineau's attack in the conversation with which this chapter opened, but by the mid-1860s her commitment was beginning to resemble a forced confinement, for she could no longer believe in the automatic facts-values continuity that once guaranteed the significance of representing the social. In *Felix Holt* she continued to represent it, but only by identifying it explicitly as that which *should* not be represented and by contrasting it with a realm that *could* not be represented. Thus in *Felix Holt* the novel begins to derive its own value from its devaluation, its unmasking, of the thing it represents. The independence of the realistic text is stressed, but only by discrediting Eliot's earlier project of realism.

Felix Holt, then, resembles all the other industrial novels we have analyzed by turning its form into its subject matter and then turning on its form. It goes beyond the others, however, by scrutinizing the general topic of realistic representation, by at once privileging it and emptying it. The politics of culture does the same thing to both literary realism and civil society: each is discredited in order to be saved. But we must ask in each case if such a simultaneous devaluation and rescue is possible. Can either the novel or the whole sphere of the social-economic be discredited without undergoing substantial transformation?

It is generally recognized that the novels of the last three decades of the nineteenth century are radically different from their midcentury predecessors. The later realism is often described as somber or disillusioned; a certain optimism and naiveté have disappeared. And yet this is the great era of realism, of Eliot's mature work, of Henry James and Thomas Hardy. There is, of course, a relationship between the sense of disillusionment in these books and our judgment that they are masterpieces of realism, for it is only after the separation of facts and values has become a programmatic element within the novel that realists can become fully conscious of the dynamics and potentialities of their own genre. The introduction of the politics of culture into the novel created just such a programmatic separation of the novel itself from the object of its representation. Flaubert had been defining realism in precisely this way for years before the English discovered that the object of representation could be deprived of value in the very process of representing it and that the value thus subtracted from the thing depicted could be appropriated by the representation. The English, however, did not learn this technique from Flaubert; it followed readily from the logic of the politics of culture, conditioned as that was by the Condition of England Debate. Although the English version of the new realism differed greatly from the French, an emphatic facts-values discontinuity became a commonplace of English fiction. Even *Middlemarch*, with all of its ardently professed meliorism, gets its power from the felt distance between the realm of exchange that Dorothea must enter ("I will learn what everything costs") and the plane on which the novel itself exists. Indeed, the narrator's very hope in a facts-values continuity at the end of *Middlemarch*, precisely because it is expressed as hope in some very distant resolution, leaves us with Dorothea's humbler excuse for representing the social: "no one stated exactly what else that was in her power she ought rather to have done" ("Finale"). Perhaps if Eliot had renewed her earlier conversation with Harriet Martineau a dozen years later (before the messianic solution of *Daniel Deronda* occurred to her), she might have concluded it with just those words.

Realism, then, is reshaped within the discourse about representation in the 1860s; it cannot remain the same after it has made war on its previous justifications by stressing the necessary discontinuity between facts and values. Some historians, moreover, are now beginning to come to a similar conclusion about the effect of the politics of culture on the social and economic life of England. The discrediting of the interests of the "ordinary self," the devaluation of merely social and economic goals, it is currently being argued, worked directly on the pride and the will of the industrial bourgeoisie, forcing it to accept the passive, rural, rentier goals of the gentry and to forego consolidating its economic, cultural, and political power.[29] Harold Transome himself would make an excellent illustration of this dynamic. When Harold's membership in the gentry is exposed as a fiction, he becomes obsessed with behaving like a gentleman. The self-confident, egotistical, entrepreneurial side of Harold is shamed out of existence when it recognizes its likeness to the arriviste, Jermyn, reflected in a mirror. After perceiving that devaluing reflection, Harold must protect himself against the charge that he is not really a gentleman, and hence he must cease to be an ambitious, progressive force in the region.

In this analysis, the politics of culture (that which provides the devaluing reflection) is one very significant component within a larger ideological battle between the gentry, with its allies in the intelligentsia, and the industrial middle class, a battle that was handily won by the gentry.[30] Their ideological victory, it seems, contributed to the decline of England as an industrial power. One might argue with this account of the sources of the politics of culture, but the record of its effects suggests that emptying and preserving are antithetical activities. Installing a facts-values discontinuity at the heart of English institutions preserved only some of the facts; others were necessarily altered by the values that no longer protected them. Moreover, industrial novels ceased to be written not because the values of laissez-faire industrial capitalism came to be widely accepted,[31] but because those values, like the Condition of England Debate they spawned, were so swiftly outdated.

Notes

Introduction

1. In the 1950s Kathleen Tillotson, Arnold Kettle, and Raymond Williams discussed the definitive criteria for this subgenre and selected the major novels it should include. I have not thought it necessary to dispute their selections, and although I have included a great deal of minor fiction in this study, I have used Raymond Williams's list of the most important novels. Kathleen Tillotson's discussions of these novels are in *Novels of the Eighteen-forties* (London, 1954); Arnold Kettle's, in "The Early Victorian Social Problem Novel," in *Dickens to Hardy*, ed. Boris Ford, *The Pelican Guide to English Literature* 6 (Baltimore, 1958), pp. 169–87; Raymond Williams's, in "The Industrial Novels," in *Culture and Society, 1780–1950* (New York, 1958), pp. 78–109. For definitions of the subgenre of the industrial novel, see P. J. Keating, *The Working Classes in Victorian Fiction* (London, 1971), pp. 10–24. For other book-length studies of this fiction, see Louis Cazamian, *The Social Novel in England, 1830–1850*, trans. Martin Fido (London, 1973); Ivan Melada, *The Captain of Industry in English Fiction, 1821–1871* (Albuquerque, 1970); and Ivanka Kovačević, *Fact into Fiction: English Literature and the Industrial Scene, 1750–1850* (Leicester, 1975). Some scholars have included Charlotte Brontë's *Shirley* among these novels, but I have chosen to exclude it because industrial conflict in *Shirley* is little more than a historical setting and does not exert any stong pressure on the form.

2. My use of this word is informed by but not identical to the complex and

idiosyncratic use made of it by Michel Foucault and the simpler but no less eccentric one of Mikael Bahktin.

3. See George Lukacs, *History and Class Consciousness: Studies in Marxist Dialectics*, trans. Rodney Livingstone (Cambridge, Mass, 1971), pp. 110–48.

4. To make Lukacs's adjective meaningful, it would be necessary to engage in his own dangerous pastime of "imputing" oppositional consciousness outside the dominant discourse to groups who cannot be demonstrated to possess it.

Chapter 1

1. The two major histories of the factory reform movement used throughout this chapter are J. T. Ward, *The Factory Movement, 1830–1855* (New York, 1962), and Alfred [Samuel] Kydd, *The History of the Factory Movement from the Year 1802, to the Enactment of the Ten Hours' Bill in 1847*, 2 vols. (London, 1857).

2. *Leeds Mercury*, October 16, 1830.

3. For an account of Oastler's early abolitionist activities, see Cecil Driver, *Tory Radical: The Life of Richard Oastler* (New York, 1946), pp. 18–20.

4. The wide variety of applications of the master/slave metaphor in England since 1066 is a striking feature of Christopher Hill's succinct account of the theory of "The Norman Yoke," in *Democracy and The Labour Movement* (London, 1954), pp. 11–66, passim.

5. "Remarks by S. T. Coleridge on Sir Robert Peel's Bill," Appendix I in Lucy E. Watson, *Coleridge at Highgate* (London, 1925), p. 179.

6. Samuel Martin, *An Essay upon Plantership, Humbly Inscribed to His Excellency George Thomas, Esq., Chief Governor of All the Leeward Islands, as a Monument to Antient Friendship*, 5th ed. (London, 1773), pp. vii–viii.

7. "On Slavery," *General Magazine* 6 (1792):477–80, for example, gave extracts from the *Wealth of Nations*. Two other popular pamphlets associated the ideas of slave emancipation and classical economics in the public mind: [H.P. Brougham], *A Concise Statement of the Question Regarding the Abolition of the Slave Trade* (London, 1804), and William Thornton, *Political Economy: Founded in Justice and Humanity* (Washington, 1804). It must be admitted that many of the leaders of the anti–slave trade and antislavery movements were not political or economic liberals at all but Tory or independent Evangelicals. William Wilberforce was the leader of this group of "Saints," as they were called. For an account of the Saints, see R. Coupland, *Wilberforce: A Narrative* (Oxford, 1923), pp. 503–4. Much of their support, however, came from liberals who opposed slavery on economic as well as humanitarian grounds. The pamphlets listed here are examples of their propaganda; they show that many antislavery arguments did rely on laissez-faire ideas, although the extent to which the abolitionists were free traders is debatable. See Eric Eustace Williams, *Capitalism and Slavery* (Chapel Hill, 1945); Eric Eustace Williams, "Laissez Faire, Sugar and Slavery," *Political Science Quarterly* 58 (1943):67–85; and Dale Herbert Porter, *The Abolition of the Slave Trade in England* (Hamden, Conn., 1970).

8. William Knox reprinted the testimony of over a dozen witnesses on this point in his pamphlet *A Country Gentleman's Reasons for Voting against Mr. Wilberforce's Motion for a Bill to Prohibit the Importation of African Negroes into the Colonies* (London, 1792), pp. 45–68. The same argument can be found in other proslavery speeches and pamphlets of the 1790s, despite Coleridge's claim (see note 4 above) that such arguments were recognized by the reactionary defenders of slavery to be "suited only to the sowers of sedition and the advocates for

insurrection." Anti-Jacobin fears moderated but failed to silence the accusations of domestic poverty and oppression; for an illustration of this point, see the anonymous pamphlet *An Appeal to the Candour of Both Houses of Parliament, with a Recapitulation of Facts Respecting the Abolition of the Slave Trade, by a Member of the House of Commons* (London, 1793), pp. 15–17.

9. The author of *An Appeal to the Candour of Both Houses of Parliament*, for example, gently chided the abolitionists: "Their philanthropy, it would seem, soars far above the vulgar transactions and common-place misfortunes of their own country, and winging its visionary way to the remotest corners of the earth, only expands its wings for the benefit of mankind over the inhabitants of terra incognita" (p. 17).

10. "Slave Trade," *Cobbett's Weekly Political Register* 7 (1805): 372.

11. "Slave Trade," *Cobbett's Weekly Political Register* 9 (1806):845.

12. Ibid., p. 867.

13. "To William Wilberforce, on the State of the Cotton Factory Labourers, and on the Speech of Andrew Ryding, Who Cut Horrocks with a Cleaver," from *Political Register*, 27 August 1823. Reprinted in *Selections from Cobbett's Political Works*, eds. John M. Cobbett and James P. Cobbett (London, n.d.), 6:351.

14. *Selections from Cobbett's Political Works*, 6:353.

15. The Combination Acts forbade all "conspiracies" of both masters and workers to take action to impose certain wages or working conditions. Both strikes and lockouts were proscribed under the laws, but they were used almost exclusively to keep workers from unionizing and striking. Liberal political economists as well as radicals like Cobbett were opposed to the laws, and their repeal was, of course, sought by the working class. They were repealed the year after this letter was written.

16. *Selections from Cobbett's Political Works*, 6:352.

17. Cobbett here refers to the sunset-to-sunrise curfew imposed on the Irish peasantry.

18. *Selections from Cobbett's Political Works*, 6:354.

19. Quoted by Coupland, *Wilberforce*, p. 433.

20. Subsequent chapters will investigate the theological and philosophical as well as the social and political roots of this controversy in greater detail and with reference to specific industrial narratives.

21. Robert Owen, *A New View of Society and Other Writings*, ed. G.D.H. Cole (New York, 1963), p. 5.

22. Ibid., p. 6.

23. Ibid., p. 45.

24. There is an overview of the freewill-determinism controversy under "Determinism" in the *Encyclopedia of Philosophy*, ed. Paul Edwards, vol. 2 (New York, 1972). My primary sources for this general discussion are Frederick Copleston's *History of Philosophy* (Westminster, Md., 1960), vols. 2, 5, and 6; Sidney Hook, ed., *Determinism and Freedom in the Age of Modern Science* (New York, 1958); J.J. Rickaby, *Free Will and Four English Philosophers* (Freeport, N.Y., 1969); George Lukacs, *History and Class Consciousness*, trans. Rodney Livingston (Cambridge, Mass., 1971), pp. 110–38.

25. Owen, *A New View of Society*, p. 33.

26. For clarification of the ideas of positive and negative freedom, see Isaiah Berlin, *Four Essays on Liberty* (Oxford, 1969), p. 7.

27. Owen, *A New View of Society*, p. 122.

28. Ibid., p. 142.

29. Ibid., p. 143.

30. Ibid., p. 144.

31. See for example the report of a *Public Discussion, between Robert Owen and the Rev. J.H. Roebuck* (Manchester, 1837). Owen wanted to found his own rational and humanitarian religion; see *The New Religion, or Religion Founded on Immutable Laws of the Universe* (London, 1830).

32. Robert Owen, "To the British Master Manufacturers," in *A New View of Society*, p. 144.

33. Ibid., p. 143.

34. Ibid.

35. Owen was often characterized as a mistaken (but not quite harmless) philanthropic crank in the propaganda of the cotton manufacturers between 1816 and 1819. This passage is taken from a pamphlet entitled *An Inquiry into the Principle and Tendency of the Bill Now Pending in Parliament, for Imposing Certain Restrictions on Cotton Factories* (London, 1818), p. 31: "Late years have been wonderfully prolific of ostentatious and useless schemes of philanthropy, from humble Evans and his nation of happy landholders, to Mr. Owen with the millennium dawning over the ruins of Christianity in a cotton-mill; not quite the spot, and not quite the circumstances, in which the beginnings of that blissful period were to be expected. Of all these schemes the present [Peel's second Factory Bill] is one of the strangest. It is in truth a part of Mr. Owen's dreams."

36. *Hansard's Parliamentary Debates*, ser. 1, vol. 31 (May–July 1815), pp. 625–26.

37. Review of *A New View of Society, or Essays on the Principle of the Formation of the Human Character*, in *Philanthropist* 3 (1813):114.

38. Most Parliamentary supporters of the 1819 Factory Act were even more careful than Owen to reconcile the legislation with the doctrine of free labor. *Hansard's Parliamentary Debates*, ser. 1, vol. 33 (1816), p. 884, reports the first Sir Robert Peel pleading: "It might, perhaps, be said that free labour should not be subjected to any control, but surely it could not be inconsistent with our constitution to protect the interests of those helpless children." This rather conditional support for the doctrine of free labor ("It might, perhaps, be said . . .") was echoed by other M.P.s. It should be noted, however, that the conditional language sometimes became ambivalent: "We are sufficiently aware of the difficulties the question would meet with, were a legal restraint on the labor of adults to be a part or a consequence of the measure proposed; but if, in shielding the children from mischiefs to *them* more peculiar, the adults should be incidentally benefited, without the least encroachment made on free labor, there can be no possible harm in the good thus accidentally accruing, nor even in the congratulation which some may, perhaps, be inclined to offer to the fortunate subjects of it." Here Sir Nathaniel Gould is certainly talking on both sides of the issue at once in his pamphlet *Information Concerning the State of the Children Employed in Cotton Factories, Printed for the Use of the Members of Both Houses of Parliament* (Manchester, 1818), p. 19.

39. See the following publications: Peter Gaskell, *The Manufacturing Population of England* (London, 1833); Edwin Chadwick, *Report to Her Majesty's Principal Secretary of State for the Home Department, from the Poor Law Commissioners on an Inquiry into the Sanitary Condition of the Labouring Population of Great Britain*, House of Lords Sessional Papers, session 1842, vol. 26; Hector Gavin, *The Habitations of the Industrial Classes: Their Influence on the Physical and on the Social*

and Moral Condition of These Classes (London, 1851); and George Goldwin, *London Shadows: A Glance at the "Homes" of the Thousands* (London, 1854).

The amount of medical testimony given at the various Parliamentary enquiries into conditions in cotton mills varies, but there is a general trend toward proportionately more medical testimony as the century progresses. My rough estimate of the testimony contained in the Irish University Press Series of Parliamentary Papers is that not less than 10 percent of the testimony in 1816–18 was from medical men, 20 percent was from medical men in 1831–32, and 60 percent was from medical men in late 1833. See *Industrial Revolution: Children's Employment*, vols. 586–89 of *British Parliamentary Papers*, Irish University Press Series (Shannon, 1968), passim.

Even in 1818, however, the factory reformers made much of the medical testimony favorable to their cause, publishing long extracts from it in anonymous pamphlets. See for example *Information Concerning the State of Children Employed in Cotton Factories* (Manchester, 1818), and *Answers to Certain Objections Made to Sir Robert Peel's Bill for Ameliorating the Condition of Children* (Manchester, 1819). Both pamphlets are reprinted in *The Factory Act of 1819: Four Pamphlets*, one of an unnumbered series of volumes, *British Labour Struggles: Contemporary Pamphlets, 1727–1850*, ed. Kenneth E. Carpenter (New York, 1972).

40. There is no doubt that Coleridge read Cobbett. He criticized the radical's rhetorical techniques at length in his second *Lay Sermon* and planned a third sermon to the working classes in order to combat the writings of William Cobbett and John and Leigh Hunt; see R.J. White, "Editor's Introduction," *Lay Sermons*, vol. 6 of *The Collected Works of Samuel Taylor Coleridge* (London, 1972), pp. xxxi–xxxii. Despite his war of words on the radicals, though, he sometimes adopted their tone when criticizing society and made many similar arguments. Note for example that his argument about paper money and the national debt is almost identical to Cobbett's (*Lay Sermons*, p. 212). At least one radical acknowledged the kinship between Coleridge's concerns and complaints and his own: William Hone quoted Coleridge on the state of the manufacturing poor in his *Hone's Reformists' Register* in 1817. See White, "Editor's Introduction," p. xl.

41. Quoted by Watson, *Coleridge at Highgate*, p. 75.

42. "Remarks by S.T. Coleridge on Sir Robert Peel's Bill," reprinted in Watson, *Coleridge at Highgate*, pp. 174–75.

43. Ibid.

44. See Martin, *An Essay upon Plantership*, p. ix; and William Knox, *Letter from W.K., Esq., to W. Wilberforce, Esq.* (London, 1790), p. 15.

45. "Remarks by S.T. Coleridge on Sir Robert Peel's Bill," p. 179.

46. Ibid., pp. 179–80. Another pamphlet writer for the bill made a similar comparison, characterizing the friends of the bill as disinterested men who were willing, "in common with the friends of African emancipation, to have their motives and their characters decried, so that they may but succeed at length in placing under some control, a trade which is any thing but humane and *free*, though subsisting in the very heart of a free and happy country," in *Answers to Certain Objections Made to Sir Robert Peel's Bill*, p. 17.

47. "A Lay Sermon Addressed to the Higher and Middle Classes on the Existing Distresses and Discontents," in *Lay Sermons*, ed. R.J. White, *Collected Works of Samuel Taylor Coleridge*, 6:227.

48. Ibid., p. xxxii.

49. Ibid., p. 31.

50. Ibid., p. 182.

51. Ibid., p. 183.

52. For a thorough discussion of Romantic ideas about the will, see Michael Cook, *The Romantic Will* (New Haven, 1978).

53. Kydd, *History of the Factory Movement*, 1:88–89.

54. According to his own testimony, Oastler knew nothing about the situation in the factories prior to his talk with John Wood, a worsted manufacturer, a few days before he wrote his letter. We can assume, then, that he had not read the publicity of earlier reformers.

55. See "To the Editor of the *Leeds Intelligencer*," *British Labourer's Protector, and Factory Child's Friend*, no. 1 (1832), pp. 7–8; repr. (New York, 1969).

56. *British Labourer's Protector*, no. 1 (1832), p. 62.

57. Ibid., p. 55.

58. Ibid., p. 203.

59. Driver, *Tory Radical*, p. 75.

60. *British Labourer's Protector*, no 1 (1832), p. 32.

61. "Report from the Select Committee on the Bill to Regulate the Labour of Children in Mills and Factories of the United Kingdom," 1831–32 (706.) xv.1.

62. *British Labourer's Protector*, no. 1 (1832), p. 55.

63. Ibid., p. 46.

64. Ibid., p. 64.

65. "Report from the Select Committee," 11:462–63.

66. Ibid., p. 463.

67. *British Labourer's Protector*, no. 1 (1832), p. 47.

68. P.M. McDouall, "What Have We Done, and What Are We To Do?" *McDouall's Chartist Journal and Trades Advocate* 1 (1841):1.

69. Ibid.

70. Ibid.

71. "Common Sense, Addressed to the Inhabitants of America," in *Life and Writings of Thomas Paine*, ed. Daniel Edwin Wheeler (New York, 1908), 2:27.

72. "African Slavery in America," in *The Complete Writings of Thomas Paine*, ed. Philip S. Foner (New York, 1945), 2,18.

73. "Emancipation of Slaves," *Complete Writings of Thomas Paine*, 2:21.

74. "A Favorite Song," *Politics for the People* 2 (1795):270.

75. *Gorgon* 1 (1818):35.

76. Ibid., p. 14.

77. Ibid., p. 15.

78. *McDouall's Chartist Journal* 2 (1841):13.

79. "Corn Law Agitation," *Chartist Journal and Trades Advocate*, no. 25 (1841), pp. 198–99.

80. The first of these claims, that the novels' formal problems can be traced to the authors' middle-class fears was made originally by Raymond Williams in "The Industrial Novels," in his book *Culture and Society, 1878–1950* (New York, 1958), pp. 87–109. The second, that the "social problem novel" is a contradiction in terms, was made by Arnold Kettle in "The Early Victorian Social-Problem Novel," in *Dickens to Hardy*, ed. Boris Ford, vol. 6 of *The Pelican Guide to English Literature* (Baltimore, 1958), pp. 169–86.

81. General discussions of free will and determinism in the novel that I have found suggestive are W.J. Harvey, *Character and the Novel* (Ithaca, N.Y., 1965); John Goode, "William Morris and the Dream of Revolution," in *Literature and Politics in the Nineteenth Century*, ed. John Lucas (London, 1971); Patrick Brantlinger, *The Spirit of Reform: British Literature and Politics, 1832–1867* (Cam-

bridge, Ma., 1977), pp. 35–59; Ferenc Feher, "Is the Novel Problematic?," *Telos*, no. 15 (Spring, 1973) 47–74.

82. A very good discussion of this contradiction as a trait of narrative in general and of historical narratives in particular can be found in Gorden Leff, *History and Social Theory* (Garden City, N.J., 1971), passim.

83. Samuel Taylor Coleridge, in a letter to Thomas Allsop, April 8, 1820, on the subject of Walter Scott's novels. Printed in *Scott: The Critical Heritage*, ed. John O. Hayden (New York, 1970), pp. 180–81.

84. Ralph W. Rader identifies this as the definitive principle of coherence of most nineteenth-century novels in his article "Defoe, Richardson, Joyce and the Concept of Form in the Novel," in *Autobiography, Biography and the Novel* (Los Angeles, 1973), pp. 29–72.

85. Robert Colby's *Fiction with a Purpose* (Bloomington, Ind., 1967) documents the emergence of the novelist as a moral guide in the nineteenth century. Carlyle's criticism of Scott also illustrates the point. He writes, "The composition of the Waverley Novels, slight as it often is, usually hangs together in some measure, and *is* a composition. There is a free flow of narrative, of incident and sentiment; and easy master-like coherence throughout." But this mere narrative coherence, he later insists, is not enough, for "Literature has other aims. . . . Under this head there is little to be sought or found in the Waverley novels. Not profitable for doctrine, for reproof, for edification, for building up or elevating, in any shape!" (Unsigned review by Thomas Carlyle quoted here from *Scott: The Critical Heritage*, pp. 364, 366. See also an extract by Harriet Martineau in the same volume, pp. 340–42.)

Chapter 2

1. Hannah More, "Turn the Carpet; or, The Two Weavers: A Dialogue between Dick and John," in Hannah More and others, *Cheap Repository Tracts: Entertaining, Moral, and Religious* (New York, n.d.), 3:96–98.

2. Leslie Stephen points out that the idea of the Almighty Watchmaker, popularized by William Paley in his *Natural Theology* (1802), was anticipated by Bolingbroke. See his *History of English Thought in the Eighteenth Century* (New York, 1802), 1:180, 408–15. The concept of the absentee Watchmaker God was common to the late eighteenth- and nineteenth-century philosophical deists. See Jacob Viner, *The Role of Providence in the Social Order: An Essay in Intellectual History* (Princeton, 1972), pp. 16–17. For a discussion of the differences between philosophical and historical deists, see A. R. Winnett, "Were the Deists 'Deists'?" *Church Quarterly Review* 161 (1960):70–77.

3. The Evangelicals, both inside and outside the Church of England, considered the conversion of the "lower orders" to be their special mission. Although Hannah More had begun writing tracts to improve the morality of the London social elite, with which she was closely associated, her contributions to *Cheap Repository Tracts* were an important and effective part of the mission to convert the poor in the late eighteenth and early nineteenth centuries. She designed many of her stories to appeal to workers, choosing working-class heroes and heroines and considering them in their relationship to their work and their employers. Although none of her characters is employed in a mechanized trade, her stories should be considered early examples of industrial fiction because they portray the workers *as workers*, as a specific group with a definitive productive and social role.

For further information on Hannah More, see Mary Gladys Jones, *Hannah More, 1745–1833* (Cambridge, 1952).

4. Hannah More on *Candide*. See *Tracts*, 8:122.

5. See chapter 1, pp. 18–19.

6. Hannah More, "Patient Joe; or, The Newcastle Collier," *Tracts*, 8:152.

7. For a succinct account of the Evangelicals' battle against both Calvinists and contemporary philosophers on the issue of free will, see Bernard Semmel, *The Methodist Revolution* (New York, 1973), pp. 81–93, or John Wesley, "A Thought on Necessity," *Works* (New York, 1975), pp. 474–79. For an example of how the Calvinists used the new determinist philosophers, see A.M. Toplady, "Doctrine of Absolute Predestination," in *Works* (London, 1825), 5:160–66, or "The Scheme of Christian and Philosophical Necessity Asserted: In Opposition to Mr. John Wesley's Tract on the Subject," in *Works*, 6:48–66.

8. "The Lancashire Collier-girl," *Tracts*, 5:144. Further references to this story will be given in the text.

9. For a discussion of the relationship between the doctrines of universal salvation and free will, see Semmel, *Methodist Revolution*, pp. 81–96.

10. "History of Diligent Dick; or Truth Will Out, Though It Be Hid in a Well," *Tracts*, 8:68.

11. There was no necessary connection between Evangelicalism and support for factory reform. However, as a biographer of Lord Ashley has pointed out, "one of the great achievements of Evangelicalism was to make clear the essential connection between privilege and responsibility" (Georgina Battiscombe, *Shaftesbury: The Great Reformer, 1801–1885* [Boston, 1975], p. 80). The Ten Hours Movement was for Ashley and for many other Evangelicals what the anti–slave trade movement had been for Wilberforce: a consequence and an expression of religious enthusiasm. Certainly the Ten Hours movement was consonant with Ashley's Tory politics, and most nonworking-class Northern leaders of the movement (John Wood, George Bull, Richard Oastler, and William Ferrand) were also Tories. John Wood and Richard Oastler were both touched by Evangelicalism early in their careers, however, and Michael Sadler, Ashley's predecessor as Parliamentary spokesman for factory reformers, was both an Anglican and Methodist. For many of these reformers Ashley's remark to George Bull would have seemed valid: "The Ten Hours Bill appeared an affair less of policy than of religion" (Battiscombe, *Shaftesbury*, p. 84).

12. The book was first serialized in *The Christian Lady's Magazine* (1839–40) and was published in a single volume by R.B. Seeley and W. Burnside in 1841.

13. For a discussion of Tonna's appeal to the individual to resist the system, see Angus Easson, *Elizabeth Gaskell* (Boston, 1979), p. 67.

14. See *Personal Recollections of Charlotte Elizabeth, Continued to the Close of Her Life* (London, 1847), p. 310.

15. Charlotte Elizabeth [Tonna], *Helen Fleetwood* (London, 1841), pp. 80–81.

16. For a discussion of the relationship between *Helen Fleetwood* and the publications of the factory reformers, see Ivanka Kovačević and Barbara Kammer, "Blue Book into Novel: The Forgotten Industrial Fiction of Charlotte Elizabeth Tonna," *Nineteenth-Century Fiction* 25 (September 1970): 152–73.

17. For a discussion of Tonna's sources, see Kovačević and Kammer, "Blue Book into Novel."

18. This strain of thought is not completely foreign to Wesleyan Evangelicalism. In the very act of arguing against Calvinist ideas of predestination,

Evangelical theologians claimed that God could not punish people for failing to fulfill duties of which they were wholly ignorant. Thus, in disproving the claims of one of their deterministic adversaries, the Calvinists, they strengthened the hand of another, the social and psychological determinists. See, for example, chapter 9 of John Plaifere, *An Appeal to the Gospel for the True Doctrine of Divine Predestination, Concorded with the Orthodox Doctrine of God's Free-Grace, and Man's Free Will,* in *The Arminian Magazine: Consisting of Extracts and Original Treatises on General Redemption* 2 (1790):5–15. This chapter instances the fact that the creed of general redemption had drawn Evangelicals toward a kind of social determinism. In debating whether or not a person is to be held responsible for ignoring the Gospel of Christ, for example, the author argues: "A neglect in acquiring a knowledge of the Christian faith, is faulty or excusable, according as man had, or wanted, motives to think it reasonable or necessary" (p. 14).

19. *Harriet Martineau's Autobiography*, ed. Maria Weston Chapman (Boston, 1877), 1:84.

20. Although this was Martineau's general belief, she did try to correct certain specific abuses. Several of her stories have reformist intentions, for she believed that change was both a necessary and an inevitable part of providence and that she could be an instrument for change. The changes she advocated, however, led in the direction of less, not more, government interference with the "laws" of economic development.

21. In *The Eighteenth-Century Background* (New York, 1940), p. 183, Basil Willey points out that the religious beliefs of Deists and Unitarians were often identical. The two groups differed primarily in their degree of organization and in the social class of their adherents: Deists tended to be "Gentlemen," while Unitarian congregations were largely middle class. The Watchmaker, however, is an apt metaphor for the God of both the Deists and those Unitarians of the late eighteenth and early nineteenth centuries who adhered to the beliefs of Joseph Priestley.

22. *Autobiography*, 1:85.

23. For a full and systematic exposition of Joseph Priestley's materialistic determinism, see *A Free Discussion of the Doctrines of Materialism, and Philosophical Necessity, In a Correspondence between Dr. Price, and Dr. Priestley* (London, 1778).

24. A succinct discussion of Hartley's contribution to Priestley's thought is contained in Geoffrey Rowell, *Hell and the Victorians: A Study of the Nineteenth-Century Theological Controversies Concerning Eternal Punishment and Future Life* (Oxford, 1974), pp. 34–38.

25. *Autobiography*, 1:85. Martineau thought Owen's determinism was too simple-minded, since it did not take into consideration any innate differences among people. See *Autobiography*, 1:175.

26. *Autobiography*, 1:86.

27. This remark was made in an 1829 review by Martineau of a Necessarian work entitled *Essays on the Pursuit of Truth, the Progress of Knowledge, and on the Fundamental Principle of All Evidence and Expectations*, by Samuel A. Bailey. The essay was reprinted in *Miscellanies* by Harriet Martineau (Boston, 1836), 2:174–96. The political economist under discussion is Adam Smith (p. 184).

28. *Autobiography*, 1:86.

29. For a discussion of Martineau's sources, see R.K. Webb, *Harriet Martineau: A Radical Victorian* (New York, 1969), pp. 116–17.

30. Rowell, *Hell and the Victorians*, p. 38.

31. In her *Autobiography*, 1:88, she says she had no "literal notion of being dammed—any more than any other born and bred Unitarian."

32. I use the term here in Coleridge's sense of religiosity that is primarily motivated by promises of rewards or threats of punishment in an afterlife.

33. In a rather confused discussion of *A Manchester Strike*, Ivanka Kovačević, in *Fact into Fiction: English Literature and the Industrial Scene, 1750–1850* (Leicester, 1975), accuses Martineau of simply being ambivalent and illogical. She adds, on p. 120, "Had Harriet Martineau held consistently to her theories, the story would have been the poorer for it." Kovačević has a rather scanty knowledge of Martineau's intellectual tradition and fails to recognize how contradictory the writer's own theories were. N.E. Rivenburg, *Harriet Martineau: An Example of Victorian Conflict* (Philadelphia, 1932), errs in the opposite direction and attributes everything in Martineau's *Illustrations* to the classical political economists, taking Martineau as a perfect representative of that tradition alone. Valerie Kossew Pichanick offers a more helpful treatment of the ambiguities in Martineau's position by tracing the development of Martineau's ideas and placing specific works at specific points in that development in *Harriet Martineau: The Woman and Her Work, 1802–76* (Ann Arbor, 1980), pp. 47–72.

34. For a discussion of how uncharacteristic Martineau's optimism was among political economists, see Mark Blaug, *Ricardian Economics: A Historical Study*, Yale Studies in Economics, no. 8 (New Haven, 1958), pp. 129–39. And for the importance of providential thought to eighteenth- and nineteenth-century economic theory, see Viner, passim.

35. Harriet Martineau, *A Manchester Strike*, in *Illustrations of Political Economy*, vol. 3 (London, 1834).

36. See, for example, James Mill on how competition sets wages in *Elements of Political Economy* (1826), reprinted in *Selected Economic Writings*, ed. Donald Winch (Edinbugh, 1966), pp. 229–31.

37. This new interest in the worker is not unique to the political economists, of course, but is a part of the widespread elevation of the "common man" that is a hallmark of the Romantic movement.

38. R. K. Webb has pointed out (*Harriet Martineau*, p. 39) that in Martineau's theory "the callings of novelist and preacher are identical." She believed that all "good art" taught general principles, and consequently she had no compunction about giving her stories over completely to their didactic purposes.

39. For a discussion of Martineau's didacticism in response to public interest, see Pichanick, *Harriet Martineau*, pp. 50–52.

40. Blaug, *Ricardian Economics*, p. 123.

41. Webb, *Harriet Martineau*, pp. 122–23.

Chapter 3

1. George Rowell, *Hell and the Victorians*, pp. 49–57, gives a succinct account of the sources and impact of James Martineau's thought. See also James Drummond, *The Life and Letters of James Martineau* (New York, 1902), vol. 1, passim.

2. *Harriet Martineau's Autobiography*, ed. Marie Weston (Boston, 1877), 1:83.

3. Quoted in Drummond, *Life and Letters of James Martineau*, 2:262–63.

4. Quoted in Webb, *Harriet Martineau*, p. 96.

5. Drummond, *Life and Letters of James Martineau*, 2:262.

6. James Martineau, "Three States of Unitarian Theology," in *Essays, Reviews, and Addresses*, (London, 1891), 4:574.

7. Ibid.

8. Rowell, *Hell and the Victorians*, p. 52.

9. W. Arthur Boggs, "Reflections of Unitarians in Mrs. Gaskell's Novels" (Dissertation, University of California, Berkeley, 1950), p. 23.

10. Two of Elizabeth Gaskell's letters indicate that she rather disliked James Martineau and was probably not strongly influenced by him personally. See *The Letters of Mrs. Gaskell*, ed. J.A.V. Chapple and Arthur Pollard (Manchester, 1966), pp. 177, 239. One as deeply immersed in Unitarianism as Gaskell was, however, could hardly have escaped being influenced by the emphasis he gave to man's "capacity . . . for voluntary righteousness" (see note 1). *Mary Barton* itself provides sufficient evidence that Gaskell had entered "the second stage of Unitarian theology."

11. Quoted in William Robbins, *The Newman Brothers: An Essay in Comparative Intellectual Biography* (Cambridge, Mass., 1966), p. 152.

12. Gaskell's admiration for Francis Newman and her attention to his thought are evident in this description: "We first knew Mr. Newman from his coming here to be a professor at the Manchester College—and the face and voice at first sight told 'He had been with Christ.' . . . Oh dear! I long for the days back again when he came dropping in in the dusk and lost no time in pouring out what his heart was full of, (thats [sic] the secret of eloquence) whether it was a derivation of a word, a joke or a burst of indignation or a holy thought" (*Letters*, pp. 87–88).

13. From Francis Newman, *Four Lectures on the Contrasts of Ancient and Modern History* (1846), quoted in Robbins, *Newman Brothers*, p. 93.

14. Catholic Union, *Essays towards a Church of the Future as the Organization of Philanthropy* (London, 1854), p. 13; first published in 1844.

15. *Four Lectures*, p. 93.

16. From *Biographical Memoranda*, by James Martineau, quoted in Drummond, *Life and Letters of James Martineau*, 2:273.

17. Ibid.

18. In one of her explanations of John Barton's crime, Gaskell traces it to his reification of the masters. Barton only understands the true nature of his error after Carson ceases to be a capitalist in Barton's eyes and becomes a mere man: "The mourner before him was no longer the employer; a being of another race, eternally placed in antagonistic attitude . . . but a very poor and desolate old man" (p. 435).

19. *Letters of Mrs. Gaskell*, p. 70.

20. Ibid., p. 74. See Jeannette King, *Tragedy in the Victorian Novel: Theory and Practice in the Novels of George Eliot, Thomas Hardy, and Henry James* (New York, 1978) for a discussion of the ways in which Victorian writers tried to reconcile their proletarian subject matter and their ideas of social determinism with classical models of tragedy that emphasized the noble status of the hero and the universal, unchanging nature of Fate.

21. *Letters of Mrs. Gaskell*, p. 47. Gaskell here complains about the narrative structure of Martineau's *Hour and the Man* (1841).

22. See note 2.

23. Angus Easson discusses the formal significance of Barton's crime in *Elizabeth Gaskell* (Boston, 1979), pp. 76–77.

24. The ending of *Mary Barton* strikingly recalls the idea of Providence elucidated in Francis Newman's essay "On the Existence of Evil" (1841), in F. W. Newman, Miscellanies (London, 1888), pp. 1–10. In his essay, Newman argues that the idea of free will reconciles the idea of Providence with the existence of evil. God does not will but merely permits the evil created by man. The evil, he insists, is only temporary because it is self-obliterating: "believe

that goodness alone is eternal; and it remains clearly intelligible, how the divine wisdom may have ordained, on the one hand, that man should gain a stable independent holy will, so as to be capable of friendship with his infinite creator; but that, on the other hand, this essentially demanded that he should be left free to sin, and consequently moral evil has abounded and abounds, but only for a time. Sin and its effects, remorse and misery, are to be abolished, and the fruit of holiness shall flourish to everlasting life" (p. 8).

25. *British Quarterly Review* 9 (1849):128.

26. The formal discontinuity of this novel has been remarked by most of its critics. Various sources of the discontinuity have been advanced, and I will mention only three of the most important. In *Culture and Society, 1780–1950* (New York, 1958), pp. 87–91, Raymond Williams divides the novel into halves: the first half is a successful evocation of "everyday life in the working-class"; the second, however, is dominated by the "orthodox plot of the Victorian novel of sentiment." He attributes the split to a shift of emphasis away from John Barton that takes place when "the flow of sympathy with which [Gaskell] began was arrested." The flow of sympathy is arrested, moreover, by a fear of violence, which was part of the middle-class "structure of feeling" that Elizabeth Gaskell inhabited. In "The Early Victorian Social-Problem Novel," in *From Dickens to Hardy*, ed. Boris Ford, vol. 6 of *The Pelican Guide to English Literature* (Baltimore, 1958), pp. 169–87, Arnold Kettle also divides the book between the near-tragic story of John Barton (p. 181) and the love story of his daughter. Although Kettle sees connections between the two, he believes the love story was imposed by the demands of the novel form. Stephen Gill, in his introduction to the Penguin edition of *Mary Barton*, agrees with both Kettle and Williams, but he adds a point of his own: Gaskell could not find a solution to the vast social problems she portrayed because her historical perspective was limited by the immediacy of those problems. All of these judgments are sound; all contribute to our understanding of the novel. But they leave certain things out. First, they do not seem to recognize the generic multiplicity within the two halves of the book. Second, they ignore the fact that John Barton's tragedy is more than merely frightening to a middle-class sensibility; it is also unmanageable because it is self-contradicting. Its paradoxical nature is not explicable in terms of a vague "structure of feeling"; it must be traced to the author's precise intellectual context. Third, these three important analyses do not take the author's own formal self-consciousness into account. For a more recent discussion of the problem, see Angus Easson, for whom the formal ambiguities of *Mary Barton* mark the work of a developing novelist working within a "context of change and debate" in *Elizabeth Gaskell*, p. 58.

27. *Mary Barton: A Tale of Manchester Life*, ed. Stephen Gill (Baltimore, 1976), p. 121. All subsequent references to *Mary Barton* are to this edition, and page numbers are given in the text.

28. As Harry Levin has pointed out in *The Gates of Horn: A Study of Five French Realists* (New York, 1966), p. 19, "the movement of realism, technically considered, is an endeavor to emancipate literature from the sway of conventions."

29. It is Stephen Gill who suggests in footnote 58 of the Penguin edition of *Mary Barton* that this is the quotation, from *Henry IV, Part 1*, 4.3, to which Gaskell alludes. However, my colleague Paul Alpers suggests informally that, although these are his most famous lines in the scene, Falstaff has a much longer speech that yields lines possibly more appropriate to Carson's purpose,

such as "ragged as Lazarus in the painted cloth", and "a hundred and fifty tattered prodigals lately come from swine-keeping."

30. *Letters of Mrs. Gaskell*, p. 74.

31. See note 6.

32. Patrick Brantlinger, in "Bluebooks, the Social Organism, and the Victorian Novel," *Criticism* 13 (1972):328–44, contrasts the detailed evocation of working-class life with the "melodrama of the murder plot," and Stephen Gill ("Introduction") also contrasts the realistic sketches of the first half with the conventional "romantic" sensationalism of the second half (p. 22).

33. My paradigm of melodrama is based primarily on the discussions by Peter Brooks in *The Melodramatic Imagination: Balzac, Henry James, Melodrama, and the Mode of Excess* (New Haven, 1976), pp. 11–20, and by R.B. Heilman, *Tragedy and Melodrama* (Seattle, 1968), passim. Brooks stresses that melodramas portray uncompromising struggles between good and evil. Their mode of action is excessive and parabolical. Heilman discusses the affective difference between tragedy and melodrama, arguing that the former, by portraying an irresolvable internal conflict, produces a complex emotional response, while the latter, by portraying a heroic fight against an external evil force, produces a simpler, self-righteous emotional reaction in the audience.

34. Kathleen Tillotson, *Novels of the Eighteen-Forties* (London, 1956), p. 214.

35. Gaskell's description from a letter to Mary Howitt, *Letters of Mrs. Gaskell*, p. 33. The sketch was published in *Blackwoods Magazine* 41 (1837):48–51, under the title "Sketches among the Poor, No. 1."

36. *Letters of Mrs. Gaskell*, p. 74.

37. Tillotson, *Novels of the Eighteen-Forties*, p. 222.

38. The often-repeated story is that Gaskell was inspired to write *Mary Barton* while on a mission of mercy to a poor family during the depression of the early 1840s: "She was trying hard to speak comfort, and to allay those bitter feelings against the rich which were so common with the poor, when the head of the family took hold of her arm, and grasping it tightly said, with tears in his eyes, 'Ay, ma'am, but have ye ever seen a child clemmed to death.' " The story is from M. Hompes, "Mrs. E.C. Gaskell," *Gentleman's Magazine* 55 (1895):124.

39. For a discussion of the various narrative modes in *Mary Barton* as deviations from a dominant domestic mode, see Rosemarie Bodenheimer, "Private Grief and Public Acts in *Mary Barton*," *Dickens Studies Annual: Essays on Victorian Fiction* 9 (New York, 1981): 195–216.

40. Tillotson, *Novels of the Eighteen-Forties*, pp. 215–21, contains an excellent discussion of the two London stories.

41. For a discussion of a possible source for this scene in the work of Caroline Bowles, see Michael D. Wheeler, "The Writer as Reader in *Mary Barton*," *Durham University Journal* 67 (1974): 92–106.

Chapter 4

1. Information about Kingsley's education comes from two biographies: Susan Chitty, *The Beast and the Monk: A Life of Charles Kingsley* (London, 1974); Brenda Colloms, *Charles Kingsley: The Lion of Eversley* (New York, 1975). The influence of Carlyle, Coleridge, and Maurice on Kingsley is discussed in Stanley E. Baldwin, *Charles Kingsley*, Cornell Studies in English, no. 25 (Ithaca, 1934), pp. 48–73; and in Roger LeRoy Tarr, "Carlyle's Influence upon the Mid-Victorian Social Novels of Gaskell, Kingsley, and Dickens" (Dissertation, University of Southern California, 1970), passim.

2. For an account of the Victorian Anglican thinkers who were most influenced by Coleridge in their philosophies and religious views, especially in their beliefs about Providence and free will, see Duncan Forbes, *The Liberal Anglican Idea of History* (Cambridge, England, 1952), passim.

3. Long before Kingsley began investigating the sanitary conditions of England (1844, according to Chitty, *The Beast and the Monk*, pp. 90–91), he was introduced to materialist accounts of behavior by his reading in the natural sciences and by the arguments of Charles Mansfield, a Cambridge friend. Under Mansfield's influence, Kingsley for a time became an outspoken ontological materialist and free thinker. Although Kingsley was swiftly reconverted to Anglicanism by his future wife, Fanny Grenfell, he never completely purged himself of his materialist tendencies, which often resurfaced as a vague species of pantheism. See Chitty, *The Beast and the Monk*, p. 80.

4. Kingsley struggled to purge himself of Lockean empiricism and yet hold fast to inductive scientific methods: "till we work clear of Locke and return to Bacon," he wrote to Thomas Cooper in 1854, "we shall do no good" (Charles Kingsley, *His Letters and Memories of His Life*, ed. Fanny Kingsley [London, 1877], 1:180).

5. The quotation is from a wall poster written by Kingsley on the day after the failed Chartist mass meeting of 10 April 1848. It is reproduced in *His Letters and Memories of His Life*, 1:156–57. Although he saw the Charter as a potential extension of the purely negative idea of freedom (freedom merely to do what one wants as opposed to what one should), he also sympathized with the Chartists and thought the extended franchise could lead to a truly cooperative and Christian social organization.

For a discussion of the ways in which the English Romantics both absorbed and challenged the Lockean empiricist tradition, see Robert Langbaum, *The Mysteries of Identity: A Theme in Modern Literature* (New York, 1977), pp. 25–47.

6. For a discussion of crisis autobiography, the Romantic form into which both *Sartor Resartus* and *Alton Locke* loosely fit, see M.H. Abrams, *Natural Supernaturalism: Tradition and Revolution in Romantic Literature* (New York, 1973), pp. 307 ff. Abrams argues that the reconciliation of self and world is actually accomplished by the Romantics, albeit often by absorbing the world into the self. For an argument that denies the reconciliation of the two terms in Romantic literature, see Michael G. Cooke, *The Romantic Will* (New Haven, 1976), pp. 52–144. Cooke argues that self and system are normally irreconcilable in Romanticism. Contesting Northrop Frye's opinion that self and world are united in Romanticism, he contends: "Frye is, I think, unduly positive when he declares that 'in the romantic construct there is a center where inward and outward manifestations of a common motion and spirit are unified, where the ego is identified as itself because it is also identified with something which is not itself. [See Northrop Frye, "The Drunken Boat," in *Romanticism Reconsidered* (New York, 1963), passim.] This Fichtean terminology . . . deals with a *proposed* identification, a perpetual and perpetually unfinished process of approach, à la Zeno, toward identification. Partly this results from the fact . . . that it is impossible to do justice at once to the self and to the place where it finds itself—each emphasis is jealous of the other. But partly also the uncertainty arises from a desolidification of the meaning of self and not-self (and not-self may be equally nature, society, or free mental construct)" (p. 54).

Cooke's description here of the antithetical relationship between self and not-self and of the "desolidification" of both terms make the contradictions of *Alton Locke* seem typical of the Romantic tradition, but we might grant that

Romanticism is thus self-contradictory on this point and still argue that Kingsley's irrepressible materialism exaggerates the contradiction within Romanticism.

7. For a discussion of the circuitous journey in *Sartor Resartus*, see Abrams, *Natural Supernaturalism*, pp. 307–12. See also G.B. Tennyson, *"Sartor" Called "Resartus"* (Princeton, 1965), passim.

8. Thomas Carlyle, *Sartor Resartus: The Life and Opinions of Herr Teufelsdröckh* (London, 1871), pp. 67–68.

9. For a discussion of the post-Romantic elements of *Sartor Resartus*, see Masao Miyoshi, *The Divided Self: A Perspective on the Literature of the Victorians* (New York, 1969), pp. 138–51.

10. In its most exploitative form the sweating system herded half-starved workers together into unsanitary workrooms, where they both lived and worked. They were paid very low price rates, and often became deeply indebted to the middleman who employed them. For a discussion of this practice in the London clothing industry, see Beatrice Webb [Potter] and Sydney Webb, *Problems of Modern Industry* (London, 1902).

11. Chitty, *The Beast and the Monk*, p. 129.

12. From a letter by F.D. Maurice to Kingsley in which Maurice agrees with Kingsley's judgment about Wordsworth's *Prelude*. Quoted in Abrams, *Natural Supernaturalism*, pp. 122–23.

13. *Alton Locke: Tailor and Poet*, ed. Herbert Van Thal (London, 1967), p. 1. All other quotations from *Alton Locke* are from this edition, and page numbers are given in the text.

14. See, for example, *His Letters and Memories of His Life*, 1:187, where he writes that our "piecemeal and partial minds" are not yet capable of "binding" the idea of "Free Will" with its true "correlative," "predestination."

15. This may be what Arnold Kettle means when he says Alton's sensibility is never placed. See "The Early Victorian Social-Problem Novel," in *From Dickens to Hardy*, ed. Boris Ford, vol. 6 of *The Pelican Guide to English Literature* (Baltimore, 1958), p. 184.

16. According to Allan John Hartley, in *The Novels of Charles Kingsley: A Christian Social Interpretation* (Folkestone, 1977), p. 77, Alton follows a "perversion pattern": he suffers from self-imposed blindness rather than from obstructed vision. This "perversion pattern" argument, however, ignores the rhetorical structure of Alton's confessions of wilfulness: they almost always end by accusing the reader of hypocrisy and by insisting that *anyone* would have done what Alton did in his "circumstances."

17. Kingsley was very interested in the philosophical dispute that revolved around the idea of identity. He wanted to believe in the Romantics' response to such skeptical challenges to the concept of identity as Hume's. "I am very anxious to get your definition of a *person*," Kingsley wrote to Thomas Cooper. "I have not been able yet to get one, or a proof of personal existence which does not spring from a priori subjective consciousness, and which is, in fact, Fichte's 'I am I.' . . . How I get this idea I know not: but it is the most precious of all convictions, as it is the first; and I can only suppose that it is a revelation from God, whose image it is in me, and the first proof of my being his child." Yet for all the attraction of this essentialist view of identity, Kingsley cannot rid himself of the idea that dominates *Alton Locke*, the idea that one's identity depends on what one does and how one exists. Later in the same letter, he attributes to Lange's *Leben Jesu* a curious blend of the essentialist and existential ideas of identity: Lange, he claims, "(deriving person from persona, a mask—a charac-

ter in a play—at last an office, or functionary of any sort) says that the true idea of a person is a being inspired by God, and called by Him to certain functions in His world, persons *per* quam *sonat* spiritus, through whom God's spirit speaks" (*His Letters and Memories of His Life*, 1:384–85). Applying this theory of personality to *Alton Locke*, we can see that because Alton is prevented from performing the function to which God called him, he is prevented from being a person.

18. Articles exposing the sweating system appeared in the *Morning Chronicle* in 1849. For a discussion of the relationship between these articles and *Alton Locke*, see Louis Cazamian, *The Social Novel in England, 1830–1850*, trans. Martin Fido (London, 1973), pp. 266–88.

19. Kingsley's habit of discussing other writers is reminiscent of Carlyle, but Carlyle seldom names a book. He normally conjures up, addresses, and dismisses other authors. Compare, for example, Carlyle's treatment of Voltaire with two samples of Kingsley's treatment of his own opposition. Authors are imagined as speaking through their books in *Sartor Resartus*. The book is a mere medium, an extension of the voice: " 'Cease, my much-respected Herr Von Voltaire,' thus apostrophises the Professor: 'shut thy sweet voice, for the task appointed thee seems finished.... Take our thanks, then, and—thyself away' " (pp. 133–34).

In *Alton Locke*, on the other hand, Kingsley's Swiftean imagination reduces the writer to the physical book containing his ideas: "From the ceiling . . . dangled various books to which [Mackaye] had taken an antipathy, principally High Tory and Benthamite, crucified, impaled through their covers, and suspended in all sorts of torturing attitudes" (p. 61); "Bell's *Life in London* and the *Ecclesiologist* had, between them, got down *McCulloch on Taxation*, and were sitting, arm-in-arm, triumphantly astride of him" (p. 145).

Chapter 5

1. Raymond Williams, *The Long Revolution* (New York, 1966), p. 278.

2. See Francis Mulherne, "Ideology and Literary Form—A Comment," *New Left Review*, no. 91 (May–June 1975), p. 86.

3. Sarah Ellis, *The Women of England: Their Social Duties and Domestic Habits*, 11th ed. (London, n.d.), p. 52.

4. Sir Arthur Helps, *The Claims of Labour: An Essay on the Duties of the Employers to the Employed*, 2d ed. (London, 1845), p. v.

5. Ellis, *Women of England*, pp. 52, 58.

6. Helps, *Claims of Labour*, p. vii.

7. Ibid., p. 157.

8. See David Roberts, *Paternalism in Early Victorian England* (New Brunswick, 1979), for an account of the early Victorian social paternalists and their achievements.

9. Christopher Hill describes the earliest English conceptions of a paternalistic state in "The Norman Yoke," *Democracy in the Labour Movement*, ed. John Saville (London, 1954), pp. 19–20.

10. For a thorough discussion of the origins and uses of patriarchal theories in English political thought, see Gordon J. Schochet, *Patriarchalism in Political Thought: The Authoritarian Family and Political Speculation and Attitudes Especially in Seventeenth-Century England* (New York, 1975).

11. The founders of the cult of domesticity include Elizabeth Sandford (*Woman and Her Social Domestic Character*, 1831; *Female Improvement*, 1836); Anna Jameson (*Characteristics of Women*, 1832); Sarah Lewis (*Woman's Mission*,

1839); and C.M. Sedgwick (*Means and Ends or Self-Training*, 1840). One of the best discussions of the impact of the ideology of domesticity on English writers is in the first chapter of Inga-Stina Eubank's *Their Proper Sphere: A Study of the Brontë Sisters as Early-Victorian Female Novelists* (Cambridge, Mass., 1968). Other discussions of domestic ideology in Victorian literature are included in Robert R. Utter and Gwendolyn B. Needham, *Pamela's Daughters* (New York, 1937); Aina Rubenius, *The Woman Question in Mrs. Gaskell's Life and Works* (Cambridge, Mass., 1950); Patricia Thomson, *The Victorian Heroine: A Changing Ideal, 1837–1873* (London, 1956); John Killham, *Tennyson and 'The Princess': Reflections of an Age* (London, 1958); Ellen Moers, *Literary Women: The Great Writers* (Garden City, N.Y., 1976). For a general discussion of Victorian ideas of the family, see Walter E. Houghton, *The Victorian Frame of Mind, 1830–1870* (London, 1966), pp. 341–93. See also Martha Vicinus, ed., *Suffer and Be Still* (Bloomington, Ind., 1972).

12. Ellis, *Women of England*, p. 53.

13. For Locke's account of the differences between parental and political power and between conjugal and political societies, see his *Two Treatises on Government*, ed. Peter Laslett (New York, 1960), pp. 209–10, 427–29.

14. The Infants' Custody Bill of 1840, for example, was defeated on the strength of patriarchal arguments that the bill would promote public disorder by undermining the authority of the heads of families. Even liberals argued that political representation for women was unnecessary because a woman's interests were identical with her husband's. See, for example, the article entitled "Woman, and her Social Position," *Westminster Review* 35 (1841): 24–52.

15. Richard Oastler, "Letter," *The British Labourer's Protector and Factory Child's Friend*, November 30, 1832, p. 83.

16. Lord Ashley, "Ten Hours' Factory Bill, The Speech of Lord Ashley, M.P., in the House of Commons, on Friday, March 15th, 1844," p. 4, reprinted in *Prelude to Victory of the Ten Hours Movement: Two Speeches, One Letter and a Report, 1844*, one of an unnumbered series, ed. Kennth E. Carpenter, *British Labour Struggles: Contemporary Pamphlets 1727–1850* (New York, 1972).

17. Robert Southey, *Sir Thomas More; or Colloquies on the Progress and Prospects of Society* (London, 1829), 1:128. Southey continues, "and whenever a state shall duly exercise its parental duties, there will surely be none which shall either wholly hebetate the faculties or harden the heart."

18. For a discussion of the economic, political, and social reasons for this shift in strategy, see A. Harrison and B. L. Hutchins, *A History of Factory Legislation* (London, 1966), pp. 81–85.

19. Richard Oastler, "Select Committee Evidence," *British Labourer's Protector and Factory Child's Friend*, 28 September 1832, pp. 14, 15.

20. Ashley, pp. 18, 21.

21. Ibid., pp. 24, 26.

22. In her exhaustive *Women and Trade Unions: An Outline History of Women in the British Trade Union Movement* (London, 1977), pp. 53–54, Sheila Lewenhak points to a pragmatic ulterior motive behind the male reformers' sentimental idealization of family life: "After the 1833 Factory Act was passed, considerably restricting the use of child labour in cotton factories, women replaced children. So, similarly, it was hoped that a restriction of women's hours of work would cause employers to replace women with men. It was true that men trade unionists hoped in the long run to reduce the length of the working-day for themselves, but the immediate battle was for work."

23. Ibid., p. 29.

24. There were, of course, liberal objections to including any adults, male or female, under legislative protection. Sydney Smith, for example, remarked that "it does seem to be absurd to hinder a woman of thirty from working as long as she pleases; but mankind are getting mad with humanity and Samaritanism" (quoted in John Trevor Ward, *The Factory Movement, 1830–1855* [London, 1962], p. 289).

25. For a discussion of the moral force behind Lord Ashley's position in terms of his personal idealism and unassailable credibility as an impeccably motivated philanthropist, see Patricia L. Schmidt, "The Role of Moral Idealism in Social Change: Lord Ashley and the Ten Hours Factory Act," *Quarterly Journal of Speech* 63 (February 1977): 14–27.

26. It is to this ideological crisis that J.S. Mill was referring in his 1845 review of Helps, *The Claims of Labour,* when he said that the old system was losing its prestige (review of *The Claims of Labour,* in the *Edinburgh Review,* April 1845; reprinted in *Dissertations and Discussions Political, Philosophical, and Historical,* 2d ed. [London, 1867], 2:181). Discussions of the crisis can be found in Eduard Heimann, *History of Economic Doctrines* (London, 1945); Ronald Meek, "Decline of Ricardian Economics," in *Economics and Ideology and Other Essays* (London, 1967); M. Blaug, *Ricardian Economics: A Historical Study* (New Haven, 1958).

27. The fifth chapter of Sidney Pollard's *The Genesis of Modern Management: A Study of the Industrial Revolution in Great Britain* (Baltimore, 1968), pp. 189–242, documents the growth of management and of the ideological control over workers in British industry. Another economic historian, John Foster, tells us in his *Class Struggle and the Industrial Revolution: Early Industrial Capitalism in Three English Towns* (London, 1974) that a new social perspective was reached by the manufacturers of Oldham in the late 1840s, and that it signified a retreat from rationality. "Its language," he writes, "was simplistic, its ultimate explanations founded on divinity, not economics, and its view of society reduced to that of a family" (p. 188).

28. Harold Perkin, in *The Origins of Modern English Society, 1780–1880* (London, 1972), p. 343, argues that "the essential change in the climate from early Victorian social conflict to mid-Victorian stability was not in living standards or production but in prices, not from depression to prosperity but from long-term deflation to long-term inflation."

29. See Perkin, *Origins,* pp. 365–80, for a description of how the middle class made its peace with the aristocracy, how it succeeded in dominating legislation while allowing the landed classes to dominate the legislature numerically.

30. Helps, *The Claims of Labour,* p. 142.

Chapter 6

1. Frances Trollope concentrates exclusively on child workers in her description of both Matthew Dowling's mill and Deep Valley Mill. See *The Life and Adventures of Michael Armstrong, the Factory Boy* (London, 1839), 1:197 ff. and 2:148 ff.

2. "The Factory Child's Last Day," *British Labourer's Protector and Factory Child's Friend,* no. 1 (1832–33), p. 247.

3. Charlotte Elizabeth Tonna, *The Wrongs of Women* (New York, 1843–44)

4. See Louis James, *Fiction for the Working Man, 1830–1850: A Study of the Literature Produced for the Working Classes in Early Victorian England* (London, 1963), p. xii, for a definition of "cheap" or "lower class" publications.

5. For an exhaustive discussion of female characters as vehicles for social

themes in all the works under consideration here, see Helena Bergmann, *Between Obedience and Freedom: Women's Role in the Mid-Nineteenth Century Industrial Novel*, Gothenburg Studies in English, no. 45 (Gothenburg, 1979), passim.

6. *Second Report of the Commissioners Inquiring into the Employment of Children in Trades and Manufactures* 1843 [430], xiii.307.

7. The most sensational reports of the sweating system were carried in several issues of the *Morning Chronicle* in 1849, but extracts from the *Second Report of the Commissioners* were carried in the *Times* and in many other London papers.

8. "The Song of the Shirt," *The Complete Poetical Works of Thomas Hood*, ed. Epes Sargent (Boston, 1857), 1:148.

9. For biographical information about Rymer and Reynolds, as well as a discussion of their literary context, see James, *Fiction for the Working Man, 1830–1850*, pp. 28–44.

10. "Preface," *The White Slave: A Romance for the Nineteenth Century* (London, 1844), p. iv.

11. *The Slaves of England: No. 1, The Seamstress* in *Reynolds's Miscellany of Romance, General Literature, Science and Art*, 12 Dec. 1850, p. 43.

12. See Peter Brooks, *The Melodramatic Imagination: Balzac, Henry James, Melodrama, and the Mode of Excess* (New Haven, 1976), pp. 56–80. In a sentence particularly appropriate to our subject, Brooks writes, "Even the scenes constructed of words tend toward a terminal wordlessness in the fixed gestures of tableau" (p. 61).

13. On the metaphoric qualities of melodrama, see Brooks, *The Melodramatic Imagination*, p. 72: "The gestures which fill the gap reach toward other meanings which cannot be generated from the language code. They often take the form of the message . . . expressed in an immediate inarticulate language of presence: a moment of victory of pure expression over articulation. In terms of Roman Jakobson's two poles of language, metonymy could represent the model of traditional discourse, of the spaced, articulated phrase; while metaphor appears here as an effort to collapse spaced, articulated language back into a direct, presented meaning: a meaning made visible."

14. Thomas Carlyle, *Past and Present* (London, 1960), p. 154.

15. As Louis James has shown, "domestic tale" was often used in the nineteenth century to refer to melodramatic stories like Rymer's and Reynolds' (*Fiction for the Working Man*, pp. 97–113). I use it here, however, as I used it in chapter 3, to denote unsensational, largely antiromantic fiction that describes the daily occurrences of domestic life.

16. See, for example, two stories published in cheap periodicals in 1850 in addition to the tales discussed in this chapter: "The Seamstress," *Eliza Cook's Journal*, 3 (May 11, 1850): 17–19; H. M. Rathbone, "The Seamstress," *Working Man's Friend and Family Instructor* 1 (1850):306–8. For additional titles see Margaret Dalziel, *Popular Fiction 100 Years Ago* (London, 1957), pp. 89–90.

17. Ralph Barnes Grinrod, L.L.D., *The Slaves of the Needle: An Exposure of the Distressed Condition, Moral and Physical of Dressmakers, Milliners, Embroiderers, Shopworkers & C.* (London, n.d.), p. 19.

18. These include such periodicals as *The People's Journal, Howitt's Journal, Mother's Friend, The True Briton,* and *Sunday at Home*. For discussions of these and other "improving" magazines, see Dalziel, *Popular Fiction*, pp. 46–76, and James, *Fiction for the Working Man*, pp. 114–29.

19. Quoted in Silverpen [Eliza Meteyard], *Lucy Dean: The Noble Needlewoman*, in *Eliza Cook's Journal*, 3 (January 1850–January 1851): 312.

20. For other didactic industrial tales using contrasting models of conduct, see Sarah Patterson, *Masters and Workmen: A Tale for the Times* (n.p. [1858]); *The Strike* (London, [1858]); Hugh Vernon, *The Weaver's Son*, in *The True Briton*, vol. 2 (1853); and *The Harnetts: A Tale of North English Life*, in *The Cottage Economist*, vol. 1 (1854).

21. Other such periodicals were *The Cottage Economist, Household Words, Illustrated Family Paper, The British Workman* and *Sunday at Home*. For information on these periodicals, see Dalziel, *Popular Fiction*, pp. 46 ff.

22. "The Three Homes: A Tale of the Cotton Spinners," *Working Man's Friend and Family Instructor* 4 (November 5–20, 1850):93.

Chapter 7

1. See "The Preston Strike: A History," in the *Annual Register*, May 1854, reprinted in *Hard Times*, eds. George Ford and Sylvère Monod (New York, 1966), pp. 279–82.

2. Humphry House has noticed and discussed Dickens's social paternalism and has suggested that the novels should be read in the context of such books as Arthur Helps, *The Claims of Labour*. See *The Dickens World* (London, 1941), p. 45. Dickens, of course, knew Helps; it was Helps who arranged Dickens's 1865 interview with Queen Victoria. Helps was then Clerk of the Privy Council. See Edgar Johnson, *Charles Dickens, His Tragedy and Triumph*, rev. ed. (London, 1976), p. 574.

3. Of these novels, Raymond Williams says, "Recognition of evil was balanced by fear of becoming involved. Sympathy was transformed, not into action, but into withdrawal" (*Culture and Society: 1780–1950* [New York, 1966], p. 109). According to Williams, *Hard Times* withdraws into personal feeling, into an innocence that "shames the adult world, but also essentially rejects it" (p. 96). In *North and South*, Williams notes, there is a more serious attempt to come to terms with industrial society, but he believes Margaret's legacy and her marriage to Thornton to be forms of escape: "Once again Mrs. Gaskell works out her reaction to the insupportable situation by going—in part adventitiously—outside it" (p. 94). In his essay "The Early Victorian Social-Problem Novel" in *From Dickens to Hardy*, vol. 6 of *The Pelican Guide to English Literature* (Baltimore, 1973), pp. 169–87, Arnold Kettle blames the difficulties of the industrial novels on the "abstraction" that comes from seeing "a living complex of forces and people as a 'problem.' " He specifically exempts *Hard Times* from this charge, but the ending of *North and South* seems to Kettle a tepid compromise of a conflict that was never fully ripe emotionally.

4. Charles Dickens, *Hard Times*, ed. George Ford and Sylvère Monod (New York, 1966), p. 9. All further page references in the text are to this edition.

5. In " 'Divorce and Matrimonial Causes': An Aspect of *Hard Times*," *Victorian Studies*, Summer 1977, pp. 401–12, John D. Baird argues persuasively for Dickens's use of actual cases in his portrait of Stephen Blackpool, whose wife, Baird suggests, is not only alcoholic but adulterous and syphilitic as well. Nevertheless, under then-current divorce laws, Stephen's only remedy lies in the procedure Bounderby outlines—three separate lawsuits and a private act of Parliament, at an estimated cost of two thousand pounds—in order to be free to marry Rachael. So, with his fellow "average Englishman," Stephen is, as Baird points out, "more likely to be struck by lightning than to be divorced."

6. Carlyle's influence is partly responsible for this pessimism, but a number of other factors contribute to the book's bleak outlook. Edgar Johnson attributes the darkness of vision in *Hard Times* to Dickens's earlier experience in the north of England: "the roots of the story . . . were twisted in the flaring gloom of the Black Country and his first horrified vision, sixteen years ago, of mines like underground dungeons and mills filled with clamour and cruelty. He had sworn then 'to strike the heaviest blow in my power' for their victims" (*Charles Dickens*, p. 404). Dickens's own family troubles must also have contributed to the novel's advocacy of easier divorces and to its general pessimism about family life. The dispersal of the Gradgrinds at the end of the book may be related to the author's own restlessness during the period of composition. "I am in a state of restlessness," he wrote in a letter, "impossible to be described— impossible to be imagined—wearing and tearing to be experienced" (quoted in Johnson, *Charles Dickens*, p. 422).

7. Such scenes were staples of didactic domestic tales, which frequently portray the redemption of women by other women. In *Lucy Dean*, for example, Mary Austen saves the fallen Nelly Dean by the same means that Sissy uses to save Louisa. The two scenes are strikingly similar:

> For a moment, the wretched girl, with a sort of blind ferocity, strove to elude the restraining arms, and in the struggle, griped them as a vice its wedge or nail; then as the voice entreated once again, crouched like a hound beneath the keeper's lash; and then at last, all woman, fell weeping down before the feet of her, who of all women, most could save and most could pity!
>
> "My poor one, my unhappy one," spoke Mary, half kneeling too in the fervency of her extreme pity, "I know you . . . and I must save you if I can."

(Silverpen [Eliza Meteyard], *Lucy Dean: The Noble Needlewoman*, in *Eliza Cook's Journal* 3 [January 1850–January 1851]:361).

8. John D. Baird traces interesting ironic inverse parallels between the nonmarriages of Bounderby and Stephen Blackpool in " 'Divorce and Matrimonial Causes,' " pp. 410–12.

9. For a discussion of Dickens's own perceptions and manipulations of fact, fancy, and public opinion, see Joseph Butwin, "*Hard Times*: The News and the Novel," in *Nineteenth-Century Fiction* 32 (1977), pp. 166–87.

10. To contend, as F.R. Leavis has in "*Hard Times*: An Analytic Note," in *The Great Tradition* (London, 1960), pp. 227–48, that the circus in unambiguously depicted as a center of vitality and human sympathy is to ignore much of the evidence of the text. For a full discussion of the ambiguity of the circus in *Hard Times*, see Joseph Butwin's "The Paradox of the Clown in Dickens," in *Dickens Studies Annual*, ed. Robert B. Partlow, 5 (Edwardsville, Ill., 1967):115–32.

11. Leavis's discussion of Sissy, which stresses her vitality, makes her seem a representative member of Sleary's troupe. See *The Great Tradition*, pp. 230–35.

12. Dickens is here playing off the growing Victorian mania for statistical data in aid of scientific authority. According to the London Statistical Society Report of 1836, "The spirit of the present age has an evident tendency to confront the figures of speech with the figures of arithmetic. . . . In the business of social science principles are valid for application only inasmuch as they are legitimate inductions from facts, accurately observed and methodically qualified" (quoted in T. S. Ashton, *Economic and Social Investigations in Manchester*,

1833–1933: A Centenary History of the Manchester Statistical Society [Manchester, 1934]).

13. *The Letters of Charles Dickens*, ed. Walter Dexter (Bloomsbury, 1938), 2:598. Dickens was also annoyed at *North and South* because the sales of *Household Words* had been decreasing since the novel began to appear.

14. Elizabeth Gaskell, *North and South* (Harmondsworth, 1970), p. 166. All further references to this edition will be cited in the text.

15. See *The Mothers of England: Their Influence and Responsibility* (London, 1843), pp. 40 ff.

16. "At the root of all good influence is example," wrote Sarah Ellis in *Mothers of England* (p. 43), and she expands on this precept for several pages.

17. Ibid., p. 40.

18. John Pikoulis identifies public and private concerns as complementary aspects of one theme, that of human aspiration among two manifestly oppressed groups, nineteenth-century workers and nineteenth-century women, and explores this theme in the lives and works of both Elizabeth Gaskell and Charlotte Brönte, in *"North and South*: Varieties of Love and Power," *Yearbook of English Studies* 6 (1976): 176–93.

19. In *Elizabeth Gaskell: The Novel of Social Crisis* (London, 1975), p. 113, Coral Lansbury wrongly celebrates the "rightness" of Margaret's response to Thornton's proposal, thinking it shows Margaret to be a "master at heart" and compensates for any undercutting of Margaret's authority in a novel that locates women's power over men primarily in maternal influence.

20. In the above-cited section of *Mothers of England*, Ellis repeatedly states that mothers should neither preach nor blame. They should, rather, accept the faults of family members and yet try to improve them by example. The ideal mother of Ellis's book is thus somewhat inconsistently conceived, for she must be a moral guide without being a moral judge. The home is thus also inconsistently characterized both as a place where children and men feel pressure to improve themselves and as a place where children and men are accepted and loved despite their faults. The nature of private life is not settled in Ellis's work.

21. In "Price's Patent Candles: New Light on *North and South*," *Review of English Studies* 27 (1976): 313–21, Stephen Gill argues that the character of Thornton is actually based on one James Wilson, managing director of a Vauxhall factory, who instituted impressive reforms in his own firm and at his own expense, and with whom Gaskell was personally acquainted.

22. In *Culture and Society*, Raymond Williams comments on the social significance of this ending. He sees it almost entirely, however, in geographical, not class, terms: "The relationship of Margaret and Thornton and their eventual marriage serve as a unification of the practical energy of Northern manufacturer with the developed sensibility of the Southern girl" (p. 92).

23. Rosemarie Bodenheimer discusses, as an organizing dynamic in *North and South*, the fluidity of associative vision and the ability to adapt to changing social and personal perspectives, in *"North and South*: A Permanent State of Change," *Nineteenth Century Fiction* 34 (December 1979): 281–301.

Chapter 8

1. For a general discussion of the Utilitarian theory of value see Leszek Kolakowski, *The Alienation of Reason: A History of Positivist Thought*, trans. Norbert Guterman (Garden City, N.Y., 1969), pp. 79–87.

2. Elie Halevy, in *The Growth of Philosophical Radicalism*, trans. Mary Morris

(Boston, 1955), points out that Utilitarians were never able to integrate fully their reliance on the individual pain-pleasure principle with their desire for achieving the greatest good for the greatest number. By mid-century their individualist and communitarian tendencies had become very distinct and even opposed to one another. Early in the century, however, these contradictions were less apparent.

3. Much of the following discussion of descriptive and symbolic representation is based on Hanna Fenichel Pitkin's *The Concept of Representation* (Berkeley, 1967), pp. 60–111. See also A. H. Birch, *Representation* (New York, 1971), especially pp. 50–96.

4. "A Lay Sermon," in *Lay Sermons*, ed. R. J. White, *The Collected Works of Samuel Taylor Coleridge*, 6 (Princeton, 1972): 189.

5. For a general discussion of Coleridge's theory of the State, see David P. Calleo, *Coleridge and the Idea of the Modern State* (New Haven, 1966).

6. "A Lay Sermon," p. 206.

7. "The Statesman's Manual," in *Lay Sermons*, p. 50.

8. *Lay Sermons*, p. 70.

9. Ibid., p. 70 n.

10. Ibid., p. 49.

11. Ibid.

12. Ibid., p. 51.

13. Ibid., p. 30.

14. "Statesman's Manual," p. 109, editor's note 3: Coleridge "had (he believed) inherited the mantle of Burke."

15. See Pitkin, *The Concept of Representation*, pp. 168–89.

16. "The State is actual only in the Idea. The Idea is the Reality of the State, yea, *is* the State" (Notebook 44, fol. 64ʳ; quoted in Calleo, *Coleridge and the Idea of the Modern State*, p. 77. Calleo mistakenly comes to the conclusion that the state, for Coleridge, is a psychological entity. Coleridge, however, is quite clearly defining the state as a metaphysical entity.

17. "A Lay Sermon," pp. 214–16.

18. Ibid., p. 217.

19. See, for example, Frances Ferguson, "Coleridge on Language and Delusion," *Genre II* (Summer 1978), pp. 191–207; and Jerome C. Christensen, "The Symbol's Errant Allegory: Coleridge and His Critics," *FLH*, 45 (1978): 640–59.

20. For a full discussion of Carlyle's complex reactions to the politics of his time see John P. Farrell, *Revolution as Tragedy: The Dilemma of the Moderate from Scott to Arnold* (Ithaca, 1980), pp. 187–245.

21. *Sartor Resartus: The Life and Opinions of Herr Teufelsdröckh* (London, 1871), p. 150. All further references to this work appear in the text.

22. *Past and Present* (London, 1960), pp. 276–77.

23. Disraeli the Younger, *Vindication of the English Constitution in a Letter to a Noble and Learned Lord* (London, 1835), pp. 60–80.

24. For other interpretations of the irony in *Sybil* see Patrick Brantlinger, "Tory Radicalism and 'the Two Nations' in Disraeli's *Sybil*," *Victorian Newsletter*, no. 41 (Spring 1972), pp. 13–17; and Bernard McCabe, "Disraeli and the 'Baronial Principle': Some Versions of Romantic Medievalism," *Victorian Newsletter*, no. 34 (Fall 1968), pp. 7–12.

25. *Sybil; or The Two Nations* (London, 1969) p. 67. All further references to this work appear in the text.

26. *Past and Present*, p. 177.

27. See for example McCabe, "Disraeli and the 'Baronial Principle' "; and

Arnold Kettle, "The Early Victorian Social-Problem Novel," in *From Dickens to Hardy*, ed. Boris Ford, *The Pelican Guide to English Literature*, 6 (Baltimore, 1958): 175–76.

28. See McCabe, "Disraeli and the 'Baronial Principle,'" p. 11.

29. Daniel R. Schwarz, (*Disraeli's Fiction* [New York, 1979], p. 114) makes a slightly different point when he argues that the marriage unites spirituality and politics.

30. Brantlinger, "Tory Radicalism," pp. 16–17.

Chapter 9

1. This story, originally recorded in a letter from Harriet Martineau to Henry Reeve (May 7, 1861), is retold by R. K. Webb in *Harriet Martineau: A Radical Victorian* (New York, 1960), p. 39.

2. Dorothy Van Ghent, "On *Adam Bede*," in *The English Novel: Form and Function* (New York, 1953), p. 172. For a summary of the debunking criticism of the 1890s and 1910s, see David Carroll, Introduction, *George Eliot: The Critical Heritage*, ed. David Carroll (London, 1971), pp. 41–43; and Elaine Showalter, "The Greening of Sister George," *Nineteenth Century Fiction*, December 1980.

3. *Adam Bede*, ed. Stephen Gill (Harmondsworth, 1980), ch. 17.

4. Twentieth-century commentators have softened the outlines of Martineau's reputation. R. K. Webb, for example, defends her against charges of hard-heartedness (see *Harriet Martineau*, passim); and Mark Blaug, *Ricardian Economics: A Historical Study*, Yale Studies in Economics, 8 (New Haven, 1958): 129–39, sees her as an optimistic humanitarian when contrasted to the political economists she popularized.

5. See Martineau's review of Samuel Bailey's *Essays on the Pursuit of Truth, on the Progress of Knowledge, and on the Fundamental Principle of all Evidence and Expectation*, reprinted in her *Miscellanies*, 2 vols. (Boston, 1836), 2:174–96.

6. U.C. Knoepflmacher and Walter M. Kendrick have made similar points by directing our attention to Eliot's "latent idealism." See Knoepflmacher, *George Eliot's Early Novels: The Limits of Realism* (Berkeley, 1968), passim; Kendrick, "Balzac and British Realism: Mid-Victorian Theories of the Novel," *Victorian Studies*, 20 (1976): 5–24.

7. Miriam Allott, in "George Eliot in the 1860s," *Victorian Studies*, 5 (1961): 97, rightly notes that "ill-health and the emotional depressions of middle age" were quite "possibly deepened by the scepticism which is usually associated with this decade's movement of ideas"; George Eliot, she stresses, "was now facing for the first time the more sombre implications of her own doctrines. Yet Allott does little to connect the artistic impasse that the novelist reached after *Silas Marner* with her changing social and political doctrine, the skepticism about reform and amelioration that now distanced her from thinkers like Harriet Martineau. Joseph Butwin does show Eliot's growing discomfort with the principle of mere aggregation in politics in his "The Pacification of the Crowd: From 'Janet's Repentance' to *Felix Holt*," *Nineteenth Century Fiction*, 35 (1980): 349–71.

8. See James Mill, "Essay on Government" (1820). For a discussion of the logic and consequences of his position as well as a reprint of the essay see *Utilitarian Logic and Politics: James Mill's 'Essay on Government,' Macaulay's Critique, and the Ensuing Debate*, ed. Jack Lively and John Rees (Oxford, 1978). For a general discussion of descriptive representation see Hannah Fenichel Pitkin, *The Concept of Representation* (Berkeley, 1972), pp. 60–91.

9. George Eliot, "The Natural History of German Life: Riehl," in *Miscellaneous Essays, Poetical Works,* vol. 8, *The Works of George Eliot* (New York, n.d.) p. 143.

10. "Speech on Reform" (no. 11), December 4, 1866, in *Studies in Rhetoric in the Nineteenth Century,* 3 (Wiesbaden, 1970): 131.

11. Ibid., p. 130.

12. On Lowe's reputation as a Benthamite see Asa Briggs, "Commentary," in *Studies in Rhetoric in the Nineteenth Century* 3: 41.

13. "Speech on the Representation of the People Bill and the Redistribution of Seats Bill, 31 May 1866," in *Studies in Rhetoric in the Nineteenth Century* 3: 3.

14. Ibid., p. 9.

15. Ibid., p. 134–35.

16. Ibid., p. 18.

17. See R. J. Pole, *Political Representation in England and the Origins of the American Republic* (New York, 1966), on the Whig theory of interest representation.

18. For a short discussion of the debate over J. S. Mill's politics see Dennis F. Thompson, *John Stuart Mill and Representative Government* (Princeton, 1976), pp. 5–9. See also Pitkin, *(The Concept of Representation)* (p. 263, n. 19), who denies that Mill is interested strictly in "the relationship of Parliament as a body to the nation as a whole, or whether it is representative of the nation."

19. Richard Wollheim discusses problems of meaning, with respect to fact and value, of the term "political representation," particularly as used by Mill, in "How Can One Person Represent Another?" *The Aristotelian Society,* supp. vol. 34 (1960):209–20.

20. "On Representative Government," *Three Essays* (London, 1948), p. 256. All further references to this work appear in the text.

21. For a detailed discussion of the origins of Mill's disaffection with Utilitarianism, see Gertrude Himmelfarb, *On Liberty and Liberalism: The Case of John Stuart Mill* (New York, 1974), pp. 5–22.

22. Although both James Mill and Bentham recognized a distinction between public and private interests, they tended to gloss over it in their political writings by naming the "public" interest enlightened self-interest. See Lively and Rees, *Utilitarian Logic,* pp. 39–45.

23. *Culture and Anarchy,* ed. D. Wilson (London, 1960), pp. 80–81. All further references to this work appear in the text.

24. *Felix Holt, the Radical* (London, 1967), pp. 54–55. All further references to this work appear in the text.

25. Carlyle's *Latter-Day Pamphlets* (1850) also use the metaphor of the pig's desire for "pig-wash" to stigmatize the wants of the "ordinary self."

26. George Rowell, *The Victorian Theatre, 1792–1914* (Cambridge, 1978), pp. 66–70.

27. "Debasing the Moral Currency," in *Miscellaneous Essays, Poetical Works,* p. 86. All further references to this work appear in the text.

28. For a complete account of the correspondence between Harrison and Eliot, see Fred C. Thompson, "The Legal Plot in *Felix Holt,*" *Studies in English Literature* 7 (1967): 691–704.

29. This and related arguments are assembled in Martin J. Wiener, *English Culture and the Decline of the Industrial Spirit, 1850–1980* (Cambridge, 1981).

30. See also W. D. Rubinstein, "The Victorian Middle Classes: Wealth, Occupation, and Geography," *FHR,* 2d ser., 30 (1977): 602–23. This article argues that the industrial middle class had the disadvantage of significantly less

personal wealth than businessmen engaged in commerce, finance, and transportation. These wealthier businessmen, according to Rubinstein, were London-based, Anglican, and tended to mix freely with the gentry. Rubinstein argues that these men, and not the northern industrialists, were the real financial backbone of the nation. Rubinstein could be used to claim that the politics of culture was nothing more than an ideological reflection of the material ascendancy of a commercial capitalism allied with the gentry. Suggestive as Rubinstein's argument is, however, it fails to explain why London financial interests consistently ignored investment opportunities in indigenous, northern English industries. What were the cultural and ideological assumptions that prevented a national financial-commercial-industrial amalgamation?

31. Terry Eagleton, in *Criticism and Ideology: A Study in Marxist Literary Theory* (London, 1976), rightly notes the growth of organicist, anti–laissez-faire rhetoric in Eliot and Hardy, which he links to the advance of "corporatism." Corporatism, however, does not explain the general devaluation of the social sphere in late nineteenth-century novels.

Bibliography

I. Primary Works: Fiction

Ainsworth, William Harrison, *Mervyn Clitheroe*. London, 1858.
Anon. *David Lloyd's Last Will*. In *Leisure Hour*, January 1, 1869–June 1, 1869.
———. *The Harnetts: A Tale of North English Life*. In *The Cottage Economist* 1 (1854).
———. "The Honest Workman." In *Eliza Cook's Journal* 4 (1851): 337–40.
———. *Hugh Vernon, the Weaver's Son*. In *The True Briton* n.s. 2 (October 20–December 29, 1853).
———. "The Incendiary." In *Bradshaw's Manchester Journal*, 1842.
———. "The Mill and the Manor," In *Chamber's Edinburgh Journal*, n.s. 47–48 (1844): 327–29; 338–41.
———. "Nothing," by an Old Hand. In *Fraser's Magazine*, n.d.[c. 1838].
———. "The Seamstress." In *Eliza Cook's Journal* 3 (May 11, 1850): 17–19.
———. "Slow Sam; or, The Orphan Family in London." In *The True Briton*, 1852.
———. *The Strike*. London, n.d. [c. 1858].
———. "The Three Homes: A Tale of the Cotton Spinners," by One Who Has Been Among the Spindles. In *The Working Man's Friend and Family Instructor* 4 (November 5–26, 1850).
Brierly, Benjamin, *Tales and Sketches of Lancashire Life*. London, n.d. [c. 1865].
Brontë, Charlotte. *Shirley: A Tale*. London, 1849.

[Chichester, Richard Frederick, Lord Belfast]. *Masters and Workmen; Illustrative of the Social and Moral Condition of the People*. London, 1851.

Cobden, John. *The White Slaves of England*. Buffalo, 1853.

Cooke, James. *Jack Cade*. London, 1850.

Cooper, Thomas. *Captain Cobbler*. London, 1856.

Dickens, Charles, *Hard Times*. Edited by George Ford and Sylvère Monod, New York, 1966.

———. *Nicholas Nickleby*. London, 1833–39.

Disraeli, Benjamin. *Coningsby; or, The New Generation*. London, 1844.

———. *Popanilla*. London, 1827.

———. *Sybil; or, The Two Nations*. London, 1845.

Egan, Pierce, Jr. *Wat Tyler*, London, 1844.

Eliot, George. *Felix Holt: The Radical*. London, 1866.

Ellis, Sarah, *Social Distinction; or, Hearts and Homes*. London, 1848–49.

Fothergill, Jessie, *Probation: A Novel*. London, 1880.

Frost, John. *The Young Mechanic*. London, n.d.

Frost, Thomas. *The Secret*. In *National Instructor*, 1850.

Galt, John. *Annals of the Parish* (1821). New York, 1967.

Gaskell, Elizabeth. "Life in Manchester: Libbie Marsh's Three Eras." *Howitt's Journal* 1 (1847): 310, 334-35.

———. *Mary Barton* (1848). Baltimore, 1976.

———. *North and South*. Harmondsworth, 1972. Originally published in *Household Words*, September 2, 1854–January 27, 1855.

Gilbert, William. *Dives and Lazarus; or, The Adventures of an Obscure Medical Man in a Low Neighborhood: A Tale Illustrative of the Anomalies of the Poor Law*. London, 1858.

Glyn, Herbert. *The Cotton Lord*. London, 1862.

Gore, Catherine. *The Man of Business; or, Stokehill Place*. London, 1857.

———. *Progress and Prejudice*. London, 1854.

Gresley, William. *Colton Green: A Tale of the Black Country*. London, 1848.

Howitt, Mary. *Work and Wages*. London, 1842.

Howitt, William. "The Miner's Daughters." *Household Words*, 1850.

Jewsbury, Geraldine. *Marian Withers*. London, 1851.

Jones, Ernest. "The Working Man's Wife." In *Woman's Wrongs: A Series of Tales*. London, 1855.

Kay-Shuttleworth, Sir James. *Scarsdale: Life on the Lancashire and Yorkshire Border, Thirty Years Ago*. London, 1860.

Kingsley, Charles. *Alton Locke: Tailor and Poet*. Edited by Herbert Van Thal. London, 1967.

———. *Yeast: A Problem* (1848). London, 1860.

Martineau, Harriet. *The Hill and the Valley* (1832). In *Illustrations of Political Economy*, vol. 1. London, 1834.

———. *A Manchester Strike* (1833). In *Illustrations of Political Economy*, vol. 3. London, 1834.

———. *The Rioters*. London, 1827.

Mayhew, Augustus. *Kitty Lamere*. London, 1855.

———. *Paved with Gold; or, The Romance and Reality of the London Streets: An Unfashionable Novel*. London, 1858.

Mayne, Fanny. *Jane Rutherford; or, The Miners' Strike*. In *The True Briton*, 1 (1853).

Miller, Thomas. *Gideon Giles*. In *The London Journal*, 1848.

More, Hannah, and others. *Cheap Repository Tracts* (1793–98). Vols. 3. 5. and 8. New York, n.d.

Overs, John. *Evenings of a Working Man*. London, 1844.

Paget, Francis Edward. *Luke Sharp; or, Knowledge without Religion: A Tale of Modern Education*. London, 1845.

Patterson, Sarah B. *Masters and Workmen: A Tale for the Times*. N.p., n.d. [c. 1858].

Pimlico, Paul. "The Factory Girl: A Tale in Six Chapters." In *Reynolds's Miscellanies*, n.s. 3 (October 20–November 24, 1849).

Rathbone, H. M. "The Sempstress." *The Working Man's Friend and Family Instructor* 1 (1850): 306–8.

Reade, Charles. *It Is Never Too Late To Mend*. London, 1853.

———. *Put Yourself in His Place*. London, 1870.

Rendle, E. "Edward Smith. A Narrative of the Sweating System." *The Working Man's Friend and Family Instructor* 3 (September 4, 21, 28, 1850).

Reynolds, G. W. M. *The Slaves of England, No. 1: The Seamstress*. In *Reynolds's Miscellany of Romance, General Literature, Science and Art* 5 (1850).

Rowcroft, Charles. *Fanny, the Little Milliner; or, The Rich and the Poor* (1846). London, 1853.

Rymer, James Malcolm. *The White Slave: A Romance for the Nineteenth Century*. London, 1844.

Silverpen [Eliza Meteyard]. "The History and Present Condition of the Metropolitan Omnibus Drivers and Conductors." *The Working Man's Friend and Family Instructor* 3 (August 10, 1850).

———. *Lucy Dean: The Noble Needlewoman*. In *Eliza Cook's Journal* 3 (January 1850–January 1851).

Simpson, Wharton. "Colliers and Coal Mining." *The Working Man's Friend* 3 (1850).

Staton, J. T. *Rays fro' th' Loominary: A Selection of Comic Lancashire Tales*. N.p., n.d. [c. 1854].

Stone, Elizabeth. *William Langshaw, the Cotton Lord*. London, 1842.

Taylor, Rev. Charles. *Social Evils, and their Remedy*. London, 1833.

[Tonna]. Charlotte Elizabeth, *Helen Fleetwood*. London, 1841.

———. *The Wrongs of Woman*. London, 1843–44.

Toulmin, Camilla. "A Story of Factories." In *Chamber's Miscellany*, 1846.

Trolloppe, Frances. *The Life and Adventures of Michael Armstrong, the Factory Boy*. 3 vols. London, 1839–40.

Wheeler, Thomas Martin. *Sunshine and Shadow: A Tale of the Nineteenth Century*. In *Northern Star*, 1849–50.

Wright, Thomas. *Johnny Robinson*. [London], n.d.

II. Other Primary Sources

Alfred [Samuel Kydd]. *The History of the Factory Movement from the Year 1802 to the Enactment of the Ten Hours' Bill in 1847*. 2 vols. London, 1857.

An Appeal to the Candour of Both Houses of Parliament, with a Recapitulation of Facts Respecting the Abolition of the Slave Trade, in a Letter to William Wilberforce, Esq., by a Member of the House of Commons. London, 1793.

Ashley [later Shaftesbury], Lord Anthony. "Ten Hours' Factory Bill, The Speech of Lord Ashley, M.P., in the House of Commons, on Friday, March 14, 1844." In *Prelude to Victory of the Ten Hours' Movement: Two Speeches, One Letter, and a Report, 1844*. In Carpenter series (see below).

"Associative Efforts of Working Men." *Eliza Cook's Journal*, 25 January 1851, pp. 193–94.

Ayton, Richard. *A Voyage Round Great Britain*. London, 1814.

The Battle for the Ten Hours Day Continues: Four Pamphlets 1837–1843. Carpenter series (see below).

Bayly, Mary. *Ragged Homes and How to Mend Them*. American Edition. Philadelphia, 1859.

Bentham, Jeremy. *Deontology; or, The Science of Morality*. Edited by John Bowring. London, 1834.

———. *Four Early Works on Motivation*. Edited with introduction by Paul McReynolds. Gainesville, 1963.

———. *The Works of Jeremy Bentham*. Published under the superintendence of his executor John Bowring. Vol. 2. Edinburgh, 1843.

Bowring, John. *Minor Morals for Young People: Being an Application of the Greatest-Happiness Principle to Early Instruction*. London, 1843–49.

British Labourer's Protector and Factory Child's Friend 1 (September 21, 1832– April 19, 1833). Repr., New York, 1969.

British Quarterly Review 9 (1849).

[Brougham, H. P] *A Concise Statement of the Question Regarding the Abolition of the Slave Trade*. London, 1804.

Browning, Elizabeth Barrett. "The City of Children." *Blackwoods Magazine*, August 1843.

Bull, George Stringer. *A Respectful and Faithful Appeal to the Inhabitants of the Parish of Bradford on Behalf of the Factory Children*. Bradford, 1832.

Butterforth, James. *Trade of Manchester*. Manchester, 1822.

Carlyle, Thomas. *Chartism*. London, 1839.

———. *Latter-Day Pamphlets*. London, 1850.

———. *Past and Present*. London, 1960.

———. *Sartor Resartus: The Life and Opinions of Herr Teufelsdröckh*. London, 1871.

———. "Signs of the Times." London, 1829.

Carpenter, Kenneth E., ed. *British Labour Struggles: Contemporary Pamphlets, 1727–1850*. An unnumbered series of volumes. New York, 1972.

Chadwick, Sir Edwin. *Report on the Sanitary Condition of the Labouring Populations of Great Britain*. Edited with introduction by M. W. Finn. Edinburgh, 1965. Originally published in 1842 under the title *Report to Her Majesty's Principal Secretary of State for the Home Department from the Poor Law Commissioners on an Inquiry into the Sanitary Condition of the Labouring Population of Great Britain*.

Close, Francis. *An Apology for the Evangelical Party: Being a reply to the pamphlet of the Rev. W. Gresley, A.M., on "The real danger of the Church."* London, 1846.

———. *The Chartists' Visit to the Parish Church: A Sermon Addressed to the Chartists of Cheltenham*. London, 1839.

———. *The Female Chartists' Visit to the Parish Church: A Sermon Addressed to the Female Chartists of Cheltenham*. London, 1839.

———. *Lectures on the Evidence of Christianity Addressed to the Working Classes*. Carlisle, 1860.

Cobbett, William. *Cobbett's Weekly Political Register*. Vols. 5, 6, 7, and 9. London, 1804–6.

———. *A History of the Protestant Reformation in England and Ireland*. London, 1846.

———. *Rural Rides*. London, 1967.

————. *Selections from Cobbett's Political Works.* Edited by John M. Cobbett and James P. Cobbett. Vol. 6. London, n.d.

Coleridge, Samuel Taylor. *First and Second Circular* (1818). In *Coleridge at Highgate.* Edited by Lucy E. Watson. London, 1925.

————. *Lay Sermons.* In *The Collected Works of Samuel Taylor Coleridge.* Edited by R. J. White. Vol. 4. Princeton, 1972.

Combe, William. *A Word in Season to the Traders and Manufacturers of Great Britain.* London, 1792.

Conditions of Working and Living (5 pamphlets, 1838–44). *Cooperation and the Working Class: Theoretical Contributions* (4 pamphlets, 1827–34). *Cooperative Communities: Plans and Descriptions* (11 pamphlets, 1825–47.) In Carpenter series (see above).

Darwin, Charles. *Autobiography of Charles Darwin.* Edited by Nora Barlow. London, 1958.

————. *The Origin of the Species by Means of Natural Selection* (1859). Edited by Morse Peckham. Philadelphia, 1959.

Darwin, Erasmus. *The Botanic Garden.* London, 1789–91.

Dawes, Richard. *Lessons on the Phenomena of Industrial Life and the Conditions of Industrial Success.* 2d ed. London, 1857.

"Demands for Early Closing Hours" (3 pamphlets, 1843). In Carpenter series (see above).

Dickens, Charles. *The Letters of Charles Dickens.* Edited by Walter Dexter. Bloomsbury, 1938.

————. "On Strike." *Household Words*, 1854.

Disraeli the Younger. *Vindication of the English Constitution in a Letter to a Noble and Learned Lord.* London, 1835.

Drummond, James. *The Life and Letters of James Martineau.* 2 vols. New York, 1902.

Eliot, George. *Miscellaneous Essays, Poetical Works.* Vol. 8 of *The Works of George Eliot.* New York, nd.

Ellis, Sarah. *The Mothers of England: Their Influence and Responsibility.* London, 1843.

————. *The Mothers of England: Their Influence and Responsibility.* London, 1843.

————. *The Women of England: Their Social Duties and Domestic Habits.* 11th ed. London, n.d.

Engels, Frederick. *The Condition of the Working-Class in England in 1844* (1845). In *Marx and Engels on Britain.* Moscow, 1953.

The Factory Act of 1819: Six Pamphlets, 1818–1819. In Carpenter series (see above).

The Factory Act of 1833: Eight Pamphlets, 1833–1834. In Carpenter series (see above).

The Factory Education Bill of 1843: Six Pamphlets, 1843. In Carpenter series (see above).

"A Favorite Song." *Politics for the People* 2 (1795): 270.

Ferguson, Adam. *An Essay on the History of Civil Society.* Edinburgh, 1767.

————. *Institutes of Moral Philosophy.* 2d ed. Edinburgh, 1872.

The Framework Knitters and Handloom Weavers: Their Attempts to Keep up Wages. Eight Pamphlets, 1820–1845. In Carpenter series (see above).

Freeling, Arthur. *The Railway Companion, from London to Birmingham, Liverpool and Manchester; with Guides to the Objects Worthy of Notice in Liverpool, Manchester, and Birmingham.* London, 1837.

Gaskell, Elizabeth Gleghorn. *The Letters of Mrs. Gaskell.* Edited by J.A.V. Chapple and Arthur Pollard. Manchester, 1966.

————. *The Life of Charlotte Brontë.* London, 1857.

Gaskell, Elizabeth Gleghorn, and William Gaskell. "Sketches among the Poor, No. 1." *Blackwoods Magazine* 41 (1837): 48–51.

Gaskell, Peter. *The Manufacturing Population of England.* London, 1833.

Gavin, Hector. *Sanitary Ramblings: Being Sketches and Illustrations of Bethnal Green.* London, 1848.

————. *The Habitations of the Industrial Classes: Their Influence on the Physical and on the Social and Moral Condition of These Classes.* London, 1851.

Godwin, George. *London Shadows: A Glance at the "Homes" of the Thousands.* London, 1854.

————. *Town Swamps and Social Bridges.* London, 1859.

Gould, Sir Nathaniel. *Information Concerning the State of the Children Employed in Cotton Factories, Printed for the Use of the Members of Both Houses of Parliament.* Manchester, 1818.

Greg, William Rathbone. *Essays on Political and Social Science, Contributed Chiefly to the Edinburgh Review.* London, 1853.

————. *Literary and Social Judgments.* Boston, 1873.

Grinrod, Ralph Barnes. *The Slaves of the Needle: An Exposure of the Distressed Condition, Moral and Physical, of Dressmakers, Milliners, Embroiderers, Shopworkers &c.* London, n.d.

Hansard's Parliamentary Debates, ser. 1, vol. 31 (May–July 1815).

Hansard's Parliamentary Debates, ser. 1, vol. 33 (1816).

Helps, Sir Arthur. *The Claims of Labour: An Essay on the Duties of the Employers to the Employed.* 1844; 2d ed., London, 1845.

Hompes, M. "Mrs. E. C. Gaskell." *Gentleman's Magazine,* n.s. 55 (1895) 124.

Hone, William. *Hone's Reformists' Register.* London, 1817.

Hood, Thomas. "The Song of the Shirt." In *The Complete Poetical Works of Thomas Hood,* 1:147–49. Edited by Epes Sargent. Boston, 1857.

Jameson, Anna. *Characteristics of Women: Moral, Poetical, and Historical.* 2 vols. London, 1832.

Kingsley, Fanny, ed. *Charles Kingsley: His Letters and Memories of His Life.* 2 vols. London, 1877.

Knight, Charles. *The British Almanac: Appropriate for the Tradesman, Manufacturer, Merchant, and Professional Upper Classes Generally.* London, 1836.

————. *The British Working-Man's Almanac.* London, 1836.

————. *Capital and Labor.* London, 1845.

————. *Industrial Guide Books.* London, 1838.

————. *The Working-Man's Companion.* London, 1836.

Knox, William. *A Country Gentleman's Reasons for Voting Against Mr. Wilberforce's Motion for a Bill To Prohibit the Importation of African Negroes into the Colonies.* London, 1792.

————. *Letter from W. K., Esq. to W. Wilberforce, Esq.* London, 1790.

Kovalev, Yuri V., ed. *An Anthology of Chartist Literature.* Moscow, 1958.

Labour Disputes in the Mines: Eight Pamphlets, 1831–1844. In Carpenter series (see above).

Lewis, Sarah. *Woman's Mission.* London, 1839.

Locke, John. *Two Treatises on Government.* Edited by Peter Laslett. New York, 1960.

Manners, Lord John James Robert. *England's Trust, and Other Poems.* London, 1841.

Marcet, Jane. *Conversations on Political Economy in Which the Elements of That Science Are Familiarly Explained*. London, 1816.

——. *Rich and Poor*. London, 1851.

Martin, Samuel. *An Essay upon Plantership, Humbly Inscribed to His Excellency George Thomas, Esq., Chief Governor of all the Leeward Islands, as a Monument to Antient Friendship*. 5th ed. London, 1777.

Martineau, Harriet. *Harriet Martineau's Autobiography*. Edited by Maria Weston Chapman. Boston, 1877.

——. *Miscellanies*. Vol. 2. Boston, 1836.

Martineau, James. *Essays, Reviews, and Addresses*. Vol. 4. London, 1891.

Mayhew, Henry. *London Labour and the London Poor*. London, 1851.

McCulloch, John Ramsay. *The Literature of Political Economy: A Classified Catalogue of Select Publications in the Different Departments of That Science, with Historical, Critical, and Biographical Notices*. London, 1845.

——. *Outlines of Political Economy*. Edited by John McVickar. New York, 1966. First published in 1824 under the title *Political Economy* in the Edinburgh Supplement to the *Encyclopædia Britannica* over the signature "S.S."

McDouall, [J.]. "What Have We Done, and What Are We To Do?" In *McDouall's Chartist Journal and Trades Advocate*, 1841. Repr. in *Radical Periodicals of Great Britain*. New York, 1969.

Mill, James. *Elements of Political Economy* (1820). In *Selected Economic Writings*. Edited by Donald Winch. Edinburgh, 1966.

Mill, John Stuart. *Autobiography of John Stuart Mill* (1873). Indianapolis, 1957.

——. *Collected Works*. Indianapolis, 1951. Toronto, 1963.

——. *An Examination of Sir William Hamilton's Philosophy and of the Principal Philosophical Questions Discussed in His Writings*. 3d ed. London, 1867.

——. Review of *The Claims of Labour*. *Edinburgh Review*, April 1845; repr. in *Dissertations and Discussions Political, Philosophical, and Historical*, 2:175–85. 2d ed. [London, 1867.]

——. *Three Essays by John Stuart Mill*. London, 1912.

Newman, Francis W. *Catholic Union: Essays Towards a Church of the Future as the Organization of Philanthropy* (1844). London, 1854.

——. "On the Existence of Evil." In *Miscellanies*, pp. 1–10. London, 1888.

Oastler, Richard. *King of Factory Children: Six Pamphlets 1835–1861*. In Carpenter series (see above).

——. "Letter." *British Labourer's Protector and Factory Child's Friend*, no. 11 (November, 30 1832), p. 83.

——. "Select Committee Evidence." *British Labourer's Protector and Factory Child's Friend*, no. 2 (September 28, 1832), p. 14.

"On Slavery." *General Magazine* 6 (1792): 477–80.

Owen, Robert. *An Inquiry in the Principle and Tendency of the Bill Now Pending in Parliament, for Imposing Certain Restrictions on Cotton Factories*. London, 1818.

——. *Lectures on the Rational System of Society*. London, 1841.

——. *The New Religion; or, Religion Founded on Immutable Laws of the Universe*. London, 1830.

——. *A New View of Society and Other Writings*. Edited by G.D.H. Cole. New York, 1963.

——. *Public Discussion, between Robert Owen . . . and the Rev. J. H. Roebuck . . .* Manchester, 1837.

Owenism and the Working Class: Six Pamphlets and Four Broadsides, 1821–1834. In Carpenter series (see above).

Paine, Thomas. *The Complete Writings of Thomas Paine.* Edited by Philip S. Foner. Vol. 2. New York, 1945.

―――. *Life and Writings of Thomas Paine.* Edited by Daniel Edwin Wheeler. Vol. 2. New York, 1908.

Parliamentary Papers. "Select Committee on the State of the Children in Manufactures of the United Kingdom." 1816 (397.) iii. 235.

―――. "Second Report from the Select Committee on the State of Education among the Lower Orders in the Metropolis." 1816 (427.) iv. 1.

―――. "Report from the Select Committee on the Bill for Regulation of Factories; Together with Minutes of Evidence." 1831–32 (706.) xv. 1.

―――. "First Report of the Commissioners Appointed to Collect Information in the Manufacturing Districts, Relative to the Employment of Children in Factories . . . : with Minutes of Evidence and Reports of District Commissioners." 1833 (450.) xx. 1.

―――. "Supplementary Reports from Commissioners Appointed to Collect Information in the Manufacturing Districts, Relative to the Employment of Children in Factories . . . with Minutes of Evidence and Reports of District Commissioners." 1834 (167.) xix. 253. xx. 1.

―――. "Reports from each of the Four Factory Inspectors on the Education Provisions of the Factories Act; Together with Joint Reports." 1839 (42.) xlii. 353.

―――. "Reports of the Assistant Commissioners on Hand-loom Weavers." 1839 (159.) xlii.511; Part 2, 1840 (43-I.) xxiii.49.; Part 3, 1840 [43-II.] xxiii.367; Part 4 (Midland District), 1840 (217.) xxiv.1.

―――. "Report of the Commissioners on Hand-loom Weavers." 1841 (296.) x.273.

―――. "First Report of Commissioners For Inquiring into the Employment and Condition of Children in Mines and Manufactories." 1842 (380.) xv.1.

―――. "Reports and Evidence of Sub-Commissioners, Appendix to First Report," Part 1, 1842 [381.] xvi.1; "Appendix to First Report," Part 2, 1842 [382.] xvii.1.

―――. "Second Report of the Commissioners Inquiring into the Employment of Children in Trades and Manufactures." 1843 [430.] xiii.307. "Appendix to Second Report, Part 1, with Reports and Evidence from Sub-Commissioners." 1843 [431.] xiv. [432.] xv.1.

―――. "Report of the Commissioners Appointed to Inquire into the Condition of the Framework Knitters." 1845 [609.] xv.1.

―――. "Appendix to Report of the Commissioners Appointed to Inquire into the Condition of the Framework Knitters: Part I. Leicestershire." 1845 [618] xv.151.;" Part II. Nottinghamshire and Derbyshire." 1845 [641.] xv.665.

Plaifere, John. *An Appeal to the Gospel for the True Doctrine of Divine Predestination, Concorded with the Orthodox Doctrine of God's Free-Grace, and Man's Free Will.* In *The Arminian Magazine: Consisting of Extracts and Original Treatises on General Redemption* 2 (1790).

Priestley, Joseph. *A Free Discussion of the Doctrines of Materialism and Philosophical Necessity, in a Correspondence Between Dr. Price and Dr. Priestley.* London, 1778.

Pugin, Augustus Welby. *Apology for the Revival of Christian Architecture in England.* London, 1843.

―――. *Contrasts: Or a Parallel Between the Noble Edifices of the Middle Ages, and Corresponding Buildings of the Present Day, Shewing the Present Decay of Taste.* 2d ed. London, 1841.

Rebirth of the Trade Union Movement: Five Pamphlets, 1838–1847. In Carpenter series (see above).

Repeal of the Combination Acts: Five Pamphlets and One Broadside, 1825. In Carpenter series (see above).

Report of the Debate on a Motion for the Abolition of the Slave Trade, in the House of Commons, on Monday and Tuesday, April 18 and 19, 1791. London, 1791.

Ricardo, David. *Notes on Malthus' "Principles of Political Economy."* Edited by Jacob Hollander and T. E. Gregory. London, 1928.

———. *On the Principles of Political Economy, and Taxation.* 3d ed. London, 1821.

Ruskin, John. *Political Economy of Art.* London, 1912.

———. *Sesame and Lilies.* London, 1882.

———. *"Unto This Last": Four Essays on the First Principles of Political Economy.* London, 1862.

Sandford, Elizabeth. *Female Improvement.* London, 1836.

———. *Woman and Her Social and Domestic Character.* London, 1831.

Sedgwick, Catharine Maria. *Means and Ends, or Self-Training.* Boston, 1839.

Senior, Nassau, W. *Industrial Efficiency and Social Economy.* New York, 1928.

Shaftesbury, Seventh Earl of (Anthony Ashley). *Speeches of The Earl of Shaftesbury, K.G., upon Subjects Having Relation Chiefly to the Claims and Interests of the Labouring Class.* London, 1868. (See also Ashley, Lord Anthony, above.)

Smiles, Samuel. *Self Help.* (1859) London, 1876.

Southey, Robert. *Sir Thomas More: or Colloquies on the Progress and Prospects of Society.* Vol. 1. London, 1829.

———. "The State of the Poor: The Principle of Mr. Malthus's Essay on Population and the Manufacturing System 1812." *Essays Moral and Political.* Vol. 4. London, 1832.

Substance of the Debates on a Resolution for Abolishing the Slave Trade. 1806; repr. London, 1968.

The Ten Hours Movement in 1831 and 1832: Six Pamphlets and One Broadside, 1831–1832. In Carpenter series (see above).

Thornton, William. *Political Economy; Founded in Justice and Humanity.* Washington, 1804.

[Tonna], Charlotte Elizabeth. *Personal Recollections of Charlotte Elizabeth, Continued to the Close of Her Life.* London, 1847.

Toplady, A. M. *Works.* Vols. 5 and 6. London, 1825.

Trade Unions in the Early 1830s: Seven Pamphlets, 1831–1837. In Carpenter series (see above).

Watson, Lucy, ed. *Coleridge at Highgate.* London, 1925.

Wesley, John. *Works.* Vol. 10. New York, 1975.

Westminster Abbey Sermons for the Working Classes. London, n.d. "Woman, and Her Social Position." *Westminster Review* 35 (1841): 24–52.

The Working-Classes, by a Daughter of the People. London, 1869.

"The Working Man. Reciprocal Duties of Employers and Work People." *Working Man's Friend and Family Instructor* 2, nos. 15, 16, 17 (1850).

The Working Man's Wife. London, 1844.

Wright, Thomas. *The Great Unwashed.* London, 1868.

———. *Our New Masters. London, 1873.*

III. Secondary Works: Literary Studies

Abrams, M. H. *Natural Supernaturalism: Tradition and Revolution in Romantic Literature.* New York, 1973.

Allott, Miriam. "George Eliot in the 1860s." *Victorian Studies* 5 (1961): 97.

Altick, Richard D. *The English Common Reader: A Social History of the Mass Reading Public, 1800–1900.* Chicago, 1967.

Arac, Jonathan. *Commissioned Spirits: The Shaping of Social Motion in Dickens, Carlyle, Melville, and Hawthorne.* New Brunswick, 1979.

Aydelotte, William O. "The England of Marx and Mill as Reflected in Fiction." *Journal of Economic History,* suppl. B, 1948.

Baird, John D. "Divorce and Matrimonial Causes: An Aspect of *Hard Times.*" *Victorian Studies* 20 (Summer 1977): 401–12.

Baker, E. A. *The History of the English Novel.* Vol. 8. London, 1937.

Baldwin, Stanley Everett. *Charles Kingsley.* Cornell Studies in English, no. 25. Ithaca, 1934.

Bergmann, Helena. *Between Obedience and Freedom: Women's Role in the Mid-Nineteenth Century Industrial Novel.* Gothenburg, 1979.

Bodenheimer, Rosemarie. "*North and South*: A Permanent State of Change." *Nineteenth-Century Fiction* 34 (1979): 281–301.

———. "Private Grief and Public Acts in *Mary Barton.*" *Dickens Studies Annual: Essays on Victorian Fiction* 9 (1981): 195–216.

Boggs, W. Arthur. "Reflections of Unitarianism in Mrs. Gaskell's Novels." Dissertation, University of California, Berkeley, 1950.

Brantlinger, Patrick. "Bluebooks, the Social Organism, and the Victorian Novel." *Criticism* 14 (Fall 1972): 328–44.

———. *The Spirit of Reform: British Literature and Politics, 1832–1867.* Cambridge, Mass., 1977.

———. "Tory Radicalism and 'the Two Nations' in Disraeli's *Sybil.*" *Victorian Newsletter* 41 (Spring 1972): 13–17.

Brooks, Peter. *The Melodramatic Imagination: Balzac, Henry James, Melodrama, and the Mode of Excess.* New York, 1976.

Buckley, Jerome. *The Triumph of Time: A Study of the Victorian Concepts of Time, History, Progress, and Decadence.* Cambridge, Mass., 1966.

Butwin, Joseph. "*Hard Times*: The News and the Novel." *Nineteenth-Century Fiction* 32 (1977): 166–87.

———. "The Pacification of the Crowd: From 'Janet's Repentance' to *Felix Holt.*" *Nineteenth-Century Fiction* 35 (1980): 349–71.

———. "The Paradox of the Clown in Dickens." In *Dickens Studies Annual,* 5:115–32. Edited by Robert B. Partlow. Edwardsville, Ill., 1967.

Calleo, David P. *Coleridge and the Idea of the Modern State.* New Haven, 1966.

Carroll, David. *George Eliot: The Critical Heritage.* New York, 1971.

Cazamian, Louis. *The Social Novel in England, 1830–1850: Dickens, Disraeli, Mrs. Gaskell, Kingsley.* Translated by Martin Fido. London, 1973.

Chaloner, W. H. "Mrs. Trollope and the Early Factory System." *Victorian Studies* 4 (1960): 159–66.

Chapman, Raymond. *The Victorian Debate: English Literature and Society.* London, 1968.

Chitty, Susan. *The Beast and the Monk: A Life of Charles Kingsley.* London, 1974.

Christensen, Jerome C. "The Symbol's Errant Allegory: Coleridge and His Critics." *English Literary History* 45 (1978): 640–59.

Colby, Robert. *Fiction with a Purpose: Major and Minor Nineteenth Century Novels.* Bloomington, 1967.

Colby, Vineta. *Yesterday's Woman: Domestic Realism in the English Novel.* Princeton, 1974.

Collin, D. W. "The Composition of Mrs. Gaskell's *North and South.*" *Bulletin of the John Rylands Library* 54, no. 1 (Autumn 1971).

Collins, H. P. "The Naked Sensibility." *Essays in Criticism* 3 (January 1953).

Colloms, Brenda. *Charles Kingsley: The Lion of Eversley.* New York, 1975.

Cooke, Michael G. *The Romantic Will.* New Haven, 1976.

Craig, David. "Fiction and the Rising Industrial Class." *Essays in Criticism* 17 (1967): 64–74.

————. *The Real Foundations: Literature and Social Change.* London, 1974.

Culler, A. Dwight. "The Darwinian Revolution and Literary Form." In *The Art of Victorian Prose.* Edited by George Levine and William Madden. New York, 1968.

Dalziel, Margaret. *Popular Fiction 100 Years Ago.* London, 1957.

Dickens and the Twentieth Century. Edited by John Gross and Gabriel Pearson. Toronto, 1962.

Eagleton, Terry. *Criticism and Ideology: A Study in Marxist Literary Theory.* London, 1976.

Easson, Angus. *Elizabeth Gaskell.* Boston, 1979.

Empson, William. *Some Versions of Pastoral.* London, 1935.

Ewbank, Inga-Stina. *Their Proper Sphere: A Study of the Brontë Sisters as Early Victorian Female Novelists.* Cambridge, Mass., 1968.

Farrell, John P. *Revolution as Tragedy: The Dilemma of the Moderate from Scott to Arnold.* Ithaca, 1980.

Feher, Ferenc. "Is the Novel Problematic?" *Telos* 15 (Spring 1973): 47–74.

Ferguson, Frances. "Coleridge on Language and Delusion." *Genre* 2 (Summer 1978): 191–207.

Fielding, Kenneth J. "*Hard Times* and Common Things." In *Imagined Worlds.* Edited by Maynard Mack and Ian Gregory. London, 1968.

Fielding, K. J., and Anne Smith. "*Hard Times* and the Factory Controversy: Dickens vs. Harriet Martineau." *Nineteenth-Century Fiction* 24 (1970): 404–27.

Fulmer, Constance Marie. *George Eliot: A Reference Guide.* Boston, 1977.

Furbank, P. N. "Mendacity in Mrs. Gaskell." *Encounter* 40 (June 1973) 6:51–55.

Gerin, Winifred. *Elizabeth Gaskell: A Biography.* Oxford, 1976.

Gill, Stephen. "Price's Patent Candles: New Light on *North and South.*" *Review of English Studies* 27 (1976): 313–21.

Goldmann, Lucien. *Toward a Sociology of the Novel.* Translated by Alan Sheridan. London, 1975.

Goode, John. "William Morris and the Dream of Revolution." In *Literature and Politics in the Nineteenth Century.* Edited by John Lucas. London, 1971.

Haberman, Melvyn. "The Courtship of the Void: The World of *Hard Times.*" In *The Worlds of Victorian Fiction.* Edited by Jerome H. Buckley. Cambridge, Mass., 1975.

Hartley, Allan John. *The Novels of Charles Kingsley: A Christian Social Interpretation.* Folkestone, Kent, 1977.

Harvey, W. J. *Character and the Novel.* Ithaca, 1965.

Hayden, John O. *Scott: The Critical Heritage.* New York, 1970.

Hazen, Lynn Shuford. "Vessels of Salvation: Fathers and Daughters in Six Dickens Novels. Ph.D. diss., University of Wisconsin—Madison, 1978.

Heilman, R. B. *Tragedy and Melodrama.* Seattle, 1968.

Holloway, John. *The Victorian Sage: Philosophy and Rhetoric in the Work of Carlyle, Disraeli, George Eliot, Newman, Arnold, and Hardy.* Hamden, Conn., 1962.

Hopkins, Annette. *Elizabeth Gaskell: Her Life and Work.* London, 1952.

House, Humphrey. *The Dickens World*. London, 1941.

Howard, David, John Lucas, and John Goode. *Tradition and Tolerance in Nineteenth Century Fiction*. London, 1966.

James, Louis. *Fiction for the Working Man, 1830–1850: A Study of the Literature Produced for the Working Classes in Early Victorian England*. London, 1963.

Johnson, Edgar. *Charles Dickens: His Tragedy and Triumph*. Rev. ed. London, 1976.

Jones, Mary Gladys. *Hannah More, 1745–1833*. Cambridge, 1952.

Keating, Peter. *The Working Classes in Victorian Fiction*. London, 1971.

Kendrick, Walter M. "Balzac and British Realism: Mid-Victorian Theories of the Novel." *Victorian Studies* 20 (1976): 5–24.

Kettle, Arnold. "The Early Victorian Social-Problem Novel." In *From Dickens to Hardy*. Edited by Boris Ford. Vol. 6 of *The Pelican Guide to English Literature*. Baltimore, 1973.

Killham, John. *Tennyson and 'The Princess': Reflection of an Age*. London, 1958.

King, Jeanette. *Tragedy in the Victorian Novel: Theory and Practice in the Novels of George Eliot, Thomas Hardy, and Henry James*. New York, 1978.

Knoepflmacher, U. C. *George Eliot's Early Novels: The Limits of Realism*. Berkeley, 1968.

———. *Religious Humanism and the Victorian Novel: George Eliot, Walter Pater, and Samuel Butler*. Princeton, N.J., 1965.

Kovačević, Ivanka. *Fact into Fiction: English Literature and the Industrial Scene, 1750–1850*. Leicester (U.K.), 1975.

Kovačević, Ivanka, and Barbara Kammer. "Blue Book into Novel: The Forgotten Industrial Fiction of Charlotte Elizabeth Tonna." *Nineteenth-Century Fiction* 25 (September 1970): 152–73.

Langbaum, Robert. *The Mysteries of Identity: A Theme in Modern Literature*. New York, 1977.

Lansbury, Coral. *Elizabeth Gaskell: The Novel of Social Crisis*. London, 1975.

Larkin, Maurice. *Man and Society in Nineteenth Century Realism: Determinism and Literature*. London, 1977.

Lawrence, D. H. "Letter to A. W. McLeod (June 2, 1915)." In *Selected Literary Criticism*. Edited by Anthony Beal. London, 1967.

Leavis, F. R. *The Great Tradition*. London, 1960.

Levin, Harry. *The Gates of Horn: A Study of Five French Realists*. New York, 1966.

Levine, George. *The Boundaries of Fiction: Macaulay, Carlyle, Newman, and Pater*. Princeton, J.J., 1968.

———. *The Realistic Imagination*. Chicago, 1981.

Lucas, John. *Literature and Politics in the Nineteenth Century*. London, 1971.

———. *The Literature of Change: Studies in the Nineteenth Century Provincial Novel*. Totowa, N.J., 1980.

Lukács, Georg. *History and Class Consciousness: Studies in Marxist Dialectics*. Translated by Rodney Livingston. Cambridge, Mass., 1971.

———. *The Historical Novel*. Translated by Hannah and Stanley Mitchell. London, 1962.

———. *The Theory of the Novel*. Translated by Anna Bostock. Cambridge, Mass., 1971.

Lyons, David. "Mill's Theory of Justice." In *Values and Morals*. Edited by A. I. Goldman and J. Kim. Dordrecht, Holland, 1978.

Marx, Paul. "Matthew Arnold and Culture." *Essays in Arts and Sciences* 4 (1975): 45–63.

Matthews, William. *British Autobiographies*. Berkeley, 1955.

Matthews, William, and Ralph J. Rader. *Autobiography, Biography, and the Novel.*" William Andrew Clark Memorial Library Papers. Los Angeles, 1973.

McCabe, Bernard. "Disraeli and the 'Baronial Principle': Some Versions of Romantic Medievalism." *Victorian Newsletter* 34 (Fall 1968): 7–12.

Melada, Ivan. *The Captain of Industry in English Fiction, 1821–1871*. Albuquerque, 1970.

Miyoshi, Masao. *The Divided Self: A Perspective on the Literature of the Victorians.* New York, 1969.

Moers, Ellen. *Literary Women: The Great Writers*. Garden City, N.Y.,1976.

Mulherne, Francis, "Ideology and Literary Form—A Comment." *New Left Review* 91 (May–June 1975): 79–86.

Neff, Emery. "Social Background and Social Thought." In *The Reinterpretation of Victorian Literature*. Edited by Joseph E. Baker. Princeton, N.J., 1950.

Oddie, William. *Dickens and Carlyle: The Question of Influence*. London, 1972.

Phillips, Walter C. *Dickens, Reade, and Collins. Sensation Novelists: A Study in the Conditions and Theories of Novel-writing in Victorian England*. London, 1919.

Pichanick, Valerie Kossew. *Harriet Martineau: The Woman and Her Work, 1802–76*. Ann Arbor, 1980.

Pikoulis, John. "*North and South*: Varieties of Love and Power." *Yearbook of English Studies* 6 (1976): 176–93.

Rader, Ralph. "Defoe, Richardson, Joyce, and the Concept of Form in the Novel." In *Autobiography, Biography, and the Novel*. William Andrew Clark Memorial Library Papers. Los Angeles, 1973.

Rance, Nicholas. *The Historical Novel and Popular Politics in Nineteenth-Century England*. London, 1975.

Rivenburg, N. E. *Harriet Martineau: An Example of Victorian Conflict*. Philadelphia, 1932.

Rosenberg, Philip. *The Seventh Hero: Thomas Carlyle and the Theory of Radical Activism*. Cambridge, Mass., 1974.

Rubenius, Aina. *The Woman Question in Mrs. Gaskell's Life and Works*. Cambridge, Mass., 1950.

Ruskin, John. "A Note on *Hard Times*" (1860). In *The Dickens Critics*. Edited by George H. Ford and Lauriat Lane, Jr. Ithaca, N.Y., 1961.

Schwartz, Daniel R. *Disraeli's Fiction*. New York, 1979.

Selig, Robert L. *Elizabeth Gaskell: A Reference Guide*. Boston, 1977.

Sharps, J. G. *Mrs. Gaskell's Observation and Invention*. London, 1970.

Showalter, Elaine. "The Greening of Sister George." *Nineteenth-Century Fiction* 35 (December 1980): 292–311.

Shumaker, Wayne. *English Autobiography: Its Emergence, Materials and Form.* Berkeley, 1954.

Smith, David. "*Mary Barton* and *Hard Times*: Their Social Insights." *Mosaic* 5 (Winter 1971): 97–112.

Smith, James L. *Melodrama*. The Critical Idiom, edited by John D. Jump, no. 28. London, 1973.

Smith, M. Sheila. "Willenhall and Wodgate: Disraeli's Use of Blue Book Evidence." *Review of English Studies*, n.s. 2, (1962): 368–84.

Stang, Richard. *The Theory of the Novel in England, 1850–1870*. London, 1961.

Sussman, Herbert L. *Victorians and the Machine: Literary Response to Technology.* Cambridge, Mass., 1968.

Sypher, Wylie. *Literature and Technology: The Alien Vision*. New York, 1971.

Tarr, Roger Leroy. "Carlyle's Influence upon the Mid-Victorian Social Novels of Gaskell, Kingsley, and Dickens." Ph.D. diss., University of Southern California, 1970.

Tennyson, G. B. *"Sartor" Called "Resartus."* Princeton, 1965.

Thompson, Fred C. "The Legal Plot in *Felix Holt.*" *Studies in English Literature* 7 (1967): 691–704.

Thomson, Patricia. *The Victorian Heroine: A Changing Ideal, 1837–1873.* London, 1956.

Tillotson, Kathleen. *Novels of the Eighteen-Forties.* London, 1956.

Utter, Robert P., and Gwendolyn B. Needham. *Pamela's Daughters.* New York, 1937.

Van Ghent, Dorothy. "On *Adam Bede.*" In *The English Novel: Form and Function.* New York, 1953.

Vicinus, Martha. *The Industrial Muse: A Study of Nineteenth Century British Working-Class Literature.* London, 1974.

Vicinus, Martha, ed. *Suffer and Be Still.* Bloomington, Ind., 1972.

Webb, Igor. *From Custom to Capital: The English Novel and the Industrial Revolution.* Ithaca, N.Y., 1981.

Webb, R. K. *The British Working Class Reader, 1790–1848.* London, 1955.

———. *Harriet Martineau: A Radical Victorian.* New York, 1960.

Weintraub, Karl J. "Autobiography and Historical Consciousness." *Critical Inquiry* 1 (June 1975): 821–48.

Welch, Jeffrey. *Mrs. Gaskell: An Annotated Bibliography, 1929–1975.* New York, 1977.

Wheeler, Michael D. "The Writer as Reader in *Mary Barton.*" *Durham University Journal* 67 (1974): 92–106.

Wiesenfarth, Joseph. *George Eliot's Mythmaking.* Heidelberg, 1977.

Williams, Raymond. *The Country and the City.* London, 1973.

———. *Culture and Society, 1780–1950.* New York, 1960.

———. "Dickens and Social Ideas." In *Sociology of Literature and Drama: Selected Readings.* Edited by Elizabeth and Tom Burns. Baltimore, 1973.

———. *The Long Revolution.* Rev. ed. New York, 1966.

Wright, Edgar. *Mrs. Gaskell: The Basis for Reassessment.* London, 1965.

IV. Secondary Works: Intellectual, Cultural, and Social History

Anderson, Michael. *Family Structures in Nineteenth Century Lancashire.* Cambridge, 1971.

Appleman, Philip, William A. Madden, and Michael Wolff, eds. *1859: Entering an Age of Crisis.* Bloomington, Ind., 1959.

Ashton, T.S. *Economic and Social Investigations in Manchester, 1833–1933: A Centenary History of the Manchester Statistical Society.* Manchester, 1934.

Backstrom, P. N. "The Practical Side of Christian Socialism in Victorian England." *Victorian Studies* 7 (1963): 305–24.

Bagehot, Walter. *The English Constitution and Other Political Essays.* New York, 1907.

Bain, Alexander. *Mental and Moral Science.* London, 1872.

Battiscombe, Georgina. *Shaftesbury: The Great Reformer, 1801–1885.* Boston, 1975.

Benn, S. I., and G. Gaus, eds. *Public and Private in Social Life.* London, 1983.

Berlin, Isaiah. *Four Essays on Liberty.* Oxford, 1969.

Birch, A. H. *Representation*. New York, 1971.

Blaug, Mark. *Ricardian Economics: A Historical Study*. Yale Studies in Economics, no. 8. New Haven, 1958.

Bradley, Ian. *The Call to Seriousness*. London, 1976.

Brebner, J. "Laissez Faire and State Intervention in Nineteenth-Century Britain." In *The Making of English History*. Edited by Robert Livingston Schuyler and Herman Ausubel. New York, 1952.

Breton, Albert. *The Economic Theory of Representative Government*. Chicago, 1974.

Briggs, Asa. *The Age of Improvement*. New York, 1959.

———. *Chartist Studies*. London, 1959.

———. "Cholera and Society in the Nineteenth Century," *Past and Present* 19 (April 1961): 76–96.

———. "The Language of 'Class' in Early Nineteenth Century England." In *Essays in Labour History*. Edited by Asa Briggs and J. Saville. London, 1960.

Brock, Michael. *The Great Reform Act*. London, 1973.

Bythell, Duncan. *The Handloom Weavers: A Study in the English Cotton Industry during the Industrial Revolution*. London, 1969.

———. *The Sweated Trades: Outwork in Nineteenth-Century Britain*. New York, 1978.

Cantor, Milton, and Bruce Laurie, eds. *Class, Sex, and the Woman Worker*. Westport, Conn., 1980.

Chambers, J. D. "Enclosure and the Labour Supply in the Industrial Revolution." *Economic History Review* 5 (1953).

———. *The Workshop of the World: British Economic History from 1820 to 1880*. London, 1961.

Chapman, Stanley D. *The Early Factory Masters: The Transitions to the Factory System in the Midlands Textile Industry*. Newton Abbot, Devon, 1967.

Checkland, S. J. *The Rise of Industrial Society in England: 1815–1885*. London, 1964.

Coats, A. W. *The Classical Economists and Economic Policy*. London, 1971.

Copleston, Frederick. *History of Philosophy*. Vols. 2, 5, and 6. Westminster, Md., 1963.

Coupland, Eric. *Wilberforce: A Narrative*. Oxford, 1923.

Coupland, Reginald. *The British Anti-Slavery Movement* (1933) London, 1964.

Court, W. H. B. *A Concise Economic History of Britain from 1750 to Recent Times*. Cambridge, 1954.

Cowling, Maurice. *1867: Disraeli, Gladstone, and Revolution: The Passing of the Second Reform Bill*. London, 1967.

Crossick, Geoffrey. "The Labour Aristocracy and Its Values: A Study of Mid-Victorian Kentish London." *Victorian Studies* 19 (1976): 301–20.

Dobb, Maurice. *Studies in the Development of Capitalism*. Rev. ed. London, 1963.

Driver, Cecil. *Tory Radical: The Life of Richard Oastler*. New York, 1946.

Dyob, H. J., and Michael Wolff, eds. *The Victorian City: Images and Realities*. Boston, 1973.

Edsall, Nicholas C. *The Anti-Poor-Law Movement, 1834–44*. Manchester, 1971.

Edwards, Paul, ed. *Encyclopedia of Philosophy*. Vol. 2. New York, 1972.

Eiseley, Loren. *Darwin's Century: Evolution and the Men Who Discovered It*. Garden City, N.Y., 1958.

Field, Clive D. "The Social Structure of English Methodism: Eighteenth–Twentieth Centuries." *British Journal of Sociology* 28 (June 1977): 199–225.

Finer, S. E. *The Life and Times of Sir Edwin Chadwick*. London, 1952.

Forbes, Duncan. *The Liberal Anglican Idea of History*. Cambridge, 1952.

Foster, John. *Class Struggle and the Industrial Revolution: Early Industrial Capitalism in Three English Towns*. London, 1974.

Frye, Northrop. "The Drunken Boat." In *Romanticism Reconsidered*. New York, 1963.

Gash, Norman, *Politics in the Age of Peel: A Study in the Technique of Parliamentary Representation, 1830–1850*. London, 1953.

————. *Sir Robert Peel: The Life of Sir Robert Peel after 1830*. London, 1972.

George, Dorothy. *England in Transition: Life and Work in the Eighteenth Century*. Baltimore, 1953.

Grampp, William Dyer. *The Manchester School of Economics*. Stanford, 1960.

Halevy, Elie. *The Growth of Philosophical Radicalism*. Translated by Mary Morris. London, 1928.

Hamer, David Allan. *The Politics of Electoral Pressure*. Brighton, Sussex, 1977.

Hammond, Barbara, and J. L. Hammond. *The Age of the Chartists, 1832–1854: A Study of Discontent*. London, 1930.

Hanham, H. J. *Elections and Party Management: Politics in the Time of Disraeli and Gladstone*. London, 1959.

Harrison, A., and B. L. Hutchins. *A History of Factory Legislation*. 3d ed. London, 1966.

Harrison, Royden. *Before the Socialists: Studies in Labour and Politics, 1861–1881*. London, 1965.

————. *Independent Collier: The Coal Miner as Archetypal Proletarian Reconsidered*. New York, 1978.

Hayek, Friedrich A., ed. *Capitalism and the Historians: Essays by T. S. Ashton and Others*. Chicago, 1954.

Hearn, Francis. *Domination, Legitimation, and Resistance: The Incorporation of the Nineteenth-Century English Working Class*. Westport, Conn., 1978.

Heimann, Edward. *History of Economic Doctrines*. London, 1948.

Hewitt, Margaret. *Wives and Mothers in Victorian Industry*. London, 1948.

Hill, Christopher. *Democracy and the Labour Movement*. London, 1954.

Himmelfarb, Gertrude. *On Liberty and Liberalism: The Case of John Stuart Mill*. New York, 1974.

Hobsbawm, Eric J. *Labouring Men: Studies in the History of Labour*. London, 1964.

Hook, Sidney, ed. *Determinism and Freedom in the Age of Modern Science*. New York, 1958.

Houghton, Walter E. *The Victorian Frame of Mind, 1830–70*. London, 1966.

Hutchins, B. L. *The Public Health Agitation, 1833–1848*. London, 1909.

Inglis, K. S. *Churches and the Working Classes in Victorian England*. London, 1963.

Irvine, W. H. *Apes, Angels, and Victorians: Darwin, Huxley, and Evolution*. New York, 1962.

Jones, Mary Gladys. *Hannah More, 1745–1833*. Cambridge, 1952.

Kinzer, Bruce. "The Failure of Pressure from Without: Richard Cobden, the Ballot Society, and the Coming of the Ballot Act in England." *Canadian Journal of History* 13 (1978): 399–422.

Kitson Clark, George. *The Making of Victorian England: Being the Ford Lectures Delivered before the University of Oxford*. Cambridge, Mass., 1962.

————. "The Romantic Element, 1830–1850." In *Studies in Social History: A Tribute to G. M. Trevelyan*. Edited by J. H. Plumb. London, 1955.

Kolakowski, Leszek. *The Alienation of Reason: A History of Positivist Thought*. Trans. Norbert Guterman. Garden City, N.Y., 1969.

Laslett, Peter. *Household and Family in Past Time.* Cambridge, 1972.

Lawson, Ina, and Leo Lowenthal. "The Debate on Cultural Standards in Nineteenth Century England." *Social Research* 30 (Winter 1963): 417–33.

Leff, Gordon. *History and Social Theory.* Garden City, N.Y., 1971.

Levine, George, ed. *The Emergence of Victorian Consciousness: The Spirit of the Age.* New York, 1967.

Lewenhak, Sheila. *Women and Trade Unions: An Outline History of Women in the British Trade Union Movement.* London, 1977.

Lively, Jack, and John Rees, eds. *Utilitarian Logic and Politics: James Mill's 'Essay on Government,' Macaulay's Critique, and the Ensuing Debate.* Oxford, 1978.

Longmate, Norman. *The Hungry Mills.* London, 1978.

Lukács, George. *History and Class Consciousness.* Translated by Rodney Livingston. Cambridge, Mass., 1971.

Magnus, Philip. *Gladstone: A Biography.* London, 1963.

Mantoux, P. *The Industrial Revolution in the Eighteenth Century: An Outline of the Beginnings of the Modern Factory System in England.* Translated by Marjorie Vernon. Rev. ed. London, 1952.

Marx, Karl. *Capital: A Critique of Political Economy.* Edited by Frederick Engels. New York, 1967.

Mathias, Peter. *The First Industrial Nation.* London, 1969.

McCord, Norman. *The Anti-Corn Law League, 1838–1846.* London, 1958.

Meakin, David. *Man and Work: Literature and Culture in Industrial Society.* London, 1977.

Meek, Ronald. "Decline of Ricardian Economics." In *Economics and Ideology and Other Essays.* London, 1967.

Morgenbesser, Sidney, and James Walsh, eds. *Free Will.* New Jersey, 1962.

Morley, John. *The Life of Richard Cobden.* New York, 1881.

Neff, Wanda. *Victorian Working Women: An Historical and Literary Study of Women in British Industries and Professions, 1820–1850.* New York, 1929.

Nichols, George. *History of the English Poor Law.* 3 vols. London, 1899.

Packe, Michael St. John. *The Life of John Stuart Mill.* New York, 1954.

Parekh, Bhikhu, ed. *Bentham's Political Thought.* New York, 1973.

Paul, Ellen Franel. *Moral Revolution and Economic Science: The Demise of Laissez Faire in Nineteenth Century British Political Economy.* Westport, Conn., 1979.

Perkin, Harold J. *The Origin of Modern English Society, 1780–1880.* London, 1972.

Peters, Richard S. *Body, Man, and Citizen.* New York, 1962.

Pinchbeck, Ivy. *Women Workers and the Industrial Revolution, 1750–1850.* New York, 1969.

Pitkin, Hannah Fenichel. *The Concept of Representation.* Berkeley, 1967.

Plamanatz, John. *The English Utilitarians.* Oxford, 1958.

Polanyi, Karl. *The Great Transformation.* Boston, 1957.

Pole, R. J. *Political Representation in England and the Origins of the American Republic.* New York, 1966.

Pollard, Sidney. *The Genesis of Modern Management: A Study of the Industrial Revolution in Great Britain.* Baltimore, 1968.

Pope, Liston. *Millhands and Preachers.* New Haven, 1976.

Porter, Dale Herbert. *The Abolition of the Slave Trade in England.* Hamden, Conn., 1970.

Pumphrey, Ralph E. "The Introduction of Industrialists into the British Peerage: A Study in Adaptation of a Social Institution." *American Historical Review* 65 (1959): 10–31.

Reed, John R. "Inherited Characteristics: Romantic to Victorian Will." *Signs Reader* 17 (Summer 1978): 335–66.

Richter, Melvin. *The Politics of Conscience: T. H. Green and His Age.* Cambridge, Mass., 1964.

Rickaby, J. J. *Free Will and Four English Philosophers.* Freeport, N.Y., 1969.

Robbins, William. *The Newman Brothers: An Essay in Comparative Intellectual Biography.* Cambridge, Mass., 1966.

Roberts, David. *Paternalism in Early Victorian England.* New Brunswick, N.J., 1979.

Rowall, George. *The Victorian Theater, 1792–1914.* Cambridge, 1978.

Rowe, D. J. "Class and Political Radicalism in London, 1831–1832." *Historical Journal* 13 (1970): 31–47.

Rowell, Geoffrey. *Hell and the Victorians: A Study of the Nineteenth-Century Theological Controversies Concerning Eternal Punishment and the Future Life.* Oxford, 1974.

Rubinstein, W. D. *Men of Property: The Very Wealthy in Britain since the Industrial Revolution.* New Brunswick, N.J., 1981.

———. "The Victorian Middle Classes: Wealth, Occupation, and Geography." *FHR,* ser. 2, vol. 30 (1977): 602–23.

Saville, John, ed. *Democracy and the Labour Movement: Essays in Honour of Dona Torr.* London, 1954.

Saville, John, and Joye Bellamy. *Dictionary of Labour Biography.* London, 1972.

Schmidt, Patricia L. "The Role of Moral Idealism in Social Change: Lord Ashley and the Ten Hours Factory Act." *Quarterly Journal of Speech* 63 (1977): 14–27.

Schochet, Gordon J. *Patriarchalism in Political Thought: The Authoritarian Family and Political Speculation and Attitudes Especially in Seventeenth-Century England.* New York, 1975.

Schultz, Harold J. *English Liberalism and the State: Individualism or Collectivism?* Lexington, Mass., 1972.

Semmel, Bernard. *The Methodist Revolution.* New York, 1973.

Smelser, N. J. *Social Change in the Industrial Revolution: An Application of Theory to the British Cotton Industry.* Chicago, 1959.

Smith, K. *The Malthusian Controversy.* London, 1951.

Stephen, Leslie. *History of English Thought in the Eighteenth Century.* Vol. 2. New York, 1902.

Sutherland, Gillian, ed. *Studies in the Growth of Nineteenth-Century Government.* Totowa, N.J., 1972.

Swart, Koenraad. "Individualism in the Mid-Nineteenth Century (1826–60)." *Journal of the History of Ideas* 23 (January 1962): 77–90.

Tawney, Richard H. *Religion and the Rise of Capitalism: A Historical Study.* New York, 1926.

Taylor, A. J. P. *The Trouble Makers: Dissent over Foreign Policy, 1792–1939.* Bloomington, Ind., 1958.

Thomas, M. W. *The Early Factory Legislation: A Study in Legislation and Administrative Evolution.* Leigh-on-Sea, Essex, 1948.

Thompson, Dennis F. *John Stuart Mill and Representative Government.* Princeton, N.J., 1976.

Thompson, E. P. *The Making of the English Working Class.* New York, 1966.

Thompson, E. P. "Time, Work-Discipline, and Industrial Capitalism." *Past and Present* 38 (1967): 56–97.

Thompson, Francis M. L. *English Landed Society in the Nineteenth Century.* London, 1963.

Treble, James H. *Urban Poverty in Britain, 1830–1914.* New York, 1978.

Trevelyan, G. M. *Life of John Bright.* London, 1913.

Vicinus, Martha. "Dark London." *Indiana University Bookman* 12 (1977): 63–92.

Viebrock, Helmut, ed. *Studies in Rhetoric in the Nineteenth Century.* Wiesbaden, 1970.

Vincent, John R. *Disraeli, Derby, and the Conservative Party: Journals and Memoirs of Edward Henry, Lord Stanlay.* New York, 1978.

Viner, Jacob. *The Role of Providence in the Social Order: An Essay in Intellectual History.* Princeton, N.J., 1972.

Ward, John Trevor. *The Factory Movement, 1830–55.* London, 1962.

Wearmouth, R. F. *Methodism and the Working Class Movements of England, 1800–1850.* London, 1937.

Webb, Beatrice, and Sydney Webb. *Problems of Modern Industry.* London, 1902.

Whitehead, Alfred North. *Science and the Modern World.* New York, 1931.

Wiener, Martin J. *English Culture and the Decline of the Industrial Spirit, 1850–1980.* Cambridge, 1981.

Willey, Basil. *The Eighteenth-Century Background.* New York, 1940.

Williams, Eustace. *Capitalism and Slavery.* Chapel Hill, N.C., 1945.

———. "Laissez Faire, Sugar, and Slavery." *Political Science Quarterly* 58 (1943): 67–85.

Wilson, D., ed. *Culture and Anarchy.* London, 1960.

Winnett, A. R. "Were the Deists 'Deists'?" *Church Quarterly Review* 161 (1960): 70–77.

Wohl, Anthony, ed. *The Victorian Family: Structures and Stresses.* New York, 1978.

Wolff, Michael. "Victorian Studies: An Interdisciplinary Essay." *Victorian Studies* 8 (1964): 59–70.

Wolin, Sheldon S. *Politics and Vision: Continuity and Innovation in Western Political Thought.* Boston, 1960.

Wollheim, Richard. "How Can One Person Represent Another?" *The Aristotelian Society,* supp. vol. 34 (1960): 209–20.

Young, George Malcolm. *Victorian England: The Portrait of an Age.* London, 1937.

Index